MOON HANDBOOKS

D1310970

KAUA'I

JADE ECKARDT

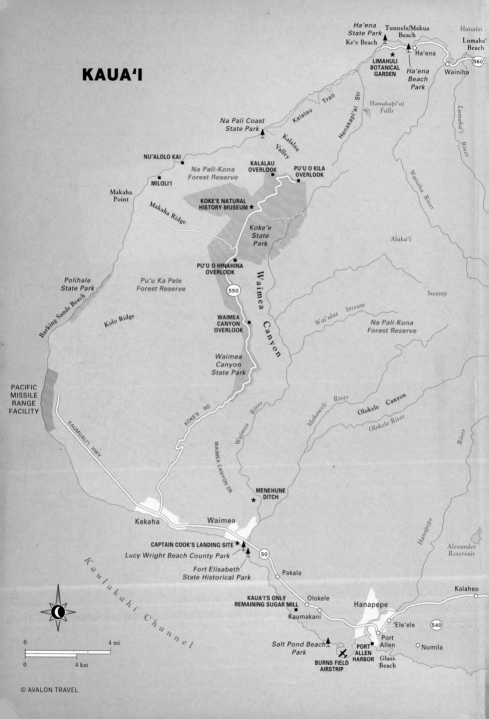

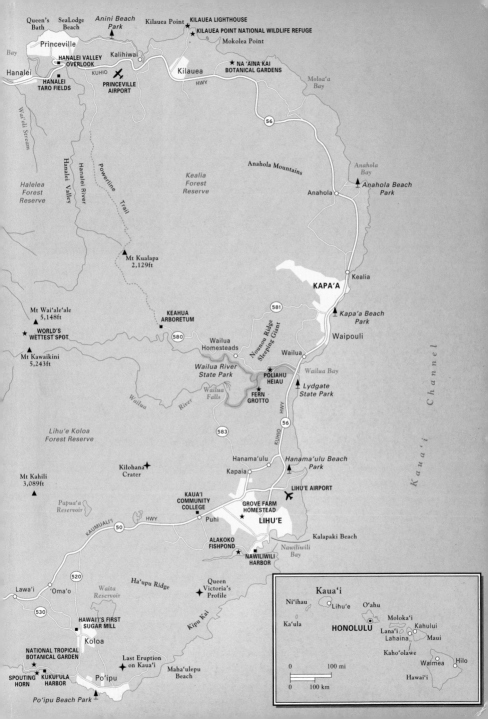

Contents

▶ **Discover Kaua'i** **6**
  Planning Your Trip 8
  Best of Kaua'i in Seven Days 11
  Best Beaches 14
  Best Snorkeling 16
  Best Hikes 18
  Best Outdoor Adventures 20
  Go Green on the Garden Isle 22
  Best Cultural and
     Historical Sites 24
  Best Waterfalls 26
  Best for Honeymooners 28

▶ **East Side** **29**
  Beaches 33
  Water Sports 38
  Hiking and Biking 44
  Adventure Sports and Tours 48
  Golf and Tennis 50
  Yoga and Spas 51
  Sights 52
  Shopping 59
  Entertainment 63

  Food 64
  Information and Services 70
  Getting There and Around 71

▶ **North Shore** **73**
  Beaches 76
  Water Sports 86
  Hiking, Biking, and Bird-Watching . . 93
  Adventure Sports and Tours 98
  Golf and Tennis 99
  Yoga and Spas 100
  Sights 101
  Shopping 105
  Entertainment 108
  Food 109
  Information and Services 114
  Getting There and Around 114

▶ **South Shore** **115**
  Beaches 118
  Water Sports 124
  Adventure Sports and Tours 127
  Golf and Tennis 128
  Yoga and Spas 130

Sights 131
Shopping 136
Entertainment 138
Food 138
Information and Services 143
Getting There and Around 143

► **West Side 144**
Beaches 149
Water Sports 155
Hiking and Biking 159
Adventure Sports and Tours 165
Yoga and Spas 166
Sights 167
Shopping 170
Entertainment 173
Food 174
Information and Services 177
Getting There and Around 178

► **Accommodations 179**
East Side 180
North Shore 187
South Shore 196

West Side 204

► **Background 209**
The Land 209
Flora and Fauna 214
History 217
Government and Economy 224
People and Culture 225

► **Essentials 233**
Getting There and Around 233
Tips for Travelers 238
Health and Safety 240
Information and Services 242

► **Resources 246**
Glossary 246
Suggested Reading 249
Internet Resources 252

► **Index 253**

► **List of Maps 261**

Discover Kaua'i

Kaua'i seduces people from all walks of life. Hawaii's oldest island is a place where everyone – locals and traveling nomads, celebrities and hippies, adventure seekers and lovers of luxe – all coexist peacefully. Yes, there are other destinations with sun, sand, and surf, but none with the unique spirit of *aloha* found here. It's as rampant as the island's wild chickens.

Approximately 90 percent of the island's land is uninhabited, thanks to Mount Wai'ale'ale (the world's wettest place) and the vast Waimea Canyon. So visitors can experience undisturbed white-sand beaches, lush jungles, and extraordinary wildlife. But Kaua'i isn't all trails, sand, and vegetation. The island has changed with the times, welcoming an influx of residents and modern-day development, including a limited number of luxury hotels, spas, and golfing greens. Epicurean restaurants are scattered throughout the island, and it boasts enough shopping to necessitate extra baggage fees on the flight home. Surfing, zip-lining, hiking, and four-wheel-driving opportunities will exhaust any adventure addict's adrenaline supply. And history buffs can explore the island's rich culture through its ancient archaeological sites, plantation architecture, and various museums.

Kaua'i isn't only a collection of stops and must-see sights, but a romance between visitor and island. Explore the Na Pali Coast, catch your first wave in Hanalei Bay, or watch the sunset over a forbidden island. Get pampered at an oceanside spa, hit par on the greens, or work on an organic farm. Your enchanting experiences of the Garden Isle will change you to your core. The memories of your time on Pele's first-born will stay with you forever.

Planning Your Trip

▶ WHERE TO GO

East Side

The east side, also referred to as the Coconut Coast, is by far the busiest side of the island. Stretching from Lihu'e to Kapa'a, it holds a vast mix of historical sites, outdoor activities, and modern comforts like restaurants, shopping, and hotels. Lihu'e is the island's main town, with Kauai's largest airport; it's also a good place to explore the island's rich history at the Kilohana Plantation and the Kaua'i Museum. Although Lihu'e serves as the go-to spot for locals seeking to fulfill daily needs such as work and shopping, those in search of activities can surf at Kalapaki Beach or stand-up paddle on the Hule'ia River. From Wailua to Kapa'a you'll find the famous Wailua Falls and Wailua River cultural sites, such as the Fern Grotto. Inland behind Kapa'a are miles of great hiking trails with amazing views, including the lovely walk to Ho'opi'i Falls.

North Shore

The magical north shore is a true tropical paradise. Its vibrant green cliffs back some of the island's most spectacular white-sand beaches with great snorkeling and world-class waves. The north side begins with Kilauea, a former sugar town that is home to the Kilauea Lighthouse and a small shopping center. The more upscale Princeville features a modern hotel and a large community

Kalalau Trail along the Na Pali Coast

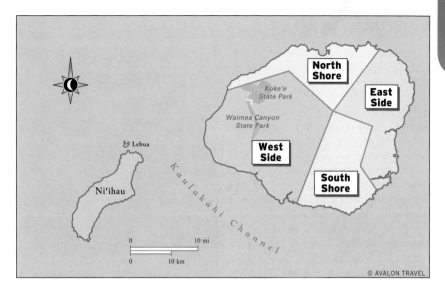

© AVALON TRAVEL

of homes resting above beautiful beaches nestled below the cliffs. Down in Hanalei Valley you'll come to quaint Hanalei town, where you will find charming shops, lovely eateries, and freshwater rivers running into the ocean. At the end of the road here is the Na Pali Coast, where miles of raw hiking trails lead adventurers to secluded beaches, waterfalls, and valleys.

South Shore

The south shore offers something for everyone: luxurious indulgences for those looking for ultimate relaxation, beaches perfect for family outings, and great snorkeling opportunities. Along the dry sunny coast, Po'ipu is lined with white-sand beaches that offer snorkeling, swimming, and surfing, with several large resorts and golf courses nearby. Po'ipu Beach and the Maha'ulepu Beaches provide exquisite beach time. On the opposite end of Po'ipu are some must-see sights, including Spouting Horn and the National Tropical Botanical Garden. Inland from here is the quaint and historical town of

Koloa, with eateries, shopping, and a more local feel. Here you'll drive through lush green pastures and dense jungle. It's a mix of locals and visitors living amid modern comforts and historical influence. Slightly inland and west is Kalaheo, a quaint, historical town where you'll also find Kukui O Lono Park, a great place for history buffs and golf lovers alike.

West Side

Out on the west side, you'll find empty land, roads, and beaches, and the very small historical town of Waimea. With its laid-back vibe, dusty red dirt, lack of rain, and small historical buildings, it almost resembles the Wild West. The landscape is extremely different than the rest of the island, but it is not to be missed. Some of the island's most spectacular viewpoints and trails can be found in Koke'e State Park. And at the end of the road lies one of the island's most beautiful beaches, Polihale State Park. In Hanapepe you'll find an artist's dreamland. The small town is home to a high number of galleries and the popular Art Night in Hanapepe.

▶ WHEN TO GO

The great thing about Kauaʻi is that it's wonderful any time of the year. As on all of the islands in Hawaii, high tourist season for Kauaʻi begins a few weeks before Christmas and lasts until late April. It then slows a bit until June and is quite busy until school starts again in August. If you are visiting during the busy season, you absolutely need to make car and hotel reservations in advance. Availability will be guaranteed, and prices will be much friendlier if you secure them early. It's not unheard of for rental cars to be completely sold out during the high season.

If your schedule allows, visiting Kauaʻi in the off season, from September to December and late April to June, is recommended. The island will still be bustling with visitors, but the beaches, hiking trails, and surf breaks will be less crowded. Perhaps more importantly, prices for cars, airline tickets, and hotels will generally be lower.

The weather on Kauaʻi is pretty consistent, with rain coming and going, and sometimes staying for longer than you'd like. Although winter is the official rainy season, it's hard to pinpoint when it will rain. As in most of Hawaii, some winters may see a lot of rain while others hardly any. But if it's rainy on the north side, there's a good chance Poʻipu or the west side is sunny, so sometimes all it takes is a short drive to find sun again.

If you're looking to surf large waves, the winter months of October to January are a good time to visit. On the flip side, if you'd appreciate a near guarantee of a calm ocean for you or your children's enjoyment of swimming, snorkeling, and simply lazing about in the water, you'll definitely prefer a trip to

If you're an avid surfer, winter is the best time to visit Kauaʻi.

Kauaʻi during the summer when the waves are small. And if you hope to kayak the Na Pali Coast, you wouldn't want to even consider it in the winter. Visitors who hope to see humpback whales must make sure they visit during whale season, from about December through May at the latest.

Weather also determines the safety and comfort level of many hiking trails. Wet weather means a great increase in the chance of slippery, crumbling, and dangerous muddy trails along the Na Pali Coast and up in the Alakaʻi Swamp. Rain also has an effect on the rivers along the Na Pali Coast and up in Waimea Canyon, which can unexpectedly swell and recede within hours, affecting hikers.

Best of Kaua'i in Seven Days

One week is the average duration of a vacation on Kaua'i. In seven days you can see the best of what the island has to offer, sans several of the island's longest hikes. Hiking the entire Na Pali Coast can take two to three days, and many of the inland hikes in Koke'e State Park require a one-day commitment, so you may have to give up some of the other activities to make room for those hikes. Of course, different sites and experiences appeal to different people, but general standout experiences appeal to people across the board. This is a basic itinerary for experiencing the best of the island in seven days.

Day 1

You'll fly into Lihu'e, and unless you've booked a separate flight from O'ahu, you'll most likely arrive midafternoon. For the first day it's a good idea to take it easy. Pick up your rental car and stop by the Kaua'i Museum for background information that will enhance the rest of your trip. If there's anything you need to shop for, such as sunblock or snorkel gear, it's a good idea to get it out of the way the first day, and Lihu'e has everything you could need. To shop for outdoor gear, drop by Da Life at Kalapaki Beach or Walmart in Lihu'e. From here it's off to your hotel to relax. Wherever you may be staying, there is no doubt a good place to eat and a beach for a leisurely stroll at day's end.

Day 2

Most visitors find Kaua'i's north shore to be the most magical experience of the island, so for the sake of instant gratification head north first. Begin the day in Kilauea with a look at the Kilauea Point National Wildlife Refuge and Lighthouse. From here head to Princeville for a visit to the beach Queen's Bath, which should only be done in the summer or spring months for safety reasons, because large surf will wash over the cliff-side pool. The hike down is an enjoyable walk in itself, featuring a small waterfall before opening to the ocean. The saltwater pool rests in the edge of the cliffs, and if the ocean is completely calm, it makes for a lovely dip. For a slightly tougher hike to a very secluded swimming area, make the trek down to SeaLodge Beach. On your way out of Princeville stop for photos and a peaceful gaze at the Hanalei Valley Overlook. In Hanalei, eat lunch at Bubba Burgers, Neide's Brazilian and Mexican Food, or, if you can hold out a little longer, Red Hot Mama's down the road in Wainiha is a great option. Before leaving town check out Hanalei Bay before heading toward the end of the road. While weaving through the coastal road, stop at the Lumahai Overlook before heading down to the Limahuli Botanical Garden for a self guided tour. Spend the remainder of the day snorkeling and sunbathing at Ke'e Beach or Tunnels

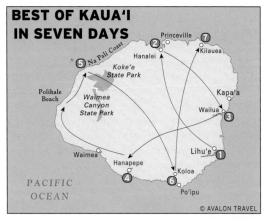

BEST OF KAUA'I IN SEVEN DAYS

Princeville ⑦
Kilauea
Na Pali Coast ⑤
Hanalei
Koke'e State Park
Polihale Beach
Kapa'a
Waimea Canyon State Park
Wailua ③
Waimea
Lihu'e ①
Hanapepe
Koloa ⑥
PACIFIC OCEAN
Po'ipu

© AVALON TRAVEL

deep in the gorge of Waimea Canyon

Beach. Enjoy the sunset at the beach out here and head back to Hanalei for tapas at the hip Bar Acuda Tapas and Wine.

Day 3

This is the day for sightseeing and activities on the east side in Wailua and Kapaʻa. For a full breakfast stop into the Kountry Kitchen, or for something quick Small Town Coffee is a good option. Take the hike down to Hoʻopiʻi Falls in the morning before heading up Kuamoʻo Road for a look at Opaekaʻa Falls. While up here take a quick stop at the sacred site Poliahu Heiau across the street. For a quick and healthy lunch try Mermaids Cafe or Caffe Coco in Kapaʻa. After lunch, take in the active underwater world while snorkeling at Lydgate Beach Park. Families with children could spend time at the Kamalani Playground at Lydgate before driving inland to look at Wailua Falls. The adventurous types can take a guided (and prebooked) kayak tour up Wailua River. End the day

with a stroll around Kapaʻa and dinner at Kintaro for wonderful sushi and Japanese food. In Lihuʻe, dine at Duke's or Gaylord's for locally grown food.

Day 4

Head out west and begin the day with a stroll through historical Hanapepe and a browse through the art galleries. While here don't forget to walk over the Hanapepe Swinging Bridge. Drop into Hanapepe Cafe and Bakery for a good breakfast. Then venture inland for the gorgeous views in Kokeʻe State Park at the Kalalau and Puʻu O Kila Overlooks. This is also your chance to take in the views of Waimea Canyon. In Waimea, Island Tacos is a great place for a tasty and very filling lunch. Then head out to Polihale Beach Park for the rest of the day. Make sure to stay to watch the sunset over Niʻihau. If it works out that you visit the west side on a Friday, stop in Hanapepe on the way out for Art Night in Hanapepe, when the community comes together to celebrate art and socialize. For a west-side dinner, try Wrangler's Steakhouse or dine at The Grove Cafe at Waimea Plantation Cottages.

Day 5

Take a prebooked helicopter tour of the island from Lihu'e over Waimea Canyon and over the Na Pali Coast or a boat tour of the Na Pali Coast. Numerous boat tours leave out of the west side and head down the Na Pali Coast. A dinner cruise is a nice way to end the day, and many combine snorkeling with the tour. If you're feeling really extravagant, book a helicopter tour for the morning and a boat cruise to end the day. Most boat tours provide lunch, but you may want to supplement your meal by bringing something additional along.

Day 6

Explore the south side, beginning with a lovely drive into Koloa through the Tunnel of Trees. A great breakfast out here can be had at the Kalaheo Cafe. A tour through the National Tropical Botanical Garden is a good idea, and at the very least a visit to the visitors center and walk around the entrance is nice. A quick stop at nearby Spouting Horn is not to be missed, and then spend the day out here on the spectacular beaches. Nearby Keoki's Paradise is a good lunch option before heading out to explore more beaches. The Maha'ulepu Beaches are a good choice if you're looking for seclusion, and Po'ipu Beach Park is ideal for anyone, especially those with children. What's often a trip-making option out here is surf lessons at Po'ipu Beach. Prebook a lesson with one of the surf schools. A perfect end to a south-side day is dinner with a sunset view at the Beach House Restaurant or from Kukui'ula Small Boat Harbor.

view of Wailua Falls

Day 7

Take your last day on the island to laze about at your favorite beach, or combine a few. In the Kilauea area, a good mix of beach-hopping includes Secret Beach for a long morning stroll or hours in the sun. Next it's down to nearby Kalihiwai Beach, which stands out because of its freshwater river, perfect for a refreshing dip and for children to play in. For breakfast and lunch in Kilauea stop at Kilauea Bakery & Pau Hana Pizza or Kilauea Fish Market. For time on a secluded beach try Donkey Beach, just north of Kapa'a, and Moloa'a Bay, located before Kilauea. For a delicious pit stop after your day at the beach try the amazing dairy-free smoothies and tropical fruit at Banana Joe's or Moloa'a Sunrise Fruit Stand. Finish the day with a sunset stroll at Hanalei Bay and a top-of-the-line seafood/sushi dinner at Hanalei Dolphin Restaurant.

Best Beaches

Of course, determining the best beaches on Kaua'i will come down to each person's preferences, but there are certain standout beaches that every beach lover is guaranteed to love.

POLIHALE STATE PARK (page 153)
The west side's Polihale State Park runs for miles with a blanket of fine white sand resting between tall sacred cliffs or sand dunes. Every visitor should experience at least one vibrant sunset over forbidden Ni'ihau out here.

PO'IPU BEACH PARK (page 120)
Home to a long strip of fluffy white sand, Po'ipu Beach is great for surfing, both for beginners and experienced surfers, and usually safe swimming. Restrooms and showers add to the convenience of the easily accessible location, which is usually quite busy.

MAHA'ULEPU BEACHES (page 118)
For a short journey into an undeveloped part of the south side, take the bumpy dirt road out to the Maha'ulepu Beaches for often-secluded beach time. You'll have your choice of Gillin's Beach and Kawailoa Bay to relax on, or you can take a cliff-side hike.

DONKEY BEACH (page 37)
Nearly almost always uncrowded, Donkey Beach offers plenty of space for sunbathing and beachcombing—the white sand is usually scattered with driftwood and other beach treasures. Accessible via a 10-minute walk from the parking lot, the east-side beach provides seclusion, but the wild ocean here can limit swimming.

LARSEN'S BEACH (page 77)
Larsen's is a generally secluded spot with a very long strip of white sand. Swimming can be rough here, but when conditions allow, the rocky area to the right offers great snorkeling.

SECRET BEACH (page 78)
Expansive Secret Beach isn't exactly a secret,

Ha'ena Beach Park

SeaLodge Beach

Hanalei Bay

but it offers plenty of space to find a spot all to yourself. You never know what you may find here—a waterfall midway down the beach, swimmable tide pools at the end, or a peaceful or raging wild ocean.

SEALODGE BEACH (page 80)
Nestled below Princeville's cliffs, SeaLodge Beach is a small cove of paradise accessible via a roughly 15-minute hike. The small crescent strip of sand is backed by shade-giving trees; the water offers good swimming and great snorkeling when conditions allow.

HANALEI BAY (page 82)
The long, crescent-moon-shaped beach offers fine white sand to stroll on, calm waters to swim in, and popular surf breaks for all levels.

HA'ENA BEACH PARK (page 84)
Nestled in front of a backdrop of lush green mountains at the end of the road on the north shore, this beach has full amenities and a life guard, and it's great for beachcombing and watching surfers.

Po'ipu Beach Park

tide pool at Secret Beach

Best Snorkeling

In Kaua'i you can always jump in the water nearly anywhere with your gear just to see what you'll find, but the island has its prime snorkel spots. Each side of the island has snorkel spots that never fail to please.

KE'E BEACH (page 88)

At the very end of the road on the north shore lies a semi-protected pool with great snorkeling, as well as an outside snorkeling area in the open ocean where the truly spectacular snorkeling exists. Beginners will enjoy the pool while only very experienced water people should explore the outer area, and only when the waves are small.

TUNNELS/MAKUA BEACH (page 87)

Possibly the most renowned snorkeling place on the island, here less experienced snorkelers will see good stuff not far from shore while experienced snorkelers will see wonderful sites out by the ledge that drops off into the deep ocean. There is a surf break here too, so it's important to only head out in periods of small surf.

ANINI BEACH (page 86)

The calm and shallow water here makes this a great family-friendly beach for snorkeling. You won't find the most lively underwater world here, but there's usually fish to see, and the peaceful water is wonderful in itself.

LYDGATE BEACH PARK (page 38)

This is one of the most popular snorkeling places on the island because the two protected pools make it a good spot to not have to worry about safety. It's a great spot for snorkelers of all ages and levels.

PO'IPU BEACH PARK (page 125)

Out on the south shore, this beach offers lively snorkeling on both the east and west ends. The water is usually pretty safe here.

Tunnels/Makua Beach

Tunnels/Makua Beach

Ke'e Beach

PK'S (page 125)

Across from the south shore's Prince Kuhio Park, this tiny strip of beach offers wonderful underwater shows. There's not much beach here, but it's a hot underwater spot for fish who like to snack on the seaweed that grows on the abundance of rocks here.

LAWA'I BEACH (page 124)

This rather small beach is a popular south-side snorkel spot. There's usually something to see here close to shore, as the rocks and seaweed attract fish.

SALT POND BEACH PARK (page 155)

This beach park with full amenities is the best bet for snorkeling on the west side. The generally calm waters here offer a place to peacefully explore the underwater world.

NA PALI COAST (page 88)

You'll find the island's most spectacular snorkeling along the Na Pali Coast, reachable only through a boat tour. Take a snorkel cruise out here and you will see jaw-dropping underwater terrain and an array of sea life from dolphins to sea turtles.

Na Pali Coast

Lawa'i Beach

Best Hikes

Kauaʻi has wonderful hikes for all levels, with most of them weaving through the interior of the island. The majority of the trails are in Kokeʻe State Park, with a few really good ones inland in the Wailua area. There are also a couple of waterfall hikes near and along the coast. The famous Kalalau Trail offers days of hiking and exploring, but a small part of the trail can be completed in a day. Generally, the other hiking trails in Kauai can all be completed in a matter of a few hours, and some in a day. Here is a list of the standout trails that avid hikers wouldn't want to miss.

NOUNOU MOUNTAIN TRAILS (page 44)

Three trails weave along the Sleeping Giant, otherwise known as Nounou Mountain, and all intersect. The East Trail, the West Trail, and the Kuamoʻo-Nounou Trail all offer sweeping views and secluded places to enjoy peaceful alone time on the east side's interior.

NORTH SHORE BEACH WALKS

One of the most peaceful and rejuvenating things to do on Kauaʻi is simply to enjoy a long beach walk. Make the short hike down to Secret Beach (page 78) and then take a stroll to the very end, where you'll encounter a small waterfall and views of the Kilauea Lighthouse. Take a peaceful stroll along Hanalei Bay (page 82) and its two miles of

white sand backed by lush mountains, or enjoy a walk along the mile-long Lumahai Beach (page 83) with a refreshing river to swim in.

KUILAU TRAIL (page 46)

This trail offers some of the most beautiful mountain views, including an amazing view of Mount Waiʻaleʻale and sweeping vistas from Kapaʻa to Lihuʻe. Taking about two or three hours to complete, this is a moderately strenuous trail with wonderful rewards.

ILIAU NATURE LOOP AND KUKUI TRAIL (page 159)

The family-friendly Iliau Nature Loop in Waimea Canyon State Park wanders through native forest for about 20 minutes of walking time. From here you can connect to

Waimea Canyon State Park

Lumahai Beach

Hanalei Bay

the Kukui Trail, which will take you down to the Waimea River in the canyon, which is roughly four hours round-trip.

PIHEA TRAIL AND ALAKA'I SWAMP TRAIL (page 163)

Known as otherworldly, these trails take you through dwarf forests, vine-covered trees, and the world's highest swamp. Amazing sweeping views to the north shore can be seen at the Kilohana Overlook.

THE KALALAU TRAIL (page 95)

The Kalalau Trail is a strenuous 11-mile hike one way, with unmatched views of the Na Pali Coast through switchbacks, mud, hills, and stream crossings. You'll pass Hanakapi'ai Beach and end on the secluded Kalalau Beach, a true escape.

HANAKAPI'AI BEACH AND HANAKAPI'AI FALLS (page 96)

Beginning at Ke'e Beach, this section of the Kalalau Trail, which is roughly four hours round-trip, features beautiful views of the Na Pali Coast, and ends with a dip in the cool freshwater pool at Hanakapi'ai Falls.

SWIMMING POOL TRAIL (page 46)

Scenes of *Jurassic Park* were filmed at the start of this trail, which offers views of Mount Wai'ale'ale and a reward of a cool natural swimming pool to dip in after cutting through a tunnel below ground.

Waimea Canyon State Park

The Kalalau Trail to Hanakapi'ai Beach

Best Outdoor Adventures

Kaua'i is a dreamland for those who enjoy being active in the outdoors. From under the sea to high above the mountains there is an intriguing and exciting activity for everyone.

KAYAKING THE NA PALI COAST (page 92)

Arms of steel are necessary for the intense 16-mile sea kayak journey along the Na Pali Coast. Outfitters Kauai offers the tour from mid-May to mid-September on Tuesdays and Thursdays.

WATERSKIING AND WAKEBOARDING ON THE WAILUA RIVER (page 43)

To mix water with adventure, try waterskiing, wakeboarding, kneeboarding, or a hydrofoil ride on the Wailua River. The only company to offer these kinds of boarding activities is Kaua'i Water Ski and Surf Co.

ATVING IN KOLOA (page 127)

For some good dirty fun, drive an ATV with Kaua'i ATV. Guided ATV tours take adventurous drivers on a waterfall, cane road, or private tour.

SURFING AT PO'IPU BEACH (page 125)

For experienced surfers, the island is your oyster, but for novice surfers Po'ipu Beach is the place to take lessons. For lessons with a true surf pioneer, try Surf Lessons by Margo Oberg for group, semiprivate, or private sessions.

WHALE-WATCHING IN PO'IPU (page 127)

Whale season runs from about November through April, so while on Kaua'i in whale season, simply keep your eye on the ocean when you're on the beach, surfing, or even in a car. There's a good chance you'll see them breaching. For whale-watching boat tours November through April, contact Captain Andy's Sailing Adventures. Another option is Blue Dolphin Charters, which offers whale-watching tours December through March.

Wailua River

Kilauea Point National Wildlife Refuge

sunset on the south shore, Po'ipu

BIRDING IN KILAUEA AND KOKE'E STATE PARK (pages 98 and 164)

Stop by the Kilauea Point National Wildlife Refuge to see huge frigate birds, dressy red-footed boobies, swift tropic-birds, the endangered Hawaiian *nene* goose, and other birds. For birding in Koke'e, try the 3.5-mile-long Alaka'i Swamp Trail, the Kaluapuhi Trail, or the 3.7-mile-long Pihea Trail. For shorter birding trails, take a stroll on the slightly over a mile Halemanu-Koke'e Trail or the mile-long Kamuwela Trail.

ZIPLINING AND TUBING IN LIHU'E (page 48)

Outfitters Kauai offers various zipline adventures on the east side. Kaua'i Backcountry Adventures offers zipline and tubing on 17,000 acres of old sugar plantation land.

HANG GLIDING AND SKYDIVING ON THE WEST SIDE (page 165)

Get a bird's-eye view of Kaua'i on a hang-gliding craft with Birds in Paradise. For skydiving excursions, Skydive Kauai will take you to freefall out of a plane at 4,500 feet.

Na Pali Coast

Dolphins are a common sight along the Na Pali Coast.

Go Green on the Garden Isle

Lush and green Kaua'i is the perfect place to travel green. Whether it's shopping at local farmers markets or waking up under the stars, Kaua'i has a lot of options for those who wish to go green and travel lightly.

SHOP LOCAL AT FARMERS MARKETS

Buy fresh produce at the Sunshine Farmers Markets, which are found island-wide, to support local sales, an important effort in Hawaii's venture toward a sustainable future. You can find the markets at: Koloa Ball Park (page 139), Kalaheo Neighborhood Center (page 142), Hanapepe Park (page 175), Kilauea Neighborhood Center (page 110), and Kekaha Neighborhood Center (page 177). Also, check out the Waipa Ranch Farmers Market (page 113).

STAY AT AN ORGANIC FARM OR GREEN BED-AND-BREAKFAST

A work trade in exchange for accommodations and meals on approximately 20 organic farms on Kaua'i can be experienced through World Wide Opportunities on Organic Farms (page 181), otherwise known as WWOOFing. Most farms have guests that stay one to three weeks and move on to another farm for a new experience. WWOOFing is popular in the islands, so you'll need to book a place about four to six weeks in advance.

A very unique and "green" place to stay is Coco's Kaua'i Bed and Breakfast (page 204), which is off the electrical grid and uses hydroelectric power, compact fluorescent light bulbs, and plant-based cleaners.

CAMP

A truly green form of lodging is camping. Campsites are scattered throughout the island, but there are some standout spots. Ha'ena Beach Park (page 84) is a lovely place to camp on the north side with full amenities. On the west side, Polihale State

camping at Ha'ena Beach Park

Polihale State Park

Park (page 153) is a beautiful place to wake up by the ocean, and it has bathrooms, showers, and a few pavilions. In Koke'e State Park (page 161) there are cabins available for spending nights in the cool weather in the forest.

REDUCE WASTE

To reduce waste while spending time on Kaua'i bring reusable shopping bags. You'll undoubtedly consume a lot of water while exploring Kaua'i, and to reduce the number of disposed plastic bottles you can refill them at one of the many water dispensers for 50 cents a gallon. You can find water dispensers at Papaya's (page 69), Harvest Market Natural Foods and Cafe (page 111), and most Big Save supermarkets.

TAKE THE BUS OR DRIVE A CLEAN-ENERGY RENTAL CAR

Remember, you can always catch the bus around the island to save emissions, but another option is GreenCar Hawaii (page 235), which is a clean-energy car rental option. It has two vehicle options that go gas-free.

GreenCar Hawaii

Waipa Ranch Farmers Market

Best Cultural and Historical Sites

Sun, sand, and surf may be the main draw to the Garden Island for many people, but Kaua'i holds a rich history and there are historical and cultural places of interest on each side of the island.

HO'OPULAPULA HARAGUCHI RICE MILL (page 103)

In Hanalei, stop for a prebooked tour at the Ho'opulapula Haraguchi Rice Mill, the last remaining rice mill in all of Hawaii. It shut down operations in 1960 when the Kaua'i rice industry collapsed. The mill is within a national wildlife refuge, and the tour offers a view into the island's agricultural and cultural history, views of endangered native water birds, and information about the cultivation and uses of taro.

WAILUA RIVER SACRED SITES (page 57)

The banks of the Wailua River were once the hub for Hawaiian *ali'i* (royalty), and along the river are many cultural sites. At the Holoholoku Heiau it's believed that human sacrifice may have taken place, the Pohako Ho'o Hanau is where the *ali'i* were born, the Poliahu Heiau features a rock structure that shows a very large *heiau* (sacred place), and at the Kamokila Hawaiian Village you can wander through a replica of a traditional Hawaiian village.

PRINCE KUHIO PARK AND HO'AI HEIAU (page 133)

In Po'ipu, Prince Kuhio Park with its Ho'ai Heiau is a monument to the beloved prince who worked for the welfare of his people. The *heiau* is in great shape and the park holds a pond, a small pavilion, and a nice lawn if you wish to sit down and have a snack.

FORT ELISABETH STATE HISTORICAL PARK (page 167)

Originally built and used by Hawaiians as a *heiau*, this park in Waimea dates from 1817. Its shape resembles an eight-pointed star.

historical train at Kilohana Plantation

Kilauea Lighthouse

Kaua'i Museum

KAUA'I MUSEUM (page 52)

In Lihu'e, the best background information you'll find about the island is at the Kaua'i Museum. There are several permanent and temporary exhibits and a gift shop with great books.

GROVE FARM HOMESTEAD (page 54)

At the Grove Farm Homestead you can get a look inside the former home of one of Kaua'i's most successful sugar plantation owners, a sneak-peek into the preserved daily life of the upper class in the plantation days.

KUKUI O LONO PARK (page 135)

In Kalaheo, this park features a beautiful Japanese garden and a large collection of rocks that historically served various functional purposes.

KILOHANA PLANTATION (page 55)

The sprawling Kilohana Plantation is home to a perfectly preserved mansion built by a sugar plantation owner in the 1930s. You can browse the home and its many original pieces of decor, explore the beautiful grounds, and enjoy a historical train ride.

KILAUEA LIGHTHOUSE (page 101)

Stop for both educational and photo opportunities at the Kilauea Lighthouse and the Kilauea Point National Wildlife Refuge. For decades the lighthouse served as a beacon to ships.

LIMAHULI BOTANICAL GARDEN (page 104)

Check out the preserved wetland taro terraces and native plants at Limahuli Botanical Garden. A self-guided tour weaves through the gorgeous, vibrant green grounds.

Prince Kuhio Park

the cliffs of the Kilauea Point National Wildlife Refuge

Best Waterfalls

Considering Kaua'i is home to the wettest place on earth, Mount Wai'ale'ale, it's no surprise that there's an abundance of waterfalls on the island. From drive-up-and-look falls to falls reached after minutes or miles of hiking, there are many to enjoy.

HO'OPI'I FALLS (page 44)
The peaceful hike to Ho'opi'i Falls is actually a stroll down a sometimes muddy hill under a high tree canopy along the river that leads to two small falls.

WAIPO'O FALLS (page 161)
On the west side, a roughly three-hour strenuous hike to the 800-foot Waipo'o Falls, with beautiful views along the way, ends with a swim in a cool pool.

SECRET FALLS ON THE WAILUA RIVER (page 42)
Secret Falls, also known as Uluwehi Falls, has a swimmable pool and is reachable via a beautiful kayaking excursion on the Wailua River and a short, easy hike. Most visitors opt to do this trip with a guided kayak tour, but you can also rent a kayak and paddle to the trailhead on your own.

SECRET BEACH TIDE POOLS AND WATERFALL (page 93)
The hike to the Secret Beach tide pools and waterfall is reserved for the spring and summer *only* when the waves are flat. The oceanside cliff walk leads to a small waterfall and several swimmable tide pools.

HANAKAPI'AI FALLS (page 96)
For a quite strenuous hike with a reward of a beautiful waterfall cascading down high cliffs into a large swimming pool, make the

riverside walk to Ho'opi'i Falls

Hoʻopiʻi Falls

Waipoʻo Falls

trek to Hanakapiʻai Falls. The four-mile hike leads first to Hanakapiʻai Beach and then to the falls over generally rough terrain, but it's a rewarding experience.

WAILUA FALLS (page 57)

For gazing at waterfalls from a drive-up parking lot, Wailua Falls is an easily accessible option. You'll have a good view from the lookout point down to the falls and into the pool.

OPAEKAʻA FALLS (page 57)

On the east side, you can view Opaekaʻa Falls right from the parking lot. This is a convenient stop after looking at the sacred cultural sites along the Wailua River, such as the Poliahu Heiau across from the falls.

Wailua Falls

Opaekaʻa Falls

Best for Honeymooners

There couldn't be a better place to spend time with your *ku'uipo* (sweetheart) while on your honeymoon than Kaua'i. Some of the most romantic things to do on the island are free.

SUNSETS

One of the best places to catch the sunset is at Polihale State Park (page 153) on the west side, where you'll see the sunset with Ni'ihau island in the distance. On the south side a romantic restaurant and great place to watch the sunset is the Beach House Restaurant (page 140).

WATERFALLS AND NATURAL POOLS

Enjoying a natural swimming pool under a waterfall may perhaps be the ultimate romantic experience. Waterfalls with generally swimmable conditions include Secret Falls (page 42) on the Wailua River, the pools on the Swimming Pool Trail (page 46), and, for adventurous couples, Hanakapi'ai Falls (page 96).

EATS

Oasis (page 68) on the east side, Mediterranean Gourmet (page 108) on the north side, and Pomodoro Ristorante (page 142) in Kalaheo are all great places for a romantic dinner. What may be the most romantic meal possible is one prepared on the beach for you by Heavenly Creations (page 111). It caters unique and romantic meals to couples on the beach, complete with a dinner table and tiki torches.

CRUISES

Sunset and snorkel cruises are by far a romantic and classic Kaua'i experience. Contact one of the many boat tour companies leaving from the west side, which offer multiple cruises with combinations of snorkeling, sunset sails, and dinners. A company with romantic options is Blue Dolphin Charters (page 127). It offers a two-hour South Side Sunset Sail in the Po'ipu area. Food, cocktails, and romantic sunsets are enjoyed on this tour, along with whales during whale-watching season.

Sunsets at Polihale State Park are always exquisite.

EAST SIDE

Kaua'i's east side stretches from Lihu'e to Anahola and is a bustling area (by Kaua'i standards) lined with beaches, dotted with homes and businesses, yet still adorned with cultural sites and natural wonders. Sacred archaeological sites, dramatic waterfalls, rivers, and hikes with stunning views provide a backdrop to Kaua'i's central areas. There are many outdoor possibilities to be explored here: Have an adventurous day on ATVs and ziplines on rarely explored territory behind Lihu'e, paddle up Wailua River past cultural sites to a waterfall, hike along one of many long jungle hikes with views, or surf, swim, and sunbathe on the white-sand beaches.

Lihu'e is home to Kaua'i's most concentrated population of both people and buildings. Kaua'i's most developed district prospered as a plantation town until 1996, when the sugar mill shut down, putting an end to an era that defined the island. The area is busy, but still extremely laid-back, and is the island's central place for shopping and running errands, with a large selection of high-end dining. The main city on the island is home to big shopping centers, state and county buildings, and Kaua'i Community College, as well as important sites to visit like the Kaua'i Museum, Kilohana Plantation, and Alakoko Fishpond, which encompass the area's history. And of course, like the rest of the island, Lihu'e has its fair share of outdoor locations to satisfy water-sport lovers, beach bums, and jungle explorers.

Farther north is the **Coconut Coast,** where Kapa'a and Wailua are decorated with coconut trees planted by a copra plantation

© JADE ECKARDT

HIGHLIGHTS

LOOK FOR  TO FIND RECOMMENDED
SIGHTS, ACTIVITIES, DINING, AND LODGING.

Lydgate Beach Park: Bring your snorkeling gear and enjoy viewing the fish in the calm protected pools, which are perfect places to swim. Picnic tables, pavilions, and two awesome playgrounds make for an ideal day at the beach (page 36).

Donkey Beach: One of the more remote beaches in the area, this long, white-sand beach is perfect for sunbathing and beachcombing away from the crowds (page 37).

Surf at Kalapaki Beach: The crescent moon-shaped beach is ideal for calm swimming, surfing, and body-boarding. Take a stroll, swim, watch surfers, or catch a wave yourself (page 39).

Kayak the Wailua River: A waterfall, lush jungle, and calm waters make kayaking on the Wailua River a must-do adventure that has something for everyone (page 41).

Nounou Mountain East Trail: This strenuous yet rewarding hiking trail offers a sense of solitude and spectacular views from Mount Wai'ale'ale to far down along the coast (page 44).

Ho'opi'i Falls: This wonderful hike through a tunnel of trees along the Kapa'a Stream to two waterfalls is a gorgeous nature walk (page 44).

Kaua'i Museum: This museum is a real treat. Learn about the history and culture of Kaua'i and its people to enhance your island experience (page 52).

Kilohana Plantation: Take a trip back in time while exploring an expansive and elegant estate. Ride the sugar train, shop, and enjoy a meal at the upscale restaurant (page 55).

Wailua Falls: Gaze at the famous 80-foot gorgeous waterfall, easily accessed by car (page 57).

entrepreneur who had dreams of making it big on a plantation. The palms still tower today, moving their slender fronds in the trade winds as gracefully as hula dancers. Locals call the area home, and many independent shops, restaurants, and activity outfitters are scattered around this area. **Wailua** means "two waters," a name that makes sense considering it lies along the ocean and inland harbors freshwater rivers and waterfalls. Perhaps Wailua's

most intriguing element is the Wailua River, where *ali'i* gathered traditionally for sacred events and left archaeological remains to tell the story. That is why the *ali'i* referred to it as Wailua Nui Ho'ano (Great Sacred Wailua). The extra-tall royal palms symbolize a place of royalty in Hawaiian culture. Many *heiau* were built in the area, and their sparse remains still can be seen along the banks of the river. The road leading along the Wailua River was

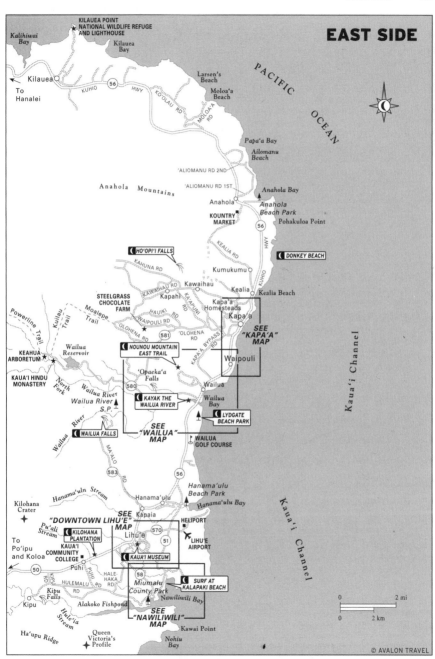

EAST SIDE

Kalihiwai Bay

KILAUEA POINT NATIONAL WILDLIFE REFUGE AND LIGHTHOUSE

Kilauea Bay

Kilauea

To Hanalei

KUHIO HWY 56

KO'OLAU RD

MOLOA'A RD

Larsen's Beach

Moloa'a Beach

PACIFIC OCEAN

Papa'a Bay

Ailomanu Beach

'ALIOMANU RD 2ND

Anahola Mountains

'ALIOMANU RD 1ST

Anahola Bay

Anahola

KOUNTRY MARKET

Anahola Beach Park

56

Pohakuloa Point

KEALIA RD

◖ HO'OPI'I FALLS

KAHUNA RD

Kumukumu

◖ DONKEY BEACH

KAWAIHAU RD

Kawaihau

Kealia

KUHIO HWY

Kealia Beach

STEELGRASS CHOCOLATE FARM

Kapahi

HAUIKI RD

KAAPUNI RD

Kapa'a Homesteads

Kapa'a

Powerline Trail

Kuilau Trail

Moalepe Trail

WAIPOULI RD

'OLOHENA RD

581

KAPA'A BYPASS RD

SEE "KAPA'A" MAP

Wailua Reservoir

'OLOHENA RD

◖ NOUNOU MOUNTAIN EAST TRAIL

Waipouli

KEAHUA ARBORETUM

KAUA'I HINDU MONASTERY

North Fork

Wailua River

580

'Opaeka'a Falls

Wailua

◖ KAYAK THE WAILUA RIVER

Wailua Bay

Wailua River S.P.

Wailua River

◖ WAILUA FALLS

◖ LYDGATE BEACH PARK

SEE "WAILUA" MAP

WAILUA GOLF COURSE

MA'ALO RD

583

56

Hanama'uln Stream

Hanama'ulu

Hanama'ulu Beach Park

Kilohana Crater

Kapaia

SEE "DOWNTOWN LIHU'E" MAP

Hanama'ulu Bay

Kaua'i Channel

Pu'ali Stream

◖ KILOHANA PLANTATION

HELIPORT

570

To Po'ipu and Koloa

KAUA'I COMMUNITY COLLEGE

Lihu'e

51

LIHU'E AIRPORT

50

Puhi

◖ KAUA'I MUSEUM

HALE-HAKA

58

KIPU RD

PUHI RD

HULEMALU RD

Kipu Falls

Kipu

Miumalu County Park

◖ SURF AT KALAPAKI BEACH

Alakoko Fishpond

Nawiliwili Bay

SEE "NAWILIWILI" MAP

Hale'ia Stream

Ha'upu Ridge

Queen Victoria's Profile

Kawai Point

Nohiu Bay

Kaua'i Channel

0   2 mi

0   2 km

© AVALON TRAVEL

THE BEST DAY ON THE EAST SIDE

To experience the best of the best on the east side, begin early and be ready for a busy day. Because Kaua'i's most spectacular beaches are found on other parts of island, a day on the east side should be spent with activities rather than lounging on the sand. Begin in Kapa'a and work your way toward Lihu'e because some of the Kapa'a and Wailua sights are best in the morning. If you begin your day early, with having breakfast around 8 A.M., you should be finished and ready for dinner around 7:30 P.M.

- Welcome the day with breakfast at **Kountry Kitchen** or the **Country Moon Rising Bakery** in Kapa'a.

- When your belly is full, either walk along the river to **Ho'opi'i Falls** or kayak the **Wailua River.** If you choose the hike, just head up the road, but if you'd rather paddle up the Wailua River make sure to book a reservation in advance. Check with your outfitter to see if they provide lunch; you can grab lunch in Kapa'a afterward if they don't.

- After your morning nature experience, head back to Kapa'a for lunch at **Mermaids Cafe** or **Pacific Island Bistro.**

- After lunch, head south to **Lydgate Beach Park** for some spectacular snorkeling and cooling off in the calm pools. Spend some time viewing the underwater world and relaxing in the sun. Don't forget your snorkel equipment here.

- Then don't miss a trip to **Wailua Falls.** This is usually a quick stop by car.

- Head over to Lihu'e for a visit to the **Kilohana Plantation.** Browse the shops and plantation grounds, or take a ride on the historical train.

- For dinner there are two great options in Lihu'e. For a spectacular dinner of local food try **Gaylord's.** To enjoy a classic Hawaiian restaurant in a semi-formal atmosphere, have a meal on the water at **Duke's.**

Wailua Falls

© JADE ECKARDT

KAUA'I'S OWN MOKIHANA FLOWER

While on Kaua'i you will most likely see and hear the word *mokihana* often. Although it's commonly referred to as a flower, it's actually a light green berry. Deemed the island's official lei-making material, the mokihana berry is strung like beads and usually intertwined with the maile plant. The berries emanate the faint scent of anise. Found in wet forests of high elevations from around 1,200 to 4,000 feet, the mokihana is found only on Kaua'i and is also the island's official flower.

with an eclectic mix of local style and hip, offbeat culture. Meaning, "to hold," as in to hold a canoe on course, Kapa'a historically served as a place for the canoes to stop and prepare for making the journey to O'ahu. Running along the coast, Kapa'a offers bohemian boutiques, elegant and healthy eateries, and a historical feel that enhances the Kaua'i experience. In downtown Kapa'a, small eateries and cafés offer a range of cuisines from local style to vegetarian to fresh fruit stands. Beaches line the area, and surfing, body-boarding, and a bike path create a beach town atmosphere. Behind the town on the northern end is Ho'opi'i Falls, where you'll find a wonderful hike along a river and to a waterfall.

Heading north from Kapa'a, you'll pass through **Anahola.** Although some like to consider this part of the northern side because of the increased greenery and lush feeling, locals stay true to Anahola remaining part of the eastern side. Out here, the white-sand beaches lining the coast are usually less crowded than the east-side beaches behind them or the northern beaches ahead.

called the King's Highway, and only those invited were allowed to approach the royal settlement. The mountains behind Wailua are lush and green and home to the mountain range Sleeping Giant, with hiking trails boasting views that can't be beat.

Just down the road is **Kapa'a,** a quaint town

Beaches

The east side's coast is dotted with numerous white-sand beaches, and each location's environment is very different. Sunbathe or surf in Lihu'e, snorkel and barbecue in Wailua, and catch some more waves or enjoy a beach-side bike ride in Kapa'a. They're all pretty, but most are some of Kaua'i's more popular and crowded beaches. If you're staying in Lihu'e and don't want to go far they will more than satisfy, but I recommend traveling north or south for Kaua'i's most spectacular beaches.

LIHU'E
Niumalu Beach Park
Just west of the Nawiliwili Small Boat Harbor, Niumalu is a county park resting along the bank of the Hule'ia River, where scenes from *Raiders of the Lost Ark* were filmed. Popular

with locals, it has with pavilions, showers, and toilets. The beach park is used mostly for launching kayaks to explore the river, for barbecues, and for family functions. If you're in the area and looking for a quick picnic stop this will do, but other beaches are much nicer. To get here, turn off of Nawiliwili Road onto Niumalu Road. Follow it to the end.

Kalapaki Beach
Although Kalapaki Beach fronts the Kaua'i Marriott Resort, access to the beach is open to anyone. The sand is white, but down by the stream it's a little darker from dirt and sediment. Because it's so popular and fronts the hotel, it lacks the feeling of seclusion that many Kaua'i beaches offer. The nice thing about Kalapaki Beach is that the waves break

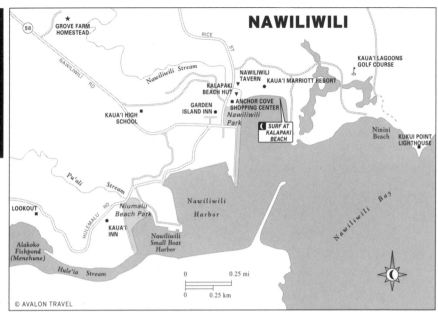

NAWILIWILI

★ GROVE FARM HOMESTEAD
KAUA'I LAGOONS GOLF COURSE
NAWILIWILI TAVERN
KALAPAKI BEACH HUT
KAUA'I MARRIOTT RESORT
GARDEN ISLAND INN
ANCHOR COVE SHOPPING CENTER
KAUA'I HIGH SCHOOL
Nawiliwili Park
SURF AT KALAPAKI BEACH
Ninini Beach
KUKUI POINT LIGHTHOUSE
LOOKOUT
Niumalu Beach Park
Nawiliwili Harbor
Nawiliwili Bay
KAUA'I INN
Nawiliwili Small Boat Harbor
Alakoko Fishpond (Menehune)
Hule'ia Stream
0   0.25 mi
0   0.25 km

© AVALON TRAVEL

pretty far out, so they've usually turned into gentle surges of water before they get to shore. It is a very good spot for swimming, bodysurfing, and occasionally snorkeling. Far out in the bay, stand-up paddlers, surfers, and body boarders take advantage of the breaking waves. The popular eatery Duke's fronts the beach here, and is another reason why it's a well-known spot.

To get here, take Rice Street down toward the ocean and stick to your right as it becomes Route 51. Access is via the hotel on your left if you park in the visitors area. Or, if you keep going, on the north end of Nawiliwili Park before the Anchor Cove Shopping Center there's a small parking lot. Look for the narrow footbridge going over Nawiliwili Stream to the hotel property and the beach.

Ninini Beach

Located to the harbor side of Ninini Point and the lighthouse, Ninini Beach is a narrow sandy beach fronting the low cliff. It's calm most of the year, but during large surf or windy days

the beach can be a little rougher. This is a small and less-visited beach that is very good for sunbathing and a secluded beach day. Snorkeling can be good on the left side by the rocks, but it's a little dangerous. To get here, take Pali Kai Road past The Marriott, walk along the edge of the Kaua'i Lagoons Golf Club, and keep to your right until you see the steep trail to the beach below. If you take the fork on your left you'll find its sister beach, also known as Ninini, which is another less-visited area for sunbathing and swimming.

Hanama'ulu Beach

Hanama'ulu is another beach that is popular with locals. People utilize the picnic tables, showers, toilets, pavilion, and camping ground for weekend getaways. The facilities are a bit run-down and there is a small playground. It's not a top choice to spend a beach day, but considering it's just north of the airport it will suffice for a lunch break or a place to recoup while figuring out your next stop. Follow Hehi Road off of Route 51 to the beach park.

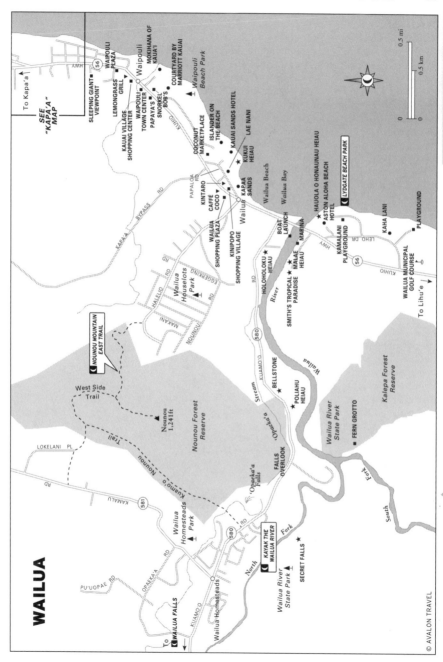

WAILUA

© AVALON TRAVEL

WAILUA
Wailua Beach

Wailua Beach reaches from the mouth of the Wailua River to the first rocky point heading north. On this point are the nearly nonexistent remains of a sacred *heiau,* one of many in the area. Surfers sometimes catch waves here, but the ocean is unprotected and often gets windy and dominated by strong currents. So, it's not the most ideal spot for swimming. However, when this beach is calm it is a local favorite for a beach stroll and sunbathing. The river mouth adds an element of action, and when the river is flowing heavily this can also be an unsafe place to hang out in the water. It's not one of Kaua'i's most spectacular beaches, but it's centrally located and rests in an area that was important to Hawaiians in the past. Petroglyphs can be seen carved into rocks at the mouth of the river when the tide is very low. It's at the mouth of the Wailua River, and you can pull up roadside off of Route 56.

◖ Lydgate Beach Park

On the south side of the Wailua River and behind the Aston Hotel lies Lydgate Beach Park. Two protected pools that create calm places to swim and snorkel are the highlight of Lydgate. The pools are protected by lava rock barriers that create perfect places to swim and snorkel regardless of surf conditions. It's safe for young children and anyone else who prefers to relax in the water worry-free. There is a lifeguard here, as well as sheltered picnic tables, grills, and restrooms and showers, but camping is not allowed.

The **Kamalani Playground** is also here and is any child's dream. The castle-like playground is about as huge and elaborate as a playground could ever get. Towers, slides, swings, interactive parts such as a huge xylophone, and a lot more are here to entertain children for a long time. A large pavilion is perfect for lunch or a birthday party.

A newly created section of the beach park has a number of bike paths and walkways as well as more restrooms, picnic benches, and another children's playground. To get to the second section drive down the paved road at the northern end of the Wailua Municipal Golf Course until it branches toward the sea. Turn onto Leho Drive and there are two access roads that head to the ocean. You can find parking along the way to the beach.

KAPA'A
Waipouli Beach

Just north of Lydgate Beach Park is Waipouli Beach. Although it's not ideal for swimming because of strong currents and a sharp reef, the paved trail here is a great place for a long oceanside jog. The beach is narrow and is an easily accessible and central spot that begins at the Coconut Marketplace. It runs a good distance in front of a number of hotels, such as the Kaua'i Sands Hotel, Islander on the Beach, Lae Nani, and Kapa'a Sands Resort.

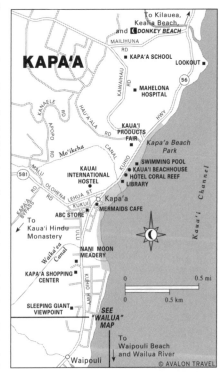

Waipouli Beach Park
(Baby Beach)

While on Kaua'i you'll probably hear the name Fuji Beach or Baby Beach. Both refer to Waipouli Beach Park, lying north of Waipouli Beach. Perfect for children and a popular spot for local families, it's a wonderful location to spend the day in the water rather than on the beach watching big waves. A large part of the ocean is protected by a long, natural stone breakwater, and unless the waves are huge, this spot is normally swimmable. Turn onto Pahihi or Makana Street and Moanakai runs parallel to the ocean. Although it's known as a great spot for children, always check out the ocean conditions first.

Kapa'a Beach Park

A little north of Baby Beach is another local-favorite beach composed of white sand and scattered rocks. The beach runs north from Waikaea for almost a mile between mile markers 8 and 9 until it ends near a community swimming pool and the Kapa'a library. Various roads lead to the beach from the highway and all are obvious; there is nothing obstructing the view from highway to coast. The beach park comprises just over 15 acres, with a pavilion, picnic tables, showers, toilets, and grills at the southern end. Several patches of sand break up the somewhat rocky beach, enabling swimming if the waves are mellow. It's a nice place for a meal or a bike ride along the coast, but otherwise it's best to move on to a sandier beach for swimming.

Kealia Beach

Shortly after Kapa'a Beach Park is Kealia Beach, a popular spot for locals and visitors alike. The half-mile-long beach has restrooms, lifeguards, and pavilions with picnic tables. The east end of the beach is usually the emptiest and is often covered with debris from the mouth of the Kapa'a Stream. Parking usually isn't a problem here as numerous parking spots back the beach. This is a popular place for surfing and body-boarding with locals, and is good for swimming when the waves are small. This is definitely one of the more crowded beaches on Kaua'i, but it makes for an easy swim while in the area. The waves here are known to be pounding, so it's best to stay near shore. The beach begins about a half mile before mile marker 10.

◖ Donkey Beach

A short distance down the road from Kealia Beach is Donkey Beach. This is a beautiful, remote white-sand beach where the swimming is less than ideal but the atmosphere is wonderful. It is a hidden treasure thanks to the 10-minute walk down to the beach. Swimming can be rough, but sunbathing is nice here thanks to the ample space and the good chance you'll be alone. The ocean here is choppy with a strong current on a regular basis and has no lifeguards. The occasional monk seal is spotted here, so if you see one stay a good distance away. This is a beach known to be a favorite for those who like nude sunbathing, but most likely you'll find the beach empty or see a few people enjoying it with their suits on.

© JADE ECKARDT

The secluded Donkey Beach is gorgeous.

To get here, turn right about a half mile past mile marker 11 at the brown sign with hikers on it. Parking is up top near the restrooms, and the easily noticeable trailhead is on the east end of the parking lot.

ANAHOLA TO KILAUEA
Anahola Beach Park

Like many of Kaua'i's beach parks, Anahola Beach Park has an open area for picnic tables, grills, showers, restrooms, and various camping spots if you have a county permit. This is a popular camping spot for locals, who like to set up elaborate camps for the weekend, so it's generally not a secluded spot, but visitors are welcome to enjoy it. The swimming is safe in the protective cove on the eastern end of the beach as well as in the river. Toward the north end the currents are usually stronger and the waves bigger. If you do plan to camp, don't leave your possessions unattended for too long; the area is known for occasional incidents of theft. The ironwood trees provide a natural shade and a break from the sun.

On the north side of the stream is **Aliomanu Beach.** Homes and vacation rentals border this less-visited beach. It's long with white sand, and there are some rocky spots in the water, but it can be a nice place to come and stroll and most likely be alone. The northern end of the beach is nicer, so take a stroll down and explore. To get here, turn right onto the second Aliomanu Road, just a bit after mile marker 15, and keep to your right to access the eastern beach or take the first left and then right to access the northern beach.

Papaʻa Bay

Papaʻa Bay is another beautiful white-sand beach. The best thing about this beach is that you'll most likely be alone. It's great for a stroll or sunbathing, but swimming can be a bit rough. To get here, turn right onto the second Aliomanu Road, just a bit after mile marker 15. Take the first left and then a right and then follow the trail on the left. Park up here and walk about five minutes down through some bushes and over large rocks for a few minutes.

Water Sports

SNORKELING AND DIVING

The east side of Kaua'i has one spectacular snorkeling spot and several worth taking out the mask just to see what you find. It's always a good idea to have some basic gear other than a mask and snorkel, like protective gloves, foot coverage, fins, and of course an underwater camera. On the east side it's easy to run to a shop to grab any last-minute items because shops and beaches are all close together.

Wailua
LYDGATE BEACH PARK

Lydgate Beach Park is a snorkeler's dreamland, with two wonderfully protected pools in the ocean that, thanks to a rock barrier, are an easy and relaxing place to snorkel and swim. The fish go crazy in this spot and never fail to present an explosion of vibrant tropical colors

underwater. The ponds are almost always swimmable and calm, unless the surf is abnormally huge. Don't forget a camera here. There will usually be quite a few other snorkelers and general beach goers, so it's not the place for seclusion, but the snorkeling is awesome.

OUTFITTERS AND RENTALS

At **Boss Frog's** (4-746 Kuhio Hwy., 808/823-0220, www.bossfrog.com, 8 A.M.–5 P.M. daily) divers and snorkelers can find pretty much anything they could need to explore Kaua'i's underwater world. Snorkel rentals include everything from the basics to full professional snorkel sets. The average snorkel set that will get you through an enjoyable session rents for $8 per day. The shop offers all other beach needs, such as board rentals and other beach gear. Service

STAND-UP PADDLING (SUP)

Since 2006, stand-up paddling has become much more popular in Hawai'i and among surfers all over the world. Unlike standard surfing, stand-up paddling, otherwise known as SUP, requires standing up on a much thicker board and using a paddle to direct the board. A surf break dotted with SUPers is a common sight in Kaua'i. Some traditional surfers find it irritating because the SUPers can catch waves much easier and from much farther out in the lineup, which means they often catch the waves before standard surfers. But SUPing is not all about catching waves. The sport is hugely popular with ocean lovers who just like to just paddle around on a flat bay or a river.

© OLEG TOVKACH/WWW.123RF.COM

is friendly and open here and the workers are happy to guide you to the best spots.

Another tried and true place for snorkel rentals is **Snorkel Bob's** (4-734 Kuhio Hwy., 808/823-9433, www.snorkelbob.com, 8 A.M.–5 P.M. daily), where you can rent all the snorkel gear you could need. They offer complete sets, including a mask, snorkel, and net gear bag with grade A surgical quality silicone for ultimate comfort and water seal. The adult package goes for $35 a week or $22 per week for children. The budget crunch package offers a basic mask, snorkel and fins, and dive bag for $9 a week. A unique rental package is what they call The 4 Eyes RX Ensemble to compensate for nearsightedness while snorkeling. This includes a mask with a prescription lens for $44 per week for adults and $32 for kids. They also offer rentals for single snorkels ($7–12 per week), various fins ($8–12 per week), wetsuits ($20 per week), snorkel vests, life jackets, and flotation belts ($20 a week), and boogie boards for $26 a week. A fish identity card is a fun thing to pick up so you can tell friends later on what you saw.

Seasport Divers (4-976 Kuhio Hwy., 808/823-9222, www.seasportdivers.com, 9 A.M.–5 P.M. daily) has been in business since 1987 and is locally owned and operated. The Kapa'a location only rents gear and takes reservations for tours. They offer complete snorkel gear sets for *kama'aina* rates of $6 a day or $19 a week and visitor rates of $8 a day or $25 a week. A unique treat with these guys is the Ni'ihau or "Forbidden Island dive," where you explore the waters around Ni'ihau and Lehua Island. Thanks to the lack of visitors and fishing on the island, Ni'ihau's waters are alive and thriving. Two- to three-tank dives off a boat are offered from $185 for just snorkeling or $310 for certified divers.

SURFING AND STAND-UP PADDLING

Surfing on the east side is usually at two main surf breaks. If you want to try surfing on the Coconut Coast and are a beginner, it's a good idea to get a surf lesson rather than renting a board and going for it alone. Experienced surfers will have fun at these breaks and should be comfortable in somewhat crowded waves with some currents. Surfers can rent gear at several shops or bring their own board. Stand-up paddling can be done at most surf spots if the paddler is experienced.

Lihu'e
◖ KALAPAKI BEACH
A great place for beginner surfing, stand-up paddling, and body-boarding, Kalapaki Beach is a

Surfers and body-boarders love the waves at Kalapaki Beach.

© JADE ECKARDT

local favorite. A rocky point lines the northern side of the bay, and a left-hand breaking wave diminishes as it gets closer to the beach. Mornings usually provide the best conditions, with light wind. Wind usually picks up in Hawaii midmorning and mellows out in late afternoon or early evening. Head down Rice Street and look for the small road behind the Anchor Cove Shopping Center. There's a small dirt parking lot by the river and Duke's Canoe Club.

OUTFITTERS

For lessons at the popular Kalapaki Beach try **Kalapaki Beach Boys** (808/821-1000, li-likoi@trykauai.com), which offers 90-minute classes at the beach with no more than four people in a class. Classes begin with about 30 minutes on land with the instructor giving tips and sharing information, and the rest of the class in the water. Classes include land demo, boards, rash guards to protect against sun and rash, and booties for foot protection. Lessons are daily and usually at 10 A.M., noon, and 2 P.M. Price with tax totals $78.12 per person.

To explore a river on a board, try the stand-up paddle tour offered by **Outfitters Kauai** (2827A Po'ipu Rd., 808/742-9667, www.outfitterskauai.com, $122). The tour takes you on an adventure up the Hule'ia River. You will paddle downwind on the calm river, hike to waterfalls, and even get some water zipline action. The two-mile paddle lasts about a half day.

Kapa'a
KEALIA BEACH

Kealia Beach is very popular, and is generally crowded with locals for surfing and body-boarding. The waves can get very pounding here, and the conditions can make for a strong current and windy surf session. For the experienced surfer it's a fun wave. The waves break both right- and left-handed. For beginners, it's possible for mellow conditions but with the usual crowd it can be a bit tough. If you're a surfing novice and you feel the conditions are good for you, try to sit on the very inside of the waves where they're smallest. The farther out you go the waves get bigger and the talent gets better. You can't miss Kealia in full view from Route 56, near mile marker 10 at the northern end of Kapaʻa.

OUTFITTERS
Kauaʻi Water Ski & Surf Co. (4-356 Kuhio Hwy., Kinipopo Shopping Village, 808/822-3574, www.kauaiwaterskiandsurf.com, 8 A.M.–6 P.M. Mon.–Sat. and 9 A.M.–4 P.M. Sun.) offers surf gear rentals and private surf lessons. Surfboards 6–10 feet long are for rent. Body boards and stand-up paddle boards are also available for rent.

They also provide private surf lessons one on one with an instructor, or you and a friend with an instructor. Both lessons last two hours, and if you still have energy afterward they allow you to play around with your board for a few extra hours at no charge. They do lessons in Wailua Bay but say that if you feel that the conditions aren't right for you they are happy to move to another location that you are more comfortable with. Lessons are available any time and day, but you must call and book in advance.

The surf shop offers all the surf gear you need for the water or just for style. Men and women's swimwear, clothing, accessories, and other surf-themed products are available in the shop.

KAYAKING
Kayaking is popular on east-side rivers. Avid kayakers will find exciting adventures to embark on, and those new to the sport will have plenty to choose from too.

Lihuʻe
OUTFITTERS
Visit **Aloha Canoes and Kayaks** (Kalapaki Marketplace, Ste. 106, 808/246-6804, 7:30 A.M.–6 P.M. Mon.–Fri.) to rent gear to paddle up the Huleʻia River through the rainforest. Guided trips will take you up the river and help you navigate your way through the terrain.

Kapaʻa
◖ WAILUA RIVER
The Wailua River is Kauaʻi's most popular spot for kayaking. The vast river holds a lot

© JADE ECKARDT

Home to numerous sacred sites along its banks, the Wailua River is a fun place for a kayak tour.

of gorgeous sights. Up the river you'll find **Fern Grotto,** a natural amphitheater where ferns hang in abundance; **Secret Falls** with its swimmable pool; and gorgeous views inland and on the banks. **Uluwehi Falls,** also known as Secret Falls, lies on the north side and is reachable after a paddle and a hike. It's about five miles round-trip and roughly three hours without stopping to explore the river. The most common way to navigate the river is with guided kayak tours. Only a few companies rent kayaks for independent paddling up the river. The Hollywood film *Outbreak* was filmed on north side of the river.

OUTFITTERS
Ali'i Kayaks (174 Wailua Rd., 808/241-7700, www.aliikayaks.com, 7:30 A.M.–7:30 P.M. Mon.–Sat., $40) offers a Wailua River kayak tour. The tour is led by a local guide who shares Hawaiian history and legends as you kayak along. The tour heads up the river's north fork and takes a short hike through the rainforest, ending at Secret Falls. Offered every day except for Sunday, the trip's check-in time is either 8:30 or 10:30 A.M., and reservations are required. They provide kayak equipment, a dry bag, and walking sticks. The tour lasts approximately 4.5 hours and includes four miles of kayaking and 1.5 miles of moderate hiking.

Another reliable option is **Kayak Kaua'i** (5-5070 Kuhio Hwy., 808/826-9844, www.kayakkauai.com, 7 A.M.–8 P.M. daily, $85 plus tax adults, $60 children under 12). They offer a one-day guided paddle up the Wailua River and hike to Secret Falls. The five-hour tour is fitting for families and allows you to swim in the freshwater stream or pool of the falls. Offered daily except Sunday, this tour has a 12-person capacity. Several tours are offered daily beginning with 7:45 and 8:45 A.M. check-ins, then 12:15 and 12:30 P.M. They provide kayaks with foot pedals and rudders, dry bags, life vests, juices and water, and a deli sandwich lunch with snacks and a vegetarian option.

Kayak Kaua'i is one of the few selected by the state to be an exclusive outfitter for lone kayaking up the Wailua River. They rent kayaks to those who wish to go unguided. The Wailua River Rental package includes double kayaks with a permit, life preservers, car racks, paddles, back rests, a map, and bow line. Dry bags, coolers, and walking sticks can also be rented separately. Kayakers need to bring lunch and other necessary supplies on this trip. The kayaks are dispatched between 8:30 and 11:30 A.M. and can be returned after sunset or before 8 A.M. the next day to the Kapa'a shop. No singles are available and price is $27 per person.

Kayak Wailua (4564 Haleilio Rd., 808/822-3388, www.kayakwailua.com, Mon.–Sat., $48) offers guided tours up the Wailua River. They offer dry bags and coolers to bring your own refreshments and food. They even offer adult sized triple kayaks for a family or group of friends. A trip up the river and a hike and swimming usually lasts about 4.5 hours. Tours depart at 9 and 10 A.M. and noon and 1 P.M.

Wailua Kayak Adventures (6575 Kuamo'o Rd., 808/822-5795, www.kauaiwailuakayak. com, Mon.–Sat.) offers four tours a day. The roughly 4.5-hour tour provides paddlers with a two-mile round-trip paddle and a hike to Secret Falls for a swim. They offer cruise ship shuttle services for $80 per van load. Price is $47.87 with tax per person.

A favorite with many is **Outfitters Kauai** (2827A Po'ipu Rd., 808/742-9667, www.outfitterskauai.com), which offers a guided Wailua River tour to Secret Falls. A lunch is included with a choice of a turkey watercress wrap or Mediterranean veggie wrap. Lunch comes with pasta salad and a cookie. Cold drinks are available throughout the day. Prices are $102 per adult and $82 for children 5–14 years old. The company asks that participants are comfortable kayaking for 60–90 minutes and walking two miles of rugged trail.

One of the original kayak companies on the Wailua River, **Wailua Kayak and Canoe** (169 Wailua Rd., 808/821-1188, www.wailuakayakandcanoe.net) offers both four-hour guided kayak tours as well as five-hour kayak rentals (single $45, double $75). The four-hour waterfall guided tour includes a class one easy paddle and a short hike to Secret Falls for $49. The company does not provide lunch.

WATERSKIING, WAKEBOARDING, AND OTHER POWER SPORTS
Wailua

The only company to offer these kinds of boarding opportunities is **Kaua'i Water Ski and Surf Co.** (4-356 Kuhio Hwy., Kinipopo Shopping Village, 808/822-3574, www.kauaiwaterskiandsurf.com, 9 A.M.–5 P.M. Mon.–Fri. and 9 A.M.–noon Sat.). For a unique experience on the gorgeous Wailua River, hop on some water skis for an experience you'll never forget. The company also offers wakeboarding on the river, kneeboarding, and hydrofoil, where your board rises above the water while supported by a hydrofoil wing that remains under the water. The company offers the experience for beginners as well as experienced boarders who want to work on their technique while in Kaua'i. The boat fits five extra passengers, who can come along for free and watch while you board around the river.

FISHING
Lihu'e

Departing from Lihu'e's Nawiliwili Harbor, **Kai Bear Sportfishing Charters** (808/652-4556, www.kaibear.imoutdoorshosting.com, reservations required) offers a variety of shared and exclusive private charters for a range of interests and budgets. Charters go out on one of their two boats, the 38-foot *Kai Bear* or the 42-foot *Grander*. The boats offer at least one custom-made Blue Water Rod and Penn International Gold two-speed reel. Beverages are included. Four-hour charters range $130–945. Six-hour charters range $130–1,395. Eight-hour charters range $1,400–1,795, and for a to-be-determined price you keep all the fish, a unique offer considering the catch usually belongs to the captain. Bottled water and

soft drinks are provided, and guests are allowed to bring their own food and alcoholic beverages but no glass containers.

Lahela Sportfishing (Slip 109, Nawiliwili Small Boat Harbor, 808/635-4020, www.lahela-adventures.com, reservations required) leaves out of Nawiliwili Harbor and takes guests out on the 34-foot *Lahela*. The boat is the only fishing boat certified by the Kauai Coast Guard in operation on the island and takes up to 14 passengers. Private fishing charters range from $575 for four hours to $1,725 for 12 hours. Deluxe shared charters are priced at $219 with spectators at half price. Economy shared charters require a minimum of four anglers at $135. Guests must be at least seven years old.

Kapa'a

C-Lure Charters (Nawiliwili Harbor, 808/822-5963, www.clurekauai.com) takes anglers out on the Mele Kai, a custom-built 41-foot Noosa cat equipped with Shimano tackle, depth sounders, and a GPS. It seats six people in the shade and has a fighting chair. Guests must bring their own food and alcoholic beverages, but C-Lure provides fishing tackle, bait, soft drinks, and water. They cannot take more than six people but can arrange for additional boats to caravan if you want to bring more people. Charters range from half-day to whole-day trips and custom charters. Prices range from $100 for non-fishing spectators to $1,050 for a full day up to six anglers.

Going out with **Hawaiian Style Fishing** (1651 Hoomaha Pl., 808/635-7335, www.hawaiianstylefishing.com) means you go out to sea on a 25-foot Radon. They do sport and bottom fishing and say they're prepared for any fish. You're invited to bring along your lucky lure or pole and the captain will most likely give it a try. Four-hour shared charters run from $130 per person, while private are $600. Eight-hour private charters are $900.

Hiking and Biking

HIKING

Miles of trails weave through the east side's interior behind Wailua and Kapa'a. Much hiking here winds through lush green forest, while some goes through dry and shadeless areas. A great thing about hiking in this area is that vistas are abundant, offering sweeping views from the island's center and all along the coast.

Wailua

The Nounou Mountain Trails comprise three trails. They are all inland in the mountains above Wailua and zigzag over Nounou Ridge, the Sleeping Giant.

◖ NOUNOU MOUNTAIN EAST TRAIL

Many feel the nearly two-mile-long (each way) east trail is the prettiest of the three and can easily take up most of the day if you take your time enjoying views and lunch. The trail is rather tough but can be done by a fit family and sees a nearly 1,000-foot elevation gain while hiking.

The east side of the trail begins off of Haleilio Road. The trailhead leads to a series of well-defined switchbacks. It continues with an incline through lush forest providing some shade. As you walk along look for flowers and guavas and passion fruit, and feel free to enjoy some. At the half-mile mark there is a fork; *be sure not to go to the left here.* It's dangerous, as are most side trails on this hike. At the 1.5-mile marker the west trail intersects, but stick to the east trail. Farther along at the main fork in the trail, take the left path, which leads to a picnic table, shelter, and bench. Take in the views because they're wonderful here. At the table, where you hopefully enjoyed a meal, a trail goes south up to the giant's head and face. The view is truly amazing!

However, as gorgeous as this part of the trail is, it's what locals would call gnarly. It goes across the giant's throat, up the head, and is dangerous, narrow, and steep. But for the truly adventurous folks, the view is one of the biggest rewards you could ever get. So, the picnic table

is a good idea for the end of this trail unless you are fearless. If you proceed, you'll walk along the spine of the mountain with deadly drops of hundreds of feet on each side. From the face, you'll be treated to an amazing all-around view. To get here, drive 1.2 miles up Haleilio Road. Parking is by the 38th pole on the right, which has a sign indicating it is pole 38.

KUAMO'O-NOUNOU TRAIL

The Kuamo'o-Nounou Trail is about two miles one way and is tough, but suitable for a fit family. The trail begins with a wooden bridge over the Opaeka'a Stream. From here you veer left gradually at an incline. It takes about one hour each way and sees about an 800-foot elevation gain or loss depending on which way you're going. This trail is steeper than the east trail. The end of the trail intersects with the west side trail. About three-quarters of a mile from the trailhead is a shelter on a perch with great views of Kaua'i's highest point, Kawaikini, Wailua Homesteads, and views to the northwest. At the 1.8-mile point it begins the decline to the west trail. You can usually see waterfalls if it's been raining. To get here, head up Kuamo'o Road, after Opaeka'a Falls. There is a pasture on the near corner of Maile Street on the right side and a home on the far corner. You'll see the Nounou Trail sign.

NOUNOU MOUNTAIN WEST TRAIL

The Nounou Mountain West Trail is 1.5 miles and one hour each way. A little shorter and less steep than the east-side trail, the west trail has more shade, provided by tall pines, and meets up with the Kuamo'o Nounou Trail after about a half mile in. The trail ascends faster than the others, making it quite a workout. Keep going and you'll meet up with the east-side trail and then have access to the incredibly dangerous trail to the summit and giant's head.

Kapa'a
◖ HO'OPI'I FALLS

This low-impact hike is more of a forest walk

© JADE ECKARDT

The long riverside walk to Ho'opi'i Falls is a great way to start the day.

and brings explorers to two falls on the Kapa'a Stream, accessed by a lovely walk along it. It's hard to say how long the walk is—it just keeps following the stream—but the good news is that you can walk five minutes down the dirt hill just to meet the stream under a magical canopy and enjoy time there (while braving mosquitos). Or, you can continue to walk for a half hour or so. As you head down the trail look for *liliko'i* (passion fruit) on the ground; they fall from very high up on the jungle canopy. You'll probably run into the occasional resident going for a jog or walking a dog. Along the trail are thimbleberry bushes that have bright red berries similar to raspberries. Give one a try. When you come down to the river, hang a right slightly up from the river and continue on the well-worn, narrow trail. You'll see multiple offshoot trails going down to the river. They're a bit steep, and the red dirt can be slippery. When you can hear the falls, this is most likely the right side trail down to the top of the falls. Here you can sit, spend some time, eat, or just hang out near the falls and along the river.

To get to the bottom of the falls you'd have to continue downstream then head back up in the water. When you're done, backtrack up the side trail and continue on.

Eventually you'll have to go down to the river and walk along the edge. Stay near the water's edge to stay off of private land. Right before the second waterfall the trail goes over the river to the top of the falls, and this is the end of the trail. Don't forget your camera on this hike, and make sure you have enough time to leisurely explore. If you want to really enjoy it bring mosquito repellent.

To get here, turn onto Kawaihau Road from Kuhio Highway. Head inland for about 12 minutes and then take a right onto Kapahi Road. Look for the yellow metal post on your left at the trailhead. Right past here is a dirt pull-off spot that fits about three cars. Please go very slow on the road; this is a very local and mellow neighborhood.

POWERLINE TRAIL

This 13-mile, strenuous trail will take you from

the east side to the north over the course of the day. If you choose to complete the whole thing, you'd need a pickup on the north side, or you could take the bus back to the east side. The problem with trekking the whole path, though, is that you'd have to get a taxi or ride a couple miles back up to the trailhead, so I'm recommending to just go as far as you like and turn around back to the beginning. The rough road was built for the installment of power transmission lines between Lihu'e and Hanalei, although some believe the trail was originally a connection between the two areas for Hawaiians.

Starting at the Kapa'a trailhead, you'll encounter a rather steep incline for a little while, and from there it's pretty level traveling with an eventual descent into Hanalei. Not too far from the beginning you'll see **Kapakaiki Falls** on your right, and soon after is **Kapakanui Falls.** These falls aren't close enough to access but make a nice sight. The part of the island the trail weaves through is densely lush and green and creates a feeling of strolling through a magical forest. But the road itself is bare, dry, and hot. This means that although the surrounding foliage is thick, the trail itself provides no shade. Remember to bring water for this trail. Roughly halfway down you begin to see the ocean, and glorious views are offered along the way. Random roads jut off the main road, but I don't recommend following any. Footing off the main road can be unstable, and the biggest thrills are found by sticking to the road. After completing the incline from the trailhead you'll be treated to great views of **Mount Wai'ale'ale.**

Others you may see on this trail are mountain bikers, dirt bikers, and hunters and their dogs in season. Still, you'll most likely have the trail to yourself. To get here, head up Kuamo'o Road and pass the Wailua Reservoir till the pavement ends and then go about a mile to the Keahua Arboretum. At the arboretum, cross the stream and walk up the steep road; you'll see a four-wheel-drive track heading uphill to your right. This is the start of the trail.

KUILAU AND MOALEPE TRAILS
The 4.5-mile Kuilau Trail begins about 200

yards before the entrance to the Keahua Arboretum and takes about 2–3 hours round-trip. There are a few parking spots at the trailhead marker on the right side of Kuamo'o Road. This somewhat mellow trail leads to a picnic area with tables and shelter after about a mile. Not long after this, the prize of this trail is the mountain views, which are some of the best you can find. Views to Mount Wai'ale'ale and the crater, and down to Kilohana and Ha'upu Ridge, are in sight. From here, keep following the trail circling around the hill until you come to a small wooden footbridge. Here, about two miles from where you began your nature stroll, the Kuilau Trail meets the Moalepe Trail. After crossing the bridge the Kuilau Trail weaves through a tunnel of trees to an open flat spot and then turns east. The Moalepe Trail begins at the end of Olohena Road. This trail is popular with local horseback riders and offers awesome views before joining back with the Kuilau Trail almost three miles from Olohena Road.

SWIMMING POOL TRAIL
For a cool pool and Mount Wai'ale'ale views, take this hike. The best thing about this adventure is the two pools of water you are treated to, depending on how far you go. This trail heads into the center of the island and leads to a stream-gauging station and dammed section of the river. The locked gate at the beginning of the trail is where scenes of the entrance gate were filmed for *Jurassic Park.* Walk around the gate and head up the road for roughly 45 minutes up an incline and you will be at the gauging station and the dammed part of the river. Here, you are very close to the center of the island. This is a great place to just relax, meditate, or enjoy a picnic lunch. From here you can see the crater, and if it's been rainy, as the center of Kaua'i usually is, you may see many waterfalls cascading down the green cliffs.

From here it's about an hour and a half via either a walk through a tunnel in the hill that requires most people to hunch over or a trek over the hill to the falls and the refreshing pool at the bottom. A flashlight is a good idea for the tunnel, and of course the water level has a lot to do with safety. Soon after you'll see the chilly and refreshing pool, and if you swim through it and stick to the right for just a few minutes you'll come to the falls, with another small and refreshing bubbling pool. Only go in if the water flow isn't too treacherous—it's a highly enjoyable experience.

To get here, head to the Keahua Arboretum off of Kuamoʻo Road and follow the gravel road running across the stream at the arboretum. Stick to the main road for about four miles. The road is marked as being for four-wheel-drives, but it is usually fine for two-wheel-drives unless it is very muddy. At the fork in the road keep to the left, then there's another fork with a gate. If the gate is open keep driving, and if it's closed park here and you'll just have to walk longer. The second gate is the *Jurassic Park* gate. Go around the gate and begin your adventure.

HIKING TOURS AND GEAR

For all the hiking gear you could need, stop by **Da Life** (3500 Rice St., on Kalapaki Beach, 808/246-6333, www.livedalife.com, 9 A.M.–5 P.M. Mon.–Fri. and 10 A.M.–4 P.M. Sat. and Sun.). The shop offers a thorough array of outdoor gear. Name brands fill the store, providing all the hiking gear you could need. Stop by for anything you may need, especially before any serious hikes.

For a private guided tour contact **Kauaʻi Hiking Adventures** (808/634-1018, www.kauaihikingadventures.com, full-day tours $285, half-day tours $185). According to the company, the tours are suitable for all fitness and ability levels. Each tour is customized to the hiker's personal preference, ability, and weather conditions. The guide shares knowledge of Hawaii's plants, history, and culture while hiking. Prices include you and up to three of your friends. The guide is a National Outdoor Leadership School Certified Outdoor Skills and Ethics Trainer and has explored Kauaʻi extensively.

BIKING

Much of Kauaʻi has narrow, winding roads without shoulders. Therefore, it can be quite

© JADE ECKARDT

Take a ride along the coastal Ke Ala Hele Makalae bike path.

unsafe for biking around. But if you really enjoy cruising on two wheels, you're in luck because the east side is home to the **Ke Ala Hele Makalae bike path.** The name translates to "the path that goes by the coast," and true to its name, the bike path stretches along part of the east coast while staying almost entirely level. Multiple beaches, swimming, and picnic spots are located along the path. The path begins at the Lihi Boat Landing to the south and winds north to Kealia Beach.

Lihu'e

Long-time bike doctor **Bicycle John** (3142 Kuhio Hwy., 808/245-7579, 10 A.M.–6 P.M. Mon.–Fri. and 10 A.M.–3 P.M. Sat.) offers a thorough selection of road and mountain bikes to rent and own. Also available is a selection of other biking gear including bikes, helmets, lights, repair services, and more. Bicycle John himself is known to be straight-to-the-point kind of guy, no bells (except for bikes) or whistles, but he knows what he's doing.

Kapa'a

At **Coconut Coasters Beach Bike Rentals** (4-1586 Kuhio Hwy., 808/822-7368, www.coconutcoasters.com, 9 A.M.–6 P.M. Tues.–Sat., 9 A.M.–4 P.M. Sun.–Mon.), you will find a variety of bikes: classic and three-speed cruisers ($22 half day, $25 full day, $95 weekly) for adults and children, tandem bikes (half day $36, full day $45, weekly $190), mountain bikes (half day $25, full day $30, weekly $120), trainers that attach to adult bikes for 6–9 year olds, and covered trailers for toddlers that connect to the back of the bike. The classic beach cruiser is slightly less expensive, but I would recommend the three-speed; it makes it a lot easier to go uphill. Rates for kids' mountain bikes and cruisers vary. Reservations are required for rentals.

Kauai Cycle (934 Kuhio Hwy., Kapa'a, 808/821-2115, www.kauaicycle.com, 9 A.M.–6 P.M. Mon.–Fri. and 9 A.M.–4 P.M. Sat.) offers cruisers, road bikes, and mountain bikes for rent. It also provides maps, trail information, clothing, accessories, and guidebooks. Rentals include a helmet and a lock and start at $20 per day. Multiday rates are also available, as well as car racks. It also has a full certified repair shop in case your own bike needs help.

Adventure Sports and Tours

LIHU'E
Ziplining and Tubing

You flew to Kaua'i on a plane, so why not fly through the air on a harness? **Kaua'i Backcountry Adventures** (3-4131 Kuhio Hwy., 808/245-2506, www.kauaibackcountry.com) offers ziplining and tubing on 17,000 acres of old sugar plantation land. You have the choice of seven different courses for your zipline experience. Zipline sessions begin at 8 and 10 A.M., noon, and 2 P.M. daily for $99.

Tubing begins at 9 and 10 A.M. and 1 and 2 P.M. daily for $102. The ride takes you down the plantation's old irrigation system. Float through open canals and several tunnels dug in the late 1800s.

Another option is **Outfitters Kauai** (2827A Po'ipu Rd., 808/742-9667, www.outfitterskauai.com), which offers ziplining in the Kipu area on the southern border of Lihu'e. The Zipline Trek Nui Loa offers an 1,800-foot tandem zipline over the Ha'upu Mountains, valleys, waterfalls, and huge trees. You fly for about a quarter mile, enjoying over 90 seconds of air time. This tour includes a picnic lunch of a turkey or veggie wrap, pasta salad, a cookie, and cold water. It costs $152 for adults and $132 for children 14 and under. Another zipline trek is the Kipu Zipline Safari, which includes kayaking two miles up a river, exploring swimming holes and waterfalls, views of features that appeared in the films *Jurassic Park* and *Raiders of the Lost Ark,* and ziplining through jungle terrain. This tour includes snacks, a picnic lunch, and cold drinks. It costs $182 for adults and $142 for those 14 and under.

ATVing

Muddy family fun can be had when driving an all-terrain vehicle (ATV) with **Kipu Ranch Adventures** (Kipu Rd., 808/246-9288, www.kiputours.com, 6:30 A.M.–6 P.M. daily). Guided ATV tours take adventurous drivers into 3,000 acres of Kaua'i's uninhabited interior. Driving yourself into otherwise inaccessible parts of the island offers awesome views, mud puddles to plow through, and exciting terrain in Kipu Ranch just outside of Lihu'e. The land is former plantation property turned working cattle ranch and offers adventure driving through its pastures and up to Kilohana Crater. Drivers must be 16 or older, but there are other vehicles available for younger guests. Long pants and shoes are a must. After getting muddy and dusty drivers can cool off in a stream. Three different tours are offered and range $75–160 depending on guests' ages and the tour chosen.

Aloha Kaua'i Tours (1702 Haleukana St., 800/452-1113, www.alohakauaitours.com) offers a range of tours into the interior of the island. The rainforest hike is actually a combo of four-wheel-driving and hiking. The tour goes inland from Wailua into the heart of the island. After a bumpy ride, the tour walks from the gate where scenes from Jurassic Park were shot. Guests walk for about three miles to freshwater pools while learning about Hawaiian culture and history. The guides provide umbrellas, ponchos, and walking sticks, as well as backpacks, snacks, and beverages. Groups are required to be a minimum of four and maximum of 12. Adults cost $80 and children 5–12 are $62.50. They also offer a Kaua'i backroads four-wheel-drive tour over the 22,000-acre Grove Farm Plantation, offering a scenic route of the interior. The half-day tour departs at 8 A.M. and 1 P.M. from Kilohana Plantation. The tour covers 33 miles of mostly private roads from the top of 1,250-foot Kilohana Crater, along the rugged coastline of Maha'ulepu, and through a cane tunnel.

Prices are $80 for adults and $62.50 for children under 12. Tours run seven days a week.

Helicopter Tours

Blue Hawaiian Helicopters (3501 Rice St., Ste. 107A, 808/245-5800 or 800/745-5800, www.bluehawaiian.com, 7 A.M.–5 P.M. daily) offers a tour they call the Kaua'i ECO adventure. The company's new American Eurocopter ECO-Star offers more interior room to take you over the Hanapepe Valley, then on to Manawaiopuna, otherwise known as Jurassic Park Falls. Then it's on to the Olokele and Waimea Canyons, then over the Na Pali Coast, Bali Hai Cliffs, and Hanalei Bay. If weather permits, you get to explore the crater of Mount Wai'ale'ale by air for a finale. Regular price is $240 with special online prices.

Near the airport is **Jack Harter Helicopters** (4231 Ahukini Rd., 808/245-3774, www.helicopters-kauai.com, 8 A.M.–6 P.M. daily), which offers two tours. The 60- to 65-minute tour hits all of Kaua'i's major scenic areas in their AStar and Hughes 500 helicopters. Price totals $259 including fuel surcharge. A longer tour of 90–95 minutes flies at slower speeds and explores deeper into Kaua'i's valleys and canyons. In this tour the helicopter takes more turns than in the other, providing more photo opportunities. The only tour on the island of this length, it takes place only on the Astars. Regular price is $384 including fuel surcharge.

With **Safari Helicopters** (3225 Akahi St., 808/246-0136, www.safarihelicopters.net, 7:30 A.M.–5:30 P.M. daily) you have the opportunity to tour a waterfall owned by the owner of Ni'ihau. The Deluxe Waterfall Safari is a 60-minute trip to Wai'ale'ale Crater, Waimea Canyon, and the Na Pali Coast. Regular price is $254 per person with special web fares. For the Kaua'i Refuge Eco Tour they offer a 90-minute trip over the same sites as the other tour as well as a stopover at the Kaua'i Botanical Refuge overlooking Olokele Canyon. The price is $279 per person or a special web price of $268.

Sunshine Helicopters (Kahului Heliport

#107, 866/501-7738, www.sunshinehelicopters.com/kauai/tours/kauai.html, 6 A.M.–8 P.M. daily, $244 or online price of $194) offers a tour called the Ultimate Kaua'i Adventure, which leaves out of Lihu'e before 8:30 A.M. The tour flies over Waimea Canyon, Mount Wai'ale'ale and the nearby Alaka'i Swamp, and Wailua Falls. Views of the Na Pali Coast are also offered. The flight is about 45–55 minutes.

Island Helicopters (Ahukini Rd. across from the Lihu'e Airport helipads, 808/245-8588 or 800/829-5999, www.islandhelicopters.com, 7 A.M.–6 P.M. daily) flies over the sought-after Manawaiopuna Falls, otherwise known as Jurassic Falls. The Kaua'i Grand Circle Tour provides views of Waimea Canyon, the Na Pali Coast, and the north shore. The tour lasts 50–60 minutes but doesn't include a landing at the falls. The Jurassic Falls Tour lasts about 75–85 minutes and includes all views from the Grand Circle Tour as well as a stop at the 400-foot falls.

Golf and Tennis

LIHU'E
Kaua'i Lagoons Golf Club
The Kaua'i Marriott Resort's new and improved Kaua'i Lagoons Golf Club (3351 Ho'olaule'a Way, 808/241-6000, www.marriottgolf.com) reopened in 2011 after being refurbished and renamed. This golf course has won many awards and was recently rated one of the top 50 golf resorts by *Golf World Magazine*'s Readers' Choice Award. In 2009 *Golfweek* rated it #5 for America's Best Courses You Can Play in Hawaii. The course, which sits atop a bluff over the ocean, can be experienced two ways. The Kiele Moana Nine features all new putting surfaces and bunkers, boasting the longest stretch of continuous ocean holes of any course in Hawaii. These nine holes have been paired with the original front nine holes, the Kiele Mauka Nine, to create 18 holes of Jack Nicklaus–inspired golf.

Children under 15 years old play for free after 3 P.M. when accompanied by a full-paying adult. One child is allowed to play for free per round for each full-paying adult. Also, free instruction is available for children under 15 when accompanied by an adult who is paying for a lesson at the same time with the same instructor. Proper golf attire is required for all ages at Kauai Lagoons Golf Club. Golfers must be at least six years old to play. Single ride golf is available here but you must contact the golf shop in advance for reservations and availability.

To accommodate a range of golfers, the 18-hole course offers gold tees with a 7,120 yardage, blue with a 6,675 yardage, white with a 6,252 yardage, and red with a 5,377 yardage.

Tee times can be made up to 30 days in advance. Golf shoes are available, and rentals include a shared golf cart, two bottles of water, a cooler, and a warm-up bucket of range balls.

Eighteen-hole prices range $75–120 depending on the time of day, $75–175 for visitors. Nine-hole fees range $65–75 depending on time of day, and $95–100 for visitors. Guests at select hotels can receive discounted rates. Juniors pay $60 before 3 P.M. for 18 holes and $20–35 for nine holes. The clubhouse at Kaua'i Lagoons has an upscale ambience on a lake, providing a convenient spot to enjoy a drink and recap your game while overlooking the lagoon.

Kaua'i Lagoons Golf Club also has **tennis courts.** For island residents it's $10 an hour and it's free for hotel guests. The courts are open 7 A.M.–5 P.M. daily. Call 808/241-6000 for reservations. Check in at the golf shop and they will give you a key for the courts.

Puakea Golf Course and Pro Shop
A favorite with local and visiting golfers, Puakea Golf Course (4150 Nuhou St., 808/245-8756, www.puakeagolf.com) was ranked by *Golfweek* magazine as 15th in Hawaii, and in 2009 it ranked 14th in *Golf* magazine's Reader's Choice Awards. Just

several minutes from the Lihue Airport, the course travels up, down, and around deep ravines. Beautiful Ha'upu Mountain views are in sight on about three-quarters of the course, and ocean views are in sight for the rest of it. Shopping center "views" are also there, but the course is fun enough to keep your eyes off of them. Golfers love that each hole is sharply different from the rest, inspiring a new challenge at each hole. Robin Nelson was the golf course architect, and golfers report repeated satisfaction with the course.

Avid golfers say the course ranks about medium on the difficulty scale. The course begins on the easier side and increases in difficulty as you move along. It lies behind the Kukui Grove Shopping Center in Lihu'e and offers golf club rentals for those who don't want to haul clubs on the plane.

The Pro Shop (866/773-5554) offers a wide spectrum of golf accessories and clothing. Anything you might need to complete your gear selection can be found here.

After a long 18 holes, you can relax and enjoy a meal at The Grille. It serves up sandwiches, salads, pupu, and burgers. The laid-back restaurant serves up food that will satisfy after a day on the greens.

Golf Gear

To meet all your golf needs, stop by the **Pro-Am Golf Shop** (4303 Rice St. #B9, Lihu'e, 808/632-0609). It offers a variety of name-brand gear for a day on any of Kaua'i's courses.

For a unique golf shirt or quality useable souvenir, check out **Garden Island Golf Co.** (3411 Hinahina St., Lihu'e, 808/822-7135, www.gardenislandgolf.com). The locally owned and operated shop offers quality golf wear. The idea for the company originated with former pro surfer Cody Graham and former pro body boarder Chris Burkart. The apparel is marked with their petroglyph-like logo of a golfer.

WAILUA
Wailua Municipal Course

Just a few miles north of the Lihue Airport, the Wailua Municipal Golf Course (3-5350 Kuhio Hwy., 808/241-6666, www.kauai.gov/golf) offers 18 holes, a golf shop, locker rooms with showers, a driving range, putting and chipping greens, and a practice bunker. For two players, tee times can be booked up to seven days in advance, while single golfers go out on a stand-by basis. The course offers blue tees at a 6,991 yardage, white tees at a 6,585 yardage, and red tees at 5,974 yardage. The course lines the ocean, and the ocean breeze enhances the experience. Visitor weekday price is $48, and weekends and holidays are $60. *Kama'aina* rates are $15 weekdays, weekends and holidays $20. Twilight prices are offered in the morning and afternoon for half the daily rate. Junior and senior rates are also offered. A motorized cart available for $18. Don't be shocked that it's directly across from the Kaua'i Correctional Facility.

Yoga and Spas

LIHU'E

Get pampered at the **Alexander Day Spa and Salon** (Kaua'i Marriott Resort, 3610 Rice St., Suite 9A, 808/246-4918, www.alexanderspa.com, 8 A.M.–7 P.M.) and you will truly get lost in a luxurious experience. Massages in the spa or beachside cabana range $70–175, and in your room they cost $150–200. Various modalities are offered, including couples, sports, deep tissue,

Hawaiian *lomilomi,* aroma massage, and more. Body treatment combos of masks, scrubs, massage, and more range $70–185 and all involve island-themed scents and ingredients. Facials with delicious scents like green tea, ginger, and fruit range $70–180. For the ultimate luxurious experience packages are offered with a combo of a facial, massage, mani-pedi, and more for $160–310. Full bridal services are offered.

KAPA'A

Relax and get centered at **The Yoga House** (4-885 Kuhio Hwy., 808/823-9642, www.theyogahousekauai.com), which offers a wide array of classes and styles. In the Hot Power and Yoga Blast classes, yogis will strengthen the body and relax the mind during a 75-minute heated session. During Hot Flow yoga, participants will spend 75 minutes combining postures, breathing, and vinyasa. Yin yoga addresses the health and suppleness of the joints, fascia, ligaments, and bones. Slow Flow Vinyasa encourages a balanced practice of challenging sun poses along with relaxing moon poses. Times and rates vary widely, so it's a good idea to call or visit the website.

The name says it all for **Kaua'i Yoga on the Beach** 808/635-6050, www.kauaiyoga-onthebeach.com), where beach yoga is offered at 6 A.M. on various east-side beaches. Classes

are $15 per person, and private lessons are offered for $50. Bring a beach towel, a yoga mat, and water. Mats can also be rented for $2.

Spa by the Sea at Waipouli Beach Resort (4-820 Kuhio Hwy., 808/823-1488, www.spabytheseakauai.com) has a thorough array of options to indulge in. The experienced therapists offer a variety of massage techniques, from traditional Hawaiian *lomilomi* and hot stone to therapeutic deep tissue. Couples and beach massages are also available and massages range $125–330. The spa uses the high-quality skin-care line Epicurean and offers organic skin-care treatments, including volcanic clay and custom facials from $20 for an exfoliant to $1,140 for an anti-aging series. It also offers Hawaiian sea salt body scrubs, volcanic wraps, and many more decadent choices. Ayurvedic, body, and foot treatments range $20–290.

Sights

LIHU'E
◀ Kaua'i Museum

The Kaua'i Museum (4428 Rice St., 808/245-6931, www.kauaimuseum.org, 10 A.M.–5 P.M. Mon.–Sat., $10 adults, $8 *kama'aina* and seniors 65 and up, $6 students 13–17, $2 children 6–12, and under 5 free) is a real treat. This two-building complex is in downtown Lihu'e, and although it's a good place to visit anytime, exploring it at the start of your trip leaves you with a background that enhances the rest of the visit. The island art exhibits change on a regular basis; however, the museum focuses on displaying ethnic heritage such as koa furniture, feather lei, and more. Permanent exhibits include the Story of Kaua'i, which takes up two floors in the Rice Building. The exhibit constructs the island's past, highlighting the geological aspects of the island and settlement by the Hawaiian people. Island chiefs, Captain Cook, traders, and whalers are highlighted. The exhibit even features a life-size camp house to walk through,

shedding light on the many different people who came to the island.

The William Hyde Rice Building was built in 1960 to house the museum, and the Albert Spencer Wilcox building was built in 1924. Although small on the scale of national museums, the Kaua'i museum exudes a strong presence with arches, a cement front, and broad steps. The building has a lava rock exterior, sloped roof, barrel-vaulted ceilings, original antique light fixtures, and a mezzanine with a balcony overlooking the first floor. The building is on the National Historic Register. The museum shop sells books, cards, Hawaiian prints, a magnificent selection of Hawaiian craft items, and a fine selection of detailed U.S. geological survey maps of the entire island.

In the Juliet Rice Wichman Heritage Gallery exquisite finds are on display. Beautiful and rare N'ihau shell lei and items that belonged to Kaua'i *ali'i* and monarchs are out for viewing. Furniture and other household items are on display. In the Oriental Art Gallery

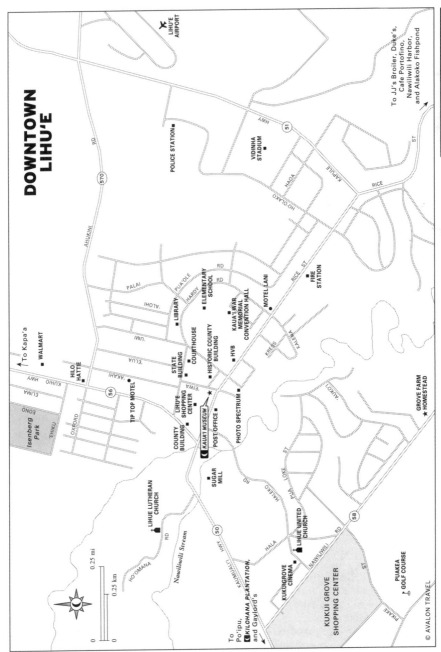

DOWNTOWN LIHU'E

To JJ's Broiler, Duke's, Cafe Portofino, Nawiliwili Harbor, and Alakoko Fishpond

LIHU'E AIRPORT

To Kapa'a

WALMART

Isenberg Park

HILO HATTIE

TIP TOP MOTEL

POLICE STATION

VIDINHA STADIUM

LIBRARY

ELEMENTARY SCHOOL

STATE BUILDING

COURTHOUSE

HISTORIC COUNTY BUILDING

KAUA'I WAR MEMORIAL CONVENTION HALL

HVB

MOTEL LANI

FIRE STATION

LIHU'E SHOPPING CENTER

COUNTY BUILDING

KAUA'I MUSEUM

POST OFFICE

PHOTO SPECTRUM

GROVE FARM HOMESTEAD

SUGAR MILL

LIHUE LUTHERAN CHURCH

Nawiliwili Stream

LIHUE UNITED CHURCH

KUKUIGROVE CINEMA

KUKUI GROVE SHOPPING CENTER

PUAKEA GOLF COURSE

To Po'ipu, KILOHANA PLANTATION, and Gaylord's

0.25 mi

0.25 km

© AVALON TRAVEL

MOVIES MADE IN KAUA'I

Kaua'i's vast uninhabited land with its unique landscape has long been a favorite location for Hollywood film makers. Movies have been shot on the island for decades, and the trend doesn't appear to be stopping. Take a look around and you may recognize some of the island from these films. Or later when watching them you may see a familiar place. Here are some of the more well-known movies.

- *Blue Hawaii*
- *Dragonfly*
- *Fantasy Island*
- *George of the Jungle*
- *Honeymoon in Vegas*
- *Hook*
- *Jurassic Park*

- *King Kong*
- *Lord of the Flies*
- *Mighty Joe Young*
- *Outbreak*
- *Pirates of the Caribbean: On Stranger Tides*
- *Raiders of the Lost Ark*
- *Six Days/Seven Nights*
- *Soul Surfer*
- *South Pacific*
- *Starsky & Hutch*
- *Tropic Thunder*
- *White Heat*

exhibit, housewares from Asia are on display. Asian china, sculptures, and art that had been in homes on the island are shared with viewers here.

There are also temporary exhibits. These include exhibits on the Kekaha train robbery, various art exhibits, textiles, and an aviation history of Kaua'i.

It's a good idea to dedicate at least a couple of hours for a thorough visit to the museum. The entrance fee is valid for several days and includes docent tours, so ask for a pass if you'd like to return. Free family admission is offered the first Saturday of every month.

Alakoko Fishpond

The Alakoko (Rippling Blood) Fishpond is commonly known as Menehune Fishpond. Overlooking the Hule'ia River and the Ha'upu ridge on the far side, the pond tells the story of Hawaiian history and myths. This fishpond has been used to raise mullet and other commercial fish. But unlike most other fishponds, which are built along the edge of the ocean, this pond was constructed along the riverbank and is said to have been built by the *menehune* in just one night.

Legend says that these little people built the rock wall surrounding this pond for a royal prince and princess and made only one demand: that no one watch while they were working. It's said that throughout the night the *menehune* passed the stones needed from hand to hand in a 25-mile-long line. Meanwhile, the prince and princess grew curious and watched from nearby. The *menehune* saw them and turned the royal pair into two pillars of stone that you can see on the mountain overlooking the pond. The small workers stopped their work and left holes in the wall. To get here, follow Hulemalu Road until you see the overlook. It's a beautiful sight.

Grove Farm Homestead

The Grove Farm Homestead (4050 Nawiliwili Rd., 808/245-3202, www.grovefarm.net, tours Mon., Wed., and Thurs. 10 A.M. and 1 P.M., $20 donation for adults or $10 for children 5–12) is a former sugar plantation that was

© JADE ECKARDT

Local lore says the *menehune* built the expansive Alakoko Fishpond in one night.

started in 1864 by George Wilcox, the son of Congregational missionary teachers who worked for the original owner of the bordering land. Wilcox bought 500 acres for $12,000 through a lease-to-purchase arrangement. The property had been chopped out of a large grove of kukui trees—hence the name Grove Farm. Bringing water down from the mountains, Wilcox formed one of the most profitable sugar plantations in Hawaii. He purchased more land as the years went by, and now the property encompasses 22,000 acres (one of the five largest landholdings on the island).

The homestead was a working plantation until the mid 1930s when Wilcox died. His nieces went on to care for the property, and in 1971 Mabel Wilcox created a nonprofit organization to preserve Grove Farm Homestead as a historical living farm. Reservations for tours are preferred, but the staff will most likely accommodate unexpected visitors. They ask that visitors call at least 24 hours in advance to book a tour. Reservations are also accepted by snail mail up to three months in advance

by writing to Grove Farm Homestead (P.O. Box 1631, Lihu'e, HI 96766). Exact directions will be given on the phone. Wear comfortable shoes that can be slipped off because, as in most homes in Hawaii, shoes are not worn indoors here. Tours are sometimes canceled on rainy days.

◀ Kilohana Plantation

For an elegant trip back in time visit the Kilohana Plantation (3-2087 Kaumuali'i Hwy., 808/245-5608, www.kilohanakauai.com, shops open 9:30 A.M.–9:30 P.M. Mon.–Sat. and 9:30 A.M.–5 P.M. Sun.), a sprawling estate with manicured lawns, fruit, flowers, a train, and the former mansion of Gaylord Wilcox. At the time that Gaylord Wilcox moved the business offices of Grove Farm from the homestead site, he had the 16,000-square-foot Kilohana plantation house built in 1936. After decades of family use, the building was renovated in 1986 and turned into shops that sell arts and crafts. Exploring the antique mansion's rooms, still decorated with original

© JADE ECKARDT

carriage in front of the historic Kilohana Plantation

furnishings, jewelry, and other elegant artifacts, serves as a tangible experience of history.

Kilohana Plantation has several restaurants, as well as Lu'au Kilohana every Tuesday and Thursday evening. A horse-drawn carriage operates 11 A.M.–6 P.M. daily. Just show up and stand in line near the front entrance to take a ride. The 20-minute carriage ride is $12 for adults and $6 for children; call 808/246-9529 for reservations.

The **Kauai Plantation Railway** (www.kauaiplantationrailway.com) is a popular attraction here also. With a whistle to get the excitement going, the 1939 Whitcomb diesel engine, named Ike, pulls mahogany coaches modeled after King Kamehameha's personal car. The first stop is at a housing of wild pigs, goats, sheep, horses, and other farm animals. You can even feed the animals with the bread supplied by the conductor. Go on the tour that includes riding the train, hiking in the surrounding rainforest into a valley with streams, and having a picnic with a dessert of fresh fruits right off the tree.

WAILUA
Fern Grotto

The Wailua River's Fern Grotto, a natural rock amphitheater where a dense forest of ferns hangs from the grotto, is a popular place to visit. An upriver tour run by **Smith's Kauai** (Kuamo'o Rd., 808/821-6895, www.smiths-kauai.com, boats depart at 9:30 and 11 A.M. and 2 and 3:30 P.M. daily, $20 adults, $10 children 3–12) is the way to access it. A two-mile, 90-minute round-trip river journey takes you to the grotto. On the trip you'll also be treated to a hula dance and Hawaiian music.

It's a pretty sight, but some say the grotto isn't as romantic as it used to be. This is due to Hurricane 'Iniki taking a toll on the overlying canopy and ferns in 1992 and a lack of water seepage from the close of the sugar plantation. Although it has regrown, it isn't quite as wonderful as it once was. In efforts to reestablish the ambience, improvements have been made to bring back the irrigation to the ferns. Many couples come here to get married.

Kamokila Hawaiian Village

For a cultural experience explore Kamokila Hawaiian Village (on Kuamo'o Rd. along the Wailua River, 808/823-0559, www.villageka-uai.com, 9 A.M.–5 P.M. daily, $5 adults, $3 children 5–12). Kamokila means stronghold, and is Kaua'i's only re-created Hawaiian village. It has been formed on the site of an ancient royal village, the first of seven ancient villages in this valley. Resting on four acres, the location was once home to the last reigning king of Kaua'i, King Kaumuali'i. Village sites include the canoe house, the *Outbreak* movie set, a birth house, taro patches, wood-carving house, village lagoon, petroglyphs, medicinal plants, and a lot more.

When fruit is in season visitors are welcome to help themselves to it, and several huts have been reconstructed with traditional methods. In the courtyard traditional Hawaiian games are featured, such as spear throwing and Hawaiian bowling. Kamokila has been resurrected to give visitors a glimpse of what island life was for ancient Hawaiians. It opened in

© KENNETH SPONSLER/WWW.123RF.COM

Wailua Falls

trails down to the falls, but they are slippery and can be dangerous.

Smith's Tropical Paradise

Smith's Tropical Paradise (5971 Kuhio Hwy. 808/821-6895, www.smithskauai.com, 8:30 A.M.–4:30 P.M. daily, $6 adults, $3 ages 3–12) is a 30-acre botanical and cultural garden along the Wailua River. On the property many plants are labeled, including an array of fruit and common island foliage as well as other plants that are rare and hard to find. There are two main buildings here; one is home to a *lu'au* and the other is a lagoon theater used for music shows. A path over one mile long leads you around the property. A Japanese garden is nice to roam around.

Opaeka'a Falls

Two miles up Kuamo'o Road are the roughly 150-foot majestic Opaeka'a Falls. The scenic lookout is on the right after the first mile marker and has a large parking lot and restrooms. The beautiful falls are easy to see and make for a good photo opportunity. Along Kuamo'o Road on the way to the falls look out for sacred *heiaus,* such as the Poliahu Heiau.

Kuamo'o Heiau

Along the Wailua River off of Route 580 are seven sacred *heiau* from the pre-contact period that are easily accessible. At the river mouth are several ancient petroglyphs that can be seen at low tide—if they're not covered by sand or sediment. The first *heiau* is called **Hauola O Honaunau** and was where *kapu* (rule) breakers came to make up for their indiscretions by having a priest redeem them. This is located on the south side of the river mouth. Near the marina entrance is **Malae Heiau,** which is said by some to have been constructed by the *menehune.* It's on the road into Smith's Tropical Paradise and is believed to be the biggest *heiau* on Kaua'i. There really isn't much to see here; it's the cultural significance that counts. On the outcrop of land at the end of Wailua Beach is the **Kukui Heiau.** There is only a tiny part of the structure left, but it once measured 230 by 70 feet. It's not really

1981 and was almost destroyed by Hurricane 'Iwa in 1982, only to be damaged again in 1992 by Hurricane 'Iniki. The village also offers outrigger canoe rides, hiking and swimming, access to Secret Falls, weddings, and a *lu'au.*

◖ Wailua Falls

One of Kaua'i's most beautiful and easy-to-view waterfalls is the 80-foot Wailua Falls, which was featured on the opening credits of the television show *Fantasy Island.* Legend says the Hawaiian *ali'i* would dive off the falls to prove their physical prowess, and commoners were not allowed to participate. The ride up Ma'alo Road to the falls is gorgeous itself, as the road is surrounded by wide open pasture. The falls are about four miles up at the end of the road, so you can't miss them. The falls can be viewed from a lookout spot where there is a parking lot, which is a perfect place for a photo op. There is usually a line of onlookers here and hat makers selling their shade-providing palm hats. The lookout spot is the only place to view the falls unless you take one of the two

© JADE ECKARDT

Opaeka'a Falls

worth the walk over, but knowing of it enhances the sacredness of the area. Traditionally it was used as a makeshift lighthouse, a fire beacon to lead canoes to shore. It's located on what is now property belonging to a condominium.

Holoholoku Heiau is up Kuamo'o Road right after the state park boat-launch area along the river on your left. Some say this place was used for human sacrifice, and some say for animal sacrifice. There is a big flat stone near the front of the area that was the altar. Very close is **Pohako Ho'o Hanau,** the royal birthstones where the royal women came to give birth. The mother rested her back on one of the two stones and placed her feet on the other while giving birth.

Along the river and just before Opaeka'a Falls is **Poliahu Heiau.** This was once a very sacred site and is said to have been built by the *menehune* and used by King Kaumuali'i, Kaua'i's last king. Although its exact function is not known and the structures inside are long gone, the size of it leads archaeologists to believe that it was a *luakini heiau* (human sacrifice). A rock wall in the shape of a rectangle is all that's left, which is more than most other *heiau.* Please don't walk on the wall. Enjoy, and use your imagination to think of what may have gone on in that very

spot generations ago. There is a great lookout here over Wailua River and a good photo opportunity. Farther up the road, turn down a dirt road after the first mile marker, head to the end of the road, and walk down the path past the guard rail till you see a few large stones. One is known as the **Bellstone.** When it is struck a certain way the stone produces a metallic sound, which historically announced the birth of a royal child.

KAPA'A
Kaua'i Hindu Monastery

A very intriguing place to visit is the Kaua'i Hindu Monastery (Kaholalele St., 888/735-1619, www.himalayanacademy.com, 9 A.M.–noon daily). Located up the Wailua River, the monastery is built completely from hand-carved stones from India. Each stone takes seven years to carve and there are 4,000 of them. Free guided tours are offered once a week, but it is open for visitation daily. The holidays vary with the Hindu calendar. Wear long plants and shirts that cover the shoulders; no mini skirts for women or going shirtless for men. On-site are the Kadaval Hindu Temple building, Ganesha Shrine, and Bangalore

Gallery. Call for specific guided tour dates and to reserve a parking space.

Nounou, the Sleeping Giant

Legend says that a long time ago, a giant lived in Kawaihau behind Kapa'a town. He was very friendly and helped the people of the area. He had a hard time staying awake for more than a hundred years at a time, and when he would sleep, he would use a small hill as a pillow. The people called him Kanaka Nunui Moe, the sleeping giant. After a chief requested that the people bring rocks and trees from Koke'e and Waimea to build a *heiau* for him, the giant helped, bringing all the material down. To show appreciation, the people provided the giant with a wonderful meal of poi, pig, and fish. He filled his belly and was so full he laid down to rest for the last time.

At Kipuni Place is the **Sleeping Giant Viewpoint** pull-off. From this angle you can see the mountain, and with some imagination you can see why they call it Sleeping Giant. You can see the vague outline of legs and an incline going up to a chest and head. Wonderful trails go up both the front and the back of this hill, bringing you up to a picnic spot on the chest; from there a narrow trail leads over the throat to the chin and forehead, but these hikes are very dangerous.

Honey Wine Tasting at Nani Moon Meadery

Nani Moon Meadery (Yasuda Center, 4-939 D Kuhio Hwy., 808/823-0486, www.nanimoon-mead.com, noon–5 P.M. Tues.–Sat.) offers an opportunity to enjoy the tastes of the islands at the state's only producer of honey wine. Made with local ingredients, the tasty honey wine is produced, bottled, and sold on-site at the tasting room. Try the Cacao Moon mead, made with macadamia nut blossom honey and Kaua'i cacao.

Steelgrass Chocolate Farm

Steelgrass Chocolate Farm (808/821-1857, www.steelgrass.org, 9 A.M.–noon Mon., Wed., and Fri., $60 adults, under 12 free) offers a tour entitled Chocolate from Branch to Bar. The eight-acre farm specializes in vanilla, bamboo, and cacao, the chocolate tree. The tour reveals to visitors everything about growing and harvesting cacao fruit and turning it into chocolate. Smelling and tasting is part of the three-hour tour, where you explore the gardens and the orchard and enjoy an 11-course chocolate tasting. Exploring a chocolate farm in Hawaii is an experience unique from what the rest of the United States has to offer, as Hawaii is the only state with an environment hospitable to cacao.

Shopping

LIHU'E

Shopping in Lihu'e is best explored in the main shopping centers. This is because much of the town serves daily functional needs, so quaint independent boutiques aren't as common here as on other parts of the island. Yet Lihu'e is the best spot for mall shopping and to find the best hiking and beach gear.

Shopping Centers
KUKUI GROVE SHOPPING CENTER

In Lihu'e's largest shopping center, you will find an array of stores. Department stores such as

Macy's and **Sears,** as well as **Kmart,** offer their standard products. **Jeans Warehouse** offers low-priced clothing for trendy teens and young women. **Deja Vu Surf Hawaii** provides extensive surf gear and clothing, and **San Lorenzo Bikinis** offers top-quality bikinis very popular in the island as well as clothing and accessories. For footwear stop into **Footlocker** or **Payless Shoe Source.** If you're looking for electronics there is a **Radio Shack.** Several jewelry stores can be found here, along with a **GameStop** for the kids and a few salons. The center is located at 3-2600 Kaumualii Highway and you can't miss it. There are some basic eateries. The shopping center is open 9:30 A.M.–7 P.M. Monday–Thursday and on Saturday. Friday it opens at the same time but closes at 9 P.M., and on Sundays it's open 10 A.M.–6 P.M.

KILOHANA PLANTATION

The historic plantation estate (3-2087 Kaumuali'i Hwy., 808/245-5608, 10:30 A.M.–9:30 P.M. Mon.–Sat., 10:30 A.M.–3 P.M. Sun.) holds a nice selection of shops with art, knick-knacks, hand-made items, clothing, and other island-style products. The shops can be found on both levels of the house and include **Grande's Gems and Gallery,** offering jewelry with Tahitian black pearls, opals, tanzanite, and other unique items. At **Sea Reflections** you can find unique objects from the sea as well as Hawaiian shells. The **Artisans Room** on the lower level of the house is decorated with work from local artists. Originals, prints, and sculptures can all be found here. A fun shop is **The Country Store,** where distinctive gifts, collectibles, and local crafts like quilts and things made with local woods are found. A popular shop is **Clayworks at Kilohana,** a working ceramics gallery. Browse work by local artists or take a workshop and clay-making class yourself. **The Hawaiian Collection Room** has an array of intriguing island finds, like Ni'ihau shell lei, Hawaiian collectibles, and local jewelry and gifts.

WALMART

Walmart (3-3300 Kuhio Hwy., 808/246-1599, 6 A.M.–midnight daily) offers all of the usual things Walmarts do but with an island twist. This is an affordable place for basic snorkeling, fishing, beach, and camping gear. There is a Hawaii souvenir section with a pretty thorough selection of fun stuff. Adult, baby, and children's clothing and accessories often have a Hawaiian theme and style. This store does not give out plastic bags, so bring your own or carry your items out.

COSTCO

Costco (4300 Nuhou St., 808/241-4000, 10 A.M.–8:30 P.M. Mon.–Fri., 9:30 A.M.–6 P.M.

Sat., 10 A.M.–6 P.M. Sun.) is a good place to stock up on food if you're going on a camping trip (if you have a Costco membership card). The card also enables you to fill up with some of the lowest priced gas around. They also usually have a basic stock of camping and beach gear.

KAPA'A AND WAILUA
Galleries

Aloha Images (1467 Kuhio Hwy., 877/821-1382, www.alohaimages.com, 10 A.M.–6:30 P.M. Mon.–Sat., 11 A.M.–3 P.M. Sun.) has prided itself on being a "candy store for art lovers" for 15 years. It's a good slogan as the shop is loaded with affordable local art. Hundreds of original works line the walls, along with giclees, prints, and other things for the home. Featured artists paint in the gallery daily.

Noticeable by the mural of a ship on the northern wall of the gallery, **Ship Store Galleries** (4-484 Kuhio Hwy., 800/877-1948 or 808/821-1249, www.shipstoregalleries.net, 8:30 A.M.–5 P.M. Mon.–Fri., 10 A.M.–5 P.M. Sat. and Sun.) is decorated with ocean-themed art, such as paintings of ships, canoe paddlers, and beautiful landscape and ocean paintings.

Inside **Kela's-A Glass Gallery** (4-1354 Kuhio Hwy., 888/255-3527 or 808/822-4527, 10 A.M.–7 P.M. Mon.–Sat., noon–5 P.M. Sun.) is a dreamy, glistening underwater world of pretty things. With over 150 glass artists' work on display, Kaua'i's natural beauty is represented in jewelry to wear and things to decorate the home with. Staff is friendly and happy to help you find that perfect gift. It can be pretty pricey in here, but it's at least worth window shopping. **Earth and Sea Gallery** (4504 Kukui St., Ste. 3, 808/821-2831, 10 A.M.–8:30 P.M. daily) is stocked with locally made products from over 30 artists. The boutique has something to offer for everyone, with shell jewelry, children's clothing and toys, artwork, bath and body products, and more. The staff is always friendly and outgoing and the products are unique.

Clothing and Accessories

At **Island Hemp and Cotton** (4-1373 Kuhio Hwy., 808/821-0225, www.islandhemp.com,

10 A.M.–8 P.M. Mon.–Sat., 11 A.M.–5 P.M. Sun.) you can find a wide selection of clothing made from, you guessed it, hemp. The airy shop is in the center of downtown Kapa'a, and here you can find dresses, boxers, surf shorts, shoelaces, smoking pants, and even some really nice aloha shirts.

A lovely shopping stop is **Bamboo Works** (4-1388 Kuhio Hwy. #C-109, www.bambooworks.com, 808/821-8688, 10 A.M.–6 P.M. Mon.–Sat., 11 A.M.–4 P.M. Sun.). The shop offers women's clothing, accessories, and home decor made from bamboo with a down-to-earth elegance. The bamboo clothing is amazingly soft with a classy look. The owners also offer prefabricated buildings and other supplies made from the sustainable wood.

Women will love the clothing at **The Root** (4-1435 Kuhio Hwy., Ste. 101, 808/823-1277, 9:30 A.M.–7 P.M. Mon.–Sat., noon–5 P.M. Sun.), where quality clothing is available in a combination of relaxed and classy. The skirts, dresses, and shirts are comfortable yet stylish and perfect for island wear or anywhere else. Clothing is a little on the pricey side, but it's a nice break from cookie-cutter clothing.

Sweet Bikinis (4-871 Kuhio Hwy. #B, 808/821-0780, 10 A.M.–6 P.M. daily) offers a selection of swimwear in a seemingly infinite array of colors and styles. Separates, tankinis, Brazilian cut bottoms, and accessories like beach wraps and jewelry can also be found. They're cute, they're fun, and there are some for sunbathing or for being active. The staff is usually knowledgable about which fabric holds up well for surfing and about sizing.

With all of the hikes and beaches on the island, a stop at **Work It Out, Kaua'is Active Clothing Store** (4-1312 Kuhio Hwy., 808/822-2292, www.workitoutkauai.com, 10 A.M.–6 P.M. Mon.–Sat.) may be necessary. The store is loaded with stylish apparel for hiking, biking, jogging, yoga, martial arts, and paddling. A running and walking group meets at the shop on Wednesdays at 6 P.M. and runs the path, a three- to seven-mile jaunt before returning to the shop for refreshments. The staff is always happy to share input on Kaua'i activities.

Shopping Centers

Located on the ocean side of the highway, **Coconut Marketplace** (4-484 Kuhio Hwy., www.coconutmarketplace.com, 9 A.M.–9 P.M. Mon.–Sat. and 10 A.M.–6 P.M. Sun.) is home to many shops and eateries. From high-end souvenirs and locally made ones to classy resort wear and amazing jewelry, you'll find it all here. Apparel can be found at **Crazy Shirts,** which has an abundance of souvenir clothing; **By the Sea,** which offers jewelry and resort clothing; and **Nakoa Surf Co.,** which has loads of surf-related stuff. Other highlights include **Paradise Music,** a great source for Hawaiian music; **Island Rush/Mystical Dreams,** offering fine gifts, souvenirs, clothing, and more; as well as **Elephant Walk Gift Gallery & Boutique,** where you find unique art, home decor, jewelry, accessories, and clothing. The **Coconut Marketplace Farmers Open Market** takes place every Tuesday from 9 A.M. to noon and is worth a look with locally made gifts and locally grown food.

Surf Shops

At the **Deja Vu Surf** outlet (4-1419 Kuhio Hwy., 808/822-4401, www.dejavusurf.com, 9:30 A.M.–6 P.M. daily) in Kapa'a an extensive selection of surf gear is provided: clothing, swimwear, boards for rent and sale, and everything else for catching waves or relaxing on the beach.

The locally owned and operated **Tamba Surf** (4-1543 Kuhio Hwy., 808/823-6942, www.tambasurfcompany.com) is a popular shop and brand with locals. They carry their own brand of clothing, as well as name-brand clothing, accessories, gear, and boards. Boards for rent and sale are offered.

Gifts and Souvenirs

Densely stocked with souvenirs and beach gear, the **ABC Store** (4-831 Kuhio Hwy., 808/822-2115, www.abcstores.com, 8 A.M.–9:30 P.M. daily) is a bit of a tourist trap, but it's fun. The store is loaded with all kinds of not-one-of-a-kind souvenirs, shirts, snacks, and general store basics. Drinks and alcoholic beverages are also for sale, along with Underwater cameras, limited snorkel and beach accessories, and beach supplies.

Shell lovers must make a stop at **Shell World Kaua'i** (4-1621 Kuhio Hwy., 808/821-9070, www.shell.com, 8 A.M.–8 P.M. daily) or the **Shell Factory** (4-901 Kuhio Hwy., 808/822-2354, www.shellskauai.com, 9 A.M.–5 P.M. Mon.–Sat. and 10 A.M.–5 P.M. Sun.). Both are adorned with beautiful tropical shells, although most are not from Hawaii. Still, they are perfect, fully intact, and exhibit some of nature's most intricate work.

Jewelry

Imperial Jewelers (4-831 Kuhio Hwy., 808/822-0094, 10 A.M.–6 P.M. Mon.–Sat.) sells Hawaiian hand-crafted heirloom jewelry. Pendants, bracelets, rings, and earrings are available in the local style of carved 14-karat gold with a name in black if you like. The carvings come in an array of Hawaiian designs like whales, sea turtles, flowers, and more. A highlight is the plumeria lei flowers collection, where elegant small plumerias are connected in a permanent lei.

Jim Saylor Jewelers (1318 Kuhio Hwy., 808/822-3591, 9:30 A.M.–5:30 P.M. Mon.–Sat.) is another nice jewelry store selling unique designs. The designer uses precious stones, black pearls, and diamonds in his unique settings and styles. He's been designing on Kaua'i for over two decades.

A very fun stop is **Kauai Crafters** (4-1176 Kuhio Hwy., 808/346-7700, www.kauaicrafters.com, 9 A.M.–6 P.M. daily). The small shop is jam-packed full of local crafts with a strong shell theme. They sell *kahelelani* jewelry, koa and mammoth ivory fishhook necklaces, coconut faces, and a lot more. It's a fun store to check out, everything is gorgeous, and there are some affordable items.

Outdoor Markets

The **Kaua'i Products Fair** (4-1613 Kuhio Hwy., 808/246-0988, www.thekauaiproductsfair.com, 9 A.M.–5 P.M. Mon.–Sun.) is an outdoor market with a wide variety of souvenirs, clothing, jewelry, and more sold in tents and on tables. Mostly everything here has an island theme and style, although many of the products aren't from Hawaii. It's a fun place to shop and is a great souvenir stop. Vegetables and fruits are also available here.

A "no import" market, **Kealia Kountry Market** (4100-4199 Kealia Rd., 808/635-5091, www.kealiakountrysundaymarket.com, 11 A.M.–4 P.M. Sun.) brings local vendors together offering shoppers locally grown and made products. Live music usually takes place, and local crafts, produce, and ready-to-eat food are available. Locals come to shop and socialize; it's definitely worth a stop while on Kaua'i.

On the way north out of Kapa'a is the **Anahola Marketplace** (4523 Ioane Rd., 808/820-8029, www.ahha96703.org, 9 A.M.–5 P.M. Wed.–Sun.), another place for residents to sell fruit and veggies, locally made crafts, and other things. It's worth a stop to or from the north shore.

Supermarkets and Drugstores

For basic drugstore needs stop at **Longs Drugs** (4-831 Kuhio Hwy. #500, 808/822-4915, www.cvs.com, 7 A.M.–9 P.M. Mon.–Sat., 8 A.M.–8 P.M. Sun.). The store has a pharmacy, body products, alcoholic beverages, limited stationery supplies, souvenirs, and limited camping gear, baby products, and housewares. It also has an electronics area to save you a trip to Lihu'e for a digital camera emergency.

In the same parking lot is **Safeway** (808/822-2464, 24 hours daily), with the usual supermarket products.

Health Food Stores

A newer Kapa'a health food store is **Hoku Natural Foods** (4585 Lehua St., 808/821-1500, www.hokufoods.com, 10 A.M.–6 P.M. daily), which has a thorough array of natural products and food. Natural and organic baby and body products, household cleaners, and food fill the spacious store. They also sell BPA-free water containers and other products.

Papaya's (4-831 Kuhio Hwy., 808/823-0190, www.papayasnaturalfoods.com, 8 A.M.–8 P.M. Mon.–Sat., 10 A.M.–5 P.M. Sun.) has long been the east side's staple health food store (and where the hippies gather). They have a full selection of vitamins, body products, cleaning supplies, books, food, and a lot more. If you're going to be around for a while ask for their deli and frequent shopper card.

Wine and Spirits

The small **Kapa'a Liquor and Wine** (4-1397

Kuhio Hwy., 808/822-4151, 8 A.M.–5 P.M. daily) has a good selection of beer in the old fridge behind the counter, but you have to read the handwritten lists on the front of the fridge and ask the worker to get it for you. Liquor lines the walls, and although they don't have an infinite stock, they'll probably have what you want.

Entertainment

LIHU'E
Cinema

Kukui Grove Cinema (4368 Kukui Grove St., 808/245-5055, www.kukuigrovecinema.com, $10) is the movie theater for the east side, and the island. It's in the Kukui Grove Shopping Center, and four screens show the latest blockbuster hits. Matinees are only $5.

Polynesian Dance, *Lu'au*, and Theater

Luau Kalamaku takes place at Kilohana Plantation (3-2087 Kaumuali'i Hwy., 808/245-5608, www.kilohanakauai.com) and entertains with hula, poi, food, music, and a full-scale theater experience. Luau Kalamaku is Kauai's only theatrical *lu'au*. Hula dancers, fire poi ball twirlers, traditional Polynesian fire knife dancers, and a vivid story line all combine for an exciting evening and view of Hawaiian culture. Your main course is cooked in the plantation's *imu*, an underground oven, and is unearthed while you are there. Then it's time for live Tahitian music, Hawaiian games, and hula dancing.

The evening begins outside in the estate's garden for fun and games before entering the theater. A storyteller tells of the settling of the island by voyagers from Tahiti. The evening is enchanting, fun, and educational.

WAILUA
Lu'au and Theater

A riverside *lu'au* takes place at **Smith's Tropical Paradise** (5971 Kuhio Hwy.,

808/821-6895, www.smithskauai.com, 5 P.M. Mon.–Fri. Jun.–Aug.; 5 P.M. Mon. and Wed.–Fri. Feb.–May and Sept.–Oct.; 4:45 P.M. Mon., Wed., and Fri. Nov.–Jan.; $88 adults, $30 7–13, $19 3–6). The location is home to a garden *lu'au* where your belly will be full as you enjoy music and hula. Dinner includes *kalua* pig cooked in an *imu*, teriyaki beef, mahimahi, chicken adobo, poi, and more. Hula is presented later on, and guests may go on stage to try out some moves. Tahitian drum dances and a Samoan fire knife dance are also treats.

Guests are welcomed at 5 P.M. with an *imu* ceremony, cocktails, and music, followed by the *lu'au* feast and ending with the rhythm of an *aloha* show. Those who choose to eat dinner elsewhere can purchase show-only tickets.

In the 1950s, the film *South Pacific* was filmed on Kaua'i, and paying homage to it is **South Pacific Dinner and Theater** (4331 Kaua'i Beach Dr. at the Kaua'i Beach Resort, 808/346-6500, www.southpacifickauai.com, 5:30 P.M. Wed., $85 adults, $30 6–12, under 5 free, premier seating $105). Based on the original Broadway show, the production has been brought to Kaua'i by the Hawaii Association of Performing Arts and producer Alain Dussaud. In its eighth year of production, the show tells the love story set on the island during World War II.

An all-you-can-eat buffet is included with the show and offers salad, pasta salad, teriyaki chicken, vegetables, desserts, coffee, and more. Tickets include the show, a buffet dinner, gratuity, and parking. A no-host cash bar is offered.

Food

Kaua'i's east side is home to many great restaurants and eateries. This is where you'll find the majority of the island's high-end and elegant restaurants, but there's also a great array of hole-in-the-wall local eateries.

LIHU'E
American
The **Kaua'i Bakery** (4-356 B Kuhio Hwy., 808/821-0060, 6 A.M.–2 P.M. Sun.–Tues., 6 A.M.–2 P.M. and 5–8 P.M. Wed.–Sat.) serves tasty pastries to start the day. They don't have the broadest selection, but what they do have is very good. The pumpkin crunch pie is wonderful when in season, and the pastries and cakes are great daily. A local favorite. Service is quick and to the point.

Eat, drink, and be merry at the **Nawiliwili Tavern** (3488 Paena Loop, 808/245-1781, www.nawiliwilitavern.com, 2 P.M.–2 A.M. daily). The tavern is a very casual place to throw back a few drinks, watch some sports, and grab wireless Internet at Nawiliwili Bay.

A Lihu'e staple is ◖ **JJ's Broiler** (3416 Rice St., 808/246-4422, 11 A.M.–11 P.M. daily) on Kalapaki Bay. A chart house feel with sailboats hanging from the ceiling, it is a classic Lihu'e stop. Meats and local fish are offered on their extensive menu. The bilevel restaurant overlooks Kalapaki Bay, which enhances the experience greatly. The bottom level is more casual, offering a full bar and a veranda. Upstairs is a bit more formal and romantic. Their claim to fame is the Slavonic Steak, a thin broiled tenderloin dipped in butter, wine, and garlic sauce. Portions are large, the food is good, and it rarely disappoints.

The tried and true **Kalapaki Beach Hut** (3474 Rice St., 808/246-6330) serves up breakfast and lunch with burgers that have proved to be a local favorite and never a letdown. The restaurant offers views of the harbor and for breakfast has the standard fare plus local dishes like *loco moco*. Lunch includes fish and chips and sandwiches along with buffalo, turkey, fish, veggie, and beef burgers. A good reliable choice for a relaxed meal.

During football season a good stop is **Kalapaki Joe's** (3501 Rice St., 808/245-6266, www.kalapakijoes.com, 11 A.M.–10 P.M. daily, opening at 7 A.M. Sat.–Sun. during football season). Basic drinks and food along with a fun atmosphere create a fun environment.

Hawaiian Regional
◖ **Gaylord's** (3-2087 Kaumualii Hwy., 808/245-9593, www.gaylordskauai.com, 11 A.M.–2:30 P.M. and 5:30–9:30 P.M. Mon.–Sat., 9 A.M.–2:30 P.M. Sun. for brunch, $21–32) is a farm-to-table restaurant at the Kilohana

---

THE COCONUT

While on the Coconut Coast, make sure to try a coconut. Available at several fruit stands in Kapa'a, the coconut water is a refreshing and very healthy drink. Although the name calls it a nut, it is in fact a seed and fruit. Packed with electrolytes, coconut water is also full of fiber, protein, antioxidants, vitamins, and minerals. It's become a hot packaged commodity in recent years and now is stocked on supermarket shelves, but for many islanders there is nothing more satisfying and refreshing than a coconut straight from the tree. When you sample coconut water, make sure to ask the supplier if you can try the coconut meat. Lining the inside of the coconut, the fleshy white meat is also a tasty treat. The coconut meat in a young green coconut is generally softer and more gelatinous than an older one. In an older coconut the meat is usually thicker, firmer, and sometimes even rather hard. Don't miss out on this Coconut Coast treat.

LOCAL FISH

Fresh fish from the waters of Kaua'i is a treat for many. Called *i'a* in Hawaiian, fish is a local staple and fishing is a favorite pastime for islanders. Because many of Hawaii's fish are found elsewhere they have names that will be familiar to you but will usually be referred to by their Hawaiian name on a menu. So here's a quick breakdown of what fish is what.

- **Mahimahi** is a favorite for fish lovers. Often found in burgers or as an entrée, mahimahi is otherwise known as "dolphin fish." The meat is generally white, flaky, and moist and should not be overdone. The fish is identifiable by its broad head.

- A real island favorite is **ono,** otherwise known as wahoo or king mackerel. A deep-sea fish, the ono is known as one of the all-time best fish to eat, which makes sense considering that *ono* is also a Hawaiian term for delicious.

- The **ulua** is also known as a jack crevalle. Many local fishers test themselves with the ability to catch a large ulua, over 100 pounds or so. You may see stickers of the fish on trucks, or even hear the term "ulua hunter." The ulua is also a popular and tasty eating fish.

- The oh-so-popular **ahi** is a well-known fish, also called yellowfin tuna. The deep pink meat is another favorite eating fish for many and is great served raw as *poke* (fish salad) or sashimi, or seared.

- The silver *moi* is an especially savored fish, as it can only legally be caught in certain times of the year. Meaning "king" in Hawaiian, *moi* was traditionally reserved for royalty. You probably won't see it in restaurants often, but it is considered an exquisite eating fish by locals.

Plantation. Using local ingredients, the classy restaurant features American comfort food and Asian-fusion cuisine options. They use produce grown in the fields at Kilohana, and their meat and fish comes from Kaua'i ranchers and fishers. Some of the main dishes include potato-crusted mahi mahi, sesame seed-seared ahi tuna, chipotle barbecued pork chop, and grilled ribeye steak. Dinner main dishes run $21–32, with limited vegetarian options. Lunch mains include salads, sandwiches, fish and chips, steak frites, and vegetarian quiches ranging $9–19.

A classic eatery in the islands, **❰ Duke's** (3610 Rice St., 808/246-9599, www.dukeskauai.com, 11 A.M.–11 P.M.) is a must-stop on the to-eat-at list in Hawaii. Named after the legendary Hawaiian surfer Duke Kahanamoku, the restaurant is split into two levels, where of course railing-side seats with unobstructed ocean views are the best. The downstairs Barefoot Bar is steps from the sand and serves up sandwiches, burgers, fish tacos,

Hawaiian plates, and more for $11–16. The Dining Room serves dinner daily and offers fresh fish and seafood, steaks and prime rib, and a salad bar for $15–30. Lanai seating is the best and music is offered several nights of the week.

On Kalapaki Beach is **Kukui's** (Kaua'i Marriott Resort, 808/246-5166, www.kukuis.kauaimarriott.com, 6:30–11 A.M. and 5–10 P.M. Mon.–Sat., 6:30–10 A.M. and 5–10 P.M.), offering Pacific Rim food for breakfast and dinner. The poolside seating adds to the romantic and elegant experience. Sunday brunch is also offered. Service is always on point here.

Italian

The open air and views over Kalapaki Bay from **❰ Cafe Portofino** (3481 Ho'olaule'a Way, 808/245-2121, www.cafeportofino.com) offer one of the most ideal backdrops, especially to enjoy always-great Italian food. The food is good and the wine selection is well done. The owner is a genuine Italian, which

KAU KAU: FAVORITE LOCAL DISHES

There's really no better way to experience a culture than to *kau kau* (pidgin slang for eat) the food of the people. Most of these foods are available in restaurants, supermarkets, and delis. So if you stumble across some, give it a try.

- Often found in supermarket delis or on restaurant menus, *poke* is a local favorite. Usually served as an appetizer, although *poke* and rice bowls are often available at delis, poke is cubed raw fish with seasonings. The fish of choice is usually ahi (yellowfin tuna), but it's not uncommon to find it made with *tako* (octopus), other types of tuna, or other fish. Seasonings are usually a combination of chopped onion, soy sauce, oil, sea salt, seaweed, and garlic. With *poke,* the fresher the fish the better the dish.

- A Hawaiian staple is **poi,** a form of taro that has been cooked, pounded, had water added, and fermented. The consistency can be from runny to thick. There is "two-finger" or "three-finger" poi, referring to how many fingers it takes to eat it depending on how thick it is.

- The often roadside-roasted **huli huli chicken** is simply barbecued chicken, but Hawaiian style. *Huli* means to turn, a reference to the rotisseried whole chicken continuously turned during cooking.

- The **plate lunch** is a local favorite composed of two scoops of rice, one scoop of macaroni salad, and a main meat course. The lunch is often served on a disposable plate. Lunch wagons usually serve plate lunches.

- Cooked in an *imu,* or earth oven, **kalua pig** is a flavorful dish usually found at celebratory gatherings. Birthday parties, *lu'au,* and other holiday feasts are usually reason to go through the long process, which entails hours of slow cooking.

- The locally loved **loco moco** is basically a bowl of rice topped with a meat patty, egg, and gravy. In Pacific Rim cuisine, the modernization of the *loco moco* with unique ingredients is becoming a trend.

- *Lomilomi* **salmon** is a popular side dish in Hawaii consisting of raw salmon and tomatoes. It's called "massaged" *(lomilomi)* salmon because the fish is massaged with the ingredients by hand, including salt, onions, and sometimes chili pepper. The dish is commonly found at *lu'au,* on menus, and in delis.

---

reflects in the quality of the food. Seafood, pasta, veal, filet mignon, and other meat dishes are available, along with enough meat-free options for vegetarians. Homemade gelato and fruit sorbets are also served. This is romantic fine dining.

A local favorite, **Kaua'i Pasta** (4-939B Kuhio Hwy., 808/822-7447, www.kauaipasta. com, 11 A.M.–9 P.M. daily, $12–22 d) offers a not-over-done sleek atmosphere. Tasty appetizers, wonderful and unique salads, paninis, and an array of main dishes with several suitable for vegetarians are combined with a few Pacific-inspired apps on the lounge menu. There are locations in Lihu'e and Kapa'a. The atmosphere is modern yet warm.

Mexican

At the Kukui Grove Shopping Center, **La Bamba Mexican Food** (3-2600 Kaumualii Hwy., 808/245-5972, 11 A.M.–9 P.M. daily) will fill the stomach. The food is standard mall food—basic Mexican fare on the slightly greasy side. Drop in only if you're shopping in the mall.

Another stop in Nawiliwili is **Mariachie** (3501 Rice St., 808/246-1570, 8 A.M.–9 P.M. Mon. and 8 A.M.–10 P.M. Wed.–Sun.), where basic Mexican food is served up. The menu is quite extensive and offers many common Mexican options. Nothing is bad, but nothing is really amazing either. This is a decent stop while exploring Nawiliwili Bay.

Thai, Japanese, and Filipino

At Kalapaki Bay is **Gingbua Thai Restaurant** (3501 Rice St., 808/245-9350, 11 A.M.–3 P.M. and 4–9 P.M. Mon.–Sat., dinner only Sun.). The restaurant serves up standard Thai cuisine that can be either really good or just average. Service is usually good but can be slow.

A homestyle place is **Mama Lucy's Kitchen** (4495 Puhi Rd., 808/245-4935, 6 A.M.–6 P.M. Mon.–Fri., 6 A.M.–4 P.M. Sat.), where you can get authentic Filipino food served with a smile. The desserts and treats are good too. The environment is nothing fancy.

Shaved Ice

Shakas Shave Ice (3474 Rice St., 808/652-1793) serves up standard shave ice beachside at Kalapaki Bay. Portions are good sized and I recommend trying local flavors.

WAILUA AND KAPA'A
American

The quaint and simple 🔲 **Kountry Kitchen** (1485 Kuhio Hwy., 808/822-3511, 6 A.M.–1:30 P.M. daily, $7.50–11) is a perfect place to grab a classic breakfast of eggs, omelets, pancakes, French toast, coffee, and more. The place is a favorite with locals and visitors, and you may have to wait a few minutes on a weekend morning. True to its name, a country theme sets a homey feeling for the decor. Portions are large and service is friendly and on top of it.

Killah Steaks (across from the Waipouli Town Center, 808/631-1935, 11 A.M.–5 P.M. Tues.–Thurs. and Sun., 11 A.M.–5:30 P.M. Fri.–Sat., $6.50–10) is a local favorite. Customers leave stuffed and satisfied every time. The roadside restaurant in a wagon serves up steaks at decent prices to go or to enjoy at a picnic table. Two local guys own and operate the portable restaurant, and serve up "killah" affordable steaks. There is no menu here, just two options: the salt and pepper steak or a mushroom onion steak with gravy. Both options come with a side salad and rice. Sometimes they sell out and close early.

At **Olympic Cafe** (1354 Kuhio Hwy., 808/822-5825, 6 A.M.–9 P.M. daily), the open-air side of the café overlooks the sidewalk in downtown Kapa'a. Usual breakfast fare like eggs and pancakes is offered for breakfast. Lunch is wraps, burgers, salads, and sandwiches. Dinner offerings include pasta, fish, burgers, Mexican dishes, steaks, and more. The restaurant is known for its large portions. You won't leave here hungry.

Chicken in a Barrel (4-1586 Kuhio Hwy., 808/823-0780, 10 A.M.–8 P.M. Mon.–Sat., $5–15) is famous for its smoked foods and classic barbecue. Service is generally great with the occasional slow meal. For lunch or dinner it makes a perfect stop while cruising Kapa'a. The chicken is known to be tender and moist. Indoor and outdoor seating are available. Try the sampler or the chicken burrito in the casual atmosphere.

Coffee and Bakeries

Country Moon Rising Bakery (4-1345 Kuhio Hwy., 808/822-0345, www.roxysquare.com/countrymoonrising.htm, 3 A.M.–8 P.M. Sun.–Thurs., 8 A.M.–5 P.M. Fri.–Sat.) is a sweet place to get fresh baked breads and pastries. The bakery uses only organic flour in its hand-formed breads and bagels. Hawaiian sweet breads to take home include macadamia nut ginger and cinnamon raisin; they are so good! Stop by for a tasty pastry.

Sweet describes **Sweet Marie's Hawaii Bakery** (4-788 Kuhio Hwy., 808/823-0227, www.sweetmarieskauai.com, 7 A.M.–2 P.M. Tues.–Sat.), a quaint and cute bakery. The small bakery is in with today's health trends of serving up gluten-free baked goods, desserts, and wedding cakes, as well as gluten-free catering. Freshly baked pastries, muffins, and cookies are a delightful treat. Try the amazing *liliko'i* (passion fruit) burst. You can even take home some gluten-free muffin mixes and pizza dough. Great for breakfast or dessert.

Java Kai (4-1384 Kuhio Hwy. 808/823-6887, www.javakaihawaii.com, 6 A.M.–7 P.M. daily) serves locally roasted coffee along with other Fair Trade varieties. Muffins, scones, croissants, and cookies are baked on-site. Egg sandwiches, bagels, and a decadent waffle are

---

ONO SNACKS: LOCAL TREATS

Try this *ono* (delicious) local treats.

- The sweet and refreshing **shave ice** is a local staple. Although it's similar to the Mainland snow cone, shave ice is made with ice that is much finer. The heavy shave ice machine shaves away at a block of ice, and the shavings are then piled into a paper cup. A modern and helpful advancement in the world of shave ice is the flower-shaped plastic tray cup. Most shave ice shops offer traditional flavors like vanilla and strawberry, along with local flavors like coconut, *liliko'i* (passion fruit), and melon. These local flavors really make a shave ice a treat. Many shops offer the option of cream on top, which is really the icing on the cake, or chunks of coconut or ice cream under the ice.

- Brought to Hawaii by the Portuguese, a **malasada** is basically a doughnut without a hole, sprinkled with sugar. They're soft inside. Similar to a morning pastry, they are commonly found in bakeries or in stand-alone *malasada* wagons. Enjoy one for breakfast or even for a treat or dessert.

- A local and tasty take on the standard potato chip is **taro chips.** Thinly sliced with a coat of salt, the taro chip is a yummy snack. Most supermarkets and sandwich shops offer packages of taro chips, so give them a try.

- **Pupu** is a common term in Hawaii for finger food. Many restaurants offer a pupu platter, which can be anything from cheese and crackers to caviar. Some bars offer free pupu platters during happy hour. The term pupu often replaces "appetizers" on a menu.

- While in the islands you will probably see the term **li hing mui** all over the place, as *li hing mui* powder, shave ice, plums, candies, and even in margaritas. It's a unique flavor of sweet, sour, salty, and tart. *Li hing mui* means "traveling plum" or dried plum in Chinese, and it's this form that you'll probably see the most.

---

the closest they have to a real meal. Service is order at the counter and to the point.

The artsy and funky **(Small Town Coffee** (4-1495 Kuhio Hwy., 808/821-1604) serves up an array of tasty quality coffee to get your day started. The staff is friendly, usually young, hip, and tattooed. The decor is simple and offers seats and free wireless Internet. The coffee is always good and never burnt, and various breakfast bagels and pastries are available for a quick eat.

Hawaiian Regional

A sea of seafood is available at **Wahooo Bar and Grill** (4-733 Kuhio Hwy., 808/822-7833, www.wahooogrill.com, 11 A.M.–9:30 P.M. daily, $13–50), bordering a coconut grove on the Coconut Coast. They have a wide array of all the seafood you could ask for, from local fish to wonderful lobster tail. For those not in the mood for seafood there is a cheeseburger

for the lowest priced meal, as well as beef dishes and ribs. There's not really much for vegetarians here except for a grilled cheese and dessert. And for dessert, try the baked papaya, a unique twist on a fruit usually reserved for breakfast.

An eclectic mix of Asian and Pacific cuisine is offered at **Pacific Island Bistro** (4-831 Kuhio Hwy., 808/822-0092, 10:30 A.M.–9:30 P.M. daily, $10–37). Although hidden behind a modest front, the bistro offers tasty, flavorful, and unique options. The menu is extensive and offers a variety of food even for vegetarians. Some of their best is the Peking duck, herb-crusted lamb chop, and vegetarian stir-fry. It serves lunch and dinner, with lots of seafood and meat dishes as well as a good selection of vegetarian meals.

Escape reality at **(Oasis** (4-820 Kuhio Hwy., in Waipouli Beach Resort, 808/822-9332, 5:30–9 P.M. daily, $10–17), which offers oceanfront dining in an environment that is truly an oasis from the outside world. Service is always on point, and the eatery focuses on local cuisine, using 90 percent ingredients from Kaua'i, from veggies to fish. A perfect location for a romantic dinner or celebratory meal. The eatery opens to a white-sand beach.

Lemongrass Grill (4-885 Kuhio Hwy., 808/821-2888, 4–9:30 P.M. daily) offers a beautiful atmosphere of island style combined with Asian decor. The menu offers seafood, steak, full bar, and Thai and American dishes. The food is usually good, but steaks can be mostly hit and sometimes miss. Try to sit indoors; the outdoor seating is roadside. There is a lot of meat but several dishes provide a sufficient vegetarian dinner. There is also a children's menu. Service can be slow.

◖ **Caffe Coco** (4-369 Kuhio Hwy., 808/822-7990, 11 A.M.–2 P.M. Tues.–Fri., 5–9 P.M. Fri.–Sat.) is a garden bistro emanating a relaxed island ambience. Made-to-order gourmet food with a Pacific theme and many vegetarian dishes are offered here. Outdoor seating can be enjoyed in the gravel courtyard surrounded by numerous fruit trees, tiki torches, delicate lighting, and umbrellas. Indoor seating is offered and there is also an indoor gallery. Order at the counter and don't forget to use the house's "jungle juice" if the mosquitos get bothersome. A full espresso bar and good desserts are also offered. Live music happens every evening, and it's bring your own drinks.

Named after the plant that decorates the island, the **Naupaka Terrace** (4331 Kaua'i Beach Dr., 808/245-1955, 6:30–11 A.M. and 6–9 P.M. daily) offers breakfast and dinner overlooking Kaua'i's shore. The open-air restaurant is a plantation-style building that offers steak and seafood dishes, an abundant salad bar, and other entrées suitable for vegetarians. The tranquil and elegant environment offers views of waterfalls, ponds, and the ocean. A prime rib and seafood buffet is offered every Friday and Saturday night. Breakfast starts at $9 and dinner ranges $25–40.

Health Foods

Rainbow Living Foods (4-1384 103A Kuhio Hwy., 10 A.M.–7 P.M. Mon.–Fri., 10 A.M.–5 P.M. Sat.) offers healthy and gourmet meals like Russian caviar, kale salad (a personal favorite), and delicious juices and desserts. Service is friendly and warm and they even offer catering. Check the daily specials and enjoy the healthy meals.

The Coconut Cup Juice Bar & Cafe (4-1516 Kuhio Hwy., 808/823-8630, www.coconutcupjuicebar.com, 9 A.M.–5 P.M. daily, $6–9) is the best stop for a healthy meal on your way to the beach. They serve up sandwiches, bagels, wraps, acai bowls, smoothies, and more. A real treat here is their natural shave ice, a nice break from the common artificial and sugary shave ice. Enjoy your meal on the go or at the picnic tables.

A true hole in the wall, ◖ **Mermaids Cafe** (1384 Kuhio Hwy., 808/821-2026, www.mermaidskauai.com, 11 A.M.–9 P.M. daily, $9–12) is nestled between shops in downtown Kapa'a. The food is delicious, and definitely on the healthy side, although not all vegetarian. The order-at-the-window café serves wraps, burritos, sandwiches, and stir-fry, all with unique twists and most with tofu, chicken, and fresh fish options. Check for daily specials. Try the ahi nori wrap. Good drinks include spearmint and lemongrass iced tea and hibiscus lemonade. There's limited sidewalk seating and a small bar tucked around the side.

Papaya's (4-831 Kuhio Hwy., 808/823-0190, www.papayasnaturalfoods.com, 8 A.M.–8 P.M. Mon.–Sat., 10 A.M.–5 P.M. Sun.) has an all-day hot bar and salad bar daily for $7.99 a pound. A deli that makes sandwiches, smoothies, and juices to order is also inside and there are premade foods in the refrigerator. The food is good, organic, and vegetarian but can feel repetitive if you eat there a lot. Food is served as takeout but there are seats outside to eat at.

Ice Cream

Tropical and traditional ice creams and sorbets at **Lappert's** (484 Kuhio Hwy., 808/822-0744, www.lappertshawaii.com, 10 A.M.–9 P.M. Sun.–Sat., $4 for a single scoop) are the perfect cool accent to a warm Hawaiian day. Originating on Kaua'i, the shop now has outlets statewide and has about 16 percent butterfat in its regular flavors and around 8 percent in its fruit flavors, making for some pretty creamy ice cream. There's a wide array of delicious flavors, so I recommend sampling a few before making a decision.

Another option for ice cream is **Cold Stone Creamery** (4-831 Kuhio Hwy., 11 A.M.–9:30 P.M. Sun.–Thurs., 11 A.M.–10 P.M. Fri. and Sat.). They serve up heaping piles of really good ice cream that they mix with a selection of candies, cookies, and other stuff.

Japanese

For spectacular food stop by ◖ **Kintaro** (4-370 Kuhio Hwy., 808/822-3341, 5:30–9:30 P.M. Mon.–Sat., $11–21), which has great sushi, a full bar, a lovely atmosphere, and a great teppanyaki area (where they prep the food in front of you). The fish is local and always fresh, the service is outstanding, and it's nice enough to get dressed up but still fun and not yuppy. Make reservations for the teppanyaki. Lobster, filet mignon, and other seafood are available for those not in the mood for Japanese food.

A noticeable eatery roadside in Kapa'a is **House of Noodles** (4-1330 Kuhio Hwy., 808/822-2708, 10 A.M.–9 P.M. daily). The menu is quite extensive with a lot more than noodles, such as sandwiches, smoothies, and shave ice. The food is hit or miss so stick with the noodle dishes; they're usually pretty good. The atmosphere is very simple.

Mexican

Monico's Taqueria (4356 Kuhio Hwy., 808/822-4300, 11 A.M.–3 P.M. and 5–9 P.M. Tues.–Sun.) serves up Mexican food with a local twist. Although the place is clean and the food is always quality and never bad, it can be bland and just not great. Fish tacos are a favorite for many.

Pizza

Brick Oven (4-361 Kuhio Hwy., 808/823-8561) is a local favorite. It's very child friendly with the option for the kiddos to have a free ball of dough to play with. Wheat or white crust is offered, as well as the option to have garlic butter brushed on the dough. Thursday night is all-you-can-eat buffet night. Service is friendly but sometimes on the slow side. It's a good place for a group or family dinner or a very casual date.

JJ's Pizza (4-1345 Kuhio Hwy., 808/822-5743, www.jjspizzakauai.com, noon–9 P.M. Mon.–Sat., $11–40) makes its pizza dough daily. The pizza is really good, but at JJ's the service can really be on "island time." They offer various sized pies with up to seven toppings. Calzones are also available.

Information and Services

VISITORS CENTER

Kaua'i Visitors Bureau (4334 Rice St., #101, 808/245-3971, www.kauai-hawaii.com) offers a wealth of information of all things related to visiting Kaua'i. The information hotline is 800/262-1400 and offers live and up-to-date information on visiting Kaua'i. The hotline is available to all 50 states and Canada 6 A.M.–6 P.M. Monday–Friday and 6 A.M.–2 P.M. on weekends. The KVB can direct visitors to parks and beaches, sites and attractions, local culture, island events, activities and recreation, and all things Kaua'i-made.

POST OFFICES

There are several federal post offices on the east side. United States Postal Service post offices can be found in Lihu'e (4441 Rice St., 800/275-8777, 8 A.M.–4 P.M. Mon.–Fri. and 9 A.M.–1 P.M. Sat.), near Wailua (3-4251 Kuhio Hwy., 808/275-8777, 10 A.M.–noon Mon.–Fri.), and in Kapa'a (4-1101 Kuhio Hwy., 800/275-8777, 9 A.M.–4 P.M. Mon.–Fri. and 9 A.M.–1 P.M. Sat.). The Lihu'e and Kapa'a locations both provide passport application services as well as full shipping and packing services.

INTERNET ACCESS

The **Lihue Public Library** (4344 Hardy St., 808/241-3222, 11 A.M.–7 P.M. Mon. and Wed., 9 A.M.–4:30 P.M. Tues., Thurs., and Fri.) and the **Kapa'a Public Library** (1464 Kuhio Hwy., 808/821-4422, 9 A.M.–5 P.M. Mon., Wed., Thurs., and Fri., noon–8 P.M. Tues.) offer Internet access. Residents must have a library card to get access, and visitors can get a temporary card for $5. You must use their computers.

Small Town Coffee (4-1495 Kuhio Hwy., 808/821-1604) in Kapa'a provides Internet access for the public on their desktop or via your laptop with their free wireless Internet. **Akamai Computers** (4-1286 Kuhio Hwy., 808/823-0047) provides Internet access and computer repair.

EMERGENCY SERVICES

Wilcox Memorial Hospital (3-3420 Kuhio Hwy., 808/245-1100) is central in Lihu'e and has a 24-hour emergency room (808/245-1010). The **Kaua'i Medical Clinic Urgent Care** (3-3420B Kuhio Hwy., 808/245-1532, 8 A.M.–5 P.M. daily, with 8 A.M.–2 P.M. walk-ins, 2–4 P.M. appointments by availability daily) is located right by the hospital in Lihu'e.

BANKS

Lihu'e

First Hawaiian Bank (4423 Rice St., 808/245-4024, 8:30 A.M.–4 P.M. Mon.–Thurs., 8:30 A.M.–6 P.M. Fri.) provides full teller services and a 24-hour ATM. **American Savings Bank** (4318 Rice St., 808/245-3388, 8 A.M.–5 P.M. Mon.–Thurs., 8 A.M.–6 P.M. Fri.) has teller services and a 24-hour ATM.

Kapa'a

First Hawaiian Bank (4-1366 Kuhio Hwy., 808/822-4966, 8:30 A.M.–4 P.M. Mon.–Thurs., 8:30 A.M.–6 P.M. Fri.) provides full teller services and a 24-hour ATM. **American Savings Bank** (4-771 Kuhio Hwy., 808/822-0529, 9 A.M.–7 P.M. Mon.–Fri., 10 A.M.–3 P.M. Sat. and Sun.) has teller services and a 24-hour ATM.

CLASSES

For a custom-made souvenir take an art class by **Marionette Art Classes** (808/631-9173, www.kauai-artist.net) in Kapa'a. The instructor, a local artist, art teacher, and graphic designer offers watercolor classes in Kapa'a at the Mokihana (4-796 Kuhio Hwy.) every second and fourth Tuesday of the month from 10 A.M. to 1 P.M. Check-in is at the front desk of the Mokihana. She teaches classes island-wide for a range of mediums. Beginners and children over 10 are welcome, and children under 10 are welcome with an adult.

Getting There and Around

BY CAR

The most convenient way to get to and around the east side is by car. Highway 56 heads west straight out of Lihu'e and runs all the way to the end of the road, turning into Route 560 by Hanalei. Rental cars are the best bet here and are available at the airport. Gas prices go up the farther north you go, so it's a good idea to fill up in Lihu'e.

BY BUS

The **Kaua'i Bus** (808/241-6410, www.kauai.gov/Transportation, 5:27 A.M.–10:40 P.M. Mon.–Fri. and 6:21 A.M.–5:50 P.M. Sat., Sun., and holidays) runs island-wide with numerous stops from Lihu'e to Anahola. The bus is a green, convenient, and affordable way to get around and even goes to the airport. Fares are $1 for children and seniors, and $2 for the general public. Monthly passes are also available. Bus schedules for the east side are available on the website.

BY TAXI AND LIMOUSINE

Pono Taxi (808/635-3478, www.ponotaxi.com) in Lihu'e offers taxi, airport shuttle, and tour services island-wide. They provide spacious and clean minivans. **Island Taxi** (808/639-7829) is based out of Lihu'e and provides airport rides as well as rides island-wide. Service is prompt and friendly. Lihu'e's **Ace Kaua'i Taxi Services** (808/639-4310) will take you wherever you need to go. Hawaii taxi rates are $3 per mile and 0.40 cents a minute. Prices are per minivan not per person.

SCOOTERS

Hop onto a moped to zip around the east side and save on gas at **Island Scooter Rental** (at Coconut Coasters in Kapa'a, 401586 Kuhio Hwy., 808/822-7368, www.mobilemopeds. com, 9 A.M.–5 P.M. daily). If you rent by the week the company offers free airport pickup, and they offer four-hour tours for $100. Call for prices and reservations.

NORTH SHORE

Kaua'i's north shore is a true paradise with lush green land, deep blue ocean, bright sunlight, and nourishing rain sustaining the area's fertile soil. The road through the north shore weaves through taro fields, quaint towns, valleys and jungle, and beaches, ending at the start of the Na Pali Coast.

Kilauea is the first main town you'll encounter on Kauai's north side. The dense jungle, winding rivers, and long beaches of Kilauea exist in an area without defined borders, ranging from slightly before the town to somewhere between Anini and Princeville. Kilauea town is small and sweet, built on the sugar industry, which left the area in the 1970s. Hidden from view on the highway, the town is toward the coast after you turn right near mile marker 23 and a Shell gas station. The quaint town offers a surprising array of eateries and shops that serve as bustling gathering places for visitors and locals alike. Near town is the area's claim to fame, the historic Kilauea Lighthouse, as well as marvelous white-sand beaches, secret tide pools, waterfalls, and sandy havens.

Farther north lies **Princeville** on a high bluff. It is 9,000 acres of planned luxury homes, condos, and a hotel with a view of Hanalei Bay that can't be beat. Its modern name stays true to the area's traditional uses, as it was used by the *ali'i* (Hawaiian royalty) and was also home to various sacred *heiau*. The pandanus tree grew here in abundance, providing Hawaiians with a valuable leaf called hala that was used for weaving. Because the first Europeans to the area realized the value of the location, the Russian Fur Trading Company

HIGHLIGHTS

LOOK FOR ◖ TO FIND RECOMMENDED SIGHTS, ACTIVITIES, DINING, AND LODGING.

◖ **Secret Beach:** Located at the end of a short downhill hike, Secret Beach offers a view of the Kilauea Point Lighthouse, a refreshing waterfall, and fine white sand. It's a great beach to walk and sun on, but swimming here isn't recommended (page 78).

◖ **SeaLodge Beach:** A beautiful and secluded white-sand beach, SeaLodge Beach is perfect for sunbathing, swimming, and snorkeling when the sea is calm (page 80).

◖ **Hanalei Bay:** Nearly two miles of fine white sand make up this crescent-moon-shaped heavenly beach. Several surf breaks, swimming, and full amenities can all be found here (page 82).

◖ **Snorkeling at Tunnels/Makua Beach:** When the ocean is calm, Tunnels Beach offers perhaps the best snorkeling sites on the island (page 87).

◖ **Snorkeling at Ke'e Beach:** Marking the beginning of the Na Pali Coast, Ke'e offers a semi-protected natural swimming pool and spectacular snorkeling (page 88).

◖ **Stand-Up Paddling on the Hanalei River:** The long and winding Hanalei River is a popular place for stand-up paddling. Rent a board in Hanalei and hit the river for some exercise and sun (page 90).

◖ **Hiking to Secret Beach Tide Pools and Waterfall:** Beyond Secret Beach is another hidden treasure. Scramble over rocks and hike to a beautiful area full of clear tide pools and a lovely ocean-side waterfall (page 93).

◖ **Hiking to Hanakapi'ai Beach and Hanakapi'ai Falls:** The two-mile hike to Hanakapi'ai Beach offers splendid views and time in nature, before another two miles up to the magnificent falls and icy cold pool. This is the ideal hike for a day-long nature adventure (page 96).

◖ **Kilauea Point National Wildlife Refuge and Lighthouse:** The Kilauea Point National Wildlife Refuge and Lighthouse offers great views of the north shore's coastline. Visitors can also walk through the lighthouse and learn about the sanctuary (page 101).

◖ **Hanalei Valley Overlook:** This overlook provides one of the best spots to view a wildlife preserve that is home to acres of the Hawaiian staple taro and other farmlands (page 102).

◖ **Limahuli Botanical Garden:** Take a botanical stroll through history along terraced taro fields used by ancient Hawaiians. Part of the National Tropical Botanical Garden, the property is home to native and introduced plants (page 104).

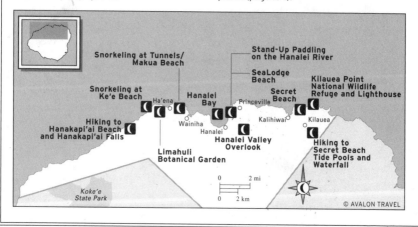

NORTH SHORE

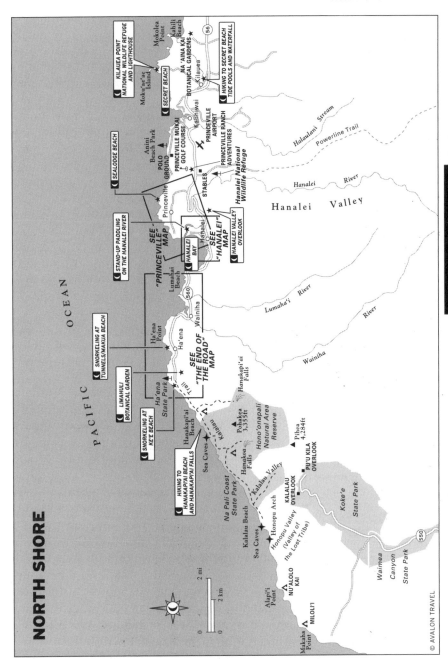

KILAUEA POINT NATIONAL WILDLIFE REFUGE AND LIGHTHOUSE

SECRET BEACH

Mokolea Point

Moku'ae'ae Island

Kahili Beach

MA 'AINA KAI BOTANICAL GARDENS

HIKING TO SECRET BEACH TIDE POOLS AND WATERFALL

Kilauea

56

Ka'aka'aniu

Halaulani Stream

Powerline Trail

SEALODGE BEACH

Anini Beach Park

POLO GROUND

PRINCEVILLE MOKAI GOLF COURSE

PRINCEVILLE AIRPORT

PRINCEVILLE RANCH ADVENTURES

STABLES

Hanalei National Wildlife Refuge

Hanalei   River

Hanalei   Valley

STAND-UP PADDLING ON THE HANALEI RIVER

Princeville

"PRINCEVILLE" SEE MAP

HANALEI BAY

Hanalei

SEE "HANALEI" MAP

HANALEI VALLEY OVERLOOK

Lumahai Beach

560

Lumahai River

Wainiha

SNORKELING AT TUNNELS/MAKUA BEACH

Ha'ena Point

Ha'ena

Lumahai River

Wainiha River

OCEAN

PACIFIC

LIMAHULI BOTANICAL GARDEN

SNORKELING AT KE'E BEACH

Ha'ena State Park

Trail

SEE "THE END OF THE ROAD" MAP

Hanakapi'ai Falls

Wainiha

HIKING TO HANAKAPI'AI BEACH AND HANAKAPI'AI FALLS

Hanakapi'ai Beach

Sea Caves

Ke'e

Pohakea 3,355ft

Hono'onapali Natural Area Reserve

Pihea 4,284ft

PU'U KILA OVERLOOK

Na Pali Coast State Park

Hanakoa Falls

Hanakoa Valley

Kalalau Valley

KALALAU OVERLOOK

Koke'e State Park

Kalalau Beach

Honopu Arch

Sea Caves

Honopu Valley (Valley of the Lost Tribe)

Alapi'i Point

NU'ALOLO KAI

Waimea Canyon State Park

550

MILOLI'I

Makaha Point

2 mi

2 km

0

N

© AVALON TRAVEL

built Fort Alexander here, one of the three forts built under King Kaumuali'i of Kaua'i. The only remains are the faint outlines of walls on the lawn in front of the St. Regis Princeville Resort, a prime spot to watch the sunset. Princeville is a destination within itself, providing accommodations, shops, eateries, a grocery store, postal services, a library, a playground, top quality golf courses, a luxury hotel, and just about anything a visitor could need or want. The area also holds beautiful beaches and a wonderful natural saltwater swimming pool, all nestled at the bottom of the cliffs.

Descending into Hanalei Valley, visitors enter into another element, one of which dreams and tropical fantasies are made of. **Hanalei town** is backed by prominent green cliffs lined with waterfalls whose numbers are relative to how much rain has fallen on the area. Where the cliffs meet the land, acres of bright and dark green taro *lo'i* (irrigated terraces) glisten in the sun. There is a great photo opportunity of the terraces from the Hanalei Overlook. The essence of old Hawaii holds strong in Hanalei, with historic buildings, a mix of homes from small plantation cabins to luxury homes owned by celebrities, and a raw

landscape. Hawaiians native to the area still live here, while celebrities, hippies, surf-happy travelers, and the upper class have all made homes in the jungle and along the beach.

From Hanalei to the start of the **Na Pali Coast** at the end of the road, the coast is made up of some of the state's most spectacular beaches. Rivers trace the land from the mountains to the ocean, and fertile dirt lends a hand in helping tropical jungle flourish. The Kalalau Trail, leading miles along the wild and gorgeous Na Pali Coast, leads to waterfalls, secluded beaches, and camping far off the beaten path.

Kaua'i's green and lush windward north side also provides the other vacation luxuries you may be looking for, with local boutiques and galleries, top-of-the-line gourmet food, and world-class surfing. Your journey to the north shore can include a range of experiences. Take a muddy hike to a waterfall or sit poolside overlooking the bay, eat a gourmet meal or enjoy lunch at a local lunch wagon, or snorkel a beautiful bay after a morning on the greens. Kaua'i's north side isn't just a destination, it's a feeling, an essence, a spirit, and it shouldn't be missed.

Beaches

The north shore holds Kauai's most exotic beaches. They instill a feeling of bliss in their visitors. Each one is covered in a thick blanket of white sand lining clear blue water, and many boast perfect waves for surfers. All are great for tanning and picnicking, many are wonderful for snorkeling, and a lot are ideal for surfing. The north shore picks up Hawaii's big swells in the winter, so make sure to be careful during winter's big waves.

KILAUEA
Moloa'a Beach
Moloa'a means "matted roots" in Hawaiian, and the relevance of the name is apparent at the river mouth, where tree roots are exposed

to the elements. Moloa'a is a beautiful white-sand beach in the shape of the crescent moon. At this lesser-visited beach, black rocks jut out through the water to the far left and right of the large bay. Oceanfront houses back the east half of the beach, but it still provides an undisturbed haven from the more crowded beaches. While several of the beaches out here have calm rivers good for swimming for children, the river mouth here is usually a little rough, and the water in it appears to be a bit more murky than others. The south side of the beach is nicer than the north, providing shade and safer swimming and body-boarding than the other end of the beach. As at all beaches out here, swimming should only be

THE BEST DAY ON THE NORTH SHORE

The best day on the north shore is all about good food, beach-hopping, colorful sunsets, snorkeling, and catching a few waves. It can all be experienced in one day if you begin early (around 9 A.M.).

- Begin your day on the north side with views of the **Kilauea Point National Wildlife Refuge.** Gaze down into the clear blue water of the cove, where birds nest and whales make wintertime visits. It's a classic photo opportunity with the lighthouse standing proudly above the cove.

- Now head back up to **Kilauea Bakery & Pau Hana Pizza** for a quick but quality breakfast of sweet and savory pastries, coffee, and other treats. If you'd like you can drop into some other shops here.

- Then it's off to Princeville for a short hike down to **Queen's Bath** or **SeaLodge Beach** (or both if you'd like). Queen's Bath is only recommended for the summer months, while SeaLodge requires more time.

- After working up an appetite hiking, stop at the **Hanalei Valley Overlook** for a photo and then head down to Hanalei for a healthy local lunch at the **Hanalei Taro and Juice Co.** This is a great place to try some healthy Hawaiian dishes.

- Now to experience what the north side is all about – surf. There are two options here: You can rent a surfboard at **Hanalei Surf Company** or **Backdoor Surf** for a self-guided surf lesson, or if you're more comfortable with a surf school, visit the **Titus Kinimaka Hawaiian School of Surfing** in Hanalei and book a lesson. Another option is renting a stand-up paddle board and hitting the **Hanalei River** or **Hanalei Bay** if the waves are flat.

- For lunch, stop at **Red Hot Mama's** in Wainiha for some unique burritos and local fish. Enjoy them on a nearby beach.

- If it's summer and the waves are small, **Tunnels Beach** is the next stop for excellent snorkeling, so don't forget your snorkel gear.

- From here drive to the **Maniniholo Dry Cave** across from Ha'ena and take a quick peek. It's fun to take photos here.

- Then it's a stop for photos and dipping your feet in the cold water at **Waikapala'e Wet Cave.** Some people like to swim here, but the cave is rather dark and eerie.

- To end the day, head down to **Ke'e Beach** for more snorkeling in the natural pool, and to enjoy some sun or the sunset.

- On the way back, stop in Hanalei at **Postcards Cafe** or **Bar Acuda Tapas and Wine** for dinner. If you're looking for entertainment check if there's live music at **Bouchons Hanalei** or **Tahiti Nui.**

attempted when the waves are very calm, and at Moloa'a the ocean can be a bit rough and windy. Moloa'a is a perfect place to watch a colorful sunset, which will most likely be enjoyed alone. To get here, turn onto the rough Ko'olau Road between mile markers 16 and 17. Then turn onto Moloa'a Road and follow it to the end to Moloa'a Bay. Parking is very limited here, but signs alert visitors of where it's okay to park. It's worth it to bring a snorkel here.

Larsen's Beach

Named after the former manager of Kilauea Plantation, L. David Larsen, Larsen's offers seclusion and enough space to stroll and see what you can find on the beach. Larsen's is another place where the crowds are usually nonexistent, and many times you will be alone or a good distance from other visitors. The very dangerous Pakala Channel is right before the point on the north end and features an extremely strong current that visitors absolutely must stay

NORTH SHORE

TOP KID-FRIENDLY ACTIVITIES ON THE NORTH SHORE

Kaua'i's north shore has a lot to offer *keiki* (children), from nature excursions to man-made fun. Out of the many beaches lining the coast of the north side, certain ones are safer and more fun for children than others. If you're looking for a *keiki*-safe beach, it's always a good idea to keep an eye on the surf and beach conditions.

- **Kaua'i Mini Golf** in Kilauea has a fun and unique course for the whole family. It takes golfers through a cultural tour of Hawaii.

- In the Kilauea area, **Anini Beach** is hands down the best beach for children. Only the beach park has a lifeguard, but the two-mile stretch of beach is bordered by a fringing reef that keeps big waves out. The seemingly endless stretch of water is only a few feet deep even yards out toward the ocean. Near the end of the beach past the beach park itself is a small river that can be fun for kids to wade in; a ways up is a swing hanging from a tree.

- Located at the top of Princeville on the right of the shopping center is a child's wonderland. Near the **Princeville Public Library**

is the **Princeville Playground.** It has two playgrounds, one for 5-12 year olds and a smaller one for toddlers. There's even a pavilion and uncovered tables to picnic at if you want to bring food from Foodland or enjoy an ice cream cone from **Lappert's Hawaii Ice Cream & Coffee.**

- Once you're down in Hanalei, **Kokonut Kids** is a fun shop for the little ones. Colorful and cute clothing for boys and girls decorates the store. Close to it is the **Hanalei Toy and Candy Store,** loaded with wonderful toys and tasty treats. Don't head in here unless you're prepared to buy something, because the kids will want to indulge.

- Also in Hanalei is the surf break called **Pine Trees** at **Hanalei Bay.** It's not only a beautiful beach but a great place for your kids to watch local surfer kids catch waves or join in themselves at a surf school.

- If the waves are flat you can snorkel in the natural pool at **Ke'e Beach.** Bring their gear and stick by them as they explore Kaua'i's underwater world.

out of. When I consulted friends while writing this book, the Pakala Channel was one of two places people warned of. If the waves are flat and conditions are very mellow, snorkeling can be marvelous here—again, only when staying out of the channel. To get here, turn down the second Ko'olau Road headed north, right before mile marker 20, and a little over one mile down take the left Beach Access road to the end. After the cattle gate is a trail and it's about a 10-minute walk to the bottom.

◖ Secret Beach

Secret Beach is a wonderful treasure at the end of a dirt road and short trail. The beach is very, very long, and when the waves are really small swimming is possible. However, in the winter

months the waves here are pounding and the current is strong. The beach is backed by steep, tall cliffs that provide a small waterfall perfect for rinsing off about halfway down the beach. Secret Beach is full of surprises, and depending on the season, wave size, rain, currents, and tides, you may find swimming ponds in the sand, exposed rock creating tide pools, or rocks to cross over about halfway down. The walk down takes about 10 minutes and is a steep trail on roots and dirt. The way back up can be pretty tough because of the incline.

Secret has always been the unofficial nude beach on the north shore, but nowadays there are flyers posted by the police department stating that it's illegal to go naked here. However, this hasn't entirely stopped dedicated nudists.

© JADE ECKARDT

Secret Beach offers plenty of space and a view of the Kilauea Lighthouse.

It's also known as Kauapea Beach, and the Kilauea Lighthouse is visible on the point at the east end. There are awesome, even more secret tide pools and another waterfall farther west past the beach. To get here, turn onto the first Kalihiwai Road heading north and take the first right onto a dirt road. Head to the end of the road; parking is behind large homes.

Kahili/Quarry Beach

A long, fine white-sand beach backed by an ironwood forest, Kahili Beach is also known as Quarry Beach. A popular spot with locals for surfing and boogie-boarding, Kahili Beach is gorgeous but doesn't provide the calmest swimming. The ironwood forest growing out of the red dirt backing the beach makes for a fun place to experiment with photography. There are two sides to the beach, with a ridge of rock dividing them, and the east side serves as an unofficial campsite. It's not a wide section of rock though, and crossing over it is simple when the waves aren't huge. A river meets the ocean on the west end of the beach, and along

the river can be a good calm place for swimming. During weekdays, there's a good chance Quarry Beach will be empty, but it's popular with locals on weekends.

Local fishers come here to catch a fish they use for bait called 'o'io. The fish is too bony to fry and eat, but the fishers get the meat off the bones by cutting off the tail, rolling a soda bottle over the body, and then squeezing the meat out of the cut. It's then made into fish balls by mixing it with water, hot pepper, and bread crumbs.

To get to Kahili Beach, head north and turn right on Wailapa Road between mile markers 21 and 22. Turn left at the yellow post and cement blocks marking the top of the road and go about a half mile down to the beach.

Waiakalua Beach

The great thing about Waiakalua Beach is that it's usually empty and secluded. The beach offers shade, which enables visitors to spend several hours here without overheating and needing to leave. Soft white sand, a fringing reef, and a spring at the north end add character to this beach. As usual, ocean conditions dictate whether it's swimmable here. When it's very mellow, snorkeling can be okay, but be careful. To get here, turn onto North Waiakalua Road and turn left on the dirt road just before you reach the end. Park at the end and walk the trail on the left. Waiakalua Beach is on the left after about a 10-minute mini hike down the steep path. To the right after the large rocks is **Pila'a Beach,** which is reachable after about 15–30 minutes of walking.

KALIHIWAI
Kalihiwai Beach

Kalihiwai is another beautiful bay nestled between two rocky points with a river at the west that usually offers a perfect place for a refreshing and calm swim. The sand is white and very fine, and the right-hand breaking wave is excellent for surfing, but it's much too advanced for beginner surfers. There are no amenities here, but there is sufficient parking under the ironwood trees. Swimming in the river is great for children, but make sure to stick by them. The edge of the water varies from a gradual slope to a steep drop. Coming from the east side, turn down the first Kalihiwai Road to get here. The road ends at the river, where the other side is visible. The road used to connect but was destroyed in a 1946 tsunami, so to reach the other side take the second Kalihiwai Road and take the right at the fork. It leads to the other side of the beach, where locals sometimes come to fish or paddle across the river to the beach.

Anini Beach

The seemingly endless white sand of Anini Beach stretches for approximately two miles. Much to the delight of beach goers who like to laze about in the water, a barrier reef creates great swimming for children and others who appreciate calm waters. The swimmable water here is a highlight. There's really no safer swimming on the north side than at Anini, and the water is surprisingly shallow very far out. Along the drive down, various pull-off stops

dot the road. They are all near small patches of beach where it's likely you'll be alone.

Anini Beach Park, about halfway down the road, is a popular beach with a camping area, restrooms, showers, picnic tables, and barbecue pits. The beach park is almost always very crowded, so if you're looking for less of a crowd try any of the spots on the way down. Past the beach park beach access continues until the end, where a stream meets the ocean. The occasional tide pool may be spotted along the way down depending on the tide, and feel free to pull over anywhere and take a dip or enjoy the beach. Near the end of the road is a swing hanging from a false kamani tree, a perfect opportunity for an ocean-side swing. To get here, take the second Kalihiwai Road headed north. Keep to the left at the fork in the road (going right leads to the north side of Kalihiwai Beach) and keep driving.

Wyllie Beach

After the stream at the end of Anini is Wyllie Beach, named after the road that accesses it from Princeville. If you want to check it out, park at the end of Anini and walk across the stream. It's the narrow strip of sand before the point and is lined with false kamani trees. The water is still really calm here.

PRINCEVILLE
◖ SeaLodge Beach

Seclusion, white sand, shade, and a pristine cove of crystal clear water compose SeaLodge Beach, offering everything a beach lover could want. Accessed by a shaded hike through the trees and then a short walk along the rocky coast, the beach provides good snorkeling when the ocean is calm. There's no lifeguard or amenities here, so it's important to be careful in the water. Located near the SeaLodge condos at the end of Kamehameha Road in Princeville, parking is in the unmarked stalls toward the top of the parking lot. The trailhead is in front of building A and marked with a sign. Here is an amazing panoramic view worth taking a minute to indulge in and snapping a few photos.

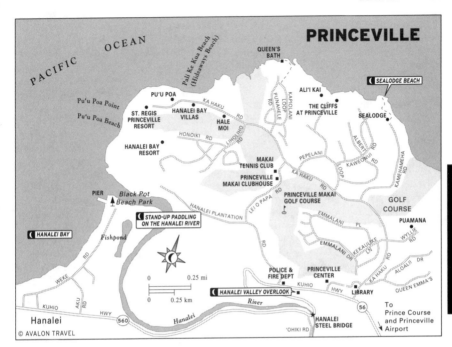

Take the dirt trail down past the small stream on the way to the ocean. Once you reach the ocean keep to your left, where you can walk along the black rocks or on the narrow trail a little up on the dirt. After a minute or so you will see SeaLodge Beach, nestled in its own cove and backed by a vertical cliff. The back of the beach is lined with trees that provide enough shade that you can spend a few hours at the beach. It's quite an amazing beach and worth the effort. The trail isn't super strenuous, but it is rather steep and tiresome on the way up.

Queen's Bath

Queen's Bath is a tide pool on the edge of a cliff looming above the ocean. Nature has created an extremely unique and picturesque combination that is at its best when the waves are small, but big enough to wash freshwater into the pool. This spot is dangerous. There's a plaque at the base of the trail with a safety warning stating that as of 2011, 28 people have died here, which speaks for itself. On very calm days, the pool is crystal clear and swimmable, but on any rough day in the winter months it's risky. There's a five-minute walk from the bottom of the trail to the pool that puts visitors at the edge of the cliff, and the pool itself isn't far from the edge and waves either. The hike down is intriguing in itself and offers several sights along the way, including a river, a couple of waterfalls, and a pool that usually has a few fish resting in it.

To get here turn right on Punahele Road and take the second right onto Kapiolani Loop. The parking lot is on the left-hand corner bordered by a green cement wall. The trailhead is easy to find, marked with both a warning sign and another one giving notice of the shearwater breeding grounds. About 10–15 minutes down the dirt trail it veers to the left at a waterfall pouring right into the ocean. Go left past the warning signs and almost right on the edge of the cliff is the pond. An important thing to know here is that during the winter months, from about September through April, the pool is pretty much unusable due to the large surf.

Hideaways Beach/Pali Ke Kua

Hideaways is a great beach for snorkeling, as is its sibling beach on the far side of the rocky point on the right. When the surf is small, snorkelers will usually see a gorgeous variety of fish and some green sea turtles. As at many other north shore beaches, false kamani trees provide shade, enabling beach goers to spend some quality time here without turning into lobsters right away. The trail leading down consists of steps for the first half before turning into a dirt path that can be muddy and slippery if it has rained. So although it's not a really strenuous hike, it takes a little agility to get down there and can be slightly tough for kids.

Check ocean conditions before going to this beach. When the waves are big in Hanalei Bay they will probably be washing far up the beach at Hideaways. To get here, take the trail that starts shortly before the St. Regis Princeville Resort gate house and next to the Pu'u Poa tennis courts. To reach the other side of the beach, either swim to the right from Hideaways (when conditions allow, of course) or walk the paved trail from the Pali Ke Kua condominiums.

Pu'u Poa Beach

Directly below the St. Regis Princeville Resort is the easily accessible and popular Pu'u Poa Beach. Swimming and snorkeling are both good here when ocean conditions allow. The white-sand beach reaches toward the mouth of the Hanalei River to the left, and the sandy bottom is enclosed by a narrow reef. When surf is up the outer reef is where experienced and elite surfers catch some of the biggest waves the north side musters up in the winter. For hotel guests, access is by the hotel pool area. For those not staying at the hotel, there is a small parking area by the guard house at the hotel entrance where the cement path begins.

HANALEI
◖ Hanalei Bay

Hanalei Bay is a crescent-moon-shaped, nearly two-mile long stretch of unbroken white sand beach consisting of several different spots that make up the heavenly stretch. The bay was used as one of Kaua'i's three main ports until recently and is still visited by large yachts. Constructed in 1912 for rice transportation, the pier on the right side of the beach is now utilized mostly by children, who love to jump off of it, and by fishers, who enjoy lazing on it with a pole.

To the left of the pier is **Queen Reef,** and to the right is **King Reef.** Surfing for both experts and beginners takes place here, along with body-boarding, sailing, swimming, and stand-up paddling. At the end of Weke Road between the pier and river is **Black Pot.** The name refers to the days when a large black pot was always cooking over a fire on the beach here with a big meal for everyone to share. Nearby and *mauka* (on the mountain side) of Weke Road is the headquarters of the Hanalei Canoe Club. You will see the sign when driving in, along with the sign for a shave ice wagon.

West of that is **Hanalei Pavilion** by the pier, recognizable of course by the large pavilion on the side of the road. Farther west and roughly in the center of the bay is **Pine Trees,** a popular surf spot for local children and families. Access to Pine Trees is at the end of He'e, Ama'ama, and Ana'e Roads. It's a good place to watch locals surf or take surfing lessons yourself. More access is available nearing the west end of the bay before the bridge. Hanalei Pavilion and Pine Trees both have lifeguards, and all of these spots are county-maintained and have showers, restrooms, picnic tables, and grills. When in Hanalei, turn off of Highway 560 onto Aku Road right before Ching Young Village. Turn right on Weke Street, and near the end you'll see the beach where the pier is. Turn left onto Weke and then right onto He'e, Ama'ama, or Ana'e Road to reach Pine Trees.

Waikoko Beach

Located at the west end of Hanalei Bay is

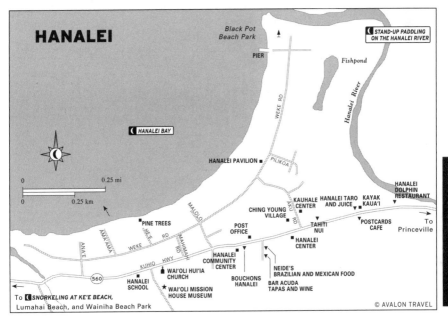

HANALEI

Black Pot Beach Park

STAND-UP PADDLING ON THE HANALEI RIVER

PIER

Fishpond

Hanalei River

HANALEI BAY

0   0.25 mi

0   0.25 km

HANALEI PAVILION

PILIKOA

HANALEI DOLPHIN RESTAURANT

WEKE RD

KAUHALE CENTER

HANALEI TARO AND JUICE

KAYAK KAUA'I

CHING YOUNG VILLAGE

AKU RD

TAHITI NUI

POSTCARDS CAFE

To Princeville

PINE TREES

POST OFFICE

HANALEI CENTER

MALOLO

AKU RD

MAHIMAHI RD

WEKE RD

HANALEI COMMUNITY CENTER

HANALEI SCHOOL

AKU RD

ANA'E

WEKE RD

KUHIO HWY

560

WAI'OLI HUI'IA CHURCH

WAI'OLI MISSION HOUSE MUSEUM

BOUCHONS HANALEI

NEIDE'S BRAZILIAN AND MEXICAN FOOD

BAR ACUDA TAPAS AND WINE

To **SNORKELING AT KE'E BEACH,**
Lumahai Beach, and Wainiha Beach Park

© AVALON TRAVEL

NORTH SHORE

Waikoko Beach and surf break. Another white-sand beach with black rocks dotting the area in the water and on the beach, it can be a less-crowded place to hang out, perhaps because the number of visitors here is limited by the road-side parking. To get here, look for the small parking area on the side of the road after the bridge and mile marker 4. If a spot is available, look for the short trail through the trees.

TO THE END OF THE ROAD
Lumahai Beach

After Waikoko Beach is the first access to Lumahai Beach. Lumahai is slightly over a mile long, running between mile markers 5 and 6, and has two accesses. The locals call the north end by the river "local" Lumahai and the east end "tourist" Lumahai. Don't be put off by nicknames, as tourist Lumahai has a nice trail down and this end of the beach is prettier. Heading north, about a mile after the last bridge at the end of Hanalei Bay is a curve in the road with several parking spots along-side. This is before mile marker 5. Look for the

trailhead, located where the trees open up to the ocean the most. Past the first access is an HVB warrior sign at a roadside lookout where you can view the beach. It will probably entice you to go down.

To access to the north end of the beach, head about a mile past the first access. If you pass mile marker 6 and the bridge you've gone too far. The best thing about this end of Lumahai is the river. The river is a great place for children to swim and play in the sand, but only upriver form the mouth. Local parents and children spend a lot of time here, and it's a good place to bring beach toys and floats. It's best to stay out of the open ocean here. Lumahai is one of the most dangerous beaches to swim on the north side, and there isn't a lifeguard, so be careful.

Wainiha Beach Park

Beachfront homes sit on Wainiha Beach, most notable by the Wainiha General Store and other small shops. A river runs into the ocean here, and the bay is almost always windy and choppy with a strong current. Access to the

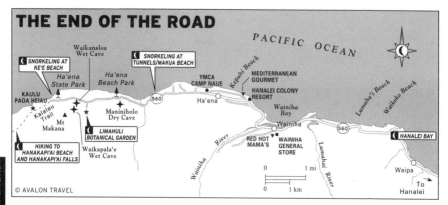

THE END OF THE ROAD

PACIFIC OCEAN

Waikanaloa Wet Cave

SNORKELING AT KE'E BEACH

SNORKELING AT TUNNELS/MAKUA BEACH

Ha'ena State Park

Ha'ena Beach Park

YMCA CAMP NAUE

Kepuhi Beach

MEDITERRANEAN GOURMET

HANALEI COLONY RESORT

KAULU PAOA HEIAU

560

Ha'ena

Maniniholo Dry Cave

Kalalau Trail

Mt Makana

LIMAHULI BOTANICAL GARDEN

Wainiha Bay

Wainiha

Lumaha'i Beach

Waikoko Beach

HIKING TO HANAKAPI'AI BEACH AND HANAKAPI'AI FALLS

Waikapala'e Wet Cave

Wainiha River

RED HOT MAMA'S

WAINIHA GENERAL STORE

Lumahai River

560

HANALEI BAY

© AVALON TRAVEL

0   1 mi

0   1 km

Waipa

To Hanalei

debris-covered beach is through trees at the far end of the bay, and it's usually so deep and muddy that only a four-wheel-drive could make it in.

Kepuhi Beach

After mile marker 7 ironwood trees line the beach; parking spots under them provide access to the start of Kepuhi Beach. The long white-sand beach can also be accessed at the Hanalei Beach Resort, where parking is free. This long beach isn't good for swimming, especially considering how nice all the other beaches are out here. It is a nice place to eat the food you might get at the Na Pali Art Gallery & Coffee Shop or for a romantic stroll before dinner at Mediterranean Gourmet.

Tunnels/Makua Beach

Named after the surf break out here, this beach offers some of the best snorkeling on the island. Reef fish can usually be found enjoying the waters not far from shore, and the sea caves to the left entertain bigger fish. There is a drop-off farther out that is intriguing, but this area is for experienced snorkelers and divers only, and should only be explored when the waves are small. The surf spot out here is a pretty intense wave, sending heavy white wash inside when the waves are breaking. This part of the beach is generally less crowded than Ha'ena Beach Park on the north end of Tunnels thanks

to the limited parking. The beach is beautiful and long and makes a perfect place for a walk or run. Access borders homes located on two narrow side roads past mile marker 8. The first is just short of a half mile past the marker, and the second is slightly farther and most recognizable by the bent metal post with red paint. It is across from the 149th telephone pole, although at press time the 9 was missing so it looks like pole 14.

Ha'ena Beach Park

A picturesque beach with a backdrop of lush green mountains highlighted by perfect surfing waves and a river, visiting Ha'ena Beach Park is a must. Before the sand is a grassy lawn for tent camping, along with restrooms, showers, and picnic tables. A river bordering the east end of the park area runs over the road as you drive in. Swimming is good here only when the waves are small, but the river makes a good spot for the kids when it's running onto the beach. The reef has great snorkeling, again only when the waves are small in the summer. If the main parking lot is filled up, which it often is, there is a bit more parking at the west end right past the showers. For those intending on camping on the north side, Ha'ena is one of the most ideal places because of its location, scenery, and surrounding sights. Past the rocks on the west end the beach keeps going, and it's a great long solitary stroll if you're up for it, passing two *heiau*

TAYLOR CAMP

In 1969, 13 young people from the Mainland moved to Kaua'i. They considered themselves refugees from campus riots, the Vietnam War, and police brutality. After a short time the group was arrested and sentenced to 90 days of hard labor for having no money and no home. Howard Taylor, brother of Elizabeth Taylor, bailed them out and invited them to camp on his oceanfront property right past Ha'ena Beach. Taylor then left them with free reign of his property, and soon throngs of hippies, surfers, and Vietnam vets joined the clothing-optional, marijuana-friendly village where people lived in treehouses. In 1977, the state of Hawaii reclaimed Taylor Camp to make it into a state park. The residents of Taylor Camp moved on, and many of them still live throughout the Hawaiian Islands and Kaua'i. For more information on the intriguing camp, watch *Taylor Camp,* a documentary of interviews with the residents 30 years after the camp came to an end.

and eventually the area formerly known as Taylor Camp. Ha'ena Beach Park is located off of Kuhio Highway after mile marker 8 and just before mile marker 9, across from the dry cave.

Ke'e Beach

The pot of gold at the end of the road is Ke'e Beach and its natural large swimming pool. The snorkeling here is truly wonderful, and between the snorkeling popularity and the fact that the base of the Kalalau Trail is here, Ke'e and its parking lot are almost always crowded. You may have to wait in the car for a few minutes for a spot to open up or drive a minute back up the road to the parking lot on the ocean side of the road. It's beautiful, provides amazing photo opportunities, and has full amenities.

and a lifeguard. Venturing east down the be will lead you to several *heiau* and the spot where Taylor Camp stood, which makes for a nice beach stroll. To get here, drive to the very end of Highway 560; the road turns into a parking area at the base of the Na Pali Coast.

NA PALI COAST
Kalalau Trail Beaches

For those who continue on foot and are dedicated to a serious hike, about a two-mile hike from Ke'e Beach is **Hanakapi'ai Beach**. There's a freshwater stream and it's a favorite campsite for hikers who make the trek out there. Brave surfers venture out here to catch some waves, but the ones who do this are serious risk takers.

After Hanakapi'ai is **Hanakoa Beach** after four strenuous miles. Hanakoa Beach is a good place to camp, but the biggest thrill here are the falls that are another half of a mile inland. In this area you'll also see wide terraces and wild coffee trees.

Five miles down the coast from Hanakoa is **Kalalau Beach.** It's important to note that this is a serious hike, requiring proper prepping and serious dedication. Kalalau Beach is about a half mile long with a small waterfall often used by campers for a shower and portable toilets. Many people who camp here like to pitch tents in the caves for wind and rain protection.

Past Kalalau is **Honopu Beach,** and the only legal way to get there is to swim from Kalalau. No surfboards, boats, or other crafts are allowed on shore, but you could paddle in a ways, anchor in the water, and swim up to the beach. Honopu Beach is actually composed of two picturesque, undisturbed beaches separated by an impressive arch. These are perhaps the most magical beaches on the island. You'll find a wonderful waterfall here and a stream to rinse off the salt water. Vertical cliff walls that are more than 1,000 feet high back these beaches.

Water Sports

SNORKELING AND DIVING

Good snorkeling is frequent on the north shore. Several beaches offer the option to break out your snorkeling gear. Because of the reefs and currents, gear in addition to a mask and snorkel is a good idea. Reef shoes, swim fins, and gloves for holding onto rocks are useful, but remember not to grab or step on coral. When snorkeling, always remember to only go out when the waves are small, and it's safest with a partner. Dive fins are always a must, not only as minor (although unofficial) foot protection, but also as an enormous help with speed and when fighting even a minor current.

A water camera is always a good idea, and even the disposable ones available at most supermarkets take pretty good photos. Snorkel gear rentals are available at the **Hanalei Surf Company** (808/826-9000, www.hanaleisurf. com, 8:30 A.M.–9 P.M. daily), **Pedal-n-Paddle** (in Ching Young Village, 808/826-9069, www. pedalnpaddle.com, 9 A.M.–6 P.M. daily), and the **Snorkel Depot** (5-5075 Kuhio Hwy.,

808/826-9983). The last chance for snorkel rentals would be the **Wainiha General Store.**

Kilauea
ANINI BEACH

The calm water and the long fringing reef make for great snorkeling at Anini Beach. The water stays shallow shockingly far out and maintains a depth of around just four feet. From the beach park down, some of the safest snorkeling on the north side can be experienced. Snorkelers who head far enough out will see the ledge dropping into the deep sea. To get here, take the second Kalihiwai Road headed north. Keep to the left at the fork in the road (going right leads to the north side of Kalihiwai Beach) and keep driving.

Princeville
HIDEAWAYS BEACH

Hideaways is the best snorkeling in Princeville as long as the waves are small. Here snorkelers will usually be treated to a colorful array of

Hideaways Beach

© ERIN RABER

tropical fish. Green sea turtles are known to cruise through the water at a leisurely pace. To get here, take the trail shortly before the St. Regis Princeville Resort gate house and next to the Pu'u Poa tennis courts. To reach the other side of the beach, either swim to the right from Hideaways (when conditions allow, of course) or walk the paved trail from the Pali Ke Kua condominiums.

SEALODGE BEACH

For more Princeville snorkeling hike down to SeaLodge Beach for seclusion and a pretty lively underwater world. There's a reef right off the beach here in a cove, which means some pretty fish like to linger around. There's no lifeguard here, so don't go out too far. If you haven't rented gear yet, you can buy some at the Princeville Foodland.

To get here, drive to the SeaLodge condos at the end of Kamehameha Road in Princeville; parking is in the unmarked stalls toward the top of the parking lot. The trailhead is in front of building A and marked with a sign. Take the dirt trail down past the small stream on the way to the ocean. Once you reach the ocean

keep to your left, where you can walk along the black rocks or on the narrow trail a little up on the dirt. After a minute or so you will see SeaLodge Beach.

Hanalei
WAIKOKO BEACH

If you're going to check out Waikoko Beach anyway, you can hop in with a snorkel and mask since you're there. The reef draws fish in and it's worth a glance, but it's not the best snorkeling on the north side. This area is rocky and waves break here, so it's a good place for snorkeling gloves and foot protection. It's at the north end of Hanalei Bay; to get here, look for the small parking area on the side of the road after the bridge and mile marker 4. If a spot is available, look for the short trail through the trees.

To the End of the Road
◖ TUNNELS/MAKUA BEACH

To see a rainbow of bright reef fish hop in the water at Tunnels. With the outer reef it's no surprise that fish like to wander in here. Reef fish spend their time not far from shore, and

© ERIN RABER

Tunnels/Makua Beach

the sea caves to the left are a favorite hangout for bigger fish, along with the outside drop-off. The outer area is for experienced snorkelers and divers only, and should be done only when the waves are small. Sea turtles, the occasional reef shark, caves, and fish can be seen. Access borders homes located on two narrow side roads past mile marker 8. The first is just short of a half mile past the marker, and the second is slightly farther and most recognizable by the bent metal post with red paint. It is across from the 149th telephone pole, although at press time the 9 was missing so it looks like pole 14.

(KE'E BEACH

Another location known for spectacular snorkeling, Ke'e offers good views inside the natural pond, where there is usually a crowd of snorkelers. Outside in the open ocean the views get even better but snorkeling here should only be attempted when the waves are flat in the summer months. Advanced snorkelers find that heading a bit to the left and snorkeling along the reef offers the best views. To get here, drive to the very end of Highway 560; the end of the road turns into a parking area at the base of the Na Pali Coast.

Na Pali Coast

The best and safest way to snorkel along the Na Pali Coast is definitely with a boat tour company. A couple leave from the north side and head down the coast, but many leave from the west side. The underwater world along the coast is nothing short of amazing. Sea turtles, a spectrum of fish, the occasional reef shark, underwater caves, and more are all out there.

Na Pali Catamaran (5-5190 Kuhio Hwy., 808/826-6853, www.napalicatamaran.com) has been launching out of Hanalei Bay for almost 40 years. People are loaded onto an outrigger canoe that takes them to a 34-foot catamaran that takes 16 passengers maximum. They offer snorkeling cruises, which they conveniently provide the gear for. A deli-style meal is provided; visitors have the option of a meat or veggie sandwich. Snack, drinks, and water

are also provided. All tours depend on ocean conditions. Adults pay $160, children 5–11 years old $130. The office is right next to the Hanalei Post Office.

Also leaving from Hanalei Bay is **Captain Sundown** (P.O. Box 607, Hanalei, 808/826-5585, www.captainsundown.com). A six-hour Na Pali snorkel sail ($199) takes you down the coast and stops at a sea-turtle cleaning station where trigger fish clean the turtles. Trampoline nets allow great views below to dolphins and other sea life. Captain Sundown also offers a three-hour Na Pali sunset sail ($144) down the coast. Snacks, soft drinks, and bottled water are provided.

Na Pali snorkeling tours leaving from the west side are much higher in number, and some include **Holo Holo Charters** (4353 Waialo Rd. Suite 5A, Port Allen, 808/335-0815 or 800/848-6130, www.holoholokauai-boattours.com), which offers a Na Pali snorkel sail ($99–139). The well-established company's cats, one motorized and one sailing, run out of Port Allen Harbor. The company has a reputation for treating guests well.

Catamaran Kahanu (4353 Waialo Rd., Port Allen, 808/645-6176 or 888/213-7711, www.catamarankahanu.com) is a Hawaiian-owned tour company offering Na Pali Coast snorkeling combined with a glimpse into Hawaiian culture. Aboard the boat passengers are treated to craft demonstrations such as basket, hat, and rose weavings, which guests take home as mementos. Rates are $80–122 with special children's rates. They also leave from the west side.

Hanalei Activity Center (kiosk near Big Save, 808/826-1898) will book you on various tours and other activities and can be visited at Ching Young Village.

SURFING AND STAND-UP PADDLING

The coast from Kilauea to the Na Pali Coast has been blessed with perfect surf breaks. The area has also produced a number of professional surfers, including Bruce Irons and his late brother Andy, Bethany Hamilton, and others. If you haven't brought a board (which is

ANDY IRONS

Three-time world surfing champion Andy Irons was born and raised in Hanalei. Irons grew up traveling the world surfing, becoming a local and national sports figure revered as one of the world's best surfers. Irons always called Kaua'i home, and his parents and his brother, professional surfer Bruce Irons, still live there. Sadly, Irons died on November 2, 2010, leaving his wife and unborn son behind. He was only 32 years old. An autopsy concluded that the cause of death was a sudden cardiac arrest due to a severe blockage of a main artery of the heart. A contributing but secondary factor might have been drugs.

Irons's death broke the hearts of surfers worldwide but especially affected the people of his home town. While driving the winding route from Hanalei to the end of the road, you'll likely see roadside surfboards and signs proclaiming "We love you, Andy" and other affectionate sayings.

On November 14, 2010, thousands gathered at Pine Trees in Hanalei Bay, where the Irons brothers grew up surfing, to pay tribute to the icon. On December 8, Irons's widow, Lyndie, gave birth to their son, Andrew Axel Irons, and the family continues to call Kaua'i home. The Irons Brothers Pine Trees Classic children's surfing competition is held each year in March or April.

a good idea for truly experienced avid surfers who just *need* their favorite board), you can rent your own and head out yourself, or take surf lessons. Surf lessons are a good idea if you're a novice to the sport. Besides the goal to eventually carve down the line there are some basic tips to learn, like how to wax your board and put on a leash (I've seen a lone novice surfer with no leash at a very crowded spot), and how to paddle for a wave and stand up.

If you'd like to learn to stand-up paddle (SUP) or are already a fan of it there are several beaches and rivers ideal for the sport. SUPs are a good thing to rent on Kaua'i; only the most serious paddlers would want to travel with a stand-up paddle board. They're huge.

If you're spending time on the north side, board rentals are available from **Hanalei Surf Company** (in Hanalei Center, 808/826-9000, www.hanaleisurf.com, 8:30 A.M.–9 P.M. daily) and **Backdoor Surf** (Ching Young Village, 808/826-1900, www.hanaleisurf.com, 8:30 A.M.–9:30 P.M.). For lessons, **Hawaiian Surfing Adventures** (5134 Kuhio Hwy., 808/482-6749, www.hawaiiansurfingadventures.com, 8 A.M.–5 P.M. daily) and the **Titus Kinimaka Hawaiian School of Surfing** (in the Quicksilver shop, 5-5088 Kuhio Hwy., 808/652-1116, www.hawaiianschoolofsurfing.

com) will take you out and most likely get you on a wave. **Hanalei Activity Center** (Ching Young Village, 808/826-1898) also arranges surf lessons.

Kilauea
KALIHIWAI BEACH AND QUARRY BEACH
When the conditions and swell direction are right, Kalihiwai Beach is home to a sometimes-perfect right-hander peeling off of a rocky point. Locals surf and stand-up paddle here, and when the surf spot is breaking, the shore break is usually intense too. The river is an ideal place for stand-up paddling, and paddlers can head up and down the river as well as across from the beach to the end of the second Kalihiwai Road. Quarry Beach offers another good wave for experienced surfers, and is mostly utilized by locals. There are no lifeguards at either beach.

To get to Kalihiwai when coming from the east side, turn down the first Kalihiwai Road. The road ends at the river, where the other side is visible. To reach the other side take the second Kalihiwai Road and go right at the fork. It leads to the other side of the beach, where locals sometimes come to fish or paddle across the river to the beach. To get to Quarry Beach when headed north, turn right on Wailapa

NORTH SHORE

BETHANY HAMILTON

At the age of 13, Bethany Hamilton, now a professional surfer, was attacked by a 14-foot tiger shark while surfing Tunnels on the north shore. It was Halloween 2003, and the shark took her left arm. After losing over 60 percent of her blood she made it through several surgeries without infection and returned to the water just one month after the attack. In January 2004, Bethany entered a surf contest and placed fifth in the open women's division (all ages) of that contest and continued to compete with no prosthetic arm. Just over a year after the attack she took first place in the explorer women's division of the 2005 NSSA National Championships and won her first national title. She's now been surfing professionally with since 2007 and competes in professional contests all over the world. Her autobiography, *Soul Surfer,* was released in October 2004, and a movie of the same title was released in major theaters in early 2011. You may see Bethany on Kaua'i catching waves.

Road between mile markers 21 and 22. Turn left at the yellow post and cement blocks marking the top of the road and head about a half mile down to the beach.

Hanalei
HANALEI BAY

All of Hanalei Bay is ideal for stand-up paddling, either on waves for experienced paddlers or around the bay when the waves are small. The outside break is known as **The Bay** and breaks when the waves are huge during the winter. This break is for experts only but is awesome to watch from the beach. Hanalei Bay has several surf breaks within the long stretch. When in Hanalei, turn off of Highway 560 onto Aku Road right before Ching Young Village. Turn right on Weke Street and near the end you'll see the beach.

PINE TREES

Roughly in the center of Hanalei Bay is Pine Trees, a perfect break for kids and beginners. Both right- and left-hand breaking waves are here and offer fun for all levels of surfers. Rent a board in Hanalei and catch a wave, if the waves are small. The fairly shallow waters and sandy bottom make it a good spot for beginners. On any given day the lineup will probably be packed with kids, so it can be a good idea to paddle out before the nearby elementary school is out for the day (around 2 P.M.). When in Hanalei, turn off of Highway 560 onto Aku Road right before Ching Young Village. Turn left onto Weke and then right onto He'e, Ama'ama, or Ana'e Road to reach Pine Trees.

◖ HANALEI RIVER

The Hanalei River is a favorite for stand-up paddlers. While crossing the Hanalei Bridge into town you'll probably see paddlers enjoying a leisurely paddle on the river. Morning is a nice time before it gets too hot, and it's a great way to start the day. You'll first notice the river as you come into Hanalei and drive over the one-lane bridge. **Kayak Kaua'i** (5-5070 Kuhio Hwy., 808/826-9844, www.kayakkauai.com) offers SUP lessons and rentals from their dock up the Hanalei River. It's about a 20- to 30-minute paddle down the river to the ocean. Lessons cost $85 and rentals are $45 per day or $225 per week. Both include leash and, if requested, a car rack.

WAIKOKO BEACH

At the north end of Hanalei Bay is Waikoko Beach, and it's a left-hand-breaking rocky reef break. Although it's not one of the *most* dangerous spots, it's a good idea to leave it alone unless you're an experienced surfer. The break requires walking out on very shallow and very sharp reef, and hopping off at the end of the wave into a shallow reef. To get here, look for the small parking area on the side of the road after the bridge and mile marker 4. If a spot is available, look for the short trail through the trees.

© JADE ECKARDT

The Hanalei River is a favorite place for a peaceful stand-up paddling adventure.

To the End of the Road
TUNNELS/MAKUA BEACH

Right before Ha'ena Beach Park, Tunnels Beach has an epic right-hand-breaking wave. Tunnels is definitely for expert surfers only, but if that's you, this is a great wave. The beach is beautiful here too, and if the waves are good it can be fun to watch people surf. This is where local surfer Bethany Hamilton lost her arm to a shark at the age of 13. If the big waves don't keep you on the beach, that might. The movie *Soul Surfer* was released in 2011, documenting the Kaua'i native's loss and her comeback.

A little west down the beach from Tunnels is the surf break known as **Cannons.** Again, this is another wave reserved for expert surfers due to the intensity of the barreling, left-hand-breaking wave as well as the shallow reef in front of it. This can be another fun spot to people-surf from the beach when the waves are good.

Access borders homes located on two narrow side roads past mile marker 8. The first is just short of a half mile past the marker, and the second is slightly farther and most recognizable by the bent metal post with red paint. It is across from the 149th telephone pole, although at press time the 9 was missing so it looks like pole 14.

KAYAKING
Hanalei

Kayak Kaua'i (5-5070 Kuhio Hwy., 808/826-9844, www.kayakkauai.com) offers a leisurely adventure on the Hanalei River with kayak rentals and guided tours where kayakers have the option of a single kayak for $29 or a double for $54.

A tour of Hanalei River and Hanalei Bay is also offered by **Kayak Hanalei** (5-5190 Kuhio Hwy., in Ching Young Village, 808/826-1881, www.kayakhanalei.com) from March through October. Suitable for all ages, the tour explores the bay and river and takes paddlers snorkeling. A complete sandwich lunch is provided, with vegetarian as an option, and is enjoyed on the beach. The price for children is $95.38, adults $106.09.

Na Pali Coast

Kayaks can be rented for a trip down the Na Pali Coast ending at Polihale, but only in summer months when seas are calm. **Outfitters Kauai** (2827A Po'ipu Rd., Po'ipu, 808/742-9667 or 999/742-9887, www.outfitterskauai.com, $230) runs a 16-mile sea kayak adventure along the coast. The trip features an exploration of sea caves; opportunities to see waterfalls, dolphins, and sea turtles; and respites on deserted beaches that feel far from civilization. The tour offers tandem, open-cockpit, or sit-on-top self-bailing kayaks with foot pedal controls, and the tour is only available from mid-May until mid-September on Tuesdays and Thursdays.

Kayak Kaua'i (5-5070 Kuhio Hwy., 808/826-9844, www.kayakkauai.com) also offers sea kayaking along the Na Pali Coast. It's a serious adventure only for the very fit and hardy and can only be done in the summer. The kayaking adventure requires 5–6 hours of paddling and runs about $200.

Na Pali Kayak (5-5070 Kuhio Hwy., 808/826-6900, www.napalikayak.com) takes adventurous day trippers, honeymooners, and campers on various trips along the Na Pali Coast. Adventures include guided day kayaking trips, camping along the coast, a honeymoon private charter for two, and private guided tours. Fees vary from $200 to $3,000 for a group charter, so please call for the most up-to-date rates and details.

FISHING
Na Pali Coast

Na Pali Sportfishing (808/635-9424, www.napalisportfishing.com) will take you down the coast, but they leave out of Kikiaola Harbor on the west side. They generally leave at 6 A.M. because, according to them, that's when serious anglers fish; that time can be hard to make if you're on the north shore, but they do schedule later trips as well. They take people out to a 35-foot Baja cruiser with a fly bridge and outriggers for a maximum of six people. Boaters must bring their own food and snacks, but the company provides soft drinks, fishing tackle, and zipper-lock bags so guests can take fish home. Half days shared run $135 an angler, full days are $220, and a full-day fishing charter runs $1,050. Check for other rates and tours. Restrictions include no pregnant women, no recent back surgeries or injuries, and no children under four years old.

WHALE-WATCHING

During the months of December through March or April, humpback whales *(kohola)* spend time in the islands singing and giving birth. After bulking up on weight in Alaska through the summer, the whales don't eat while they're here and may lose up to about one-third of their weight. During these months keep an eye out any time you look at the ocean. They breech, they spout; it's one of the best sights to be seen.

From November through March **Bali Hai Tours** (808/634-2317, www.balihaitours.com) heads north from Kapa'a, taking people out to see the whales. Although the boat can handle 12 people, they take no more than six people out on their 20-foot Zodiac with a two-stroke 100 hp Mercury motor. The company provides snorkel gear, floater noodles and boogie boards, dry bags, and snacks. Prices are $155 for adults and $90 for children.

Hiking, Biking, and Bird-Watching

HIKING

The north shore is home to some of the most outstanding hikes on the island. From short walks to secluded beaches, to hikes to hidden waterfalls, to the 19-mile trek along the Na Pali Coast, the north shore is a hiker's dream land. The value of a mile-long beach walk shouldn't go underestimated; it can be one of the most peaceful and memorable experiences to be had on Kaua'i.

Kilauea
◖ SECRET BEACH TIDE POOLS AND WATERFALL

Tide pools and an oceanside waterfall are the beautiful rewards at the end of this hike (about a half-hour long). It's important to note that this hike should only be done during the summer months when the ocean is completely flat. It's actually a combination of two hikes, one down to Secret Beach and another to the falls and tide

pools. At the northern end of the beach at the bottom of the access trail, head over the rocks. After the small sandy area is a pretty spot where the water juts into the cliffs, and you'll need to pass behind this. There's a roughly 10-foot-tall vertical cliff to climb that presents two options: climb up over the cliff and stick to the rocks, or climb up on the end that's over the water.

After passing this, stick to the trail high on the wall that backs the small cove. After going around that, it's pretty level and self explanatory. When you reach the area where the tide pools start, there will be quite a few. They are nice in size and shape, and home to different sea life. They are a little murky, but it's worth it to take a peek in them. At the end, right before another finger of water juts into the cliffs, you'll see the wonderful deep and smooth boulder-bottomed pools. Once you're here it looks like this could be the end, but it's not. There are several pools here and they're five- to

© JADE ECKHARDT

Secret Beach Tide Pools and Waterfall

six-feet deep at the deepest. These are beautiful pools that are generally clean and clear, and the rock bottom is smooth. The pool closest to the edge of the cliff needs to be avoided when the waves are anything but flat.

Where the cliff meets the finger, there is another small vertical cliff, about six- to eight-feet high. For an even better reward climb it and head a very short distance inland to see the waterfall coming out of a small lush green crevice, pouring into more tide pools. This is far from Kaua'i's tallest waterfall, but the combination of an oceanside waterfall with salt tide pools is a unique sight to see and enjoy. The falls pour down onto a fairly flat rock area, and there is a small cave in back of the water perfect for sitting in as long as the falls aren't pouring too heavily. The rock leading to the falls is extremely slippery, so taking your time is important, or walking above the falls and coming back down and around works too. In front of this are several salt tide pools that the freshwater runs into. Please note that this hike is dangerous when the waves are big and should generally be done only during the summer months. Even when the waves are small hikers need to be aware of the ocean. There's another, easier way to get here. If you take the first Kalihiwai Road and pass the road to Secret Beach, stop at the yellow fire hydrant. Take the trail here about 10 minutes down to the top of the waterfall. This isn't nearly as exciting as the hike from Secret Beach, but it's shorter and safer.

To get here, turn onto the first Kalihiwai Road heading north and take the first right onto a dirt road. Head to the end of the road, where parking is behind large homes.

Princeville
POWERLINE TRAIL

It's takes a powered-up person to attack the entire day-long journey along the roughly 13-mile Powerline Trail. Completing it is only recommended for those who have a ride waiting on the other side, where the trail ends at the Keahua Arboretum in Wailua. The sights range from a few views into Hanalei Valley to an abundance of mountain views, the north and south shores, the center of the island, and the Hanalei region. The trail is hot and dry and lacking in shade. It's best for hikers to go as far they like but to return to the Princeville trailhead. Around two hours from the start of the trail, the pass is a good place to turn around and head back. To get to the northern trailhead, turn at the Princeville Ranch Stables about a half mile east of Princeville. Head uphill for about two miles until the pavement ends. Go a little farther to the parking area near the green water tank. This is a serious trail for mountain bikers, but it's strenuous. Don't attempt to go four-wheeling here.

Hanalei
'OKOLEHAO TRAIL

This intense hike is a good hike to prep for the Kalalau Trail. *'Okolehao* refers to the Hawaiian version of moonshine, made from the ti root planted up here. It's said the literal translation is "iron bottom" for the iron pots used to ferment it. The hike provides a serious workout that will mostly likely be experienced in solitude. The trail gains about 1,200 feet and will have hikers huffing and puffing in no time. Yet the 'Okolehao Trail offers a light at the end of the steep metaphorical tunnel, with truly amazing views of the island that begin about half a mile up. From the end of the trail the Kilauea Lighthouse, Hanalei River, Wai'ale'ale, Hanalei Bay, and the area by Ke'e and as far as Anahola can be seen. When hiking after a rain, be very careful, as the trail gets slippery. To get to the trailhead, turn left right after the one-lane bridge into Hanalei onto Ohiki Road. A little over a half mile down the road there's a parking lot on the left. A small bridge marks the trailhead on the opposite side of the road.

MOKOLEA TIDE POOLS

The reward for this fairly easy, quarter- to half-mile hike (depending on how far you can drive in) is a dip in cool, refreshing tide pools. The hike is really a slow walk over lava rock along shore line. Take your time and be mindful of your footing. You'll notice very weathered metal remnants of sugar mill gear. There are two ways to get here. One is through Quarry Beach Road in Kilauea village, via a partial four-wheel-drive road that leaves only about a quarter-mile hike. The other is from the Quarry Beach access off of Wailapa Road via a two-wheel-drive road and then a half-mile walk from the river.

Na Pali Coast

The heavenly and harsh Na Pali Coast is where all of nature's wonder joins together, a world that will both amaze and test those who choose to explore it. Other than the ocean, this is the only access to the rugged coastline where sea cliffs, five lush valleys, waterfalls, and camping wait on the 15-mile stretch from Ke'e to Polihale. The cliffs rise up to 4,000 feet in certain areas, and sea level is found only at the four main beaches along the way. The largest and most magnificent valley here is the Kalalau Valley, where ancient Hawaiians lived and archaeological evidence still remains. Other valleys also hold evidence of inhabited sites, as Hawaiians lived in various locations along the way. Rain falls here in excess, creating an abundance of waterfalls and streams.

The Na Pali Coast State Park comprises 6,175 acres of raw land. The remaining cliffs, coastline, and valleys are either state forests or natural area reserves.

There is a ranger stationed at Kalalau Valley who oversees the park and who will ask campers for permits. There is a trailhead by Ke'e Beach that you can't miss, and at Kalalau Valley there's a sign-in box. Day-use permits are required to go beyond Hanakapi'ai (where there are composting toilets), about two miles in, and a camping permit is necessary to stay overnight at Hanakapi'ai, Hanakoa, or Kalalau. Camping is permitted for up to five nights total, but two consecutive nights are not allowed at Hanakapi'ai or Hanakoa. More than the basics are needed to camp out here: a waterproof tent, mosquito repellent, first-aid kit, biodegradable soap, food, sleeping bag, and whatever else you think you may need and don't mind carrying on your back

mile after mile. Water bladders as opposed to water bottles are a good idea, because they're lighter and run a constant line of water to the mouth. Tree cutting is not allowed, and there isn't much natural firewood, so bring a stove if you want to cook. Drinking out of the streams is not advised; doing so can cause serious stomach illness, so boil the water or bring purification tablets. Please remember not to litter and to take out what you carried in. Reachable only by boat or kayak, the Nu'alolo Kai can be visited for the day only, and Miloli'i can be camped at for a maximum of three nights and has very basic campsites. The most accurate idea of what to expect is from hikers who have recently made the journey, because the trail changes with the weather.

THE KALALAU TRAIL

What may be the best way to experience the coast is the 11-mile Kalalau Trail, which begins right at Ke'e Beach. Mother nature dictates what condition the trail is in, so hikers may find a somewhat dry and firm trail or a narrow trail so steep, wet, and crumbling that they must scoot along on a cliff's edge while leaning into the earth and digging their hands deep into the dirt to hang on. Upon reaching Kalalau Beach, hikers may be welcomed to the beach by nude campers, as some people take advantage of the remote location and leave swimwear in their packs.

The path was originally created by Hawaiians as a land route between Kalalau Valley and He'ena, but the Kalalau Trail but was also built in the late 1800s and rebuilt in 1930 for horses and cows to pass over. To experience the trail is to experience what old Hawaii must have been like, when people lived off the land and close to nature. It usually takes a full day to get to Kalalau Beach, and it's really the best hike in the whole state. The trail is well worn from decades of use, so you're not likely to get off track and lost. Yet roots weave through it, and it gets extremely muddy and slippery when there's been rain, a frequent occurrence out here. Small streams fill up to flooding rivers after a heavy rain but they drain out rather quickly, so instead of crossing a dangerous stream it's usually best to wait it out. Mountain climbing out here is a risky and dangerous idea because the dirt crumbles and falls easily. The trail is filled with continuous amazing views. From the impressively tall mountains to the coastal views and lush foliage, this is not a trail to forget the camera on.

The currents along the coast are dangerous too, so stay out of the water from around September through April, when the surf mellows out for the summer. In summer, the sand is usually returned to Hanakapi'ai, the most commonly visited part of the hike, after being swept away by the winter's large surf. Hanakapi'ai, like Queen's Bath, has a list of the names and ages of people who have died at this beach due to the pounding surf often washing over bare rock.

◖ HANAKAPI'AI BEACH AND HANAKAPI'AI FALLS

It's about two miles and a 1.5- to 2-hour hike from Ke'e to Hanakapi'ai Beach. The first mile goes uphill to about 800 feet, with the last mile going down and ending at the beach. Depending on the season, you may get lucky and see some brave and slightly crazy surfers out here. During low tide only during the summer, caves on the beach are good for camping, but on the far side of the stream up from the beach is the best place.

From the west side of the stream at Hanakapi'ai Beach the Hanakapi'ai Trail starts, leading two miles inland up into the valley to the wonderful Hanakapi'ai Falls, passing old taro fields and crumbling rock walls. You will cross the stream several times on the way up, so if the stream looks full and rushing, just turn around and head back. It can be dangerous during high water. If the stream is low, keep going. The hike to the 300-foot-high falls is rewarding and worth it. There is a wonderful ice-cold swimmable pool at the bottom, but don't swim directly under the falls. From Hanakapi'ai Camp near the beach, the hike should take around 2–3 hours, and it's about 5–6 hours from Ke'e Beach.

Hanakapi'ai Beach is one of the rewards along the Kalalau Trail.

© NANI MALOOF

HANAKAPI'AI BEACH TO HANAKOA

It's a strenuous 4.5-mile, three-hour trek from Hanakapi'ai Beach to Hanakoa. The trail climbs steadily and doesn't go back down to sea level until Kalalau Beach nine miles later. You are taken about 600 feet out of Hanakapi'ai Valley through a series of switchbacks, and although the trail is heavily utilized, it can be very rough in certain spots. You will walk through the hanging valleys of Ho'olulu and Waiahuakua, both parts of the Hono'onapali Nature Area Preserve and loaded with native flora, before arriving at Hanakoa. In the past Hanakoa was a major food-growing area for Hawaiians, and many of its terraces are still intact. Wild coffee plants can be seen here. Hanakoa is a bit rainy, but it's on and off and the sun usually dominates throughout the day. Numerous swimmable pools are born from the stream here. To get to Hanakoa Falls from here, which are even more amazing than Hanakapi'ai Falls you'll need to take a worthwhile half mile detour inland. Cross the Hanakoa Stream and hang a left at the trail near the shelter. Walk for about 150 feet or so and take a left at the fork and continue for 15 to 20 minutes.

HANAKOA TO KALALAU BEACH

From Hanakoa to Kalalau Beach the trek is less than five miles, but it's a tough one and takes around three hours. It's important to start this one early in the morning to get as much time as possible in before the heat sinks in. The trail gets drier and more open as you approach Kalalau, but the views along the way make it all worth it. Out here the mana of the island is strong. Try to clear your head of thoughts and concerns of the outside world and soak in the invigorating beauty and peace of the valley. Around mile marker 7 is land that until the late 1970s was part of the Makaweli cattle ranch. After Pohakuao Valley is Kalalau Valley, spanning two miles wide and three deep. Freshwater pools dot the area and look inviting after the long hot hike. The area was cultivated until the 1920s, and fruit trees are abundant in the area. Camping is only allowed in the trees along the beach, or in the caves west of the waterfall, not

along the stream, its mouth, or in the valley. The falls have a wonderful, refreshing pool. On the far side of the stream is a *heiau* on top of a little hill. If you follow the trail here inland for around two miles you'll find Big Pool, which is really two pools connected by a natural water slide.

HONOPU, NU'ALOLO KAI, AND MILOLI'I

If you somehow have it in you to keep going, other destinations include Honopu, Nu'alolo Kai, and Miloli'i. Honopu is less than a half mile west of Kalalau Valley, and is known as "Valley of the Lost Tribe" due to a legend that says the small Mu people lived out here. The beach is separated by a big rock arch that has been used in at least two movies. You can get to Nu'alolo Kai by staying on the Kalalau Trail, and it is right after Awa'awapuhi Valley, about nine miles down the coast. It has a lovely beach and dunes right up against a tall cliff. There's a pair of reefs here that provide good snorkeling opportunities when the water is calm. A community of Hawaiians lived out here until 1919, and their archaeological remnants still exist as stone walls and *heiau* platforms. Taro was cultivated out here in the adjoining Nu'alolo 'Aina Valley, and fishing was good too. The reef out here was utilized as a rest stop by canoeists, who would anchor out here while going between Hanalei and Waimea. Another mile west is Miloli'i, another ancient site that was inhabited by Hawaiians. Here there is a very basic camping area with restrooms and a simple shelter, and down the beach is another *heiau*. Miloli'i only gets about 20 inches of rain a year, a big contrast from the rest of the wet Na Pali Coast.

BIKING

Hanalei and Princeville are the best areas on the north side for biking. After Hanalei there are numerous one-lane bridges and a narrow winding road to Ke'e that could push bikers into the traffic. Princeville is the safest and most convenient place for a leisurely ride, although the steady incline heading up can be rough. To rent a beach cruiser to explore

NORTH SHORE

Hanalei stop at **Pedal-N-Paddle** (Ching Young Village, 808/826-9069, www.pedaln-paddle.com, 9 A.M.–6 P.M. daily) for hybrid road bike and cruiser rentals for $12 daily or $50 for the week. Biking accessories are also available, along with water-sport supplies.

BIRD-WATCHING

Birds can be seen all over the island, but there are few official places to go birding on the north side. Binoculars and patience are good accessories to bring. No matter how you may be exploring the island, there's a good chance various birds will be seen throughout the day, and of course, there are always the unavoidable Kaua'i chickens running wild in parking lots, hotel lawns, and shopping centers.

Kilauea

At the **Kilauea Point National Wildlife Refuge** (end of Kilauea Rd., 808/828-1413, 10 A.M.–4 P.M. daily, http://pacificislands.fws.gov/wnwr/kkilaueanwr.html), 31 acres protect numerous birds. Red-footed boobies, shearwaters, great frigate birds, brown boobies, red- and white-tailed tropic birds, and Laysan albatrosses, as well as green sea turtles and humpback whales, occupy the refuge. There's an informational plaque at the top, and if you look down into the trees right in front of this area, birds can often be seen resting in their nests.

Princeville

Shearwaters nest at **Queen's Bath** (go right on Punahele Road and take the second right onto Kapiolani Loop) and can be seen along the trail and cliffs. Residents are not allowed to bring dogs here due to a high number of dog-related deaths.

Hanalei

At the 917-acre **Hanalei National Wildlife Refuge** in Hanalei Valley, endangered native water birds such as the Hawaiian coot, black-necked stilt, koloa duck, and gallinule can be spotted, as well as several migrant species that have reclaimed their ancient nesting grounds. The area is decorated with taro plants; the root supplies about half of Hawaii's poi. Although visitors are allowed in Hanalei Valley, no one is permitted in the designated wildlife area other than for fishing or hiking along the river. After crossing the first one-lane bridge into Hanalei, turn left onto Ohiki Road.

Adventure Sports and Tours

ZIPLINING
Princeville

For the thrill of flying through the air on a beautiful Hawaiian day, **Princeville Ranch Adventures** (5-4280 Kuhio Hwy., 808/826-7669 or 888/955-7669, www.adventureskauai.com, by appt.) has three different ziplines combined with a horseback ride. The lines travel through valleys with mountain and ocean views and will get your adrenaline pumping. You can't miss the ranch entrance on the north side of Kuhio Highway before Princeville.

HELICOPTER TOURS
Princeville

For a bird's-eye view of Kaua'i, catch a ride with **Heli USA** (808/826-6591 or 866/936-1234, www.heliusahawaii.com, $267). Although the carrier currently departs from Lihu'e, the Na Pali Coast tour offers a unique view of the cliffs, beaches, and valleys without having to hike for miles and miles. Flying A-Star machines, the company offers several different routes and free hotel pickup.

Departing out of the small Princeville airport is **Sunshine Helicopters** (Princeville Airport, 866/501-7738, www.sunshinehelicopters.com). A 40- to 50-minute flight will take you over the Na Pali Coast, Waimea Canyon, and many places utilized in Hollywood films. Open seating is priced at $289, and first class is $364.

HORSEBACK RIDING
Princeville

The **Princeville Ranch Stables** (808/826-6777, www.princevilleranch.com, by appt.) offers horseback rides and other adventures through a 250-acre working cattle ranch. It's about a half mile east of Princeville Center on the *mauka* (mountain) side of the road.

Hanalei Activity Center (Ching Young Village, 808/826-1898) offers horseback rides out of Princeville. Call for rates and times.

Polo matches are open to the public every Sunday at 3 P.M. across from Anini Beach Park. Spectating makes for a unique Hawaiian experience and a great tailgate party.

Golf and Tennis

GOLF
Kilauea

To take in some lighthearted time on the greens, hit the little white ball around **Kaua'i Mini Golf** (5-2723 Kuhio Hwy., Kilauea, 808/828-2118, www.kauaiminigolf.com, 11 A.M.–9 P.M. Tues.–Sun., plus Mon. Memorial Day–Labor Day). The miniature golf course can be viewed from the highway in Kilauea and is lacking in clown mouths and other toy-inspired themes. At this course, putters take a trip through Hawaiian history as they move through botanical gardens, each inspired by different a ethnic group found in Hawaii. It's ideal to take the family or for a honeymoon date.

Princeville

At the **Princeville Makai Golf Course** (4080 Lei O Papa Rd., 808/826-1912, www.makaigolf.com), the already excellent course recently underwent a multimillion-dollar renovation. Designed by Robert Trent Jones Jr. in 1971, the course was rated one of the top 25 golf courses in America for 2004–2005 by *Golf* magazine and has been ranked by *Golf Digest* as one of Hawaii's top courses. From the central clubhouse there are three nine-hole, par-36 courses. The Makai course combines two of them and weaves around lakes, native woodlands, and the coastline with views of Bali Hai and Hanalei Bay.

The 18-hole course plays a par 72 with four different sets of tees. The renovations, also done by Jones, feature seashore paspalum turf grass on all tees, fairways, and greens, making a wonderful playing surface for all levels. All bunkers also experienced a bold reshaping. The cliff-top Ocean 7 is regarded as a tough hole, with a shot over a ravine, and the Lake 9 hole sets two lakes in the way of the shot, but the toughest hole is known to be Woods 6, with a long dogleg into the trade winds. The nine-hole Woods Course is revered as a leisurely course for the casual golfer with family and friends. The practice area at the Makai Golf Club has also been improved and includes two new practice tees, a practice fairway bunker, seven target greens with bunkers, a teaching tee, and game practice complex. The club provides rentals for men, women, and juniors. Tee time can be booked at the pros shop, and the snack shop offers decently priced sandwiches, burgers, and snacks. Greens fees are $50 for the Woods Course and $140–210 for the Makai Course, with generous discounts for juniors. Various rates are also offered for golf passes and weekly packages. *Kama'aina* rates are also offered with Hawaii state ID.

The 18-hole **Prince Course** (808/826-5070, www.princeville.com/prince_course.html) opened in 1987 on almost 400 acres of golf heaven. However, the course closed on January 29, 2011 to undergo several months of renovation and reopened in 2012. The renovation was done by the original architect, Robert Trent Jones Jr. and cost five million dollars. Named after Prince Albert, the son of King Kamehameha IV and Queen Emma, the course has both ocean and mountain views. It was ranked the number one golf course in

Hawaii and one of America's Top 100 greatest courses by *Golf Digest*.

TENNIS
Princeville
At **Makai Tennis** (4080 Lei O Papa Rd., www.makaigolf.com/tennis), tennis fans can enjoy the four newly renovated outdoor hard surface courts. Reservations can be made at 808/826-1912, and tennis pros and certified professional instructors can be reached at 808/651-0638 for lessons. Rates run from $20 per hour to $65 for private lessons. Clinics are also available for $18 per hour or $21 for 1.5 hours. Several of the Princeville condos have tennis courts only for guests, so check with your condo.

Yoga and Spas

YOGA
Yoga is a popular form of exercise throughout the north side, with each area offering places to practice. Don't forget that you can always find a secluded place on the beach to practice some poses at sunset.

Kilauea
Pineapple Yoga (2518 Kolo Rd., 808/652-9009 or 248/765-4914, www.pineappleyoga.com, 7:30 A.M.–9:30 A.M. Mon.–Sat.) offers private classes in addition to astanga mysore-style classes six days a week. They do not practice here on the new and full moons, choosing to rest instead. The studio is at the top of Kilauea behind the Shell gas station.

Princeville
The spacious Princeville park is a perfect place for some yoga poses, but **Princeville Yoga** (5-4280 Kuhio Hwy., 808/826-6688, www.princevilleyoga.com, classes at 9:15 A.M. Mon., Wed., and Fri., 8 A.M. Tues., Thurs., and Sat., and 4:45 P.M. Tues. and Thurs.) is located in the Princeville Center above Lappert's Ice Cream for classes. Specializing in the beginning bikram hatha yoga series, several teachers offer public and private classes.

Hanalei
From Hanalei to the end of the road, any secluded beach spot is there for oceanside yoga. For classes in town, bikram, astanga, mysore, and hatha yoga are all offered at **Yoga Hanalei** (5-5161 Kuhio Hwy., 808/826-9642, www.yogahanalei.com). Over 30 classes, workshops, and retreats can all be found here, so call or check the website for times. It's on the second level of Hanalei Center; a boutique there has yoga accessories and clothing.

Past Wainiha, the **Hanalei Day Spa** (808/826-6621, www.hanaleidayspa.com, A.M.– P.M.) in the Hanalei Colony Resort also offers private yoga lessons and yoga retreats.

SPAS
Kilauea
Time at **Pure Kaua'i** (4270 Kilauea Rd. Unit D, 808/828-6570 or 866/457-7873, www.purekauai.com) is not your average spa day. The luxury spa creates Hawaiian getaways as well as honeymoon vacations and romantic retreats. Luxurious accommodations, healthy meals prepared by a private chef, spa activities and services, and various sports such as yoga and surfing are all offered here. Unique services such as astrological consultations, life coaching, and relationship coaching are offered in addition to traditional services like massage ($150–195), facials ($135), manicures ($55), and pedicures ($95).

Princeville
To lounge in the lap of luxury, visit the **Halele'a Spa** (808/826-9644) at the St. Regis Princeville Resort, where a consultant will customize a wellness regime to fit each person's needs. The spa combines Hawaiian healing traditions with western techniques to create a truly heavenly experience. Massages are offered with various Hawaiian elements, including hot stones with

taro butter, traditional *lomilomi,* sports massage, pregnancy massage, and couples massage. Facials combine healing properties to rehydrate and fight aging, while the clay wrap uses Hawaiian plants to detoxify and relax. Scrubs, baths, waxing, manicures, pedicures, salon treatments, and specialized bridal treatments are also offered.

Hanalei
The **Hanalei Day Spa** (808/826-6621, www. hanaleidayspa.com, 9:30 A.M.–6 P.M. Mon.–Sat., walk-ins allowed if there's availability, otherwise by appt.) is nestled near the ocean in the Hanalei Colony Resort. Beachside and in-spa couples massage, Hawaiian *lomilomi* massage, facials, waxing, body wraps and scrubs, and Ayurveda healing treatments are all offered with the sound of the ocean in the background. Retreats, wedding services, and private yoga lessons are also offered.

Sights

KILAUEA
🌙 Kilauea Point National Wildlife Refuge and Lighthouse

A picture-perfect view of a beautiful inlet usually speckled with white birds, and whales in season, makes the Kilauea Point National Wildlife Refuge and Lighthouse (end of Kilauea Rd., 808/828-1413, 10 A.M.–4 P.M. daily, http://pacificislands.fws.gov/wnwr/kkilaueanwr.html) a must-see stop. Upon arrival, the view down is photo-worthy. After this take a stroll on the narrow peninsula to the Kilauea Lighthouse, a designated National Historical Landmark and visitors center. Originally boasting the world's largest "clamshell lens," which could send a beam of light 20 miles out to sea, it was replaced in 1976 with a small high-intensity beacon. This is also a great place for dedicated bird watchers, and people who just enjoy watching wildlife. Permanent and migrating seabirds spend their time here, including the frigate bird, boasting its eight-foot wingspan; the red-footed booby with white feathers, black-tipped wings, and, of course, red feet; as well as the *nene,* or wedgetail shearwaters; and red- and white-tailed tropic birds.

Sea turtles, dolphins, and Hawaiian monk seals can all be seen from the cliffs occasionally. The waters here are also part of the Hawaiian Islands Humpback Whale National Marine Sanctuary, and whales can be seen here during winter and spring. The visitors center holds a wealth of information worth checking out about bird and plant life, the history of the lighthouse, and Hawaiian history. To get here, turn into Kilauea at the Shell gas station near mile marker 23, then down Kilauea Road. Drive straight to the end to the lighthouse, where entrance is free for 16 and under, and all others cost $5 per person.

Na 'Aina Kai Botanical Gardens
Just past the Quarry Beach access road is Na 'Aina Kai Botanical Gardens (808/828-0525, www.naainakai.org, 8 A.M.–noon Mon. and Fri., 8 A.M.–5 P.M. Tues.–Thurs.), encompassing a whopping 240 acres of tropical hardwoods and fruit trees. Over 100 acres of the property is a tropical hardwood plantation with about two dozen types of trees, including teak, mahogany, zebra wood, rosewood, and cocobolo, along with a lot of tropical fruit trees. The gardens take a creative twist in the central areas, where theme gardens feature various types of plants and around 60 life-like bronze sculptures add life to the experience. Admission may feel a bit pricey, from $25 for a 90-minute walk to $70 for a five-hour walk and tram ride through all areas, but the view from the parking lot is enticing and it's truly an enjoyable treat. The visitors center and gift shop are a fun stop to explore the gifts, books, and plants. To get here, turn down Wailapa Road after mile marker 21 and go to the end.

NAUPAKA

Naupaka shrubs have light green, somewhat waxy leaves and distinctive white flowers; they look like half flowers with petals missing. One species grows along the coast, another in the mountains. Several Hawaiian legends explain their unique appearance.

One legend tells of Pele being so jealous that she turned two lovers into the plant, sending one to the mountains and one to the coast. Legend says that since they were soul mates, the flowers are incomplete, and when they are brought together they form a whole.

A Kaua'i legend tells of the lovers Nanau and Kapaka, who broke a hula *kapu* (taboo) the night before their graduation. It's said they fled across Limahuli Stream and passed Maniniholo Cave while chased by their *kumu* (teacher). When they reached Lumahai Beach, Nanau fled to the cliffs and Kapaka hid in a beach cave called Ho'ohila. As the teacher approached the cliffs, Kapaka tried to block the *kumu* so her lover could escape. The *kumu* was enraged and killed Kapaka, continuing to chase Nanau. Eventually, Nanau was also struck dead, and later that day fishermen at Lumahai discovered a plant they'd never seen before growing where Kapaka had died. The *kumu* noticed the same plant growing where Nanau had died.

Another Pele legend says the goddess was enamored with a young man who was greatly devoted to his lover. No matter what she did, he remained loyal to his lover. Pele was angered and chased the young man into the mountains, throwing molten lava at him. Pele's sisters saw this happen, and to save him they changed him into half of a naupaka flower and sent him to the mountains. Pele went after his young lover and chased her toward the ocean. Again, Pele's sisters stepped in and changed her into the beach naupaka. It is said that if the mountain and the beach naupaka are reunited, the young lovers will be together again.

PRINCEVILLE
Sunset on the Lawn

In front of the St. Regis Princeville Resort, where the last remnants of a *heiau*'s rock walls can be seen, is a perfect place to end a beautiful north shore day. On any clear day, drop by the lawn to take in the array of colors as the sun sets over Hanalei Bay and the green mountains backing the coast. During winter months surfers may be seen dropping in on mountainous waves at the same time.

HANALEI
◖ Hanalei Valley Overlook

The sights over Hanalei Valley tend to inspire a dreamy feeling harking back to the days of old Hawaii. Different photo opportunities present themselves as the soft morning light changes to bright afternoon sun and then to a demure sunset light, all bringing out different colors in the taro patches below. Right after the Princeville turnoff on the left is the Hanalei Valley scenic overlook. This is a view not to be missed. The Hanalei River cuts through the valley until it meets the ocean, and along its banks green radiates from the valley, which reaches back into the 3,500-foot pali for almost nine miles. Waterfalls hang in the valley, either as light curtains or heavy torrential falls when there's lots of rain. There's a saying on Kaua'i's north side: "When you can count 17 waterfalls, it's time to get out of Hanalei." Legend says that Pele sent a thunderbolt to split a boulder in Hanalei so that Hawaiians could run an irrigation ditch through the center to their fields. While Princeville was for *ali'i* (royalty), Hanalei was for the "commoners."

Originally Hanalei produced taro, which is evident far back in the valley, where the outlines of the old fields can still be seen. The bay and fishponds produced fish. When the foreigners arrived they tried and failed at coffee here, then sugar, which didn't last as in other places on the island, and all the while Hanalei was bringing in poi from the Kalalau Valley. The bay was one of the most popular ports for a long time and was

© JADE ECKARDT

Taro fields and waterfalls are visible from the Hanalei Valley Overlook.

also a whaling harbor. Chinese immigrants eventually moved in and re-terraced the valley with rice. Rice was a successful crop until the 1930s, when the valley took a turn back to taro.

Wai'oli Hui'ia Church and Wai'oli Mission House Museum

The Wai'oli Hui'ia Church (5-5363 A Kuhio Hwy., 808/826-6253) lies near the west end of town and stands tall with its colorful stained-glass windows illuminated by sunlight. Wai'oli means "joyful water," and it pays to go inside to look at the windows and take in the open-beam ceiling of the quaint church. Built in 1912, the church was part of a mission station that also included a home for the preacher, a school for Hawaiian boys, and accommodations for the teacher.

Behind and slightly to the right of the church is the Wai'oli Mission House Museum (808/245-3202, 9 A.M.–3 P.M. Tues., Thurs., and Sat.) which was originally the teacher's house. The lush green parking lot welcomes visitors to the home, which boasts a New England–style interior that was built in 1836 by Reverend William P. Alexander. It was then passed to the Wilcox family, who owned and occupied the house until recently. Wilcox family members founded the Grove Farm in Lihu'e and the nonprofit organization that operates both the Wai'oli Mission House Museum and the Grove Farm Homestead. Inside you enter the parlor, where Lucy Wilcox taught Hawaiian girls how to sew and paintings of the families are on the walls. Around the house are artifacts including dishes, knickknacks, and a butter churn from the 1800s. It's interesting to note, now that the Hawaiian language has experienced a resurgence, that Abner Wilcox, a missionary, teacher, doctor, public official, and veterinarian, wrote letters to the king urging him to make Hawaiian the first language, with English as the second.

Ho'opulapula Haraguchi Rice Mill

The Ho'opulapula Haraguchi Rice Mill (5-5070 A Kuhio Hwy., 808/651-3399, www.haraguchiricemill.org, kiosk hours 11 A.M.–3 P.M. Mon.–Fri.) is an agrarian museum nestled in the taro fields of the Hanalei Valley within a national wildlife refuge usually not accessible to the public. Dating back to the 1800s, it's listed on the National Register of Historic Places. It was purchased by the Haraguchi Family in 1924, who have restored the mill three times: after a 1930 fire, after Hurricane 'Iwa in 1982, and following Hurricane 'Iniki in 1992. This mill is the last remaining rice mill in all of Hawaii, although it stopped operating in 1960 when the rice industry ceased to thrive. A nonprofit organization was formed to preserve and share the mill, and tours (donation only) are offered for out-of-state visitors, local schools, and others. The Haraguchi family continues to farm taro on nearby land that used to grow rice. Guided tours and private tours (which can be paid for in monetary or volunteer donations) are available by reservation on Wednesdays only, so you need to call first. Tours share Hawaii's agricultural and cultural history, and visitors can view endangered native water birds and learn about taro cultivation and the uses of taro. A complimentary picnic lunch including taro grown at the farm is offered. When making a reservation, you must choose between a sandwich or Hawaiian plate lunch. The entrance kiosk is one mile after the Hanalei one-lane bridge on the north side of the road.

TO THE END OF THE ROAD
◖ Limahuli Botanical Garden

At the Limahuli Botanical Garden (5-8291 Kuhio Hwy., 808/826-1053, 9:30 A.M.–4 P.M. Tues.–Sat.) you'll take a trip back in time to see the native plants that decorated Hawaii before invasive species moved into the islands. Visitors have a choice of self-guided or guided walking tours. Self-guided tours for those 12 and under are free and cost $15 for ages 13 and up, while on guided tours children under 10 are not allowed, those 10–12 years old are charged $15, and it's $30 for ages 13 and up. Guided tours are 2–2.5 hours, and self-guided ones last 1–1.5 hours. Reservations are required for the guided tour only.

Part of the National Tropical Botanical Garden, the gardens lie in front of Mount Makana (*makana* means "gift") on 1,016 acres

that help both ancient and modern plants flourish. The original 14 acres were donated by Juliet Rice Wichman in 1976, then expanded to 17, and the final 985-acre parcel in the above valley was donated by Wichman's grandson, Chipper Wichman, in 1994. It's a good idea to wear good shoes, and umbrellas are provided. The visitors center is where the tours begin, and this is where books, crafts, gifts, and other things are on sale. Taro *lo'i* (patches) here are believed to be around 900 years old. The brochure and the tour guide share legends of the valley.

The majority of the preserve lies in the valley and is only available to biologists and botanists for research. To get to the gardens, take a left inland at the HVB warrior sign about a half mile after mile marker 9. The marker points to the gardens, which are in the last valley before Ke'e Beach. Just past this is the Limahuli Stream, which locals use as a rinse-off spot after swimming. There's only one good spot to pull off the road here. On your way to the Limahuli Botanical Garden, stop at the **Lumahai Overlook** for a view of the Lumahai Beach and a great photo op. After the fifth mile marker you'll notice a small pull off area where a Hawaii Visitors Bureau sign points to the ocean.

Maniniholo Dry Cave

Directly across from Ha'ena Beach Park is the wide, low, and deep Maniniholo Dry Cave. Take a short stroll inside the cave. There's no water in here, just a dusty dirt bottom, but it can be fun to take photos, especially from the inside facing out. Sometimes walking around in here you may look at all of the footprints on the ground and wonder how long they go undisturbed. Although the cave seems to stay dry there is no archaeological evidence that it was used for permanent habitation.

Waikapala'e Wet Cave

The earth opens up here to crystal-clear water after you've walked up a short hill to look down into the Waikapala'e Wet Cave. Also known as the "Blue Room" because of another hidden cave here that's accessible only through an underwater tunnel that turns a vibrant blue, the cave is a contradiction. It's beautiful and spacious, but since the trees have grown up and block the light, it exudes a slightly eerie feeling. Visitors will find a tranquil place to spend time, and many people swim in the cold water. It's said that the Blue Room is no longer blue due to a change in the water table height and other environmental changes, and I'm not recommending searching for it because it is dangerous! To get here, drive about three minutes past Ha'ena. It's on the left right past the big parking lot on your right, and is only identifiable by the obviously worn path up the rocky hill, and the pull-off spot across the street. It's about a 1.5-minute walk up, where you can peer into the cave from above or take a short but steep and slippery trek down into it.

Waikanaloa Wet Cave

The Waikanaloa Wet Cave is clearly seen from the road a little before Ke'e Beach. The cave is a nice sight and another good photo opportunity. There is no swimming allowed, as the sign indicates. Look at the floor of the pond itself to see some interesting patterns.

Kaulu Paoa Heiau and Kaulu O Laka Heiau

To the right of Ke'e are Kaulu Paoa Heiau and Kaulu O Laka Heiau, where it's said that the art of hula was born. Legend says the goddess Laka bestowed hula to the Hawaiians here. At these *heiau* as well as any others, please respect everything in the area, meaning do not disturb or touch. *Heiau* are the equivalent to a Christian church for Hawaiians, and respect should always be paid when visiting them. The views up here are wonderful, especially during sunrise or sunset, when the sky changes to all shades of color. For over 1,000 years the area was used as a valued hula school. It's said that the pupils were asked to swim from here down to Ke'e Beach for a final induction sort of thing. At Ke'e Beach look for the trail weaving inland through the jungle up to the *heiau*.

Shopping

KILAUEA
Kilauea Plantation Center

The Kilauea Plantation Center on Kilauea Road is home to the **Healthy Hut** (4270 Kilauea Rd., 808/828-6626, www.healthy-hutkauai.com, 8:30 A.M.–9 P.M. daily), where you'll find organic produce, fruit, and other natural foods. There are natural home wares and gifts, along with a health and beauty section, vitamins, and natural baby products. A very small wine and beer selection is also available.

Kong Lung Historic Market Square

Also on Kilauea Rd. is the Kong Lung Historic Market Square (2484 Keneke St., 808/828-1822, konglungkauai.com). The shopping center began when the Kilauea Sugar Plantation rented one of its buildings on the current market site to a Chinese businessman named Lung Wah Chee, who opened an all-in-one general store with merchandise, a barber shop, butcher shop, diner, and post office. The original wood-frame building was replaced in the 1940s by the stone building that stands there today. The building is now listed on the National Register of Historic Places for its role in the town's development.

The market square is home to an array of shops and eateries, including the **Lotus Gallery** (808/828-9898, www.jewelofthelotus.com, 10 A.M.–6 P.M. daily), selling a spectrum of antique and modern Asian art and elegant jewelry made from pearls, opals, black diamonds, jade, and other stones, as well as Hawaiian *kahelelani* and sunrise-shell jewelry. Much of the jewelry is set in gold and is designed by the owners, who share a history in jewelry design and gemology. The shop is also stocked with carvings, garden art, and various artifacts. The shop pulls you in from the outside with its outdoor waterfall and tranquil pond, and sets a high-end museum mood.

Exploring **Coconut Style** (808/828-6899, www.coconutstyle.com, 9:30 A.M.–5:30 P.M. Mon.–Sat., 11 A.M.–5:30 P.M. Sun.) leaves no one wondering why the shop was cited by *Architectural Digest* as one of Kaua'i's must-stop shopping spots. Exclusive hand-painted shirts, sarongs, bedding, and other clothing adorn the shop, which holds the title of having the largest collection of each in Hawaii. Each piece is a marriage between Hawaiian and Balinese style.

Island Soap and Candle Works outlets (808/828-1955, www.islandsoap.com, 9 A.M.–8 P.M. daily) can be found around the island. The Kilauea location is not only a retail shop, but also a working factory where visitors can watch the soap being made by hand. The shop offers a full line of all-natural products to pamper yourself with while on vacation or at home. The scents of the lotions, sugar scrubs, beeswax candles, balms, and more will make you long for a spa day, which you can do yourself after dropping into the shop.

Kong Lung Trading (808/828-1822, www.konglung.com, 10 A.M.–6 P.M. Mon.–Sat., 11 A.M.–6 P.M. Sun.) offers a spectrum of quality and Pacific-inspired clothing, gifts, and art and more. It's a great place to window shop, make a purchase to bring home, or absorb decor representing the various cultures in the islands.

PRINCEVILLE
Princeville Center

A variety of shops to fit most needs can be found in the Princeville Center (5-4280 Kuhio Hwy., 808/826-9497, www.princevillecenter.com). **Foodland** (808/826-9880, 6 A.M.–11 P.M. daily) offers the usual supermarket foods, as well as a drugstore section, beach and snorkeling supplies, and other basic needs. The large air-conditioned market is usually crowded and also has a pharmacy and a DVD vending machine requiring only a credit or debit card.

Meanwhile, clothing, accessories, and swimwear for the whole family can be found at **Taro**

Fields (808/826-6205, www.tarofields.com, 10 A.M.–6 P.M. daily). The products reflect the island lifestyle and are a perfect accent for going out on the island or wearing back at home. Service is friendly and helpful, and staff is usually happy offer tips for exploring the island.

Kaua'i-made jewelry is available at **Majestic Gems International Inc.** (808/826-7057, 10 A.M.–6 P.M. Mon.–Sat., noon–6 P.M. Sun.). Black Tahitian pearls, gold jewelry, and other stones are available. Staff here is knowledgeable about the various gems for sale.

Visit the **Hawaiian Music Store** (808/826-4223, 9 A.M.–9 P.M. daily) to find a soundtrack for your trip. It's actually a kiosk near the Foodland entrance, and listening to the music back at home will always take you back to Kaua'i. The kiosk usually has local music playing on speakers, adding an element of island style to the shopping center.

For a drink, the **Princeville Wine Market** (808/826-0040, 10 A.M.–7 P.M. Mon.–Sat., 1–7 P.M. Sun.) holds an array of wines, something for each person's palate. Pick up a bottle for a romantic night at your accommodations or a sunset glass on the beach.

At the **Magic Dragon Toy & Art Supply** (808/826-9144, 9 A.M.–6 P.M. daily), a compilation of unique and educational toys, games, activities, and kites can be found. Great art supplies are also available.

Kaua'i Shell Kreations (808/652-4338, 10 A.M.–7 P.M. daily) sells unique *kahelelani* shell jewelry, among other shells. Various shell creations like shell frames, fresh flower lei, and other accessories are available. Other services are offered here, including a hardware store, postal service, and more.

HANALEI
Kahaule Center

In the Kahaule Center (4489 Aku Rd.) on the ocean side of the road, **The Bikini Room** (808/826-9711, www.thebikiniroom.com, 10 A.M.–6 P.M. Mon.–Sat., 11 A.M.–5 P.M. Sun.) is where unique and quality Brazilian bathing suits can be found. They're stylish, small, and fit for both sunning and surfing, so this is a must-stop when bikini shopping. A sale rack can often be found in front of the shop and the staff is especially helpful with insight on what suits are best for swimming or sunning.

The Root (808/826-2575, 9:30 A.M.–7 P.M. Mon.–Sat., noon–6 P.M. Sun.) has an array of fun, funky, simple, sweet, and trendy women's clothing. From dressy to relaxed, it's of high quality and pretty.

Find the famous Tahitian pearls (among others) at **Hanalei Pearls** (4489 Aku Rd., 808/826-0230, www.hanaleipearls.com, 11:30 A.M.–6 P.M.). Designed by a long-time Kauaʻi resident, the jewelry boasts a sparkling array of pearls, larimar, and other precious stones. Tahitian pearls are a local treasure and highly valued by those raised in the islands.

Hanalei Center

At the historic Hanalei Center (5-5121 Kuhio Hwy.) on the *mauka* side of the highway lies an array of shops and eateries making a home in the old school building. **Harvest Market Natural Foods and Cafe** (5-5161 Kuhio Hwy. #F, 808/826-0089, 9 A.M.–7 P.M. Mon.–Sat., 9 A.M.–6 P.M. Sun.) brings healthy food to Hanalei. The shelves are stocked with organic and natural food, produce, body products, and vitamins. Pre-made meals are in the refrigerator at the back of the store, and a salad bar offers an array of food.

At the west and back side of the center is **Havaiki Oceanic and Tribal Art** (5-5161 Kuhio Hwy. #G, 808/826-7606, www.havaiki art.com, 10:30 A.M.–6:30 P.M. daily), where a visit feels like an exploration through the Pacific. The collection resembles what you may find while visiting a museum, with all of the most prized gifts the area has to offer. Interesting and amazing artifacts, statues, carvings, jewelry, and much more pack this store full, ranging from normally affordable to the outstanding. Every piece tells a story.

Near here is the **Yellowfish Trading Company** (808/826-1227, 10 A.M.–8 P.M. daily), an extremely interesting store that feels like a journey through Hawaiian history. The store is loaded with Hawaiiana, collectibles, hula girl lamps, aloha shirts, carvings, swords, candles, jewelry, and so much more.

At the far east end in the old Hanalei School building is the **Hanalei Surf Company** (808/826-9000, www.hanaleisurf.com, 8:30 A.M.–9 P.M. daily), which sells and rents boards and water gear, along with a good stock of clothing and swimwear for the whole family. There are more shops in the center.

Ching Young Village

The bustling Ching Young Village (5-5190 Kuhio Hwy., 808/826-7222, www.chingyoungvillage.com) has many shops, including **Divine Planet** (808/826-8970, www.divine-planet.com, 10 A.M.–6 P.M. daily) and **Aloha From Hanalei** (same phone and number), which are two connected shops, but different. The former features bamboo women's clothing, beads, Asian-themed collectibles, and pretty and fun paper star lanterns. The latter shop has a unique array of local gems, handmade creamy soaps and lotions made by a local goat dairy, and Hawaiiana.

Robin Savage Gifts & Gourmet (808/826-7500, www.robinsavagegiftsandgourmet.com, 8:30 A.M.–7 P.M. daily) may be the most fun gift shop in Hanalei. Local cards, children's clothing, books, lotions, home and kitchen wares, and gourmet foods fill the shop. The shop is stocked with an abundance of products, and it's almost hard to move, but there are a lot of good finds.

Hula Moon Gifts (808/826-9965, 10 A.M.–6 P.M. daily) offers local trinkets, jewelry, shirts, and house decorations. Located on the back strip of shops, the store offers island-inspired products and souvenirs.

On the east end of the shopping center is **Backdoor Surf** (808/826-1900, www.hanaleisurf.com, 8:30 A.M.–9:30 P.M.). It rents and sells surfboards, and offers a large array of men's, women's and children's swimwear, surf gear, and clothing.

The **Village Variety Store** (808/826-6077, 9 A.M.–6:30 P.M. Mon.–Sat., 10 A.M.–5 P.M. Sun.) has an interesting array of souvenirs,

NORTH SHORE

housewares, and a random array of things. The cashiers are usually of the no-muss no-fuss type, and the store is fun to dig around in.

Colorful and cute describes the clothing in **Kokonut Kids** (5-5190 Kuhio Hwy., 808/826-0353, www.kokonutkidskauai.com, 10 A.M.–6 P.M. Mon.–Sat., 10 A.M.–5:30 P.M. Sun.), which offers all things local for children. From play clothes to dress clothes, Kokonut Kids can deck out the children for the whole trip.

Speaking of kids, the **Hanalei Toy and Candy Store** (808/826-4400, 10 A.M.–6 P.M. daily) offers just that, and has a unique selection of quality toys. It's a good idea not to bring the little ones in here unless you're prepared to buy something.

Big Save (808/826-6652, 7 A.M.–9 P.M. daily) is also here for all the basic supermarket needs. In addition to food and liquor, beach gear and school supplies are available, along with ice for the cooler and an ATM.

Hanalei Colony Resort
Na Pali Art Gallery & Coffee Shop (5-7132 Kuhio Hwy., 808/826-1844, www.napaliart-gallery.com, 7 A.M.–5 P.M. daily) is a wonderful art gallery filled with local art, jewelry, house decorations, tribal carvings, and more. The collection of Ni'ihau and sunrise-shell jewelry at the back of the small shop should not be missed. Paintings, scratchboard art, and local shell puzzles decorate the place. Coffee, smoothies, and bagels are offered too.

Entertainment

The very best entertainment on the north side may very well be the sunset. But for those looking for a little more action, there are a few places in town with live music.

PRINCEVILLE
At the **St. Regis Lobby Bar** (inside the St. Regis Princeville Resort), those looking for a mellow social evening or date night will find a 180-degree view of Hanalei Bay accented by unique art. Live jazz or Hawaiian music will highlight the evening. The bar is open 3:30–10:30 P.M. daily.

HANALEI
Hanalei Gourmet (808/826-2524, www.hana-leigourmet.com, 8 A.M.–10:30 P.M. daily) in the Hanalei Center often has live music at night but is more of a bar scene than a nightclub. Call for music schedules.

At **Tahiti Nui** (5-5134 Kuhio Hwy., 808/826-6277, www.thenui.com, dinner and music 6–8:30 P.M. and late music 9:30 P.M.–1 A.M.) dinner is offered nightly, but more importantly

it's the only place that could be considered real nighttime entertainment in Hanalei. Karaoke and Hawaiian music are played. Check the website for monthly schedules.

Bouchons Hanalei (808/826-9701, www.bouchonshanalei.com) in Ching Young Village has live music Thursday–Sunday nights. Call for hours and music selection.

TO THE END OF THE ROAD
The oceanfront *lu'au* at **Mediterranean Gourmet** (5-7132 Kuhio Hwy., 808/826-9875, www.kauaimedgourmet.com, 6–8:15 P.M. Tues.) offers the opportunity to fill your belly with a buffet dinner of traditional Hawaiian food while taking in hula dancing, fire knife dancing, and local music. Some of the mouth-watering buffet highlights include *lomilomi* salmon, traditional *kalua* pork, *haupia,* coconut cake, and of course, Hanalei poi. Because it's limited to 80 guests, reservations are required, so call to get your spot. The adult charge is $69, which includes a drink, those ages 12–20 pay $59, and for children 11 and under it's $35.

Food

KILAUEA
Quick Bites

(**Banana Joe's** fruit stand (5-2719 Kuhio Hwy., 808/828-1092, www.bananajoekauai. com, 9 A.M.–6 P.M. Mon.–Sat., until 5 P.M. Sun.) is a family- and friend-run small yellow shop that sells smoothies, fresh fruit, baked goods, and local honey. The variety of fruit here makes Carmen Miranda's hat look boring. It's a perfect place for a pre-beach snack stop, a gift run, or an after-scenic-route stop.

Thai 2 Go (Kauai Pacific School parking lot, 4480 Ho'okui Rd., 808/652-3699, 11 A.M.–8 P.M. Mon.–Sat., $9–10) serves up Thai food quickly out of a lunch wagon. The chefs from Thailand are health conscious. The food is MSG- and GMO-free, and the chicken they use is hormone- and antibiotic-free. Try the green papaya salad and take your meal on the road or enjoy it at the on-site picnic table.

The roadside **Moloa' a Sunrise Fruit Stand** (right after mile marker 16 on Kuhio Hwy., 808/822-1441, 7:30 A.M.–5 P.M. Mon.–Sat., Sun. 10 A.M.–5 P.M.) is a tasty and easily accessible place to pick up smoothies, sandwiches, a variety of coffee drinks, juices, granola, and smoothies. Although it's a roadside stand, it sits on a well-kept piece of property with a grassy lawn and coconut trees. There are seats on the porch or you can take your food to go.

Seafood

"There's a whole lot more than fish in store" is the self-described motto of the **Kilauea Fish Market** (Kilauea Plantation Center, 4270 Kilauea Road # F, 808/828-6244, 11 A.M.–8 P.M. Mon.–Sat., $10–30), and it's true. Free-range beef, salads, and plate lunches are also available, along with vegetarian specials. For $10–30 visitors can fill up and take the food to go to eat at home or on the beach, or enjoy it in the outdoor seating area.

Natural Foods

At the **Healthy Hut** (Kilauea Plantation Center, 4270 Kilauea Rd., 808/828-6626, www.healthy-hutkauai.com, 8:30 A.M.–9 P.M. daily) you will find local produce, wine and beer, health and beauty supplies, and other natural groceries. A very small wine and beer selection is also available. They don't offer any pre-made meals; the only ready-to-eat food is fruit and snacks.

Hawaiian

Lighthouse Bistro (Kong Lung Historic Market Square, 2484 Keneke St., 808/828-0480, www.lighthousebistro.com, noon–2:30 P.M. and 5:30–9 P.M., happy hour 5:30–6 P.M. daily) is near the lighthouse, not right by it. This is the closest to fine dining for the immediate area, but it isn't entirely formal; you can dress up for fun or go low-key. Lunch includes garden and fish tacos, garden and beef burgers, fish sandwiches, soups, and salads and runs $7.50–10 or $15 for all-you-can-eat pasta. Dinner includes ginger-crusted fresh catch, shrimp parmesan, coconut-crusted pork, ribs, and a lot more, along with salads and another all-you-can-eat pasta bar. Dinner runs $14–30, and vegetarians will have plenty of options here. Wine, beer, and cocktails are available.

Deli, Pizza, and Bakery

(**Kilauea Bakery & Pau Hana Pizza** (2484 Keneke St., 808/828-2020, www.kilaueabakery. wordpress.com, 6:30 A.M.–9 P.M. daily, $15–33) in the Kong Lung Historic Market Square serves up satisfying breakfasts and coffee along with tasty pizzas. Mornings usually bring a line of loyal locals coming in for the sweet and savory breakfast pastries. Pizza starts being served at 10:30 A.M. and comes with a heap of toppings.

Kilauea Town Market and Deli (2484 Keneke St, 808/828-1512, www.kilaueatownmarket.com, 8 A.M.–8 P.M. daily for already-made food and 10 A.M.–2 P.M. for special-order sandwiches, $8–10) serves up lunch and desserts, including an ahi sandwich and a Chinese chicken sandwich or a vegetarian teriyaki tofu sandwiches. Tasty desserts include bread

NORTH SHORE

pudding with whiskey sauce and silken chocolate pie. Groceries and wines can also be found here.

Farmers Market

Sunshine Farmers Market at the **Kilauea Neighborhood Center** (4:30 P.M. Thurs.) offers fresh produce and fruits. You can also find an abundance of locally made crafts, some ready-to-eat food, and other locally made food. Bring your own shopping bag.

PRINCEVILLE
American

CJ's Steak & Seafood (5-4282 Kuhio Hwy., 808/826-6211, www.cjssteak.com, lunch 11:30 A.M.–2:30 P.M. Mon.–Fri., dinner 6–9:30 P.M. daily, $15–38) is a steakhouse in the Princeville Center with a Pacific twist to most dishes. As at many steakhouses, saddles and other western-themed decorations are found throughout. The open-beam-ceilinged restaurant has seating indoors or on the lanai. Lunch and dinner are both offered with a wide array of pupu. Lunch consists of hot and cold sandwiches, burgers, and salads, ranging $10–12. Dinner offers a salad bar, freshly caught local fish, lobster, and prime rib. A senior and children's menu offers a discount for their meals.

Paradise Bar & Grill (Princeville Center, 5-4280 Kuhio Hwy. 808/826-1775, 11 A.M.–10 P.M. daily, lunch $5–15, dinner $10–30) is a local and visitor hangout that offers the same menu all day long. It's one of the more affordable places in Princeville, which is really the appealing factor here. Burgers, some seafood, steaks, salads, and more can be found here.

The **Kaua'i Grill** (808/826-9644, www.kauaigrill.com, 5:30–9:30 P.M. Tues., Wed., and Thurs., 5:30–10 P.M. Fri. and Sat., $32–72, apps for about $15) inside the St. Regis Princeville Resort offers sweeping views of beautiful Hanalei Bay. The eatery stays true to its surroundings with a nautilus shell spiraling ceiling. Chef Colin Hazama, who was recently recognized by the James Beard Foundation as a finalist in the Rising Star Chef of the Year category, cooks up a tasting menu, unique salads, a vegetarian menu, and lamb, meats, and fish,

all with a unique island twist. A kids' menu helps keep the prices down.

Makana Terrace (808/826-2746, www.stregisprinceville.com, breakfast 6:30–11 A.M., lunch 11:30 A.M.–2 P.M., dinner 5:30–9 P.M. Thurs.–Mon.) inside the St. Regis Princeville Resort offers breakfast ($12–35), lunch ($24–35), dinner ($26–48), and a Sunday champagne brunch. The Thursday Mailani Dinner Show brings Hawaiian chant, hula, and storytelling to diners for $135.

Sweet Treats

In the Princeville Center (5-4280 Kuhio Hwy., 808/826-9497) is **Hihimanu Shaved Ice** (8 A.M.–7 P.M. Mon.–Sat., 8 A.M.–6 P.M. Sun.), which doesn't sell just shaved ice. They also offer fruit smoothies, coffee, and waffles. Twists like acai berries or spirulina powder can be added to the smoothies.

Also in the Princeville Center, for a more traditional cold treat, is **Lappert's Hawaii Ice Cream & Coffee** (808/335-6121, 10 A.M.–9 P.M. daily, single scoop $4), which scoops and serve some really good ice cream. Walk in and try a cone of ice cream. It comes in a rainbow of flavors from traditional to Hawaiian.

Thai

At **Tamarind Thai and Chinese Cuisine** (Princeville Center, 5-4280 Kuhio Hwy., 808/826-9999, www.tamarind-thai.com, noon–8 P.M. Mon., Wed., Thurs., and Fri., 5–8 P.M. Sat., and noon–8 P.M. Sun., $9–20) diners will enjoy authentic Thai food that even comes with a vegetarian and vegan meal. Entrées include soups, curries, fried rice, and vegetable, meat, and seafood dishes. Appetizers include spring rolls and green papaya salad. Tamarind even delivers.

Supermarket

Foodland (Princeville Center, 5-4280 Kuhio Hwy., 808/826-9880, 6 A.M.–11 P.M. daily) sells not only food that needs to be prepared, but deli foods like fried chicken, macaroni and cheese, fries, freshly made sushi, and much more. The made-to-order sandwiches are actually pretty good for about $6, and are perfect for a beach day.

Beachside Dining

◖ Heavenly Creations (P.O. Box 952, Kilauea, 808/651-8933, www.heavenlycreations.org, $350) caters to couples or small groups looking for unique and romantic meals on the beach. They use only natural and organic ingredients, and they specialize in catering to unique food requests, such as to avoid allergies or for vegetarians (even if it's only one diner). The menu is an array of exotic foods, such as shrimp skewers with *liliko'i* glaze, salads with edible flowers, and entrées with the option of fish, free-range chicken, tofu, or tempeh. The desserts are decadent, and other fun things, like marshmallow roasts, hula, and a romantic treasure hunt are available. I discovered this service as I stumbled upon it one night at Anini Beach, as a couple enjoyed dinner on the sand with a cute little table and tiki torches.

HANALEI
Cafés and Breakfast

The scent alone in **Java Kai** (5-5161 Ste. 210, 808/826-6717, www.javakai.com, 6:30 A.M.–6 P.M. daily, $5–10) in the Hanalei Center will make anyone who enters want to try the local coffee. The coffees are good, and food is limited but includes a really good Belgian waffle, papaya and bagels, and a small selection of breakfast dishes including a breakfast burrito. Eat and run or drink your cup of joe on the porch.

Hanalei Wakeup Cafe (5-5144 Kuhio Hwy., 808/826-5551, 7–11 A.M. daily, $5–7) in Kauhale Center keeps it simple, serving coffee, egg breakfasts, various pastries, and a papaya bowl. The decor is surf, with plastic chairs, but the breakfast gets the job done.

Harvest Market Natural Foods and Cafe (5-5161 Kuhio Hwy., 808/826-0089, 9 A.M.–7 P.M. daily) also has coffee, tea, and pastries in the morning.

Japanese and Fish

◖ Bouchons Hanalei (5-5190 Kuhio Hwy.,

808/826-9701, www.bouchonshanalei.com, 11:30 A.M.–9:30 P.M. daily, lunch $9–15, dinner $11–30) delivers what they call Pacific American cuisine. The lunch menu, served 11:30 A.M.–4 P.M., features a range of foods from burgers to ribs, to taco salads and chicken dishes. Dinner is served 5:50–9:30 P.M. and includes exquisite sushi, a Pacific-themed menu, ribs, burgers, and other Asian dishes. An array of drinks and live music on certain nights are also offered. The restaurant is the best of two previous ones fused together by the owner.

Just after entering Hanalei you'll see **◖ Hanalei Dolphin Restaurant** (5-5016 Kuhio Hwy., 808/826-6699, www.hanaleidolphin.com), consisting of the restaurant, a fish market, and sushi lounge. The restaurant (lunch 11:30 A.M.–3 P.M., $10–16, dinner 5:30–9 P.M. daily, $20–35) serves an array of Pacific Rim salads, burgers, and seafood in all of its glory. Your meals will be enjoyed on the lanai at riverside tables or in the open-air restaurant. You can go casual here, but it's also nice enough to dress up. The sushi lounge (5:30–9 P.M. daily) has a wonderful array of sushi and a good sake selection. The **Hanalei Fish Market** (10 A.M.–7 P.M. daily) offers a wide selection of fresh fish. Here you'll find a good variety of seafood, specialty cheeses, organic produce, beef, and desserts.

Hawaiian

The family-run **◖ Hanalei Taro and Juice Co.** (5-5070 Kuhio Hwy., 808/826-1059, www.hanaleitaro.com, 11 A.M.–3 P.M. Mon.–Sat., $4–10.50) serves up a modern take on traditional Hawaiian food. Established in 2000, the company is part of the Haraguchi family farm (of the rice mill) and creates the meals with local foods and taro. They put a new twist on Hawaiian food, as with the taro smoothie and taro veggie burgers, while staying traditional with *kalua* pig, *laulau*, poi, *lomilomi* salmon, and a whole lot more. *So ono, brah.*

◖ Postcards Cafe (808/826-1191, www.postcardscafe.com, 6–9 P.M. daily, $19–31) is a vegetarian's (or seafood lover's) dream, with a spectacular menu of gourmet vegetarian and seafood cuisine. No meat, poultry, or refined sugar is used here, which makes the abundance of organic ingredients and local produce stand out. Many dishes are vegan or can be made vegan.

Health Food

Harvest Market Natural Foods and Cafe

(Hanalei Center, 5-5161 Kuhio Hwy., 808/826-0089, 9 A.M.–7 P.M., hot bar $7.99 per pound) brings healthy food to Hanalei. The shelves are stocked with organic and natural food, produce, and body products. Pre-made meals are in the refrigerator at the back of the store, and a salad bar offers an array of food. Coffee and pastries are available in the morning and the deli takes orders off their menu. Slightly on the pricey side, but it's healthy.

To the left of Ching Young Village is the **Aloha Juice Bar** (808/826-6990, $5) where you can find veggie and fruit juices along with acai bowls and chocolate-dipped bananas.

American

At **Bubba Burgers** (5 Kuhio Hwy., 808/826-7839, www.bubbaburger.com, 10:30 A.M.–8 P.M. daily, $3.50–7.25) the food isn't necessarily spectacular, but the burgers are good and filling, and seem to remain so on a regular basis. The burgers come in different weights and they even offer a garden burger. They use only grass-fed Kaua'i beef and have the usual burger joint sides, like shakes, sodas, and chicken sandwiches. It's on the *mauka* side of the highway in the center of Hanalei; you can't miss it.

Hanalei Gourmet Cafe, Bar, and Delicatessen in Hanalei Center (5-5161 Kuhio Hwy., 808/826-2524, www.hanaleigourmet. com, 8 A.M.–10:30 P.M. daily, lunch $7.50–13, dinner $10–27) offers a variety of restaurants in one. It's in the old school building, so a historical element is added to the atmosphere. Happy hour is 3:30–5:30 P.M. daily. Dinner is 5:30–9:30 P.M. Early-bird specials are offered 5:30–6:30 P.M., and selected sports are available on cable TV. A really unique thing about this place is that they offer picnic services. They will help you pack your food and wine into insulated backpacks or coolers so you can hike the Na Pali Coast or paddle up a river. The meal selection is varied, from appetizers of seafood, nachos, and the tasty artichoke dip to the dinners of pork loin, poultry, steak, and pastas, many with a Pacific twist. Salads are available in abundance, as well as sandwiches and burgers. This place has plenty of vegetarian options.

Brazilian and Mexican

◖ Neide's Brazilian and Mexican Food (Hanalei Center, 808/826-1851, www.neide-salsaandsamba.com, 11:30 A.M.–2:30 P.M. and 5:30–9 P.M. daily, $10–20) serves up some really good margaritas, as well as unique dishes. The head chef from Brazil has a unique take on South American food, like adding cabbage and carrots to the dishes, but it's good and interesting. The service is very laid-back, and there is outdoor and indoor seating. It can be a good place to bring kids because the porch seating lies on a yard-like area with a picnic table and garden, so children can roll around while you enjoy a really tasty, strong, and slightly pricey margarita. Vegetarians will not leave here with an empty belly.

Tropical Taco (5-5088 Kuhio Hwy., 808/827-8226, www.tropicaltaco.com, 8 A.M.–8 P.M. daily, $5–11) is in the green Halele'a Building on the ocean side of the highway, the green being similar to the green lunch wagon the owner ran the business out of for 20 years. The tacos, burritos, and tostadas are good, simple, and can be grabbed on the run or enjoyed sitting at the location. Vegetarians will find a sufficient meal here.

Tapas

◖ Bar Acuda Tapas and Wine (808/826-7081, www.restaurantbaracuda.com, bar 5:30–10:30 P.M. daily, dinner 6–9:30 P.M. daily, $6–16) in the Hanalei Center may be home to the most modern decor in Hanalei. They serve tapas, which are defined on the menu as a variety of small savory dishes typically shared communally among friends. To never have a boring month, the menu here changes by the week and the season; offerings include local honeycomb with goat cheese, short ribs, local fish, salads, desserts, and a great wine menu.

Desserts and Snacks

Don't walk into **Pinks Creamery** (4489 Aku Rd., 808/826-1257, 11 A.M.–5 P.M. daily, $4–7) in the Kauhale Center unless you are ready to be overcome by the scent of all things sweet, such as ice cream, shakes, and other treats. The single scoop in a cone is a little on the pricey side but so wonderful.

Pizza

Hanalei Pizza (808/826-1300, www.hanaleipizza.com, 11 A.M.–8:30 P.M. daily, $12–25) in the Ching Young Village sells pizzas by the slice or by the whole pizza. Pies are available with a variety of ingredients. They offer white or whole-wheat crust, which they make daily, and whole pies can sometimes require a wait.

Farmers Market

The **Waipa Ranch Farmers Market** (5-5785A Kuhio Hwy., 808/826-9969), which takes place on Tuesdays from 2–4 P.M., is loaded with local produce, fruit, jewelry, and other crafts. It's a good idea to get here at the start, as the good stuff sells out fast.

TO THE END OF THE ROAD
Mexican

【 Red Hot Mama's (808/826-7266, 11 A.M.–5 P.M. daily but sometimes closes on Sun., $8–11) is a hole in the wall and thankfully one of the last stops before having no food options at the beach. I say thankfully because I'm thankful every time I eat there. The food always comes in a hefty serving, and fresh local fish is almost always an optional addition. Vegetarians can always find a substantial meal here. The owner has enough postings around the eatery to let you know *not* to linger right in front and keep asking if your meal is done. Browse the

neighboring shops or hang in the grass to the left and she will come out and call you.

Café

Na Pali Art Gallery & Coffee Shop (5-7132 Kuhio Hwy., 808/826-1844, www.napaliartgallery.com, 7 A.M.–5 P.M. daily, $2–5) on the Hanalei Colony Resort property provides a last chance for smoothies, bagels, and coffee—in addition to extraordinary local art, jewelry, and gifts. Note that credit card purchases require a $10 minimum.

Mediterranean

【 Mediterranean Gourmet (5-7132 Kuhio Hwy., 808/826-9875, www.kauaimedgourmet.com, 11 A.M.–3 P.M. and 4:30–8:30 P.M. Mon., 11 A.M.–3 P.M. and 6–8 P.M. (*lu'au* only) Tues., 11 A.M.–3 P.M. and 4–8:30 P.M. Wed.–Sat., 4–6 P.M. happy hour, $17–65) has been voted by *Honolulu* magazine as the best new restaurant on Kaua'i in 2007 and best restaurant on Kaua'i in 2008, 2009, 2010, and 2011. If that doesn't speak for itself, then the oceanfront location paired with the menu will amaze you. Lebanon native and chef Imad Beydoun and his wife Yarrow feature Greek, French, Spanish, Italian, and Lebanese-influenced dishes for lunch or dinner. Dinner reservations are recommended, and music is provided each night. Monday features guitar, on Tuesday a *lu'au* is offered 6–8:15 P.M., Wednesday is jazz and half-price wine night, Thursday is belly dancing, and Friday and Saturday offer more guitar. Try the homemade sangria or a mojito. Lunch includes wraps, vegetarian dishes, fish, and more. For dinner, there are vegetarian, lamb, beef, fish, chicken, and vegetarian dishes, along with their famous rack of lamb for two.

Information and Services

POST OFFICES

In Kilauea the **Kilauea Post Office** (Kaneka St., 808/828-1721, 9 A.M.–4 P.M. Mon.–Fri., 10:30 A.M.–noon P.M. Sat.) offer the usual post office shipping and packaging services. They also offer general delivery services for those in need of receiving mail but staying temporarily. To sign up for general delivery you must go to the post office and register.

The **Princeville Post Office** (5-4280 Kuhio Hwy., 808/828-0217, 10:30 A.M.–3:30 P.M. Mon.–Fri., 10:30 A.M.–12:30 P.M. Sat.) offers basic shipping services. No general delivery services or passport services are offered here.

The **Hanalei Post Office** (5-5226 Kuhio Hwy., 800/275-8777, 9 A.M.–4 P.M. Mon.–Fri., 10:30 A.M.–noon P.M. Sat. provides shipping, basic packaging materials, and general delivery. Passport services are also available here.

LIBRARY

At the **Princeville Public Library** (4343 Emmalani Dr., 808/826-4310, www.princevillelibrary.com, 10 A.M.–5 P.M. Tues., Thurs., Fri., and Sat., 1–8 P.M. Wed.) you can find Internet access along with book and video rentals. Visitors can get a library card with proof of temporary address.

GAS STATION

The last gas station on the north side is in Princeville. So when you're headed to Hanalei from another locale make sure to fill up. It's a bit of a drive from here to the end of the road, not a place you want to run out of gas.

Getting There and Around

BY CAR

The most convenient way to get to and around the north shore is by car. Highway 56 heads west straight out of Lihu'e and runs all the way to the end of the road, turning into Route 560 by Hanalei. Rental cars are the best bet here and are available at the airport. Gas prices go up the farther north you go, so it's a good idea to fill up in Lihu'e.

BY BUS

The **Kaua'i Bus** (808/241-6410, www.kauai. gov/Transportation, 5:27 A.M.–10:40 P.M. Mon.–Fri. and 6:21 A.M.–5:50 P.M. Sat., Sun., and holidays) runs island-wide with several stops through Kilauea, Princeville and Hanalei. The bus is a green, convenient, and affordable way to get around. The last stop is in Hanalei at the old Hanalei courthouse. Fares are $1 for children and seniors, and $2 for the general public. Monthly passes are also available.

BY TAXI AND LIMOUSINE

Pono Taxi (808/634-4744, www.taxihanalei. com) offers taxi, airport shuttle, and tour services in Hanalei to any destination.

North Shore Cab Co. (808/639-7829, www. northshorecab.com) provides rides to and from the airport and island-wide, and offers sightseeing tours.

For a more upscale ride, **Kaua'i North Shore Limousine** (808/828-6189, www.kauainorthshorelimo.com) offers limousine service for a special date, wedding, or corporate travel.

SCOOTERS

Hop onto a moped to zip around the north side and save on gas at **Island Scooter Rental** (5-5134 Kuhio Hwy., Kilauea, 866/225-7352, www.mobilemopeds.com, 9 A.M.–5 P.M. daily). If you rent by the week the company offers free airport pickup, and they even offer four-hour tours for $100. Call for prices and reservations.

SOUTH SHORE

The south shore, which includes the Koloa, Kalaheo, and Poʻipu areas, boasts lush green pastures above warm sunny coastlines, ocean-front accommodations bordered by the birth-place of Hawaiian royalty, and thick tropical inland jungles. A blend of vacationers and lo-cals, raw land and modern luxuries, the south shore is the island's main resort destination, with sunny skies and a coastline dotted with large hotels and condominiums, while just in-land are old plantation homes that still house local residents.

The area holds claim to what may be the most important part of Hawaiian history: the first successful sugar mill in Hawaii. Koloa was home to the mill, therefore spearhead-ing the sugar industry and bringing together many ethnicities to coexist in the island. Seven

ethnic groups became the main source of labor on the plantations and others came and went, many leaving descendants that still live in the area. The sugar mill was the central feature of society and life on the south side.

On the south side you see the area's char-acter change as you drive toward the coast. If you take Maluhia Road down to **Koloa,** you'll drive through open green pastures and then the gorgeous Tunnel of Trees. Past that and just a bit west, you'll begin your journey in-land in a lush green area called Lawaʻi Valley, where you'll notice a prominent backdrop of luxuriant jungle reaching inland to the high central part of the island. On the way down Koloa Road notice the rolling green pastures usually dotted with happily grazing sheep and horses. In Koloa, plantation homes, remnants

© JADE ECKARDT

HIGHLIGHTS

LOOK FOR 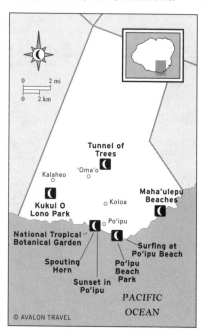 TO FIND RECOMMENDED SIGHTS, ACTIVITIES, DINING, AND LODGING.

◖ **Maha'ulepu Beaches:** The closest you'll get to venturing into the wild on this side of the island is by visiting these beaches. The long dirt road keeps many people out, and the expansive beaches offer space for everyone (page 118).

◖ **Po'ipu Beach Park:** A joy for everyone, this beach offers protected swimming and a manicured ground for picnicking and relaxing. This is a wonderful place for children and anyone who prefers a calm ocean rather than challenging waves (page 120).

◖ **Surfing at Po'ipu Beach:** A Hawaiian vacation wouldn't be complete without trying to catch a few waves. Po'ipu Beach is a popular place for surf schools and usually offers ideal conditions for beginning surfers (page 121).

◖ **Tunnel of Trees:** Eucalyptus trees that form a natural tunnel over Maluhia Road create a beautiful sight and great photo opportunity (page 131).

◖ **Spouting Horn:** Salt water erupts through a hole in the lava sea cliffs at the impressive Spouting Horn, the south shore's claim to fame (page 132).

◖ **Sunset in Po'ipu:** A wonderful end to a lovely south shore day is watching the sunset in Po'ipu. Several locations offer great views from the beach or sand-free lawns to enjoy a spectacular sunset (page 133).

◖ **National Tropical Botanical Garden:** The only tropical plant research facility in the United States boasts two gardens with a vast array of tropical plants to explore (page 133).

◖ **Kukui O Lono Park:** This lovely park is perfect for a stroll through Japanese gardens and to picnic with an ocean view (page 135).

of the mill, and small shops and eateries make up a quaint and historical central area. This is a great place to stroll through the town, sampling food, enjoying the *aloha,* and mingling with visitors while locals go about their daily business. Most of the shops in the small yet bustling town are actually remodeled old plantation buildings. Parking here is always hard to find, but the town is so small that it's fine to park anywhere and stroll around. Make a point to look inland at different points in the road. The views are gorgeous and the raw green landscape is captivating.

From 1835 to 1880 Koloa was Kaua'i's most densely populated area. Koloa Landing, down in Po'ipu, was one of the top three active whaling ports in the entire state. Sugar was a booming business for the majority of the century; the newest mill, the McBryde Sugar Co. Koloa Mill, shut its doors in 1996, ending the sugar industry for the area. Its remains can still be seen off of Maha'ulepu Road.

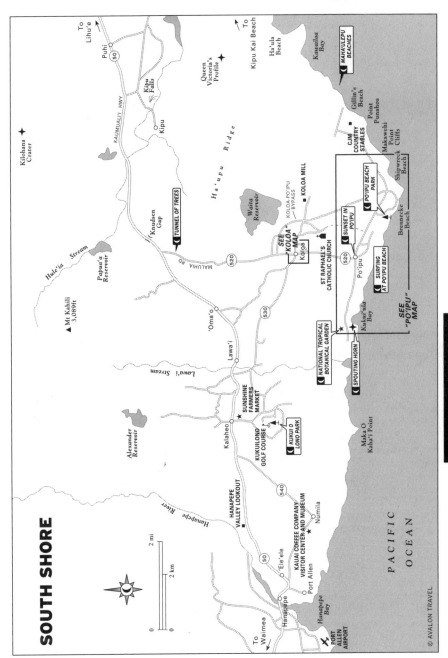

SOUTH SHORE

SOUTH SHORE

© AVALON TRAVEL

Soon after the vibrant green foliage the landscape turns to a dry and sunny beach resort area, known as **Po'ipu.** Down here the road weaves along the ocean, past historical sites, surf breaks, and numerous white-sand beaches. Po'ipu is a vacationer's paradise: gorgeous white-sand beaches, eateries galore, shopping, surf lessons, golf courses, and a few sights to see. Although mainstream development may have made its way into the area in the form of hotels and condominiums, natural sights and raw land still exist here. Locals access the surf breaks and enjoy the beaches as much as any visitor. At the end of the day you'll often see local surfers enjoying the sunset and an after-work beer across from Lawa'i Beach. Down here are some of the most intriguing sights on the island, including Spouting Horn and the National Tropical Botanical Garden. Although there is no shortage of soft white sand down here, the sandy coast also has its share of black boulders

dotting the area along with reefs, drawing in tropical fish and creating perfect waves for surfing and body-boarding. Po'ipu's resort area also offers upscale shopping and eating.

Inland on the south side and on the way to the west is **Kalaheo,** home to quaint restaurants, small shops, and a population of generations of local residents. To put it simply, Kalaheo doesn't have much going on, but the laid-back feeling is part of its appeal. Here you can find the beautiful Kukui O Lono Park and golf course. If you're headed to the west side you'll take a drive through Kalaheo because Kaumuali'i Highway is the only road that leads there.

Many visitors decide to stay on the south shore because of its sunny coast, resort options, and world-class beaches, but if you don't stay in a hotel here, make sure to schedule at least a one-day visit to this side of the island. Enjoy the popular tourist spots, but don't miss the vacant beauty of the south shore's interior jungles and the secluded coastline.

Beaches

Some of Kauai's best beaches are found on the south side. They're blanketed in fine white sand and range from popular and crowded to secluded and hardly visited. All of the beaches are in the Po'ipu area, as Koloa, Kalaheo, and Lawa'i are all inland areas. The beaches provide a selection of coveted Hawaii activities, such as snorkeling, surfing, swimming, and sunbathing.

PO'IPU
◖ Maha'ulepu Beaches
For a little adventure into the outskirts of the south side, take the drive out to the Maha'ulepu Beaches at the east end of Po'ipu. You'll travel down a long road through undeveloped land with great views of the green mountains. The road is fit for two-wheel drive cars but is usually pocked with potholes, making the ride quite bumpy. To get here, drive past the Grand Hyatt Kauai until the road turns to dirt. You'll

see the CMJ Stables sign as the road turns to dirt and a gate with a sign that states the gates are locked at 6 P.M. Access is privately owned, and locals are hoping the owners won't close it, so please respect the area and take out all that you brought. The long strip of beaches consists of Gillin's Beach, the first you come to; Kawailoa Bay, the second; and the third and most secluded, Ha'ula Beach.

Gillin's Beach is accessed via a short trail through the forest. Parking is out of sight from the beach and behind the forest, so bring any valuable belongings to the beach or leave them at home. The beach is very, very long with fine white sand. Swimming is doable, but be careful and use good judgment. Conditions can be windy with a strong current. Although the beach is very long, it's not the widest from dunes to ocean. As the tide gets higher the sand gets narrower, and you will most likely see sunbathers bordering the dunes. To the right of the beach

THE BEST DAY ON THE SOUTH SHORE

You can easily experience the best of the south shore in one day without missing out on anything. While the best days on other parts of the island require visitors to move quickly through many activities, you can see the best of the south shore in a more relaxed manner. If you start with breakfast around 8 A.M., you should be able to get it all done by sundown.

- Begin your day with breakfast at **Kalaheo Cafe.** Sit down or order takeout; either way you'll have plenty of time for the day.

- While in Kalaheo, head over to **Kukui O Lono Park.** This is a good place to bring a takeout breakfast to enjoy at a picnic table. Otherwise, take a stroll, explore the rock garden, and smell the pink plumerias.

- Now it's off to a few minutes at **Spouting Horn.** Snap a few photos, wait for a couple of big bursts, and it's on to the next stop.

- Enjoy a walk through the **National Tropical Botanical Garden.** Spend about 60-90 minutes here to make sure there's enough time for everything else on the south side.

- Head down the road to **Po'ipu Beach** for surf lessons. Make sure to book the lessons in advance, and have fun trying to catch waves.

- Now you have a choice. For a relaxing time with full amenities, bask in the sun and salt at **Po'ipu Beach Park.** This is an especially good option if you have children. For much more secluded beach time make the drive to the **Maha'ulepu Beaches.**

- To end the day, enjoy the sunset in Po'ipu. Watch the sunset over boats and Spouting Horn from **Kukui'ula Small Boat Harbor** or from the **Beach House Restaurant.**

- For dinner stay at the **Beach House Restaurant,** a good place with or without children. Otherwise, a great family and low-key place is **Brick Oven Pizza.**

© NATHANAEL DUNGAN/WWW.123RF.COM

Spouting Horn

TOP KID-FRIENDLY ACTIVITIES ON THE SOUTH SHORE

Although just about every site and activity on the south shore is fit for kids, there are a few highlights for them, especially outdoor activities.

- The south shore is filled with beaches galore, but take the kids to **Po'ipu Beach Park.** There couldn't be a more perfect beach for kids than this. Here you will find a protected shallow area for swimming, a playground, showers, and a grassy area.

- At **Spouting Horn** kids love watching the ocean water blast through a hole in the lava rock. There are also picnic tables on a well-manicured lawn.

- **Surf lessons at Po'ipu Beach** will make any Kaua'i trip complete. Kids will love a chance to try to catch some waves.

- There is a really nice **playground** on Omao Road. Swings, slides, a small rock-climbing wall, and more make for a nice break from the car. A large field and picnic table are also part of the park. Heading up from the bottom of the road, the playground is around three-quarters of the way up on your right.

- Kids love pizza and **Brick Oven Pizza** in Kalaheo is a great place for lunch or dinner. Stop by on Thursday nights for an all-you-can-eat buffet.

after Elbert Gillin's house, whom the beach is named after, is the Makauwahi Sinkhole, which is fun to explore. The open sandstone sinkhole has some fun elements to check out and has unearthed archaeological finds.

Swimming is the most protected east of Gillin's at **Kawailoa Bay.** You can keep driving and notice the beach as it becomes roadside, or walk from Gillin's east around the bend, but it's a bit of a walk. The cove is calmer here than anywhere else on the beach, but the beach isn't quite as nice as the rest. A nice aspect of Kawailoa is that since it's in a semi-protected cove, the whipping winds can be less offensive here.

To get to **Ha'ula Beach** you must walk for a while along the lithified cliffs. The cliffs look wild and prehistoric; they're rough, and you'll want shoes for this. After about 15 minutes of walking while taking in the unique landscape, you'll reach Ha'ula Beach. Swimming out here is almost always dangerous, but on the bright side, secluded beachcombing and sunbathing are plentiful. There is rarely anyone out here and you'll most likely be alone, the main appeal of making the trip.

Farther east and accessible only by boat or over the gnarly ridge is **Kipu Kai Beach.** So unless you want to rent a boat or hike over an extremely uncomfortable ridge, you shouldn't visit this beach.

Shipwreck Beach

Shipwreck Beach fronts the Grand Hyatt Kaua'i Resort and Spa. Named after an old shipwreck that used to rest on the eastern end and is now long gone, the beach is generally crowded because of its location. It offers plenty of space with about a half mile of sand, but the ocean here is usually too rough for swimming except for those who are experts in the water. Local surfers and body boarders utilize the east end of the beach for catching waves. Also on the eastern end is Makawehi Point, the high cliff that locals like to launch off of for fun. If you feel like going on a treasure hunt, a hard-to-find interesting thing here is a petroglyph carved into the base of the cliff. The ancient art is nearly always covered by sand, and you must be extremely lucky to be there when the sand is pulled away, exposing petroglyph. To get here, drive toward the Hyatt on Weliweli Road and turn right on Ainako Road. Park in the small parking lot at the end.

◖ Po'ipu Beach Park

Po'ipu Beach Park (at the end of Kuai Road) is

rocks on Po'ipu Beach

hands down the most ideal beach for families and children on the south side. A protected swimming area, playground, full amenities, and grassy lawn come together to create everything you could need for a full day at the beach. It's often crowded here, with visitors and local families, but it's a testament to how wonderful the beach is. The semi-enclosed part of the water to the east is protected by a short rock wall, providing nearly always calm and shallow water within the rock barrier. It's a great swimming pool for children to float and play. The water isn't as protected on the right side of the beach as it is on the left, but if the waves are small it's usually pretty safe. Snorkeling at the west end is pretty good too.

An elaborate playground for children is located at the east side of the park alongside a tree offering shade. Picnic tables dot the grassy lawn, showers and bathrooms are on-site, and lifeguards watch over the area. There is parking available across the street from the beach, but on most days the spots are full. You may have to wait a little while for someone to leave and open up a spot for you. The beach was mauled by Hurricane 'Iniki but has been restored to all of its glory.

Just east of Po'ipu Beach Park is **Brennecke Beach.** The waves are great for boogie-boarding and bodysurfing only, because fiberglass boards, which is what surfboards are, are not allowed. This is a good place for beginners to rent a boogie board from **Nukumoi Surf** across the street and charge the waves. To get here, turn down Ho'owili Road off of Po'ipu Road. The beach is right at the bottom along Ho'one Road.

Po'ipu Beach

Also known as Sheraton Beach (because it fronts the Sheraton Kaua'i) and Kiahuna Beach, Po'ipu Beach is a popular, and therefore a generally crowded, beautiful beach. The swimming just offshore is usually pretty mellow thanks to the reef farther out. A good wave for surfing is also created here by the reef, and it's a popular spot with local surfers and surf schools. Surf lessons are taught here frequently, and there's

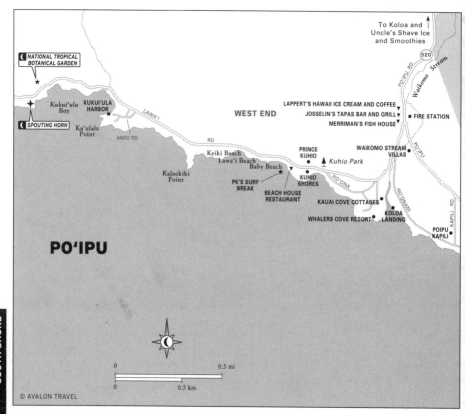

To Koloa and
Uncle's Shave Ice
and Smoothies

520

Waikomo Stream

NATIONAL TROPICAL
BOTANICAL GARDEN

PO'IPU RD

LAPPERT'S HAWAII ICE CREAM AND COFFEE

Kukui'ula
Bay

KUKUI'ULA
HARBOR

JOSSELIN'S TAPAS BAR AND GRILL

WEST END

FIRE STATION

LAWA'I

MERRIMAN'S FISH HOUSE

SPOUTING HORN

Ka'ulala
Point

AMIO RD

RD

WAIKOMO STREAM
VILLAS

PO'IPU

PRINCE
KUHIO

Kuhio Park

Keiki Beach
Lawa'i Beach

Baby Beach

KUHIO
SHORES

HO'ONA

Kalaekiki
Point

PK'S SURF
BREAK

BEACH HOUSE
RESTAURANT

KAUAI COVE COTTAGES

KOLOA
LANDING

HO'ONANI

WHALERS COVE RESORT

KAPILI RD

POIPU
KAPILI

PO'IPU

0   0.5 mi

0   0.5 km

© AVALON TRAVEL

no doubt you'll see surf school students with soft-top longboards. Body-boarding and body surfing are fun in the shore break. It's also a good spot for snorkeling if the ocean is calm, so bring your gear. There are restrooms at the grassy lawn above the sand. Parking here and along the street can be tight, so keep a lookout for several parking areas along the road. The beach is at the end of coastal Ho'onani Road.

Baby Beach

True to its name, Baby Beach is perfect for small children and babies. The small beach is nearly always calm, still, and shallow. The water here feels more like a saltwater swimming pool than the open ocean. There is a narrow strip of white sand descending into the water,

leading to a rocky bottom. Hawaiian rocks can always be a bit tough on the feet, so bringing water shoes is a good idea. Kids will love jumping around in the water with floats here. To get here, turn off of Lawa'i Road onto Ho'ona Road and look for the beach access sign. The beach is behind the oceanfront homes.

PK's

Located right across from the Prince Kuhio monument, hence the name PK's, the narrow strip of sand is most notable by the surf break-out and to the right of the Beach House Restaurant. The wave here is also called PK's. Sometimes snorkelers see a lot of fish here since the bottom is so rocky, so if you're a dedicated snorkeler hop in when the waves are very small.

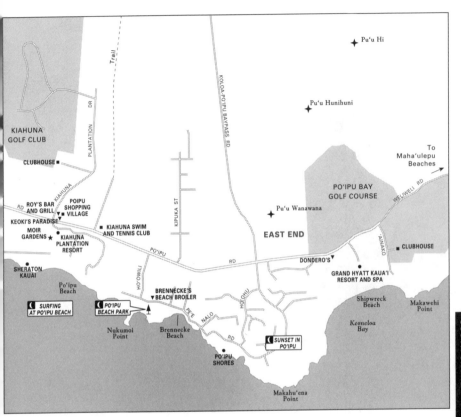

But the beach is narrow, and it's just off the road, so it's less than ideal for a day at the beach. Drive down Lawa'i Road and you'll see the small beach below the roadside rock wall directly across from the monument.

Lawa'i Beach

A small white-sand beach in an almost always sunny area, Lawa'i Beach offers swimming and decent snorkeling along a narrow strip of white sand. The grounds of the Beach House Restaurant jut out on the left side of the beach, while condominiums act as a backdrop across the road. Across the street is a small parking lot with restrooms and a small shop. This is a popular hangout for local surfers, who enjoy a few beers at day's end while watching the waves at

PK's. Head down Lawa'i Road and you can see the beach from the street right past the Beach House Restaurant.

Keiki Beach

A few yards down from Lawa'i Beach is Keiki Beach. A private and very small strip of sand just below the road, the small beach is accessible by hopping over the rock wall and stepping down past a few boulders. There's a small tide pool here for a very shallow dip or for kids, only at low tide. The nice thing about this spot is that it's nearly always uninhabited. During high tide you'll find yourself sitting up against the rock wall, so it's best at low tide. Although small, Keiki Beach is a change from Lawa'i Beach just because it's usually empty.

© JADE ECKARDT

Great for snorkeling, sunning, and surfing, Lawa'i Beach lies alongside the Beach House Restaurant.

Lawa'i Bay

Bordering the National Tropical Botanical Garden is Lawa'i Bay. The bay is usually only reached by those with a passion for serious ocean adventuring. If you kayak about a mile west from **Kukui'ula Small Boat Harbor** you will reach it. Those who make it there are asked to be respectful and not enter the gardens. Needless to say, you'll most likely be alone here if you make the trip. Park your vehicle at Kukui'ula Small Boat Harbor at the end of Lawa'i Road. Hop in the water with your kayak and paddle about a mile west down the coast.

Water Sports

SNORKELING AND DIVING

The south side has decent snorkeling at several spots. One of the highlights here is the large number of green sea turtles that frequent the waters. They move slowly and are gentle creatures, so please don't bother or touch them. Although they rarely bite, it is painful when they do. They usually cruise along leisurely, but be careful and keep board leashes away from them. They can get very tangled and angry.

Po'ipu
BEACHES

Hop in the water at **Lawa'i Beach** and you may see some colorful fish. The sea life isn't the most populated but it's definitely worth a shot if you're spending time at the beach. The bottom here is rocky, which means fish are attracted to the area because seaweed and algae grow here for them to eat. Just east of Lawa'i Beach and across from the Prince Kuhio

THE SOUTH SHORE'S OWN SION MILOSKY

While driving around the south side, you may see signs that say RIP Sion or Live Like Sion. Just as the loss of professional surfer Andy Irons was mourned by many on the north side of Kaua'i, the south side will forever be mourning the loss of Sion Milosky. Hailing from Kaua'i's south shore, Milosky rose to the top of the Hawaiian surf world in his mid-30s and drowned at big wave spot Mavericks in March 2011. During a contest at Mavericks, Milosky was held down by two huge waves, reportedly 60 feet tall, before he disappeared.

His body was eventually found about a mile down the coast.

Those who knew him enjoyed his incredible kindness and say he was a good person, great friend, and most importantly, a family man. He was a father of two and a dedicated husband. In the winter before he died, he paddled into what was believed at the time to be the largest wave ever paddled into (surfers often use Jet Skis to catch huge waves) at a break called Himalayas on the north shore. His family still resides on the south side.

monument is **PK's.** The beach is tiny, and the ocean floor is rocky, which again attracts fish into the area. The beach is rarely visited because it's right off the road, and fish seem to like to hang out here. Maybe they appreciate the lack of disturbance compared to other areas. Down the road, **Po'ipu Beach Park** is a good option for snorkeling. There's usually something to see at either end of the beach and the water is often calm here. Jump in on either end of the beach and you'll most likely see some ocean life.

SNORKELING AND DIVING GEAR RENTALS

You can rent or buy snorkel gear at **Nukumoi Beach & Surf Shop** (2080 Ho'one Rd., 808/742-8019, www.nukumoisurf.com, 7:45 A.M.–7 P.M. Mon.–Sat., 10:30 A.M.–6 P.M. Sun.). They provide all kinds of beach gear, including snorkel gear, for about $7 a day to $20 for the week. At **Snorkel Bob's** (3236 Po'ipu Rd., 808/742-2206, www.snorkelbob.com, 8 A.M.–5 P.M. daily) you'll find a wide variety of gear for rent. They offer complete sets including a mask, snorkel, and net gear bag with grade A surgical quality silicone for ultimate comfort and water seal. The adult package goes for $35 a week or $22 per week for children. The budget crunch package offers a basic mask, snorkel, fins, and dive bag for $9

a week. A unique rental package is what they call The 4 Eyes RX Ensemble to compensate for nearsightedness while snorkeling. This includes a mask with a prescription lens for $44 per week for adults and $32 for kids.

In Po'ipu **Fathom Five** (3450 Po'ipu Rd., 808/742-6991, www.fathomfive.com, 7 A.M.–5 P.M. daily) offers everything you could need for casual snorkeling or serious diving. They offer rentals for $6 daily and $35 a week. **Boss Frog's** (5022 Lawa'i Rd., 808/742-9111, www.bossfrog.com, 8 A.M.–5 P.M. daily) has rental snorkel gear for $8 a day or $30 a week. It's at Lawa'i Beach in the same building as the Beach House Restaurant.

SURFING
Po'ipu
BEACHES

If you choose to bring your own board or paddle out alone, the break at **Po'ipu Beach** is a good bet. It's rarely super intense or huge here, but of course evaluate the conditions before you paddle out. For a local spot with both left- and right-hand breaking waves, paddle out to **PK's** in front of Lawa'i Beach. The waves here mostly break as lefts, but the deepest section directly in front of the restaurant breaks as a right sometimes. Paddle out from the beach here but keep an eye out for the shallow reef below. The wave is usually dotted with locals,

A LIVING LEGEND: MARGO OBERG

Before women's surfing became the popular sport it is today, Margo Oberg was in the water paving the way for generations of female surfers behind her. A pioneer for women's surfing, Oberg dominated the sport for over three decades. Growing up in La Jolla, California, Margo Godfrey began surfing at 10 years old and won her first world championship title at 15. In her first surf contest she won the open women's division and a coed children's event, proving she had something special. She kept surfing, and by high school she had made a name for herself, winning the 1968 World Contest and the Western Surfing Association's women's title. Her early accomplishments were taking place when women's surfing was nowhere near as popular as it is today.

She moved to Kaua'i's south side in the early 1970s after marrying Steve Oberg in 1972. For three years Oberg spent time on Kaua'i, taking a break from surfing professionally. In 1975 she got back into the game, winning contests left and right. Throughout her career she won a total of seven world championships.

At home in Kaua'i, Oberg began giving surf lessons in the mid-'70s and after a few years started the Margo Oberg Surfing School. She had a strong business going that supported her life on Kaua'i. No longer competing, Oberg still lives on the south side of Kaua'i, helping out with surf contests and working with her surf school. Today, women's surfing has many more competitors, generally surfing at a higher talent level than they did 40 years ago. Oberg was truly a pioneer and an influence on many women on the surfing tour today.

so be mellow and respectful. During the right swell, the super heavy and intense right-hand breaking wave called **Acid Drops** is to the west of PK's. This wave is heavy but a coveted wave for experienced surfers. Except for Acid Drops, any of these spots are good options for experienced surfers, even children who like to surf.

SURF LESSONS AND GEAR

Po'ipu is a hot spot for surf lessons, and a Hawaiian vacation wouldn't be complete without at least trying to catch a few waves. Catching a wave is like flying, but on the ocean and in the sun. Give it a shot while you're out here. Several surf schools offer lessons at Po'ipu Beach, or the brave can rent a board and charge the waves alone.

For lessons from a company started by a true surf pioneer, try **Surf Lessons by Margo Oberg** (808/332-6100, www.surfonkauai. com) at Po'ipu Beach. You'll have the option of group lessons ($68), semi-private lessons ($90), or private lessons ($125). The surf school is known for satisfying customers and was recently named in *National Geographic Traveler Magazine* as one of the top 25 things to do on

Kaua'i. Lessons begin with a short instruction on land to learn the basics of the sport along with ocean safety. Soft boards and protective booties are provided. Instructors are locals who are previous or current professional surfers.

Also offering lessons at Po'ipu Beach is the **Garden Island Surf School** (808/652-4841, www.gardenislandsurfschool.com). They offer group lessons for $75, private lessons for $150, or $120 for two students. For something different try outrigger canoe surfing, where you'll catch waves in a canoe. They claim a 97 percent success rate.

Kaua'i Surf School (808/651-6032, www. kauaisurfschool.com) offers lessons at Po'ipu Beach as well as week-long surf clinics. For group classes of no more than four they charge $75 per person; a one-hour private lesson costs $100 while a two-hour private lesson is $175; and a two- to three-person semi-private lesson is $240. They provide a beginner surfboard, protective booties, and a rash guard.

To rent a board and paddle out by yourself contact **Progressive Expressions** (5428 Koloa Rd., 808/742-6041, 9 A.M.–9 P.M. Mon.–Sun.). Located in Koloa, they rent surfboards for $25 a day or $110 a week and body boards for $5 a day or $25 a week. **Nukumoi Beach & Surf Shop** (2080 Ho'one Rd., 808/742-8019, www.nukumoisurf.com, 7:45 A.M.–7 P.M. Mon.–Sat., 10:30 A.M.–6 P.M. Sun.) rents longboards and short boards, both hard and soft top, for $5–20.

KAYAKING
Po'ipu
You can kayak the south shore's coastline with **Outfitters Kauai** (2827A Po'ipu Rd., 808/724-9667, www.outfitterskauai.com) on their kayaking and whale-watching secluded beach adventure, which is available Tuesday–Saturday from mid-September through May. They use tandem, open cockpit or sit-on-top-type self-bailing kayaks with foot-pedal-controlled rudders to explore the coast. You'll paddle to secret beaches and snorkel and body surf at beaches that are only accessible by the water. Because the tours are done in the wintertime, whales sightings are common, as well as dolphin and sea turtle sightings. Price for adults is $152 and children 12–14 are $122.

Adventure Sports and Tours

ATVS
Koloa
A fun and wild thing to do is ride ATVs with **Kaua'i ATV** (5330 Koloa Rd., 877/707-7088, www.kauaiatv.com, 7:30 A.M.–5 P.M. daily, $125–175). They have a pretty large collection of vehicles and can take family groups or individuals. You'll go rambling through pastureland, mud, or dirt. They have clothing to loan, which means you don't have to get yours dirty. They also offer 'ohana (family) buggies to ride with your group, and lunch often happens at a waterfall.

ZIPLINING
Lawa'i
Adrenaline junkies can fly through the air with **Just Live** (P.O. Box 166, 808/482-1295, www.justlive.org, 8 A.M.–5 P.M. daily). The adventure sport company offers three different zipline eco-tours as well as a ropes course. The Zipline Treetop Tour takes place on seven different zipline courses and lets you walk over four canopy bridges for $120. The ziplines run up to 800 feet long and are suspended 60–80 feet in the air. The Wikiwiki Zip Tour utilizes three different ziplines, two of which are over 700 feet long, and three bridge crossings for $79. The Zipline Eco Adventure combines three ziplines, three bridges, rappelling, a monster swing, and rock-wall climbing for $125. Tours include snack and water.

BOAT TOURS
Po'ipu
Several boat tour companies cruise along Po'ipu waters. They also offer **whale-watching** from the months of December through April. **Captain Andy's Sailing Adventures** (4353 Waialo Rd., 808/335-6833, www.napali.com) offers various boat cruises, and each one includes whale-watching from December to May. During the winter months combine whale-watching with the two-hour Po'ipu Sunset Sail, which takes you down to the secluded Maha'ulepu Beaches and Kipu Kai. Adults cost $69, children $50, and kids under two are free. The sail includes live Hawaiian music, appetizers, beer, and wine. In season whales and dolphins are a common sight. **Blue Dolphin Charters** (4354 Waialo Rd., 808/245-8681, www.kauaiboats.com) offers a two-hour South Side Sunset Sail in the Po'ipu area. Food, cocktails, and romantic sunsets are enjoyed on this tour, along with whales in season. This company prefers December through March as whale season and rates run $62 for those 12 and up and $53 for ages 2–11.

GUIDED HIKING TOURS
Koloa
Kaua'i Nature Tours (808/742-8305, www.kauainaturetours.com) offers guided hikes in the Maha'ulepu area on the east end of the

south side. They also offer hikes in other parts of the island. The guides authored a geology book about Kaua'i, so they share insight into its geological formation and history. On this hike they'll take you around the area to see wildlife and enter a sinkhole where fossil-filled sediment has revealed island history. The 2.5-mile coastal walk begins after a 9 A.M. pickup at Po'ipu Beach Park. They provide lunch after a four-hour walk to a private beach cove, and snorkeling and swimming in Kawailoa Bay.

HORSEBACK RIDING
Po'ipu
A down-to-earth and peaceful way to explore the south side is with **CJM Country Stables** (1831 Po'ipu Rd., 808/742-6096, http://cjm-stables.com, 8 A.M.–5 P.M. daily for reservations). Located on the east end of Po'ipu, they offer scenic horseback rides through the forest and along the coast. Journeying into the undeveloped Maha'ulepu area, they take you along secluded beaches as well as into the green interior of the land. The Scenic Beach and Valley Ride includes beverages for $103, but you must bring your own lunch. They also offer the Secret Beach Picnic Ride ($130), where after riding your guide makes a good picnic lunch on a generally empty beach. Experienced riders can request private rides for $130 an hour.

Golf and Tennis

PO'IPU
Po'ipu Bay Golf Course
Golf fanatics will be in heaven at the Po'ipu Bay Golf Course (2250 Ainako St., 808/742-8711, www.poipubaygolf.com) at the Grand Hyatt Kaua'i Resort and Spa. Designed by ultimate course architect Robert Trent Jones Jr., the high-end course offers fabulous surroundings, mountain and ocean views, and open space on 210 oceanfront acres. The 18-hole course consists of 85 bunkers, five water hazards, and sometimes wild trade winds that are mother nature's way of testing your game. It is always perfectly groomed, and it's obvious here that it was designed, constructed, and maintained with attention to detail.

It's known to be not quite as tough as other courses on the island, but expert golfers as well as beginners will all have fun. A sacred *heiau* is on the grounds, along with ancient stone walls. Modern amenities are offered, like in-cart satellite navigation systems and an on-course beverage court, and daily clinics are offered by pros. The ocean-links-style course has over 30 acres of tropical plants and flowers with wonderful views. The large clubhouse is home to a golf shop open 6:30 A.M.–6:30 P.M. daily, locker room facilities, a restaurant, lounge, and club storage.

Tee times can be made up to 30 days in advance. First tee time is at 7 A.M. and they get everyone off the course at 6:15 P.M. The general public rate is $240, hotel guests pay $160, after noon the rate drops to $145, and after 2:30 P.M. it's $85. Club rentals are $55 and include Callaway, Titleist, Cobra, and TaylorMade. Carts are mandatory and appropriate attire (such as collared shirts) is required.

Kiahuna Golf Club
The Kiahuna Golf Club (2545 Kiahuna Plantation Dr., 808/742-9595, www.kiahunagolf.com) inland in Po'ipu offers 18 holes on a course also designed by Robert Trent Jones Jr. The course features remnants of ancient Hawaiian structures and good mountain views with glimpses of the ocean. The course was recently renovated, and although it's not quite as nice as Po'ipu Bay, it is more affordable and still satisfies. Notable sights on the course include the endangered state bird, the *nene* goose, which you may see wandering around the greens. The Hawaiian stilt and moorhen may also be seen here. To the left of the 15th fairway are the remnants of a house where a Portuguese immigrant lived during the early 19th century. There aren't any urban legends

SOUTH SHORE

paths leading to the first tee of the Kiahuna Golf Club

of a ghost here, but nearby is the crypt where he and his family were laid to rest.

The first tee time is 7 A.M. and the last is at 4:30 P.M., with players required to be off the course by 7 P.M. To play 18 holes with a cart costs $103, while golfers 17 and under can spend a day on the greens for $47. After 2 P.M. the price drops to $72. They offer a bounce-back rate of $88 for the duration of your stay, cart included. Club rentals are offered for $52 for 18 holes and $32 for 9 holes.

Kiahuna Swim and Tennis Club

At the Kiahuna Swim and Tennis Club (2290 Po'ipu Rd., 808/742-9533, www.kiahunatennisclub.com) players can utilize eight courts. Tennis lessons from a pro are offered and it's open to the public. Contact them for rates and to reserve court time.

Grand Hyatt Kaua'i Resort and Spa

The **Tennis Garden and Sports Center** at the Grand Hyatt Kaua'i (1571 Po'ipu Rd., 808/240-6391, 8 A.M.–noon and 1–6 P.M.) offers tennis clinics, lessons, and equipment rentals. One hour of court time daily is complimentary to all guests. Additional court time is available at $30 per hour. Call for other rates.

KALAHEO
Kukuilono Golf Course

The nine-hole Kukuilono Golf Course (854 Pu'u Rd., 808/332-9151, www.hawaiiweb.com, $7 adults, $3 under 17) is a very affordable place to spend the day on the greens. Donated to the state by Walter McBryde in 1919, the course was only the second built on Kaua'i. McBryde loved the course so much that he was buried by the eighth hole. A Japanese garden, many fragrant plumeria trees, and a Hawaiian rock collection are also on-site, and wonderful views of the ocean are enjoyed while playing. Carts can be rented for $6 a day. The course doesn't book tee times; it's first come, first served, with first play time at 6:30 A.M. For those renting clubs, last tee time is at 3 P.M., while those who brought their own can tee off at 4:30 P.M. The surroundings are gorgeous and the course is a fun one to play.

Yoga and Spas

KOLOA

Yoga is offered at a variety of places on the south side. For practice with an instructor who offers classes at several locations, try **Yoga at Koloa Hongwanji** (5521 Koloa Rd.) for hatha yoga. Classes are offered here Monday and Thursday at 8:30 A.M. for $15 for visitors and $12 for *kama'aina*. The same instructor also does classes at the Grand Hyatt Kaua'i's **Anara Spa** (1571 Po'ipu Rd.) in Po'ipu on Monday and Thursday mornings at 10:30 and Wednesday mornings at 9:30. The spa grounds are beautiful and exotic, and practice takes place in an open-air yoga pavilion. For more information contact Paul Reynolds at 650/773-3422 or check out his site at www.unlimited-ideas.com.

PO'IPU

There couldn't be a more peaceful place to practice yoga than on the beach. Yoga classes and group sessions are offered every Monday, Wednesday, and Friday at **Po'ipu Beach Park** (at the end of Kuai Road) under the ironwood trees. The session lasts from 9 to 10:30 A.M. Call **Beach Side Po'ipu** (808/651-5652) for more information.

Pure luxury can be indulged in at **Anara Spa** (1571 Po'ipu Rd., 808/240-6440, www.anaraspa.com, 7 A.M.–8 P.M. daily) at the Grand Hyatt Kaua'i. Services are offered both indoors and outdoors in the enchanting Lokahi Garden, with waterfalls, soaking pools, and open-air bungalows. You can find a full-service salon here, a spa boutique, a garden Vichy shower, a lap pool, steam rooms, saunas, fitness, and more. Hawaiian healing methods are integrated into the treatments as well as tropical scents. Relax in the lap of luxury and receive ultimate pampering here. This is a great vacation from your vacation.

Anara Spa offers massage in a variety of modalities ranging $160–235, including Hawaiian *lomilomi* and maternity. Facials with tropical scents and ingredients range $105–250. Body treatments run $165–320. Luxurious spa packages are also available and are pricey. Salon services cover all general services from nails to bridal styling and even kids' treatments for mother and daughter time.

Not far inland from the beach is **Poipu Day Spa** (3176 Po'ipu Rd., 808/742-8502, www.poipudayspa.com, 8 A.M.–6 P.M. Mon.–Sat.). Priding themselves on being a go-to spot for holistic health and beauty for visitors and residents, they specialize in massage, facials and waxing, manicures and pedicures, scrubs, wraps, and bridal services. They provide great services for lower prices than many of the big hotel spas. Massages range $50–130 while body treatments with exotic ingredients and scents run $55–185. Facials are priced $65–125. Call or visit the site for many other services, like anti-aging masks, waxing, and other treatments. A highlight here is the hot stone therapy.

KALAHEO

Inland in Kalaheo is **Kalaheo Yoga** (4427 Papalina Rd., 808/651-1568, www.kalaheoyoga.com). Here a wide variety and broad schedule of classes and yoga traditions are provided daily, so check the website for scheduling. An up-to-date calendar lists all classes. Single classes run $15, a four-class card costs $48, and a ten-class card costs $100. Workshops are also offered.

Sights

KOLOA
◖ Tunnel of Trees

Entering Koloa via Maluhia Road takes you through a grove of eucalyptus trees bending over the road and weaving together forming a natural tunnel. This is known as the Tunnel of Trees. The trees were brought in from Australia by the Knudsen family (said to be the largest landowner in the area) to stabilize the road because it was quite muddy at the time. If you can find a safe pull-off spot along the road, this is a wonderful photo opportunity if you can get a traffic-free shot. On very sunny days the tunnel is especially pretty with sparkling sunlight shining through the branches.

Koloa History Center

At the quaint Koloa History Center (Building 10 in the Waikomo Shops on Koloa Rd., www.oldkoloa.com, 9 A.M.–9 P.M. daily) get some insight into the history of Koloa via artifacts and photographs of the old days. Focused on the plantation era, since the area was home to Hawaii's first successful sugar mill, the center is very small. Yet the few small displays and photographs that offer background about the area are a good place to start a south side visit

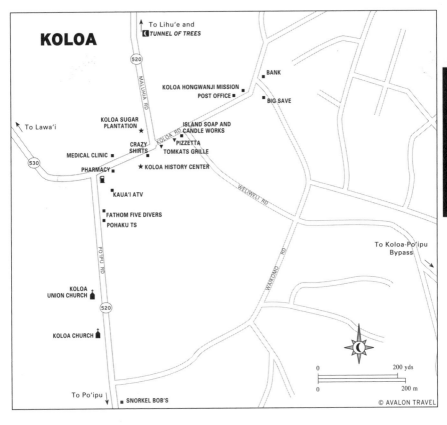

SOUTH SHORE

© JADE ECKARDT

The naturally formed Tunnel of Trees is beautiful on a sunny day.

for a deeper understanding during the rest of your stay. The visit won't take up much of your time. Near Waikomo Stream, the center is at the former site of an old hotel and provides picnic tables and a small garden to enjoy in a courtyard. Take notice of the old and huge monkey pod tree that shades much of the immediate area.

Koloa Sugar Plantation

All that's left of the foundation of Koloa town is the remnants of the old sugar mill that was the first successful attempt at a mill in Hawaii. Koloa was the birthplace of the Hawaiian sugar industry, and just across from the shops at the end of Maluhia Road is what's left of the mill, which was established in 1835. A plaque gives a brief history and explains the significance of the mill and sugar industry. You can see and touch sugar in its original form in the cluster of about 12 different varieties of sugar cane that grow on-site. There isn't really much to see here, but reading the plaque leaves visitors with an understanding of the town. A bronze

sculpture shows respect to the seven ethnic groups that worked on Hawaii's plantations: Hawaiians, Chinese, Japanese, Puerto Ricans, Filipinos, Koreans, and Portuguese. It's not a super-exciting place, but if you're shopping around Koloa it's worth a quick stop.

PO'IPU
◀ Spouting Horn

Near the end of Lawa'i Road shortly after the National Tropical Botanical Garden is the south side's claim to fame, the explosive Spouting Horn. Saltwater erupts through a hole in the lava sea cliffs, bursting very high into the air (the height of course depends on wave size). An interesting thing is that the sound follows just a second later from another hole that just blows air, and the timing is off from the initial water burst. Hawaiian legend says that a huge lizard called Mo'o (*mo'o* is Hawaiian for lizard) lived in this area. The lizard would eat anyone who tried to fish here. A man named Liko made that mistake, and Mo'o attacked him, only to get speared in the mouth and stuck where the blowhole is. According to the legend, the noise is the sound of the lizard's pain.

There is also ample parking here, a grassy lawn, and a picnic table, along with souvenir and jewelry booths. The main viewpoint is from the gated area just in front of the spout, where everyone huddles together to get the best shot. To the left of this is the end of the fence, where signs advise you not to go down to the cliffs because it's dangerous. Don't forget your camera for this one.

Koloa Heritage Trail

To explore about five million years of the south side's cultural history, follow the 10-mile-long Koloa Heritage Trail. Although Koloa is in the name, the trail is actually along the coast in Po'ipu. Weaving along the trail by car, foot, or bicycle, you will visit 14 cultural, historical, and geological sites of significance to the area. Each sight has a numbered marker, and it's a good idea to pick up the *Koloa Heritage Trail* guide, which offers descriptions of each site as you follow the trail. Call 888/744-0888

THE PEOPLE'S PRINCE

Prince Jonah Kuhio Kalanianaole was raised in Koloa. He was a worldly prince who attended the Royal School on Oʻahu and studied for four years at St. Matthews College in California. He also attended the royal Agricultural College in England and eventually graduated from a business school there. King David Kalakaua, also Kuhio's uncle, appointed Kuhio to a seat on the royal cabinet. Not long after, in 1893 the Hawaiian Kingdom was overthrown. Kuhio joined with fellow Hawaiians to restore the monarchy and the attempt was unsuccessful. He was sentenced to a year in prison while other activists were executed for treason. After getting out, Kuhio left the islands and traveled in South Africa for a few years with a vow to never return to his homeland as long as

it was inhospitable to its native people. When he came back to Hawaii it had been annexed as a territory of the United States.

For his efforts to help his people and work toward conserving the Hawaiian culture, Kuhio was nicknamed Ke Aliʻi Makaʻainana, meaning "prince of the people." While part of Congress, he was a leader in the passage of the Hawaiian Homes Commission Act, which provides land for native Hawaiians to live on. Prince Kuhio served as Hawaii's delegate to Congress from the early 20th century until his death in 1922.

He was loved and respected by his people for his efforts in working for the respect and rights of Hawaiians. Kuhio loved his home island and returned home whenever he could.

to pick up the trail guide or visit www.poipubeach.org/visitor_info/koloaheritagetrail to download a copy. It runs from Spouting Horn to down near Ainako Street to the east. It's best to obtain the guide if you want to explore it.

◖ Sunset in Poʻipu

Poʻipu has a clear view west, so there are many perfect places to watch the vibrant and colorful sunset. An ideal spot is at the **Beach House Restaurant** (5022 Lawaʻi Rd., 808/742-1424, www.the-beach-house.com, 5–10 P.M. daily, $20–40 entrées) on Lawaʻi Beach. The open-air restaurant serves dinner, pupu, and drinks overlooking the ocean. The best part of this place is the front lawn on the water, which offers tiki-torch-lit outdoor lounging while watching the sunset over wave riders at PK's. Although many locals and visitors like to spend the evening on the lawn here without eating at the restaurant, the lawn is technically part of the restaurant grounds.

At the very end of Lawaʻi Road is **Kukuiʻula Small Boat Harbor.** Here you will find a pavilion, a lawn backing a small strip of sand, picnic tables, and a small pier to watch the sunset over Spouting Horn. Swimming here isn't

recommended, but it is a great place to end the day watching the sun set over boats and the coastline.

Prince Kuhio Park and Hoʻai Heiau

Across from the ocean on Lawaʻi Road and across from Hoʻona Road is the birthplace of beloved Prince Kuhio. The well-maintained monument and park has a large lawn, a pond, a pavilion, the Hoʻai Heiau, and foliage. There isn't really much to see but it's a very pretty outdoor area worth meandering around, and a great place for culture and history buffs. The *heiau* is in great condition.

◖ National Tropical Botanical Garden

Consisting of both the McBryde and Allerton Gardens, the National Tropical Botanical Garden (visitors center, 4425 Lawaʻi Rd., 808/742-2623, www.ntbg.org, 8:30 A.M.–5 P.M. daily) is the only tropical plant research facility in the United States. In an effort to preserve, propagate, and dispense knowledge about tropical plants, the nonprofit organization is supported only by private donations. You'll want

© JADE ECKARDT

Even the entrance of the National Tropical Botanical Garden is worth exploring.

to remember your camera for this stop, and it's a fun place for photography fans to spend time trying to get good angles and lighting. If you don't have the time or the motivation to explore the gardens, go for a gander around the entrance. Even wandering around the entrance of the gardens is enjoyable. A pond with beautiful pink lilies and numerous varieties of tropical flowers to smell are here.

Over 6,000 tropical plant species flourish at the 259-acre **McBryde Garden.** Here you can explore a seemingly infinite array of plants and flowers ranging from bamboo to orchids. The gardens are divided into sections dedicated to medicinal and nutritional plants, herbs and spices, endangered species, fruits, and much more. Trams take visitors into the McBryde Garden every hour daily beginning at 9:30 A.M. until 2:30 P.M.; self-guided tours cost $20 for adults 13 years old and up, $10 for children 6–12, and children 5 and under are free.

The 80-acre **Allerton Garden** is named after John Allerton, who started the garden and was a member of a Mainland cattle-raising family that founded the First National Bank of Chicago.

The garden dates from the 1870s, when Queen Emma first planted here at one of her summer vacation homes. In 1938 Robert Allerton bought the property, and for the next two decades he and his son John cleared the land. John traveled the Pacific extensively, bringing back exotic plants to Kaua'i. Cutting through the property is the Lawa'i River, and small garden rooms and pools make it quite an enchanting experience. Here guided tours are offered beginning at 9 and 10 A.M. and 1 and 2 P.M. from Monday to Saturday. Reservations are necessary even about a week in advance, as they are often booked up, especially during holiday seasons. The price to visit the Allerton Garden is higher than the McBryde. It's $45 for those 13 years old and up and $20 for children 8–12. Children under eight are not allowed on the tour. Even for those who aren't generally interested in botany, this is an especially nice tour.

Drop by the visitors center across from Spouting Horn to check out the gift shop and displays in the former plantation manager's restored house. In here you can find Hawaiian crafts, Ni'ihau shell lei, and books

THE REAL SOUTH-SHORE LOCAL: THE WOLF SPIDER

The blind Kaua'i wolf spider is only found in three caves in the Koloa-Po'ipu area on the south side. A totally harmless spider without eyes, it was discovered in 1973. The Kauai cave wolf spider is both rare and unusual in that it is blind, unlike other wolf spiders on the island. To the left of the second fairway at the Kiahuna Golf Course are a couple of caves that are home to the spider. It's believed that the spider is at risk because of the pesticides seeping into its cave.

Wolf spiders get their name from being fast runners. Rather than catching their victims in webs like most spiders do, they chase their prey and catch it. Once they catch the prey, they bite the victim and inject poison through their fang-tipped chelicerae – which resemble miniature elephant tusks when seen through a lens. The venom paralyzes the prey and also deteriorates its tissues, breaking them down to a liquid, which the spider can suck out and swallow through its small mouth. They feed on insects like beetles and ants, leaving humans alone. And they're found exclusively on the south side of Kaua'i.

enjoyable experience. A unique combination of Japanese gardens, rocks used by Hawaiians for various purposes, abundant plumerias, and a public golf course, the park is beautiful and has a great ocean view. It was given to the people of Kaua'i in 1919 by Walter D. McBryde, a plantation owner, and a plaque in honor of his memory is on the grounds. After entering through the large stone and metal gate, go straight to find the gardens and memorial, or take the right at the fork in the road to find the golf clubhouse about a half mile up. The views in every direction are wonderful, but as you walk around exploring be mindful about flying golf balls and carts. Pink plumerias are usually flourishing here, and they smell exceptionally great. The collection of rocks used by Hawaiians for various functions is quite interesting and worth a gander. Near the front it says parking here is reserved for joggers, and if you're a runner this is a great place to get some exercise.

To get here turn onto Papalina Road in Kalaheo. About two miles up turn right at the large gate on the second Pu'u Road.

LAWA'I

Along the hillside at **Lawa'i International Center** (3381 Wawae Rd., 808/639-4300, www.lawaicenter.org), 88 Buddhist shrines replicate the 88 temples along the thousand-mile trail and pilgrimage route in Shikoku, Japan. The center was opened in 1904 in a small lush valley that had been used by Hawaiians for a place of worship for a long time and then by Japanese Taoists and Shintoists, but the area had become run-down and ignored until the 1960s, when a local woman organized the repair and eventual acquisition of the property. The area is lush and green, and dotted with orchids. During the tour you'll learn the history of the property and enjoy tea and local pastries. The tour begins through a small cave and leads to the miniature shrines, where previous visitors have left jewelry, shells, coins, and other offerings. The shrines can be viewed on the second and last Sundays of each month with tours taking place at 10 A.M., noon, and 2 P.M. There is no charge but the center accepts donations "with gratitude."

about Hawaii. Around this center, which was constructed in 1997 after the last center was destroyed in Hurricane 'Iniki, are the demonstration gardens, which are worth exploring on their own. Tours leave from the visitors center, and if you go on one remember good walking shoes and mosquito repellent, and scan the sky to determine if you want to bring an umbrella. Don't forget your camera.

KALAHEO
◖ Kukui O Lono Park

Oftentimes public parks aren't exceptional places to visit, but Kukui O Lono Park (Pu'u Rd., 6:30 A.M.–6:30 P.M. daily) is quite an

Shopping

Shopping on the south side is contained to several areas where shops are clustered together. The area is filled with many boutiques, galleries, souvenir shops, and clothing stores. Most daily shopping needs for residents are found in nearby Lihu'e.

KOLOA
Clothing

For a unique array of clothing check out **Jungle Girl** (5424 Koloa Rd., 808/742-9649, 9 A.M.–9 P.M. daily). They also have a collection of accessories and housewares. There are some locally made items as well as creations from around the world. If you're looking for aloha wear drop into **Pohaku Ts** (3430 Po'ipu Rd., 808/742-7500, www.pohaku. com, 10 A.M.–6 P.M. daily). They offer cotton aloha shirts that are designed, cut, and sewn on Kaua'i for men, women, and children. Suits galore decorate the inside of **South Shore Bikinis** (3450 Po'ipu Rd., 808/742-5200, 9 A.M.–7 P.M. daily), where they specialize in the tiny-backed Brazilian bikini. They also offer a variety of other suits along with beachwear for all ages, hats, sandals, and other accessories. A huge spectrum of Kaua'i and Hawaii souvenir shirts can be found in **Crazy Shirts** (5356 Koloa Road., 808/742-7161, www.crazyshirts.com, 10 A.M.–9 P.M.). A chain found throughout the islands, they sell shirts and a few other items for men, women, and children with a heavy Kaua'i and Hawaii theme.

Gifts, Crafts, and Souvenirs

Island-style souvenirs and gifts can be found at **Hula Moon Gifts** (5426 Koloa Rd., 808/742-9298, 9 A.M.–9 P.M. Mon.–Sat. and 10 A.M.–9 P.M. Sun.). They sell unique locally made crafts, gifts, and jewelry. At the **Emperor's Emporium** (5330 Koloa Rd. #3, 808/742-8377, 9 A.M.–9 P.M. daily) you will find a resort-style store offering jewelry, gifts, and clothing. The scent radiating out of the shop will draw you into **Island Soap and**

Candle Works (Koloa Rd., 808/742-1945, www.kauaisoap.com, 9 A.M.–9 P.M. daily). The locally run store has shops island-wide where they manufacture natural Hawaiian botanical products, beeswax candles, and other gifts. While shopping you'll get a behind-the-scenes look into how it's all made.

Wine

The lovely **Wine Shop** (5470 Koloa Rd., 808/742-7305, www.thewineshopkauai.com, 10 A.M.–7 P.M. Mon.–Sat.) in Koloa offers a great selection of wine along with other spirits. Fun and cute wine accessories can also be purchased here, along with gourmet foods to snack on while enjoying wine. Nice gift baskets are put together here.

General Store

The Koloa **Big Save** (5516 Koloa Rd., 808/742-1614, 6 A.M.–11 P.M. daily) offers a lot more than food. They have a decent array of basic fishing gear and poles. They also have limited snorkel gear, beach gear, stationery, and other basic needs.

PO'IPU
Galleries and Home Decor

For a lovely selection of island-style home decor check out **Aspire Furniture** (808/245-9015, www.aspirefurniture.com, 10 A.M.–5 P.M. Mon.–Sat.). From artwork to furniture to decorations, the store helps bring the island into the home and also offers interior design services. More island-style merchandise can be found at **Bungalow 9** (808/742-1961, www. bungalownine.com, 11 A.M.–9 P.M. daily). Here a selection of home accessories, clothing, gifts, and more can be found with a modern beach theme.

Admire the work of local crafters and artists at **Halele'a** (808/742-9525, www.haleleagallery.com). Island artisans and designers have their creations in stock here, from wall art to koa furniture and apparel. A wonderful source for locally made products is **Palm Palm** (808/742-1131, www.palmpalmkauai.com, 10 A.M.–9 P.M. daily). It's well stocked with fashionable clothing, bath products, high-end jewelry, and quality accessories, and the owner has been in the jewelry industry for a decade and brings style to the shop.

All of these shops are in the **Kukui'ula Shopping Village** (Ala Kalanikaumaka St., 808/742-9545, www.kukuiulavillage.com), open 10 A.M.–9 P.M. daily.

Clothing, Accessories, and Swimwear

In the **Kukui'ula Shopping Village** lies a selection of clothing ranging from mainstream gear to unique island-style apparel. For high-quality aloha wear stop at **Tommy Bahama** (808/742-8808, www.tommybahama.com, 10 A.M.–9 P.M. daily). The store offers high-end casual island wear for men and women. Swimwear is available at **Bikini Planet** (808/742-8860, 10 A.M.–8 P.M. daily), where you can find a huge selection of Brazilian bikinis and many other styles, along with beach accessories, workout apparel, and some clothing and jewelry.

Hopefully you brought sunglasses to Kaua'i because you'll need them. If not there's the **Sunglass Hut** (808/742-9065 www.sunglasshut.com, 10 A.M.–9 P.M. daily), which offers them in any style you could want. A combination of clothing and art can be found at **Hawaiian Salt** (808/742-6030, 10 A.M.–9 P.M. daily). Clothing here is mostly for visitors, with a lot of gear boasting Kaua'i and Po'ipu local icons. Hats, bath products, and jewelry are also sold here. In **Quicksilver** (808/742-8088, 10 A.M.–9 P.M. daily) you will find a huge selection of men's, women's, and children's surf-themed clothing for both in the water and out. Accessories like sunglasses and hats and sandals are also sold here.

Arts, Crafts, and Jewelry

At the intriguing **Red Koi Collection** (808/742-2778, www.redkoicollection.com, 10 A.M.–9 P.M. daily) you'll find an array of fine arts, from hand-painted silks to original paintings, to koa furniture and jewelry. The high-end products make it feel like a hip and modern island museum combined with the home decor of a wealthy world traveler. The prices are high, but it's at least a nice place to window shop.

Amazing Kaua'i outdoor photography decorates **Scott Hanft Photography** (808/742-9515, www.scotthanftoutdoorphotogallery.com, 10 A.M.–8 P.M. daily). Here you will find wonderful air, underwater, nature, and landmark shots from around the island. Originals and prints are both available, along with magnets, cards, jewelry, and more. Beautiful and elegant jewelry is on display at **Ocean Opulent Jewelry** (808/742-9992, www.oceanpoipu.com, 10:30 A.M.–9 P.M. daily), where semiprecious stones, freshwater pearls, and other stones are set in gold, silver, and platinum. Unique gifts and accessories are available here.

These shops are also in the Kukui'ula Shopping Village.

LAWA'I
General Store

The small **Lawai General Store** (3586 Koloa Rd., 808/332-7501, 6 A.M.–11 P.M. daily) sells snacks, beer, ice, and some general store needs. The shop is tiny and local, and much of the stock is covered in dust. They're known for their Spam *musubi,* a local concoction of a slice of Spam on top of rice.

KALAHEO
Music

In Kalaheo you won't find much shopping. **Scotty's Music** (2-2436 Kaumualii Hwy. #A3, 808/332-0090, 11 A.M.–4 P.M. Mon.–Sat.) offers an array of instruments, guitars, and ukuleles. Ukuleles are a great take-home souvenir for music lovers.

Liquor Store

Kujo's Mini Mart (2-2459 Kaumualii Hwy., 808/332-9220, 5 A.M.–11 P.M. daily) has the usual minimart array of beer, snacks, and not much else.

Bath and Beauty

A really nice shop is **Malie** (2-2560 Kaumualii Hwy. #B, 808/332-6220, www.malie.com, 9 A.M.–4 P.M. Mon.–Fri.). The locally owned line of Hawaiian luxury spa products offers glorious decadent scents from the islands with their skin care line, hand soap, and other pampering products. They use organically grown ingredients.

Entertainment

PO'IPU
Lu'au

A night well spent is at the **Grand Hyatt Kaua'i Lu'au** (1571 Po'ipu Rd., 808/240-6456, www.grandhyattkauailuau.com). No Hawaiian vacation would be complete without a *lu'au*, and on Thursdays and Sundays 6–8:30 P.M., guests are treated to cocktails and music, a *lu'au* dinner with traditional foods from Hawaii and the Pacific, along with arts and crafts and bar drinks. This includes a lovely show of Polynesian dancing, hula, and fire knife dancing.

Bars and Live Music

The Grand Hyatt Kaua'i is also home to several lounges and bars, including **Stevenson's Library.** Here you can find live jazz nightly 8–11 P.M. and enjoy it while sipping cocktails. Live music happens at the **Seaview Terrace** 6–8 P.M. daily. An evening here begins with a torch-lighting ceremony, and performances may include a Hawaiian soloist, Hawaiian duet, or a children's hula show.

Surrounded by flaming tiki torches and the Moir Gardens of the Kiahuan Plantation Resort, the **Plantation Gardens Bar and Restaurant** (2253 Poipu Rd., 808/742-2121, www.pgrestaurant.com, 5 P.M.–9:30 P.M. daily) mixes classic elegance with tropical nights. The restaurant and full bar feature a unique and delicious Pacific Rim menu with a Hawaiian flair. You can sit outside on the lanai and enjoy specially cocktails, tropical drinks, wine, and beer.

At **Lavas** (inside Sheraton Kaua'I, 2440 Ho'onani Rd., 808/742-1661 or 800/782-9488, www.sheraton-kauai.com) you can enjoy views of the sunset along with handcrafted and unique tropical drinks. Because it's located inside the Sheraton, there's a Sheraton drink of the day that changes daily. Happy hour happens daily from 3–5 P.M. and again from 9–11 P.M.

KALAHEO
Live Music

There really isn't much going on in Kalaheo at night, but **Kalaheo Steak & Ribs** (4444 Papalina Rd., 808/332-4444, www.kalaheosteakandribs.com) has live music every Friday and Saturday at 7 P.M. Along with drinks at the saloon and appetizers it adds up to a night out.

Food

KOLOA
American

Offering a nice enough setting with a garden and fishpond, **Tomkats Grille** (5404 Koloa Rd., 808/742-8887, 10:30 A.M.–midnight daily, last call at 11:15 P.M., $10–27) serves up the usual American fare. Fresh local fish, burgers, grilled sandwiches, steaks, lots of meat dishes, fried appetizers, and, well, you get the idea. There's a large beer selection as well as cocktails. The food here is far from spectacular, but it's not bad. It will fill your stomach.

Italian

If you're in the mood for really good pizza, head over to (**Pizzetta** (5408 Koloa Rd.,

808/742-8881, www.pizzettarestaurant.com, 11 A.M.–9 P.M. Mon.–Fri., 11 A.M.–10 P.M. Sat. and Sun., $11–17 for dinner, $17–25 pizza) for great pizza and other wonderful Italian dishes, such as calzones and chicken parmigiana. In honor of the Kaua'i chickens a custom beer has been brewed for the eatery called Rooster Brew, which nicely complements the dishes. The atmosphere is laid-back and casual, but you can dress up a bit if you want to. Nestled in a historic clapboard Koloa building, the restaurant is central in Koloa town. The hot spinach and artichoke dip is always great. Pizzetta uses homemade sauces, and most flavors come in the option of calzone or pizza. Vegetarians will have a sufficient array of options here.

Seafood and Local Cuisine

Koloa Fish Market (5482 Koloa Rd., 808/742-6199, 10 A.M.–6 P.M. Mon.–Fri., till 5 P.M. on Sat.) offers fish, of course, along with plate lunches and other local dishes like *laulau, poke,* cucumber salad, and sashimi. The selection is rather limited, but it's really popular with locals. It's a good option for trying out local food. Lunches run $8–11.There isn't really anywhere to sit down—it's order at the counter and take out—but what could be better with beaches to enjoy lunch on?

Local-style **Sueoka's Snack Shop** (5392 Koloa Rd., 808/742-1112, 9 A.M.–8 P.M. Tues.–Sat. and 9 A.M.–4 P.M. Sun., $5–10) is a great place for a quick stop to pick up local food. They serve teriyaki burgers, curries, chili, and plate lunches. They also have sliced up fruit available in the same style as small New York City delis. Drinks, chips, and the usual convenience store snacks are also available. A good and affordable option for a beach lunch.

Local quick eats are available at the **Big Save** (5516 Koloa Rd., 808/742-1614, 10 A.M.–6 P.M. daily), which provides groceries (of course) along with ready-made sushi rolls, hard-boiled eggs, bentos, rice, and a few other ready-to-eat meals. If you like local to-go food you'll find it here at an affordable price and decent quality, but don't expect really high quality.

Ice Cream and Shave Ice

For a treat try **Koloa Shave Ice** (Po'ipu Rd., 808/651-7104, 9 A.M.–9 P.M. daily). They generally serve up a very finely shaved cone, which is the make-or-break aspect with shave ice. The flavor selection is good, but service can be a bit slow and cold sometimes. It's worth a stop while on the south side because the treat is usually good, but it's hit or miss on the overall experience.

Koloa Mill Ice Cream and Coffee (5424 Koloa Rd., 808/742-6544, www.koloamill. com, 7 A.M.–9 P.M. daily, $4 for a single scoop) serves up items to satisfy the sweet tooth and provide a caffeine fix. They pride themselves on serving only Hawaiian-made foods, such as Kaua'i coffee, ice cream made on Maui with a lot of good local flavors, and locally made baked goods and snacks. The ice cream shop atmosphere is very classic, and free wireless Internet. From 7 to 9 A.M. they offer 50 percent off of any coffee drink.

Farmers Market

Sunshine Farmers Market in the **Koloa Ball Park** (noon Mon.) offers fresh produce and fruits. You can also find an abundance of locally made crafts, some ready-to-eat food, and other locally made food. Bring your own shopping bag.

PO'IPU
American

A wonderful atmosphere can be found at **K** **Keoki's Paradise** (2360 Kiahuna Plantation Dr., 808/742-7534, www.keokisparadise.com, 11 A.M.–10:30 P.M. daily), where ponds, a small waterfall, greenery, and a large beautiful tree make a very relaxing vibe. Here you'll find a mix of visitors and locals enjoying a drink at the bar. Service is friendly and good, and the food is pretty good but not spectacular. They have nachos, steaks, burgers, and seafood in generally large portions. It's in the Poipu Shopping Village with outdoor and open-air yet covered seating. The prices are pretty broad here and range from $8 appetizers that can fill you up if you're not starving all the way to $38 for lobster tail, but you can fill up for about $15.

The good thing about **Brennecke's Beach Broiler** (2100 Ho'one Rd., 808/742-7588, www.brenneckes.com, lunch and dinner daily) is right across from Po'ipu Beach. An open-air eatery on the second story of a building across the street from the ocean, the restaurant offers great views for lunch and dinner. Other than that it's okay, not terrible and certainly not wonderful. They serve up seafood and steak, other meats, pastas, and burgers. You could say they're famous for their *kiawe*-broiled meat and chicken. A children's menu is offered for lunch and dinner. Lunch ranges $10–20 for entrées and dinner is $16–30.

Below the broiler is **Brennecke's Beach Deli** (808/742-1582, opens 7 A.M., variable closing time), which serves up made-to-order sandwiches, cold beer, a breakfast burrito, snacks, and coffee. A meal from here is best enjoyed across the street at the beach. They offer picnic lunches for those who call ahead to take on a hike or long day at the beach. You can get a meal here for $5–10.

The popular Kaua'i eatery **Bubba Burgers** (808/742-6900, www.bubbaburger.com, 10:30 A.M.–9 P.M.) serves...burgers! They will relish your buns and they also cheat tourists, drunks, and attorneys. Well, that's what they claim on their slogan but it's not true; they're actually really nice here. The food isn't necessarily spectacular, but the burgers are good and filling, and seem to remain so on a regular basis. The burgers come in different weights so you know what to expect and range $3.50–7.25. They even offer a garden burger. They use only grass-fed Kaua'i beef and have the usual burger joint sides like shakes, sodas, and chicken sandwiches.

Asian Fusion

Located in the Grand Hyatt Kaua'i, **Yum Cha Asian Eatery** (1571 Po'ipu Rd., 808/240-6456, 5:30–9:30 P.M. Wed.–Sun.) offers a unique take on Asian dishes. Hawaiian elements are added to many dishes, and the menu consists of starters, dim sum, tempura, soups and salads, main dishes, and more. Vegetarians will find enough here to fill their bellies. Main dishes range $14–32. The atmosphere is casual and it's a good place for family or groups.

Hawaiian Regional

Two farm-to-table restaurants are **Merriman's Downstairs Cafe** (808/742-2856, www.merrimanshawaii.com, opens at 11 A.M. daily for lunch and dinner, $12–22) in Kukui'ula Shopping Village and **《 Merriman's Fish House** (808/742-8385, opens at 5:30 P.M. daily for dinner, $25–35), where good food and sustainability are combined to produce high-quality Hawaiian regional cuisine. Both eateries utilize locally grown or caught ingredients, constituting 90 percent of the food they use. The downstairs café offers casual dining while the upstairs fish house offers mountain and ocean views with a full bar. They purchase produce daily.

Overlooking the ocean is the **《 Beach House Restaurant** (5022 Lawa'i Rd., 808/742-1424, www.the-beach-house.com, 5–10 P.M. daily, $20–40 entrées). The open-air restaurant has a prime oceanfront location on Lawa'i Beach on a front lawn dotted with tiki torches that is a perfect spot for watching the sunset (although you can't bring drinks out there). Opening later in the day just for dinner, the Beach House serves seafood, steaks, and even a roasted duck dish. Vegetarians don't have many option here and what they do have is limited to the appetizers. As long as vegetarians aren't starving when they come here they probably won't mind because the atmosphere is awesome. It can get pretty crowded, so reservations are a very good idea. They also have a great wine list.

The peaceful tropical atmosphere at **Plantation Gardens Restaurant and Bar** (2253 Po'ipu Rd., 808/742-2121, www.pgrestaurant.com, 5:30–9 P.M. Mon.–Sat.) accompanies a lovely meal of good food. They serve up seafood and steaks for dinner and have a good variety of Pacific-themed appetizers. Surrounded by the tiki-torch-lit Moir Gardens at Kiahuna Plantation Resort, the rather small restaurant offers mostly outdoor seating, which is the nicest anyway. They have a nice wine list and great bar along with tasty desserts. All of their produce is said to be organically and locally grown. Entrées run $20–30 and reservations are a good idea.

Always a good choice is **《 Roy's Bar and**

Grill (808/742-5000, www.roysrestaurant.com, 5:30 A.M.–9:30 P.M. daily, $25–35) in the Poipu Shopping Village. The elegant yet island-style restaurant serves seafood, steaks, and pastas cooked perfectly consistently. Menu specials change nightly, with fresh local fish, produce, meats, and game made into creative dishes. Vegetarians are treated to a special meat-free menu with appetizers, main courses, and specials. Service is always great and you can bring your own wine if they don't carry that particular kind. Roy's doesn't require exceptionally formal attire, but don't roll in straight off the beach.

Italian

At the elegant ◖ **Dondero's** (1571 Po'ipu Rd., 808/240-6456, 6–10 P.M. Mon.–Sat., $18–42) you will be treated to a wonderful meal with a romantic and high-end atmosphere. You can sit outdoors under the stars, overlooking the ocean, or enjoy your meal inside with Italian decor of murals and tiles similar to a villa in Italy. They have a great wine list to complement their fresh local fish, veal, pastas, and decadent desserts. Vegetarians can find plenty to eat here. It's in the Grand Hyatt Kaua'i, and dressing up is required, meaning covered shoes and collared shirts for men.

Spanish

Okay, so the food here isn't entirely Spanish, but the style of eating tapas is. ◖ **Josselin's Tapas Bar and Grill** (808/742-7117, www.josselins.com, 5–10 P.M. daily, $8–32) in Kukui'ula Shopping Village inspires sharing with friends and family by serving up tapas, a variety of small dishes served to share. The chef has won numerous awards with his Pacific-inspired eateries, often named the best of the best. From fresh fish tapas to tapas made in the wood-burning oven, Chef Josselin has it covered. The truly exotic array includes tapas, scallops, oxtail, vegetarian tapas, duck, fish, and so much more. They also serve lovely *liliko'i* and pomegranate sangrias along with other signature drinks.

Ice Cream and Shave Ice

Tropical and traditional flavored ice cream and sorbet are on offer at ◖ **Lappert's Hawaii Ice Cream and Coffee** (Kukui'ula Village, 808/741-1272, www.lappertshawaii.com, 6 A.M.–10 P.M. daily, $4 single scoop). The shop originated on Kaua'i and now has outlets statewide. Its regular flavors have about 16 percent butterfat while the fruit flavors have 8 percent, making it very creamy ice cream. There's a wide array of delicious flavors; sample a few before making a decision. They let you take freshly scooped pints home, and you can mix and match flavors. This location sells coffee, too.

For a local treat head to ◖ **Uncle's Shave Ice and Smoothies** (Kukui'ula Shopping Village, 808/742-2364, www.uncleskauai.com, 11 A.M.–9 P.M. daily, $4–8), where you can expect just what the name says. Shave ice and fruit smoothies are made to cool a hot Hawaiian day. They offer 25 shave ice flavors, with extras like cream caps (really good), fruit, and ice cream. They also sell other snacks like caramel apple bites and popcorn. Sugar-free syrups sweetened naturally with stevia are a progressive option here.

Quick Bites

Shrimp is a constant throughout Hawaii, and the south side's **Savage Shrimp** (Kukui'ula Village, 808/212-2197, www.savageshrimp. com, 11 A.M.–9 P.M. daily, $12) serves up shrimp plates, fish tacos, shrimp tacos, fish and chips, and fried shrimp (am I sounding like Bubba Gump?). A favorite with beach-going locals, it used to be in a lunch wagon and now has a permanent home.

If you're in the mood for classic American fare, try **Dude Dogs** (Kukui'ula Shopping Village, 808/742-9438, www.dudedogs.com, $4–6). Here you can find hot dogs in a variety of ways with twists like beer brat mustard and passion fruit wasabi mustard. Chili is also available.

Living Foods Market and Cafe (Kukui'ula Shopping Village, 808/742-2323, www.livingfoodskauai.com, 8 A.M.–8 P.M. daily) prides itself in being a gourmet food store, not health food store, even though they offer normal snacks like regular candy bars. Here you will find standard packaged foods like drinks and snacks, along with homemade breads and dips, and made-to-order pizzas, sandwiches, and more. The shop is spacious and elegant, but it's rather expensive. They have a good array of wines and liquors. Outside tables are provided.

KALAHEO
American

The always-good 【 **Kalaheo Cafe** (2-2560 Kaumuali'i Hwy., 808/332-5858, www.kalaheo.com, 6:30 A.M.–2:30 P.M. Mon.–Sat., 6:30 A.M.–2 P.M. Sun., and dinner at 5 P.M. Tues.–Sat., $2–13) is the south side's answer to the cute, local, friendly café where you can relax reading the paper or have Sunday brunch with 10 friends. To speed along the large influx of customers, you order at the counter and then choose a table, but there's no rush to get out of the spacious hardwood floor café, which is adorned with local art and music. Coffee is served in varied forms, along with eggs, breakfast burritos, waffles, pastries, and sides. Salads and off-the-grill specialty sandwiches are available for lunch, along with bottled beer. Vegetarians can find a decent array of meat-free options. Service is good, and the only downfall is that they charge extra for additional plates.

The name says it all, almost, at **Kalaheo Steaks and Ribs** (4444 Papalina Road., 808/332-4444, www.kalaheosteakandribs.com, Tues.–Sun. 4–10 P.M., dinner 5–9:30 P.M., $17–36). For three decades the restaurant has been serving ribs, steaks, fresh fish, pastas, appetizers, and salads. As one would expect, there isn't much for vegetarians here, but there is a nice array of salads and one vegetarian entrée of veggie stir-fry with soba noodles, so meat-free diners can enjoy a night here. A full bar, the Saloon, adds to the fun. Entrées run $18–29. The atmosphere also fits the name here—a knotty pine interior with the usual steakhouse theme. At the Saloon, happy hour is held 4–6 P.M. daily with a menu of appetizers.

Italian

An island highlight, not just south side, is 【 **Pomodoro Ristorante** (2-2514 Kaumuali'i Hwy., 808/332-5945, 5:30–9:30 P.M. daily), a small gem hidden in Kalaheo, and yes, it's run by real Italians. Known for serving the best Italian food on the island, the owners have created a delightful environment as well as an upscale fee. A full bar is offered, and the ravioli is amazing, as are most dishes. The husband and wife owners are very friendly. If you have children don't be deterred by the quiet and small eatery; the wife has expressed how much she loves kids. Pomodoro is on the second floor of a small shopping center with a very nice atmosphere including Italian music and dim lighting. Since it doesn't take very long to get around Kaua'i, Pomodoro is worth making the trip to even when you're on another side of the island.

A local favorite is 【 **Brick Oven Pizza** (2-2555 Kaumuali'i Hwy., 808/332-8561, 11 A.M.–10 P.M. Tues.–Sun., 4–10 P.M. Mon.), and it's a good place for a family night or a casual date. A very kid-friendly spot, it offers free dough for kids to play with during dinner. They offer a pretty big selection of pizza, beer, and wine, and you can get your crust in white or wheat dough as well as basted with garlic butter. The decor has a countryside feel, and the walls are covered in license plates from around the country that almost all say something Hawaii-related on them. All-you-can-eat buffets on Monday and Thursday nights are fun.

Hawaiian Local

Ohana Cafe (2-2436 Kaumuali'i Hwy., 808/332-7602, $8–13, 11 A.M.–2:30 P.M. and 5–9 P.M.) serves up a combo of American food like burgers and fries, along with local food like saimin, oxtail soup, teriyaki meats, and big and sweet desserts. The atmosphere is simple, service is friendly, and the prices are good. Not gourmet, but good, simple, local food with no frills.

Farmers Market

Sunshine Farmers Market in the **Kalaheo Neighborhood Center** (3 P.M. Tues.) offers fresh produce and fruits. You can also find an abundance of locally made crafts, some ready-to-eat food, and other locally made food. Bring your own shopping bag.

Information and Services

POSTAL SERVICES

There are two United States Post Offices on the south side: **Kalaheo Post Office** (4489 Papalina Rd., 808/332-5800, 9 A.M.–3:30 P.M. Mon.–Fri., 9 A.M.–11:30 A.M. Sat.) and the **Koloa Post Office** (5485 Koloa Rd., 800/275-8777, 9 A.M.–4 P.M. Mon.–Fri., 9 A.M.–11:30 A.M. Sat.). Both post offices offer the usual shipping needs and basic packaging.

INTERNET ACCESS AND PHOTO SERVICES

Wireless Internet is available with your own computer at **Koloa Mill Ice Cream and Coffee** (5424 Koloa Rd., 808/742-6544, www.koloamill.com, 7 A.M.–9 P.M. daily) and at **Starbucks** (2360 Kiahuna Plantation Dr., 808/742-5144, 5 A.M.–8 P.M. daily) in Poipu Shopping Village. You can also bring your laptop to **Kalaheo Cafe** (2-2560 Kaumuali'i Hwy., 808/332-5858, www.kalaheo.com, 6:30 A.M.–2:30 P.M. Mon.–Sat., 6:30 A.M.–2 P.M. Sun., dinner Tues.–Sat.).

For instant vacation memory gratification, try **Poipu One Hour Photo** (3450 Po'ipu Rd. #C, 808/742-8918). Located in the Poipu Plaza, they develop prints off of memory cards.

Getting There and Around

BY CAR

The most convenient way to get around the south side is by car. Highway 50 heads west straight out of Lihu'e and runs through Kalaheo all the way to the end of the road far past the south side. To get down to Koloa and Po'ipu you can turn down Maluhia Road and drive through the pretty tree tunnel, or turn down Koloa Road and drive through lush Lawa'i. Rental cars are the best bet here and are available at the airport. Gas prices go up the farther west you go, so it's a good idea to fill up in Lihu'e; a tankful will most likely last the day.

BY BUS

The **Kaua'i Bus** (808/241-6410, www.kauai.gov/Transportation, 5:27 A.M.–10:40 P.M. Mon.–Fri. and 6:21 A.M.–5:50 P.M. Sat., Sun., and holidays) runs island-wide with many stops in Kalaheo, Koloa, and Po'ipu. Check the website for bus stops and times. The bus is a green, convenient, and affordable way to get around. Fares are $1 for children and seniors, and $2 for the general public. Monthly passes are also available.

BY TAXI

No matter which company you choose, Hawaii's standard taxi rates apply of $3 per mile and 40 cents per minute, per van. **South Shore Taxi** (808/742-1525) offers island-wide tours along with services for individual and large groups. **Pono Taxi** (808/634-4744, www.ponotaxi.com) will take you on a south-side sightseeing tour as well as usual taxi runs.

HITCHHIKING

Hitchhiking is legal on Kaua'i, as long as you stay off the paved part of the road. This could work well just around the south side, where it's a short distance between a lot of beaches, sights, and shopping. If you try to thumb it all the way out to Polihale, there's a good chance of walking a very long way in the scorching sun. Remember; hitchhiking can be very dangerous, so women and children should never hitchhike alone. Since a ride is never guaranteed with hitchhiking, just hop on the bus.

SOUTH SHORE

WEST SIDE

Locally known as the west side, Kaua'i's leeward coast is Hawaii's take on the wild west. A geologist's dreamland, the landscape out here contradicts itself with rolling white beaches, vast canyons, deep rivers, and dry desert land. The west and driest side of the island is a land without frills, but it offers something unique for art buffs, history fans, nature lovers, and beach bums alike. Everyone who visits the west side leaves with a story unique from those of other parts of the island. Art enthusiasts can view local creations and mingle with their crafters. Those hot for history can take a historical walking tour, browse an antiques shop, and visit landmarks that mark the change that led Hawaii to its current state. The outdoors types can camp in the mountains or at the beach, hike, bird-watch, and bicycle. Beach bums can surf, swim, stand-up paddle, and snorkel.

From Hanapepe to the west end of the Na Pali Coast the sun is almost always shining, and the red dirt tints everything from vehicles to buildings. The large number of historic buildings, plantation-style homes, and agricultural areas make the region seem like it is frozen in time. Most buildings have a story to tell, and towns are small, low-key, and quiet. Many locals live in this area, and it's generally not hard to define who is a resident and who's just passing through. From the longtime artist residents in Hanapepe who relocated to the area to paint Kaua'i's beauty, to the west-side born-and-raised Hawaiians in Waimea, locals are generally friendly and warm.

Hanapepe town and the still-active Port Allen near Kalaheo welcome visitors to the west.

© JADE ECKARDT

HIGHLIGHTS

LOOK FOR ◖ TO FIND RECOMMENDED SIGHTS, ACTIVITIES, DINING, AND LODGING.

◖ **Glass Beach:** The sand here is exquisite, with a colorful, sparkling layer of beach glass atop dark sand. Swimming here is best in the tide pool (page 150).

◖ **Salt Pond Beach Park:** This family-friendly beach is an ideal place for children to swim. It has a protected swimming area, a big tide pool, a large lawn, lifeguards, and restrooms (page 151).

◖ **Kekaha Beach Park:** Marking the beginning of about 15 miles of white sand, Kekaha Beach Park offers all the amenities for a full day at the beach: pavilions, picnic tables, a barbecue pit, and a lifeguard (page 153).

◖ **Polihale State Park:** Polihale State Park is a tropical dream any time of day. The fine white sand seems endless, the water is almost always a bright blue, and the sacred cliffs provide a unique backdrop. To get the best the beach has to offer arrive around 3 P.M. and stay to watch the vibrant sunset (page 153).

◖ **Snorkeling the Na Pali Coast:** Hop on a boat with Captain Andy's Sailing Adventures or any of the other outfitters in Port Allen for an unforgettable snorkeling trip along the Na Pali Coast (page 155).

◖ **Stand-Up Paddling on the Waimea River:** Explore the Waimea River on a stand-up paddle board. Kaua'i Wind and Waves offers both lessons and paddle board rentals. The leisurely paddle is a workout, but it is also a calm cruise through nature without having to ride sea waves (page 158).

◖ **Waipo'o Falls and the Canyon Trail:** Hikers who endure the trek to Waipo'o Falls will be rewarded with an 800-foot double waterfall (page 161).

◖ **Ni'ihau Helicopters:** Virtually the only way to explore Ni'ihau's beaches is through a tour with Ni'ihau Helicopters. Owned by the owner of Ni'ihau, the company offers beach-combing and snorkeling tours only with a full load of five (page 165).

◖ **Waimea Canyon State Park Overlook:** The views down into the vast and deep canyon from Waimea Canyon State Park Overlook are not to be missed. Make sure to take Waimea Canyon Drive inland because the sights from there are just as valuable (page 169).

◖ **Kalalau and Pu'u O Kila Overlooks:** Two overlooks in Koke'e State Park, regarded as the best views in the Pacific, open your eyes to untouched, looming vertical mountains reaching down to the sea (page 170).

◖ **Art Night in Hanapepe:** Around 16 galleries open their doors for a celebratory night every Friday. From 6 to 9 P.M. you can browse local art and socialize with locals (page 173).

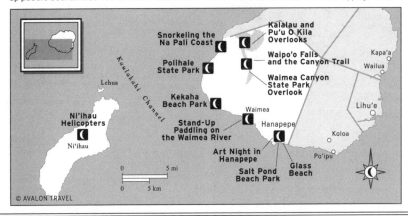

© AVALON TRAVEL

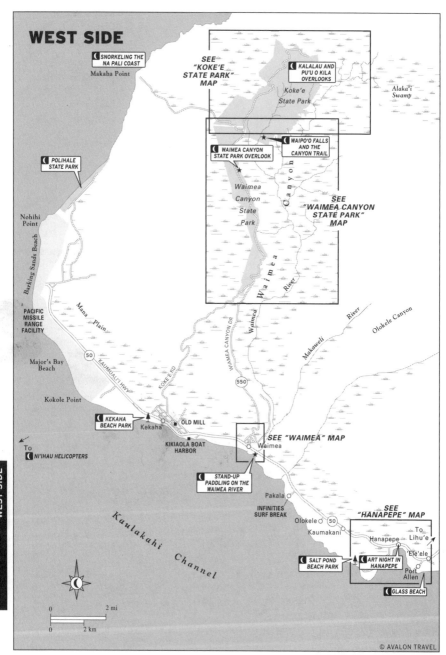

WEST SIDE

SNORKELING THE
NA PALI COAST

Makaha Point

SEE
"KOKE'E
STATE PARK"
MAP

KALALAU AND
PU'U O KILA
OVERLOOKS

Koke'e
State Park

Alaka'i
Swamp

WAIPO'O FALLS
AND THE
CANYON TRAIL

POLIHALE
STATE PARK

WAIMEA CANYON
STATE PARK OVERLOOK

Waimea
Canyon
State
Park

SEE
"WAIMEA CANYON
STATE PARK"
MAP

Nohihi
Point

Barking Sands Beach

PACIFIC
MISSILE
RANGE
FACILITY

Mana Plain

W a i m e a   Canyon

Waimea River

Makaweli River

Olokele Canyon

Major's Bay
Beach

50

KAUMUALI'I HWY

KOKE E RD

WAIMEA CANYON DR

Waimea River

550

Kokole Point

KEKAHA
BEACH PARK

Kekaha   OLD MILL

SEE "WAIMEA" MAP

Waimea

To
NI'IHAU HELICOPTERS

KIKIAOLA BOAT
HARBOR

STAND-UP
PADDLING ON THE
WAIMEA RIVER

Pakala

SEE
"HANAPEPE" MAP

INFINITIES
SURF BREAK

Olokele   50

To
Lihu'e

Kaumakani

Hanapepe

'Ele'ele

Kaulakahi Channel

SALT POND
BEACH PARK

ART NIGHT IN
HANAPEPE

Port
Allen

GLASS BEACH

0   2 mi
0   2 km

© AVALON TRAVEL

THE BEST DAY ON THE WEST SIDE

The best of the west can be experienced in one day, if you start early (around 9 A.M.). If you follow this entire itinerary, the day will end around 9:30 P.M.

- Your one-day western adventure begins with a quick stop at **Glass Beach,** where you can take a morning dip in the tide pool before heading up to **Old Hanapepe** to browse local art, walk on the swinging bridge, and have breakfast at Hanapepe Cafe and Bakery.

- Head farther west and inland to the **Waimea Canyon State Park Overlook.** It's a good idea to hit the Big Save for snacks and drinks before heading up Waimea Canyon Road (the views are much better here than on Koke'e Road). Remember to keep an eye out for the waterfall at the 1,500-foot elevation sign. The lookout is easily accessible and not to be missed or visited without a camera.

- After taking in the sweeping views, you can head back down to the coast or visit the **Kalalau and Pu'u O Kila Overlooks.** If it's cloudy and misty at the canyon, there's a good chance the Koke'e overlooks will be too cloudy to see the view, and if so, there's no need to spend the time driving up. If the sky is clear, head up there but bypass everything else in Koke'e, since time is of the essence

here. Either way, take Koke'e Road back down to the coast and turn left to Waimea for lunch at **Island Tacos,** then take a break from the heat with a Jo-Jo's Clubhouse shave ice. If you're out of snacks and drinks you'll want to restock before heading out to **Polihale State Park** for the rest of the afternoon.

- Once on the road into Polihale, you have a choice at the fork in the road, at the big tree about three miles in. From here you can go right to the parking area with showers and restrooms, or you can go about a tenth of a mile left to **Queen's Pond.** At Queen's Pond, swimming is generally safer and more mellow, and definitely better for kids. The beach access is the first right, but unless you are an experienced four-wheel driver you need to park here where the sand is still very firm. A little to the right of the end of this parking area is the pond. Once you're here it's worth it to spend the remainder of the day to see the sunset over Ni'ihau and maybe see an elusive green flash just as the sun drops below the horizon.

- Head back to Waimea for dinner. Try an island-style dinner at **The Grove Cafe,** or if you're in the mood for a good steak or vegetarian pasta dish, try **Wrangler's Steakhouse.**

Hanapepe, which means "crushed bay," calls itself "Kaua'i's Biggest Little Town." It originally thrived as a central place for taro cultivation in the Hanapepe Valley and later evolved into a rice-farming community, until it became a bustling town from the early 1900s until just after World War II. At one point the now-quiet town was an economic center and, shockingly, one of the biggest towns on the island, loaded with shops, businesses, two movie theaters, and even three skating rinks. In the 1940s, thousands of GIs were trained here before being sent for duty. The riverside town offers country charm and artisan creations that can be experienced while on a walking tour of the historic buildings, over

40 of which are listed in the National Register of Historic Places. Explore the local arts scene in historical Old Hanapepe, where art galleries have a monopoly on the main strip. Old Hanapepe is home to not only the galleries, but a general store, two banks, a post office, a playground and community park, gift shops, a swinging bridge, and a bakery. It's a good idea to pick up a *Historic Hanapepe Walking Tour Map,* available at many of the businesses in town. The newer part of Hanapepe lies along Route 50 and doesn't share its older sibling's affection for art. The newer part of Hanapepe is dotted with eateries, gift shops, a general store, and other small shops and businesses.

WEST SIDE

TOP KID-FRIENDLY ACTIVITIES ON THE WEST SIDE

Kaua'i may be a small island, but car time while sightseeing can still make children bored and antsy. The west side has an array of children-focused options to mix it up for kids. Here's a list of eateries, parks, and beaches, fun for kids to spend the day or if they just need a short break from the car.

- **Glass Beach** may not have the best swimming for the little ones, but the small tide pool in front of the beach access is suitable – under your guidance, of course – and children love hunting different colors of beach glass here. They may even get lucky and see an endangered Hawaiian monk seal. If so, take a look from a distance and don't approach the animal.

- **Salt Pond Beach Park** in Hanapepe is a perfect beach for children. The protected swimming area offers usually mellow water watched over by a lifeguard. There is a grassy lawn to run around on and play games, and a tide pool on the west end of the beach.

- Turning right onto Kona Road off of Kaumuali'i Highway leads to a park and **playground** on the left side. Located in the center of town, the playground has slides and swings for the kids to let out some energy.

- Hanapepe is home to the **Children's Media Center and Storybook Theatre of Hawaii** (3814 Hanapepe Rd., 808/335-0712, www. storybook.org), where the nonprofit organization offers a varied schedule of puppet shows, music, storytelling, and more. Art Night is a special time here, and the center participates most Fridays. Drop by or call for scheduling and events, and visit the Children's Garden of Peace adjacent to the theater. Children may also get a kick out of knowing that the historic town was featured in Disney's *Lilo & Stitch*.

- The **Hanapepe Swinging Bridge** is a hit with children, but they need to be carefully watched here. Children get a thrill from the shaking of the bridge as it's crossed.

- In Waimea, **Jo-Jo's Clubhouse** offers 60 flavors of shave ice to choose from. Let the little ones eat it outside of the car, though; it gets pretty messy.

- The safest swimming for tots in Waimea is at the **Kikiaola Boat Harbor,** where the protected swimming area is usually very mellow. There are also picnic tables here for a family lunch. There isn't a lifeguard, but down at **Kekaha Beach Park** there is one on duty daily, although the swimming there is usually a bit rough.

- At **Faye Park** in Kekaha a playground and ball field are available for public use. Turn inland off of Highway 50 onto Alae Road and the park is on the left.

Heading west from Hanapepe you will pass still-functioning old sugar towns, including **Kaumakani,** with residential homes, a post office, bakery, minimart, and the Ni'ihau Helicopters office. About a half mile farther west is Olokele, where a strip of modern oceanfront homes provide a hint of the upper-class life in the area. This is where the plantation managers and the elite of the old days lived. Right past that is Pakala, defined mostly today by the hidden beach at mile marker 21 with the same name, where locals surf the long wave called Infinities.

Waimea town is the next stop going west and claims to be Kaua'i's most historic town. Waimea, which means "reddish water," boasts a river with a red tint that is due to the dark red dirt floor. Waimea holds claim to a moment in history that changed the course of Hawaii's existence. Captain Cook first set foot in Hawaii in Waimea on January 20, 1778, and is remembered by two monuments in the small town. Once home to the last great king of Kaua'i, Kaumuali'i, for many years Waimea was one of the central towns and ports of Kaua'i until the Nawiliwili and Port Allen harbors were created. When the sugar mill closed in 1969, Waimea began to lose its place as a central area. Today the town offers opportunities to discover antique treasures, local personality, good Mexican food, great steaks, and some surprisingly good vegetarian dishes.

About 15 miles inland from here are **Waimea Canyon** and **Koke'e State Parks,** where the "Grand Canyon of the Pacific" claims part of the island. Koke'e State Park, a few miles past Waimea, is full of trails and hikes galore for all levels of hikers. The park is also home to inspiring lookouts over the Na Pali Coast.

Back down on the coast, **Kekaha** marks the beginning of the end of the road. The white-sand beaches start here and stretch for 15 miles until ending at a sacred cliff at the beginning of the **Na Pali Coast.** Out here the silence is broken only by the picturesque and dangerous waves that crash on the beaches and lull campers to sleep.

Kauai's west side is a sharp contrast to the rest of island, with a landscape and sense of aloha unique to the area. Visitors should dedicate at least one full day to explore the standout features of the west side, or more in order to spend more time on the beaches and exploring the mountains.

Beaches

Kaua'i's west coast may be on the dry side, but the beaches out here are rampant. They range from sufficient to spectacular, narrow to wide, black to white, remote to popular, and, depending on mother nature's mood, swimmable to unsafe. The Pacific is easily accessible from many areas. Check a few beaches out and find your favorite to spend some time on. As on all beaches on the island, don't leave valuables in the car. Please remember to always stay out of the water if the waves are big. If in doubt, don't go out.

© JADE ECKARDT

WEST SIDE

At Glass Beach, colorful beach glass blankets the sand.

HANAPEPE
◖ Glass Beach

The saying "one person's trash is another's treasure" fits Glass Beach, sort of. On this small black- and gray-sand beach, sand exists in its most pure and processed forms: Colored beach glass blankets the sand, making a colorful landscape that sparkles in the right light. Although near a former dump site, in front of a backdrop of large gas tanks in an industrial area, the small beach is actually quite nice and easily accessible. The water is a bit darker than at some other beaches because of the underlying reef, and it's not really the best swimming beach. You can still enjoy a dip, though, if you hop in the natural tide pool almost directly in front of the beach access. At high tide, the pool has small waves rushing into it, but at low tide it's generally mellow and provides

safer swimming than the rest of the beach. The amount of glass varies with tides and conditions, but there's usually a good amount to see. It's not uncommon to see a monk seal relaxing here for the day; let it be. To get there, head west and turn left on Waialo Road toward Port Allen. Turn left on Aka Ulu then right at the fork in the dirt road and you will see the beach.

Wahiawa Beach

Wahiawa Beach is less than a half hour east from Glass Beach on foot. This beach has black and grayish sand and is a popular fishing spot with locals, but it doesn't offer much for swimming or sunbathing. The thrill is really in the hike to the beach. Head east down the coast past the Chinese cemetery and you will find Wahiawa Beach.

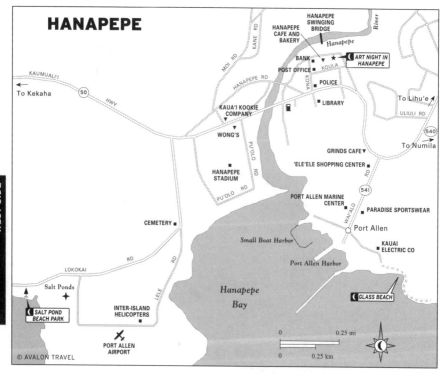

Salt Pond Beach Park is a perfect choice for a full day at the beach.

◖ Salt Pond Beach Park

Salt Pond Beach Park offers the best of Hawaii's beaches in one: white sand, black rocks, tide pools, a fairly protected swimming area, and large lawn often dotted with tents for the night or a long beach day. This beach is popular with visitors and locals, so it can be crowded. It has restrooms, showers, lifeguards, and even a local lunch wagon on a regular basis. Although it's not one of the island's remote beaches, it will give you a wonderful day at the ocean with a calm swimming area and lifeguard, making it great for children and other swimmers who prefer not to fight the surf. It's also easily accessible and convenient if you don't have time to venture into the deep west.

Its name comes from the nearby salt ponds, where locals harvest salt from evaporative basins scraped out of the earth that have been utilized for generations. The basins are lined with black clay, and after drying they're filled with sea water. When the sea water evaporates, salt is left behind and harvested. If you see any salt in them, it's spoken for, so please don't take any. Salt in Hawaiian is *pa'akai,* translating to "firm sea," while the rock salt with a reddish tint from the red dirt is *alae.* To get there turn left off of Highway 50 where you see a street sign pointing toward the ocean onto Route 543, then go right on Lele Road.

Pakala's

A three-minute walk through brush and trees brings you to Pakala's. The river mouth beach is roughly 500 yards long, and is composed of compact dark sand. It's remote and quiet, although not as picturesque as other west-side beaches. Its length makes it a great place for a morning stroll, and the compact sand is perfect for a jog or a few yoga poses. The beach is mostly used by surfers taking advantage of the long wave called Infinities. The small rock pier to the left is a good place to enjoy the morning sun while watching surfers catch waves. The water here is usually dark because of the sand flowing in from the river. It gets deep gradually, so you can wade a ways out without getting too deep. To get there, park on the side of

WEST SIDE

the road just after mile marker 21. There is a trail by the guardrail and fence.

WAIMEA

The Waimea district lies along a black-sand beach. It is long, narrow, and made of fine black sand mixed with river sediment and green olivine. Rivers are common in this area and during heavy rain cause the surrounding ocean to get dark with the red dirt, resulting in less-than-perfect swimming conditions. The beaches are still worth checking out, and are great for a picnic or walk.

Lucy Wright Beach County Park

Named after the first native Hawaiian school teacher, who passed away in 1931, Lucy Wright Beach Park is located at the mouth of the Waimea River on the western bank and is home to Captain Cook's landing site. Consisting of a small ball field, restrooms, and a couple of picnic tables, the blackish sand beach is nice and is usually covered in driftwood, but it is not one of the island's best. It's a popular hangout for locals; a canoe club launches here for practice. Swimming isn't recommended along this entire beach, and with the nearby spectacular beaches, the attraction here is really in the historical aspect. To get there, turn left after the bridge just as you enter Waimea. It's on the river and you can't miss it. Looking west down the beach, the Waimea State Recreation Pier juts off the beach into the ocean. It's a good place for picnicking and a popular spot for pole fishing. To access

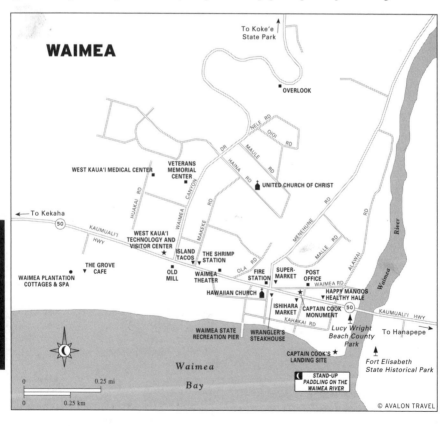

it walk along the beach or down a back street behind the Waimea Library.

Kikiaola Boat Harbor

Kikialoa Boat Harbor is not a sprawling white-sand beach with crystal-clear bright blue water, but it offers mellow, protected swimming for children and others looking to relax free from open-ocean waves. The harbor also has covered picnic tables and a small sandy area on the west end, as well as a larger sand area to the left. This is where many of the Na Pali Coast tours leave from. If you come here to swim or eat, you will probably find a group of locals enjoying the peace. Give them a wave and enjoy the park. To get there, head west out of Waimea and look for the sign after mile marker 24.

THE WILD WEST

This is where dreamy, seemingly endless beaches of tropical heaven begin and end at the Na Pali Coast. You'll encounter miles of soft sand and a multitude of opportunities for oceanside four-wheel-driving, camping, surfing, and sunbathing.

C Kekaha Beach Park

Kekaha Beach Park marks the beginning of about 15 miles of white sand that ends at the Na Pali Coast. Pavilions, picnic tables, portable toilets, and a barbecue pit set the stage for a complete day at the beach. Riptides here can be dangerous, but when the waves are small and peaceful, swimming here can be good. Locals hang out, fish, and surf here, and it's a good place to spend the day if you don't want to drive another 30 or 40 minutes to Polihale. This is the last beach with a lifeguard on duty, something to keep in mind when deciding where to spend a day at the ocean. Ni'ihau is in full view from here. Kekaha Beach Park stretches west for a few miles, but this is the last area with facilities until Polihale. The best place for kids is probably across from St. Theresa's Catholic church at the start of the beach. The beach is at mile marker 27.

Pacific Missile Range Facility

Pacific Missile Range Facility (PMRF, http://cnic.navy.mil/PMRF/index.htm) begins about six miles past Kekaha Beach Park and consists of a long strip of beach blessed with large sand dunes, surfing waves (popular with locals at Rifles, Targets, and Major's Bay), and the beach known as Barking Sands. It's a beautiful and long stretch of beach, and swimming gets dangerous when the waves are anything but small. Local lore says Barking Sands got its name from the noise the vast sand dunes make if you slide down them, resulting in the friction of sand and coral making noise similar to a barking dog. PMRF is run by the U.S. Navy, but all sectors of the U.S. military utilize the base. This area is basically a training facility for sea warfare. Its range covers 42,000 square miles to the west and south with another 1,000 square miles under the sea. Some military personnel live out here, and many more work on base. It was chosen by NASA officials because the Kaua'i weather provides 360 clear days each year, creating perfect flying conditions in unobstructed air space. Parts of the base were open for public use before September 11, 2001, but since then it has been restricted. Kaua'i residents who pass a background check can get limited access for fishing and surfing. It takes about three weeks to pass the background check required to get a base pass. For information on current access information call 808/335-4229.

C Polihale State Park

Imagine sitting on a long white-sand beach, a distant island in view, clear blue sky, looming cliffs behind you, and waves rolling in as your soundtrack. This is Polihale. The white sand stretches for miles, tall sacred cliffs are dotted with goats, chickens scamper around the beach, and the clear blue water offers good surfing and a refreshing swim. The sunsets over the "forbidden" island of Ni'ihau create a special end to a day here.

At the very end of the beach, where the cliffs meet the ocean, is **Echo Beach,** a popular beach for surfing that is reserved for very experienced surfers because of the rocks and current. The cliffs in the area, which mark the beginning of the Na Pali Coast, are home to

the seemingly endless Polihale State Park

© JADE ECKARDT

the Polihale Heiau (temple). This sacred spot is said to be where the souls of the dead leapt off the cliffs to the land of the dead, a mythical underwater mountain a few miles off the coast. This beach is also a popular four-wheel-driving and camping spot.

To get to Polihale, drive until the pavement ends on Highway 50 and turn left on the dirt road at mile marker 33. It's about a 3.5-mile, 20- to 30-minute drive to the big tree at the fork in the road. Here you can veer right to the facilities or go left for safer swimming. The left fork leads to **Queen's Pond,** where a fringing reef creates a somewhat safer swimming area. It's a long walk from the facilities, but if you're motivated and armed with sunblock and water

it can be done. Otherwise, go right at the tree and head about a tenth of a mile down. Take the first right and, unless you're prepared to four-wheel drive, make sure to park where the ground is firm. Cell phones don't get reception out here so you don't want to get stuck. Near the north end of the beach is a midsize dirt parking area with covered picnic tables, restrooms, and showers. You can park here and walk as far up or down the beach as you'd like. Lifesaving devices are attached to a post near the back of the beach in this area. The dirt road that leads to the beach is usually fit for two-wheel drive vehicles, even though a Four-Wheel-Drive Only sign is posted at the beginning of the road.

Water Sports

SNORKELING AND DIVING

Beach snorkeling on the west side isn't the best on Kaua'i, but remember that almost anywhere the sea is calm it is worth it to hop in the water with your snorkel gear. In Hawaii's lively waters there's always the chance of seeing a green sea turtle or some tropical fish. Numerous boat tour companies that leave from the west side offer guided trips along the Na Pali Coast for spectacular snorkeling. Fish, sea turtles, and reef life can be seen while snorkeling, and dolphins and whales in the winter and early spring months can be seen from the boat. Port Allen and Kikiaola Boat Harbor are the main mooring and departure points for Na Pali cruises.

Hanapepe
SALT POND BEACH PARK

West-side snorkeling is best at Salt Pond Beach Park. The water is almost always calm and the area is protected, making it a great place for children and beginners to check out the underwater life. Snorkeling is best out by the rock wall, but it's worth it to swim all over and see what's below.

◖ Na Pali Coast
BOAT TOURS FROM PORT ALLEN

Holo Holo Charters (Port Allen Marina Center, 4353 Waialo Rd., Ste. 5A, 808/335-0815 or 800/848-6130, www.holoholokauaiboattours.com) offers the only tour available to the island of Ni'ihau ($179) and a 3.5-hour Na Pali sunset tour as well as Na Pali snorkel sail ($99–139). The company uses two catamarans, one 65 feet long and another with a shaded cabin and large bar area, to get ocean goers to their destination from the Port Allen Harbor. They provide a deli-style buffet for lunch along with soft drinks, beer, and wine. The company has a reputation of treating guests well.

At **Captain Andy's Sailing Adventures** (Port Allen Marina Center, 4353 Waialo Rd., 808/335-6833 or 800/535-0830, www.na-pali.com/kauai_sailing, $69–159 with special

children's rates), Captain Andy will take you on a number of cruises on a 55-foot catamaran that are either snorkeling or dining focused. They offer a barbecue sail, prime rib sail, a snorkeling sail, and a sunset or dinner cruise along the Na Pali Coast.

Catamaran Kahanu (Port Allen Marina Center, 4353 Waialo Rd., 808/645-6176 or 888/213-7711, www.catamarankahanu.com, $80–122 with special children's rates) is a Hawaiian-owned, 22-year-old tour company offering whale-watching, Na Pali Coast swimming and snorkeling, and sunset dinner tours. They give visitors a glimpse into Hawaiian culture with craft demonstrations such as basket, hat, and rose weavings, which guests take home as mementos.

Kaua'i Sea Tours (Port Allen Marina Center, 4353 Waialo Rd. #2B, 808/826-1854, 800/733-7997, www.kauaiseatours.com) offers power sailing catamaran tours and ocean raft tours out of Port Allen. A snorkel tour is offered as well as a sunset dinner cruise.

To explore the outskirts of forbidden Ni'ihau, try **Bubbles Below Kauai** (Port Allen Marina Center, 4353 Waialo Rd., 808/332-7333 or 866/524-6268, www.bubblesbelowkauai.com, $80–310) for unique diving experiences in the waters of Ni'ihau, Lehua Island, and the Na Pali Coast, including a night crustacean dive and a twilight dive. They offer private boats and instruction as well.

Blue Dolphin Charters (Port Allen Marina Center, 877/511-1311, www.kauaiboats.com, $63–175 with special children's and Internet booking prices) offers a variety of tours. Scuba diving is available on all of them, no experience necessary. A Na Pali snorkel tour with a snorkeling stop on Ni'ihau is available, along with a Na Pali sunset and dinner cruise, a Po'ipu sunset sail, and a whale-watching tour from December through March. The company uses a 63-foot or 65-foot catamaran with freshwater showers and provides all gear needed for snorkeling.

NI'IHAU

Known as Hawaii's "Forbidden Island," Ni'ihau is really a privately owned island passed down through generations by a family known as the Robinsons. It was run as a cattle and sheep ranch until 1999, and is home to approximately 120 pure-blooded Hawaiians, who are allowed to come and go as they wish. Some even commute daily from Ni'ihau to Kaua'i for work or health care. The residents run the remote island, and outsiders can only come on shore if they are fortunate enough to have an invitation by the owners, a resident, or via tour with **Ni'ihau Helicopters.** Surfers sometimes manage to sneak in now and then by boat to catch a wave off of Lehua Island, by the northern tip of Ni'ihau. For a small island it boasts an array of unique features: the state's largest and second largest lakes; several perfect surf breaks, including one said to rival Maui's Jaws when it breaks at 40 feet; rare animals like the tall horned oryx; and, of course, the island's famous shells.

The 17-mile Kaulakahi Channel separates the island from the western tip of Kaua'i and is a popular hangout spot for whales. The island can be seen from the shores of Kaua'i's west side from Waimea to Polihale. Measuring just 18 miles long by 6 miles wide, Ni'ihau has a total area of 70 square miles, and the surrounding waters are popular with divers who spear fish. The highest point on the island, Pani'au (1,281 feet) lies on the east-central coast, and both ends are low. Like the rest of the Hawaiian Islands, which are slowly sinking, the island is the remnant of a larger old island, most of it having broken off and sunk below the ocean. Boats sometimes pull in on the northern tip at Ki'i and Lehua Landings. There are no ports on the small island. Because Ni'ihau is so low and lies in lee of Kaua'i, it gets only about 30 inches of rain each year, resulting in a rather dry island. It's said that the low rainfall has led to a lack of flowers on the island, and this is the reason Ni'ihau Hawaiians replaced flowers with shells in lei-making.

Hawaiian legend says Ni'ihau was born after the goddess Papa and her husband Wakea reconciled after he was caught with another lover while Papa was visiting Tahiti. Kaua'i was born from this pregnancy, and Ni'ihau came out as the afterbirth, along with Lehua and Ka'ulu, the last of the low reef islands. Because of the lack of rain and poor soil, Ni'ihau was never as populated as the other islands. The islanders traded with Kaua'i frequently for poi and other necessities. The abundant fish around Ni'ihau were what they used to barter, and Ni'ihau mats made from *makaloa* also became highly valuable. Today, Ni'ihau Hawaiians raise livestock, produce the famous Ni'ihau shell lei, and work on Kaua'i for an income.

So in an age where all land is owned by *someone* and it's rare for people to give oth-

BOAT TOURS FROM WAIMEA

Na Pali Explorer (9643 Kaumuali'i Hwy., Waimea, 808/338-9999 or 877/335-9909, www.napaliexplorer.com, $105–149 with children's rates) is in Waimea right next to Island Tacos and offers various tours on a 26-foot RIB, 48-foot RIB, or 46-foot inflatable hull RIB. Their expeditions include dolphins, whales, shore landings, snorkeling, a visit to an ancient fishing village, sea cave explorations, and Na Pali views. Available tours depend on the time of year.

Kaua'i native Liko Ho'okano is the captain at **Liko Kaua'i Cruises** (4516 Alawai Rd., Waimea, 888/732-5456, www.liko-kauai.com, $140 for adults and $95 for children), where a five-hour Na Pali snorkeling and sights tour is available year-round. Dolphin-watching is included, and whale-watching is part of the tour during the season. A deli lunch and soft drinks are included aboard the 49-foot powered catamaran.

Na Pali Riders (intersection of Hwy. 50 and Hwy. 550, Waimea, 808/742-6331, www.napaliriders.com, $130 for adults, $100 for children) uses Zodiac rafts for a tour combining

ers a free home, how does Ni'ihau exist like this? Well, Kaua'i and Ni'ihau became part of the Kingdom of Hawaii under Kamehameha the Great. Ni'ihau was passed down to his successors, and in 1864 Kamehameha V sold the island for $10,000 to the Sinclair family. It's said that the king offered them a swampy beach area on O'ahu, but the Scottish family didn't want it. It turns out the swampy beach was Waikiki, which means they could have had a much better investment. Ever since, the family has been the sole proprietor, but through marriage Ni'ihau became property of the Robinson family. It's not really known exactly why the Robinsons choose to let Hawaiians live on the island and even pay them to care for their sheep and cattle. One of the current owners, Keith Robinson, is said to be an environmentalist who simply wants to preserve land and culture. This must be the reason if the rumor that the family has turned down a $1 billion offer for the island is true.

Today the population on Ni'ihau is slowly declining as young people decide to move "out into the world." There's no electricity, but generators run refrigerators, TVs, and computers. Horses and old pickups are the popular mode of transportation. In the main community of Pu'uwai there is one elementary school, requiring teenagers to go to Kaua'i for high school. While strolling Polihale I recently met a woman in her 60s who grew up on Ni'ihau.

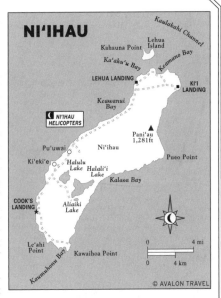

She shared her memories of the island, saying that she wished she could go back. She said that since she had married an outsider she was not allowed to go home. "I miss it," she said. "I think about how simple it is over there, and I look around life outside, and I wish I could go back and just take it easy now that I'm old."

---

snorkeling, dolphin- and whale-watching, and sea cave exploration. Departing from the Kikiaola Harbor in Waimea, the five-hour tour covers all 17 miles of the Na Pali Coast. They reach the north shore's Ke'e Beach before turning around and heading back west.

SURFING AND STAND-UP PADDLING

Some of the most intense barreling waves can be found on the west side, especially during the winter months. West-side waves in general are reserved for expert surfers due to size, currents, and lack of lifeguards. By experienced surfer I mean you've been surfing regularly for most of your life, big waves are a regular thing, and a steep drop and fast, strong riptide don't scare you. If this isn't you, it's best to wait for surf lessons on the south or north shore. A good slogan to live by is "If in doubt, don't go out."

Not all hope is lost for boarding fun on the west side, though, and stand-up paddling provides the option to catch waves or paddle along a river or calm open ocean. Lessons are available on the **Waimea River,** where it is calm and flat, or you can bring a rented board out

the Waimea River mouth at Lucy Wright Beach County Park

elsewhere. **Salt Pond Beach Park** is another calm place for stand-up paddling.

Stand-up paddling has become a hugely popular sport in recent years and is used not only for carving waves while surfing, but is popular with people who just want to cruise around in the open ocean or in rivers. While surfing requires a sideways stance, stand-up paddling requires a front-facing stance, directly facing the nose of the board while paddling along.

Waimea

Infinities (between mile markers 21 and 22) is a nearly perfect left-hand breaking wave located at Pakala's Beach. The popular but less crowded surf break is almost directly in front of the small rock pier at the east end of the beach, just past the river mouth. The wave's name refers to the seemingly endless ride surfers get out here. Although Infinities isn't the most dangerous wave, only experienced surfers should venture out. It's a very localized break, and only those with thorough knowledge of surf etiquette and respect should paddle out.

Remember to wait your turn and don't dominate the lineup or you may experience spirit lacking in aloha.

The surf break called **Tiger's** is to the right of Infinities and is named after the supposed tiger shark breeding grounds in the area. While Infinities breaks on a regular basis, Tiger's rarely breaks. Tiger's is for experienced surfers only.

◖ Waimea River

Paddle board rentals, surfing lessons, kayaks, surf and body boards, and apparel are all available at **Kaua'i Wind and Waves** (4516 Alawai Rd., on the Waimea River Bridge next to Happy Mangoes, 808/635-1791, www.Kauaiwindandwaves.com, 8 A.M.–5 P.M. daily, $39–159 daily to weekly). The locally owned surf supply store offers private and semi-private stand-up paddle lessons ($75–150) with CPR-trained instructors on the Waimea River.

The Wild West

At **Pacific Missile Range Facility** (roughly six miles past Kekaha Beach Park) the waves are heavy and dangerous. The surf breaks out here are Rifles, Targets, and Major's Bay. Very experienced surfers who obtain a base pass to access the beaches will have their pick of heavy, barreling, fast waves breaking in shallow water. Only Kaua'i's most experienced surfers come here, and the breaks have a dedicated following statewide. It's a good idea and fun on days with big waves to stay onshore and watch Kaua'i's elite surfers get barreled.

Echo Beach, by the cliffs at the north end of **Polihale Beach Park,** is a fun right-hand-breaking wave when the waves are head-high or smaller. These aren't some of the most dangerous waves on the west side, but the rocks directly in front of the waves and the persistent current out here keep it reserved for very experienced surfers.

FISHING

From trout to sport fishing, visitors have the option to reel in some fish in either freshwater or saltwater.

The Wild West

Na Pali Sportfishing (7923 Bulili Rd., Kekaha, 808/635-9424, www.napalisportfishing.com, $135–1,050) leaves out of the Kikiaola Harbor and offers the captain's lifetime of Hawaii fishing experience catching mahimahi, ahi, wahoo, blue marlin, and more. The fish caught on the trip become property of the captain, but they send you home with fillets. You must bring your own lunch on this boat. Make sure to inquire about departure time because the first cruise leaves at 6 A.M. They offer a Na Pali sightseeing cruise as well.

Koke'e State Park

Rainbow trout can be found in the **Pu'u Lua Reservoir** on the west side of Koke'e. Koke'e trout season is from the first Saturday in August for 16 consecutive days, then weekends and holidays only until the end of September. Call the **Division of Aquatic Resources, Department of Land and Natural Resources** (3060 Eiwa St., Lihu'e, 808/274-3344) for any questions. **Cast and Catch** (located in Koloa, 808/332-9707) does guided freshwater fishing trips. Fishing licenses can be obtained from **Lihu'e Fishing Supply** (2985 Kalena St., Lihu'e, 808/245-4930).

Hiking and Biking

HIKING
Waimea Canyon State Park

Waimea Canyon State Park is home to the beautiful and vast canyon, but it's also decorated with numerous trails weaving through the forest, ranging from serious hikes to short walks. Once you've gazed at the views on the drive up it's worth it to take a walk or a long hike through the area.

ILIAU NATURE LOOP

A perfect family walk, the Iliau Nature Loop begins off of Koke'e Road and also marks the beginning of the Kukui Trail. Pull all the way off of the road between mile markers 8 and 9 to access the easy, quarter-mile-long trail, which takes about 15 minutes to complete. Views of Waimea Canyon and Wai'alae Falls open up about midway along the loop. The self-guided trail sits at about 3,000 feet elevation and is home to its namesake, the *iliau* plant. The *Iliau* is a relative of the silversword, which grows high on Haleakala on Maui, and the greensword, which grows on the Big Island. This rare plant grows only on the dry mountain slopes of western Kaua'i. White-tailed tropicbirds and the brown-and-white *pueo* (Hawaiian owl) are known to fly through the area.

KUKUI TRAIL

The Kukui Trail leads down into Waimea Canyon and is home to the Iliau Nature Loop, therefore starting at the same location between mile markers 8 and 9. This 2.5-mile trail takes

WEST SIDE

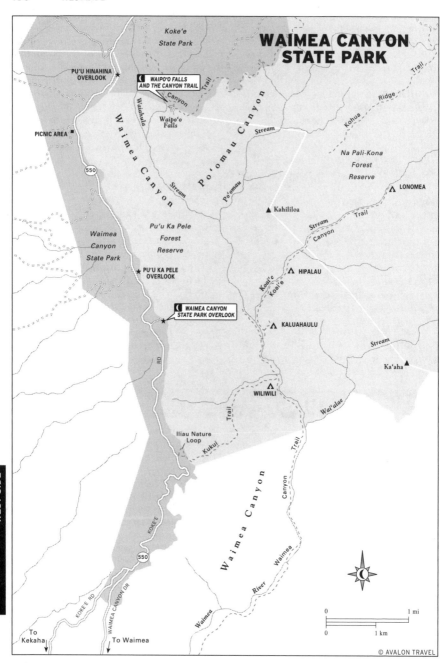

WAIMEA CANYON STATE PARK

Koke'e State Park

PU'U HINAHINA OVERLOOK

WAIPO'O FALLS AND THE CANYON TRAIL

Waipo'o Falls

PICNIC AREA

Waiahulu

Canyon

Trail

Po'omau Canyon

Stream

Kohua Ridge

Na Pali-Kona Forest Reserve

LONOMEA

Kahililoa

Stream

Canyon Trail

Waimea Canyon

Stream

Po'omau

Waimea Canyon State Park

Pu'u Ka Pele Forest Reserve

PU'U KA PELE OVERLOOK

WAIMEA CANYON STATE PARK OVERLOOK

HIPALAU

Koai'e

Koai'e

KALUAHAULU

Stream

Ka'aha

WILIWILI

KOKEE RD

Iliau Nature Loop

Kukui

Trail

Trail

Canyon

Wai'alae

Trail

Waimea Canyon

Waimea River

Waimea

KOKEE RD

WAIMEA CANYON DR

To Kekaha

To Waimea

0   1 mi

0   1 km

© AVALON TRAVEL

WEST SIDE

about 60–90 minutes to complete just the walk in. It is strenuous, as it descends over 2,000 feet very quickly, which of course you have to climb up on the way out. Thanks to the steep grade it takes longer and a lot more effort and energy on the way back up. Don't forget to bring plenty of water if you're planning on hiking all the way down and up. Water bladders are a good idea for this one; they weigh less than bottles and you can drink from the tube as you hike. There are gorgeous views of the canyon along the way, so don't forget your camera, even though it may be tempting to leave extra weight behind. The Wiliwili Campground marks the end of the Kukui Trail. You can set up camp for the night with a permit and continue on other trails or head back out the same day.

KOAI'E CANYON TRAIL

From the end of the Kukui Trail, the serious hiker can head up the Waimea River for about a half mile, where you'll have to cross the river to find the trailhead for the three-mile-long Koai'e Canyon Trail. This trail has about a 720-foot loss and gain in elevation. If the river water is high and rushing, do not cross it. Flash flooding is always a concern here. The trailhead is near the Kaluahaulu Campground on the east side of the river. The trail leads you to the south side of Koai'e Canyon, where there are many pools of freshwater, which are usually lower in summer than in winter. The canyon was once used for farming, as you might guess while walking the fertile and lush trail. There are two more campsites here. It is strongly advised to avoid this trail during rainy weather.

WAIMEA CANYON TRAIL

If you head south from the Kukui Trail, you can connect with the 11.5-mile, strenuous, and usually hot and dry Waimea Canyon Trail. This is a lengthy trail that parallels the Waimea River through the canyon. It can also be reached by hiking eight miles inland from Waimea town. This trail is popular with serious hikers who enjoy a challenge, but many regard the trail as lacking in sights and views, and don't find many interesting qualities along

the hike. The hike is well worn and passes back and forth over the river, which usually has plenty of water, but it needs to be boiled or treated before drinking.

Koke'e State Park

There are about 45 miles of trails in Koke'e with a range of difficulty levels. Most of the hikes begin along Koke'e Drive or the dirt roads that veer off of it. The trails generally fall into five categories: Na Pali Coast overlook trails, Alaka'i Swamp trails, forest trails, canyon overlook trails, and even a few bird-watching trails. Remember to bring good hiking shoes, lots of water, sunblock, food, and even swimwear, depending on which trail you take.

Trail maps and information are provided by the staff at the **Koke'e Natural History Museum** (3600 Waimea Canyon Dr. after mile marker 15, 808/335-9975, www.kokee. org, 10 A.M.–4 P.M. daily). A basic trail map put out by the state, called *Trails of Koke'e,* can be picked up at **Na Pali Explorer** (9643 Kaumuali'i Hwy., 808/338-9999 or 877/335-9909, www.napaliexplorer.com) in Waimea, but much more thorough trail maps are Hawaii Nature Guide's *Koke'e Trails* map and *Northwestern Kaua'i Recreational Map* by Earthwalk Press.

THE CLIFF TRAIL

For an easy family trail take a 10-minute walk on the Cliff Trail. Located off of Halemanu Road, it's a leisurely stroll of only a tenth of a mile and leads to a wonderful viewpoint of Waimea Canyon. From the lookout you may see some wild goats hanging out on the canyon walls. This trail also accesses the Canyon Trail.

◖ WAIPO'O FALLS AND THE CANYON TRAIL

The semi-strenuous 1.8-mile Canyon Trail branches off Cliff Trail and leads to the upper section of the 800-foot Waipo'o Falls before going up and along the edge of the canyon. It takes about three hours and could be done by a family, if the family is up for a bit of a challenge. Wonderful views of the canyon are

WEST SIDE

KOKE'E
STATE PARK

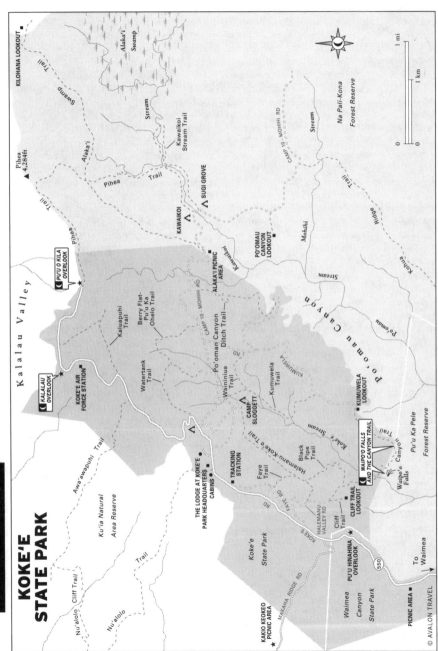

KILOHANA LOOKOUT ■

Alaka'i Swamp

Swamp Trail

Stream

Kawaikoi Stream Trail

Alaka'i

Pihea ▲ 4,284ft

Pihea   Trail

Pihea Trail

Kalalau Valley

Kawaikoi

SUGI GROVE ⋀

KAWAIKOI ⋀

Na Pali-Kona Forest Reserve

Stream

CAMP 10-MOHIHI RD

Mohihi

ALAKA'I PICNIC AREA ■

PO'OMAU CANYON LOOKOUT ■

Kohua Ridge Trail

Trail

1 mi

1 km

0

0

PU'U O KILA OVERLOOK ◖ ⚹

Kaluapuhi Trail

Berry Flat-Pu'u Ka Ohelo Trail

CAMP 10-MOHIHI RD

Po'oman Canyon Ditch Trail

Stream

Po'omau Canyon

Po'omau

KALALAU OVERLOOK ◖ ⚹

KOKE'E AIR FORCE STATION ■

Watertank Trail

Waininiua Trail

Kumuwela Trail

KUMUWELA

KUMUWELA LOOKOUT ■

Pu'u Ka Pele Forest Reserve

⋀ CAMP SLOGGETT

Awa'awapuhi Trail

Ku'ia Natural Area Reserve

Kalalau ⋀

THE LODGE AT KOKE'E ●
PARK HEADQUARTERS ■
CABINS ●

TRACKING STATION ■

Faye Trail

Halemanu-Koke'e Trail

Black Pipe Trail

Koke'e Stream

WAIPO'O FALLS AND THE CANYON TRAIL ◖

Waipo'o Canyon Trail

Waipo'o Falls

FAYE RD

KOKE'E RD

HALEMANU VALLEY RD

CLIFF TRAIL LOOKOUT ■

Cliff Trail

Nu'alolo Cliff Trail

Trail

Nu'alolo Trail

Koke'e State Park

MAKAHA RIDGE RD

PU'U HINAHINA OVERLOOK ◖ ⚹

550

To Waimea

KAKIO KEOKEO PICNIC AREA ⚹

PICNIC AREA ■

Waimea Canyon State Park

© AVALON TRAVEL

offered on this popular trail, and the reward of swimming in freshwater pools makes it a choice hike. The trail goes down into a gulch and then weaves along the cliff to the Koke'e Stream and the falls. It follows the eastern rim of the canyon. Parking is at the Pu'u Hinahina Lookout between mile markers 13 and 14. The trailhead is at the back of the parking lot. The trail ends at the Kumuwela Lookout, where you can head back on the Canyon Trail or walk back on Kumuwela Road.

FAYE TRAIL

At the end of Halemanu Road is the 0.1-mile Faye Trail, which crosses a wooded valley and accesses other trails in the Halemanu area. The trail brings you to an undrivable section of Faye Road, which leads left and back up to the highway not far from the Halemanu Road turnoff. Take a right at Faye Road to end up on the highway below the state park cabins.

NATURE TRAIL

A good trail for children is the 0.1-mile Nature Trail. Starting behind the Koke'e Natural History Museum it parallels the meadow. It's an easy and enjoyable walk through forest and offers good examples of native vegetation. Before beginning the trail pick up a free copy of a plant guide at the museum. This trail takes about 15 minutes to complete.

KUMUWELA TRAIL

Off of Mohihi Road is the one-mile Kumuwela Trail. This trail is somewhat strenuous but could be done by a tough family. It takes about one hour on the way in and offers lush native vegetation and fragrant flowers. It's a good birding trail, and you can connect to the Canyon Trail at Kumuwela Road at the end of the trail.

PU'U KA OHELO/WATER TANK/BERRY FLAT TRAIL LOOP

Near park headquarters is pole #320, which marks the beginning of Camp 10-Mohihi Road. This is generally a four-wheel-drive road, but occasionally two-wheel-drive cars can make it if the weather has been really dry. Numerous trails start here and head into the forest, along ridges with canyon views and crossing a couple of minor streams. The roughly 1.6-mile loop called the Pu'u Ka Ohelo Berry Flat Trail is a semi-tough trail that can be done with a family up for a challenge. The trail has a beautiful forest of sugi pine, California redwoods, Australian eucalyptus, and the valuable native koa as well as the 'ohi'a tree. The small, red, strawberry guava with a thick flesh and edible seeds grows here, and this is a popular spot for locals to harvest the fruit. Picking season is midsummer, so it's important to check with park headquarters before snacking on the fruit while hiking. To access this trail, begin at the Pu'u Ka Ohelo trailhead, near some cabins about a quarter mile up a road off Camp 10-Mohihi Road, and hike clockwise, which will take you downhill.

PO'OMAU CANYON DITCH TRAIL

The beautiful Po'omau Canyon Ditch Trail is less than a half mile past the Berry Flat Trail. Developed to maintain the Koke'e irrigation ditch, this trail is less than four miles long round-trip. It's pretty strenuous and it deserves plenty of time to be completed. This trail leads you to wonderful views of the Po'omau Stream, lush green forests, and a great view of two waterfalls below you from a peninsula of land that extends out into the canyon. If you bring a picnic lunch you will find a grassy overlook to sit on and enjoy the views. Take Waineke Road across from the Koke'e Museum to Mohihi Road. You will need to park well before the trailhead on Mohihi Road, a little over 1.5 miles from Highway 550. Walk about three-quarters of a mile to an unmarked trailhead on your right.

PIHEA TRAIL AND ALAKA'I SWAMP TRAIL

Beginning at the end of Waimea Canyon Drive at the Pu'u O Kila Overlook is the Pihea Trail, about 3.7 miles in length. It leads to the Alaka'i Swamp Trail, about 3.5 miles long. The Pihea Peak, accessed by a very steep trail, is about 1.3 miles after the lookout. This trail runs along the back edge of the Kalalau Valley, and you will be treated to wonderful views into the valley and out to the ocean. About 1.6 miles in, a wooden boardwalk has been constructed to help keep hikers from getting extremely submerged in mud. When you hit the Alakaʻi Trail take a left, and it's about two miles to the end. A majestic, gorgeous, and unique trail, the Alakaʻi Swamp Trail heads down toward the Kawaikoi Stream and then up a ridge across boggy forestland to the Kilohana Overlook, the trail's ultimate destination. When you can catch a very clear day, which can be tough, the views of the Wainiha and Hanalei Valleys are awesome.

The approximately five-million-year-old swamp is about 4,500 feet above sea level, and is one of the most distinctive experiences on the island. The surroundings up here feel like another world. Mossy trees, birds, and fog create an environment different from anywhere else. It's a great birding trail but the views are iffy with the lingering mist and clouds of the area. The entire trail totals about eight miles, so it's important to bring snacks, water, and energy.

NUʻALOLO LOOP/NUʻALOLO CLIFF TRAIL/AWAʻAWAPUHI TRAIL LOOP

For a nearly day-long hike with spectacular views, explore the Awaʻawapuhi/Nuʻalolo Loop. This trail is home to some of the most fantastic views on the island, and it's a must-do hike if you are up for a strenuous and long hike. It's nearly 10 miles, about 11 if you walk the paved road back to your car at the end. But, the views on this trail are picturesque and sublime. Most hikers do the full loop, beginning on the Nuʻaloalo Trail then turning right (north) about 3.2 miles in onto the Nuʻalolo Cliff Trail, which connects with the Awaʻawapuhi Trail. At the end take a left for amazing views, ending on a narrow ridge. A highlight is the thin finger of cliff where you can look down at the sea and a vibrant valley 2,500 feet below. From here you hike uphill back to the road while gaining 1,500 feet in elevation. Along the hike bright red wild berries called thimbleberries (resembling raspberries) can be snacked on, along with the sweet and sour *lilikoʻi*, or passion fruit. The damage Hurricane ʻIniki did to the area is still evident in the upland forest here.

There are no views until the end of the trails. Because they are on the western slopes of Kokeʻe,

it gets extremely sunny out here in the afternoon, so it's a good idea to begin around 9 A.M. It's a tough hike. Take your time, bring plenty of water and food, and expect to spend half to a full day on the hike. Lastly, the museum parking lot is probably safer for your car than the trailhead, and down the road after you emerge from the Awaʻawapuhi trailhead back to the museum is easier than hiking up the road to your car.

BIRD-WATCHING TRAILS

For bird-watching in Kokeʻe, try the 3.5-mile **Alakaʻi Swamp Trail.** The 1.6-mile **Kaluapuhi Trail** is also a good bet for birds, as well as the 3.7-mile **Pihea Trail.** For a shorter birding trail, take a stroll on the **Halemanu-Kokeʻe Trail,** which is slightly over a mile, or the one-mile-long **Kumuwela Trail.**

BIKING

Sunrise and sunset group bike tours are offered for an 11-mile downhill ride, but of course you can always take the ride on your own. Starting in the cool mountain air along the rim of Waimea Canyon at around 3,600 feet, the ride skirts the rim and then heads down the roller coaster foothills to the coast at Kekaha. All of the tours are done in groups and participants are given a helmet and jacket to wear. Cruiser bikes with comfortable seats are available for the half-day tour. Refreshments and information on Hawaiian culture are offered. Sunglasses, sunscreen, and sometimes pants are a necessity. A sag wagon follows for bikers who need a rest and to alert traffic from behind. If you'd like to spend about five hours on a bike tour, contact **Outfitters Kauai** (2827 Poʻipu Rd., Poʻipu, 808/742-9667 or 999/742-9887, www.outfitterskauai.com).

For the serious mountain biker, the **Waimea Canyon Trail** can be a good adventure. This lengthy eight-mile trail leads back down to the town of Waimea via an old 4WD track and crosses through a game management area. Because of this a special permit is required to walk though the area and is available at the trailhead. You can connect to the Waimea Canyon Trail by going south from the Kukui Trail. This trail is for dedicated mountain bikers only.

Adventure Sports and Tours

West-side tours explore Kauaʻi's coffee industry, history, and nature. Get a glimpse of history through town walking tours, gain insight into the tropical flora and fauna in Kokeʻe, explore the beaches of Niʻihau, and see Kauaʻi from a bird's-eye view. Unique to the west side is the opportunity for hang gliding and skydiving, offered nowhere else on the island. The adventure sports add some real action to an otherwise mellow locale.

HANG GLIDING AND SKYDIVING

If you like to live on the edge, go hang gliding with **Birds in Paradise** (Port Allen Airport, 3666 Kuiloko Rd., 808/332-0790 or 888/359-3656, www.birdsinparadise.com). Founder and one of four instructors available, Gerry Charlebois has helped over 100,000 people get their kicks high up in the air. There are three different aircraft available, and safety features include a backup rocket parachute that will bring the entire craft safely to the ground. If you would like to fly up to 100 miles per hour in the air, prices run from $165 for a mini introductory lesson to $360 for an advanced lesson. Photo packages start at $50.

For skydiving excursions, **Skydive Kauai** (Port Allen Airport, Kuiloko Rd., 808/335-5859, www.skydivekauai.com, $229) will take you to free fall out of a plane to 4,500 feet, where the chute opens and you glide back to the airfield. The ride only takes people 18 and older and under 200 pounds. They offer videos of you flying through the air on DVD for $70.

HELICOPTER TOURS
Niʻihau Helicopters

Virtually the only way to visit the beaches of Niʻihau unless invited by an islander is via a Niʻihau Helicopters tour (877/441-3500, www.niihau.us, 8 A.M.–2 P.M. Mon.–Sat., $385 including lunch and refreshments), which will take you there for a half day on the beach to snorkel and sunbathe. A safari hunting excursion is also offered ($500–1,750). Owned and operated by the owners of Niʻihau, the company offers free-chase hunting for boars, sheep, and oryx. Five people are required for both tours, and you reach the island in a twin-engine Agusta 109A helicopter that was originally set up to provide medical services for Niʻihau residents.

Inter-Island Helicopters

Niʻihau and the west side of Kauaʻi can be viewed from Inter-Island Helicopters' fast Hughes 500 four-seater machine (3441 Kuiloko Rd. Hanapepe, 808/335-5009 or 800/656-5009, www.interislandhelicopters.com). There is no back middle seat, which enables everyone to get a great view. Departing from the Port Allen Airport, a waterfall adventure is offered, along with an island tour that flies straight into the Waimea Canyon, over Kokeʻe State Park, and along the Na Pali Coast.

Island Helicopters

Movie and waterfall buffs will enjoy a trip to **Manawaiopuna Falls,** which was used in Steven Spielberg's 1993 blockbuster *Jurassic Park* and is located on land that is said to belong to the Robinsons, the same family that owns Niʻihau. The nearly 400-foot-tall falls are hidden in a valley near Hanapepe and have been restricted to the public for years. Around five years ago the owner and pilot at Island Helicopters (Ahukini Rd., Lihuʻe, 808/245-8588 or 800/829-5999, www.islandhelicopters.com) began pursuing permits from the state and county to land at the falls. He was successful and now flies people out there five days a week for a 25-minute landing at the falls as part of a 85-minute circle island tour for $269.

WALKING TOURS
Hanapepe

A self-guided walking tour through Hanapepe town can be done with or without the *Historic*

Hanapepe Walking Tour Map that is available without charge in many of the shops in the town. The map provides background information on the historical buildings and churches. For map-free walkers, plaques with information can be found on the front of most of the buildings.

The Kaua'i Coffee Company (800/545-8605, www.kauaicoffee.com, 9 A.M.–5 P.M. daily), the largest single coffee estate in Hawaii, offers a walking tour where visitors can learn about Kaua'i coffee. The tour takes you past interpretive signs that identify the five different varieties of coffee as well as the entire coffee process, from initial blossoming, through harvesting and processing, to the final roasting and into your cup.

Waimea

A local volunteer offers two tours in Waimea free of charge. A walking tour of Waimea town is offered on Mondays only and begins at the **West Kaua'i Technology Center** (9565 Kaumuali'i Hwy., 808/338-1332) at 9:30 A.M. She also guides a tour on Saturdays of a plantation neighborhood dating back to the 1900s; it meets at the lobby of the **Waimea Plantation Cottages** (9400 Kaumuali'i Hwy., 808/338-1625). Reservations are required and can be made by calling 808/337-1005.

Yoga and Spas

Yoga classes are available on this side of the island, but if you already know a few poses, practicing on a remote part of the beach can be a unique and private experience. There are two spas on the west side, both small and quaint. Yet each offers quality pampering with tropical themed scents and treatments.

HANAPEPE

Tropics Day Spa (4353 Waialo Road, Ste. #5B, 808/651-4195, www.tropicsdayspa.com, 9 A.M.–5:30 P.M. Mon.–Wed., 9 A.M.–5 P.M. Thurs.–Sat., and 9 A.M.–3 P.M. Sun.), in the Port Allen Marine Center, offers a variety of massage modalities ($45–130), including Hawaiian *lomilomi*. Body treatments ($100–195), facials ($45–100), spa packages ($155–395), and waxing are also offered, with the common theme of tropical treatments like seaweed wraps and salt scrubs. If you happen to be visiting for a wedding, spa parties are also available. A spa day could be the perfect way to spend time while the rest of the family goes sport-fishing out of the Port Allen Harbor.

WAIMEA

A Hideaway Spa (9400 Kaumuali'i Hwy., 808/338-0005, www.ahideawayspa.com, 9 A.M.–6 P.M. Mon.–Sat. and by appointment only on Sun. and holidays), at Waimea Plantation Cottages, offers beachside yoga and luxurious spa treatments. Oceanside yoga classes span 90 minutes for $15. Instructor Paul Reynolds draws from his 13 years of experience with hatha yoga and other types. The spa offers massage ($95–170), body wraps and scrubs ($65–125), facials ($60–165), waxing ($20–60), hair and nail treatments ($20–100), and traditional Indian ayurvedic treatments ($125–235). To get some serious pampering, three- and five-day spa retreats are also available ($570–745).

Sights

Sights from Hanapepe to the end of the road share two common themes: history and natural wonders. They're generally all easily accessible and camera-worthy.

HANAPEPE
Hanapepe Valley and Lookout

As you come around the bend from Kalaheo and first lay eyes on the Port Allen area, a Hawai'i Visitors Bureau sign points out an overlook pull-off spot for the Hanapepe Valley. It offers a peek down into the valley and it's easily accessible. Pull over, open your door, and you are there. The vast and beautiful valley is a reminder of the geological activity that shaped the Hawaiian Islands and is home to some overgrowth and small taro fields. It's good for a quick look since it's so easy, but the valley is tiny in comparison to Waimea Canyon.

Hanapepe Swinging Bridge

Extended over the Hanapepe River, this wooden plank footbridge runs between the historic town and the inland side of the river. With enough bounce and shake to inspire a little excitement as well as a lovely view down the river, the Hanapepe Swinging Bridge is fun to take a walk on. It's easily accessible from the town and free. Originally built to run a water line across the river and into town, the bridge ends nearly in someone's back yard. Once off the bridge take a left to walk the levee back to the old vehicular bridge and come back into town along Hanapepe Road. A stroll across the bridge fits in easily with any gander through town.

Kauai Coffee Company Visitor Center and Museum

The first coffee to be planted in the Hawaiian Islands was planted in this region over 150 years ago as the state's first coffee plantation. Years later only little success was achieved and coffee production ceased in Kaua'i and moved to the Big Island at Kona. Today coffee is grown not only on the Big Island, but on Maui, Moloka'i,

O'ahu, and again on Kaua'i. It's actually been so successful that in 2011 Italian coffee giant Massimo Zanetti Beverage bought Kaua'i Coffee Company, which grows Hawaiian arabica coffee bean plants on its 3,400-acre drip-irrigated property and produces roughly four million pounds of coffee a year.

Harvest is done mechanically and takes place September through November, resulting in the busiest time of year on the estate. The largest single coffee estate in Hawaii, Kaua'i Coffee has a hold on about 60 percent of the Hawaiian coffee market. If you use Route 540, and especially if you love coffee, stop at the Kaua'i Coffee Company Visitor Center and Museum (1 Numila Rd., 808/335-0813 or 800/545-8605, 9 A.M.–5 P.M. daily). A refurbished plantation building houses the gift shop and museum. Historical artifacts are available for viewing, and information explains how coffee is handled and processed at each stage. Gifts, clothing, food items, and of course coffee can be purchased and tasted.

WAIMEA
Fort Elisabeth State Historical Park

Just before the Waimea River and right past mile marker 22 is Fort Elisabeth State Historical Park. The shape of this Russian fort somewhat resembles an eight-pointed star, and it dates from 1817, when according to traditional history, a German doctor named Georg Anton Schaeffer constructed it in the name of Czar Nicholas of Russia and named it after the czar's daughter.

However, in 2002 University of Hawai'i at Hilo anthropologist Peter R. Mills studied the fort and drew the conclusion that "Hawaiians had been left out of their own history." Mills used hundreds of firsthand accounts along with field research to show that the fort was originally built and used by Hawaiians as a *heiau,* a Hawaiian sacred site. He shows that after the Russians' departure, Hawaiians continued to

© NANI MALOOF

The Waimea Canyon State Park Overlook offers an expansive view of the "Grand Canyon of the Pacific."

use the fort, but they did so in ways that reflected an ongoing transformation of cultural values as a result of contact with outsiders and the development of multiethnic communities in Waimea and other port settlements throughout the Hawaiian chain. For more information, read Mills' book *Hawai'i's Russian Adventure*.

History goes on to say that Schaeffer, an agent for the Russian-American Company, built two other forts on the island, one on the bluff at Princeville and another farther down in Hanalei Bay. It's said that Czar Nicholas never quite warmed up to Schaeffer's work and withdrew official support. Eventually Schaeffer was banned from Kaua'i, sent to Honolulu, and then forced to leave the islands altogether. No longer maintained and cared for, the fort fell apart and was dismantled in 1864 when 38 guns were removed. The walls were once 30 feet thick and are now rubble left to wither away from the elements. Brochures are usually available at the entrance, and plaques on the board tell the history.

Captain Cook Monuments

The Captain Cook monuments pay tribute James Cook, the explorer who is credited with "discovering" the Hawaiian Islands (for the western world, that is; let's remember the Hawaiians were already there). A life-size statue of the man himself is located on the strip of grass that is Hagaard Park, between Waimea Road and Highway 150. Benches are nearby if you'd like to have a seat and enjoy a snack. The other monument is a plaque attached to a boulder at Lucy Wright Beach Park.

West Kaua'i Technology and Visitor Center

At the bottom of Waimea Canyon Drive, audiovisual displays, books, and wall displays at the West Kaua'i Technology and Visitor Center (9565 Kaumuali'i Hwy., 808/338-1332, 9:30 A.M.–4 P.M., Mon. Wed., and Fri., noon–8 P.M. Tues. and Thurs.) offer visitors a glimpse into the history of the town and surrounding areas. There is some Ni'ihau shell

© NANI MALOOF

One of the best views on Kaua'i is from the Kalalau Overlook.

jewelry on display, and other artifacts tell the story of the area's sugar past and technological present. Brochures for Waimea businesses and restaurants, books, Internet access, and printing services are also available.

◖ Waimea Canyon State Park Overlook

Waimea Canyon State Park Overlook and the drive up offer a series of majestic sights of the varied forms mother nature appears in on the west side. The canyon's colors change throughout the day as the sun moves across the sky, so if you gaze into the 10-mile-long, 3,000-foot-deep canyon for a while different photo opportunities present themselves. Make sure to take Waimea Canyon Drive rather than Koke'e Road (which the street sign in Waimea recommends). This road provides clear views of Ni'ihau, multiple valley lookouts, and a small waterfall flowing over bright red dirt at the 1,500-foot elevation sign. Each lookout shares different views of the canyon, and you

will probably be able to spend some time at one alone. To get there, take Waimea Canyon Drive and stick to the right at the fork in the road at the Koke'e State Park sign. At the top there is a lookout with wheelchair accessibility, bathrooms, and often a snack and gift tent. On the way back down, take Koke'e Road just to see the other views. At the bottom are several gift shops and a general store.

Koke'e Natural History Museum

The Koke'e Natural History Museum (3600 Waimea Canyon Dr. after the 15 mm, 808/335-9975, www.kokee.org, 10 A.M.–4 P.M. daily, suggested donation of $1) offers several displays. The museum calls the outdoors the real plant displays, but inside is an exhibit called Treasury of Trees, Resources of a Traditional Lifestyle. The exhibit is on forest trees and their traditional Hawaiian uses. It's interesting to get an idea of how the Hawaiians utilized their natural surroundings. Game animals that were introduced to the island are also on display,

WEST SIDE

including a wild boar, a stag, goats, game birds, and trout. A weather exhibit focuses on the devastating Hurricane 'Iniki. Perhaps the most interesting display is a collection of land and sea shells from Ni'ihau and Kaua'i. A large whale vertebrae and a sea turtle shell are quite intriguing. The museum staff can help you choose which of the 19 trails and hikes in the park are right for you, which is very helpful. Detailed hiking maps are also available.

C Kalalau and Pu'u O Kila Overlooks

Many regard these two overlooks as the best views on Kaua'i, and even the best in the Pacific. At mile marker 18 the Kalalau Overlook opens to an expansive view over Kalalau Valley, the biggest one on the Na Pali Coast. The valley was inhabited until the beginning of the 1900s, and since then, occasionally hippies looking to live off of fruit in the jungle stay a while.

About a mile down the road is the even better Pu'u O Kila, which offers a window into Kalalau Valley, from the Alaka'i Swamp to Mount Wai'ale'ale. If you get there on a cloudy day there's a chance the views won't be visible at all. Earlier in the day is better, or if scheduling allows check the weather and go when it looks best. To get here go past the Koke'e Lodge and onto a road that turns into potholes and broken up pavement.

Shopping

High-end fashion and big box stores are absent on the west side. Small boutiques, local crafts, jewelry, and seemingly infinite art are abundant. The west side offers some unique souvenirs, from Ni'ihau jewelry to local art.

HANAPEPE

Art galleries featuring photography, paintings, drawings, sculptures, glass, and more line the streets of Hanapepe. The town is always worth a stroll through to window shop or take something home.

Art Galleries

Kaua'i Fine Arts (3905 Hanapepe Rd., 808/335-3778, www.brunias.com, 9 A.M.–5 P.M. daily) calls a small white building on the eastern end of Old Hanapepe home. The shop has the feel of an antiques store, as much of its stock is previously used items. Prints of local artists, shell jewelry, maps, books, antique maps, carvings, and other art objects make up the shop's unique collection. Staff is friendly and happy to let visitors browse for a while.

Colorful and unique jewelry, home decor, and handbags can be found in **Kaua'i Finds** (3890 Hanapepe Rd., 808/332-5056, www.kauaifinds.com). Dichroic glass, a glass containing multiple micro-layers of metal oxides giving the glass dichroic optical properties, is used to reflect the various colors found throughout the island in jewelry. Each piece of glass is unique and contains several colors but has one main color per piece.

Giorgio's Fine Art Gallery (3871 Hanapepe Rd., 808/335-3949, www.giorgiosart.com, 11 A.M.–5 P.M. daily) is an extravaganza of color reflecting the beauty of the islands in landscape, floral, and abstract paintings. Using a method called plein air, Giorgio creates palette knife oil paintings, often on location around Kaua'i. You will usually find a friendly staff member overseeing the spacious gallery during business hours, whose happy to chat about the island and art. The walls are covered in bursts of color that jump out at browsers, and it's definitely worth taking a look.

If you look to your left as you enter **Banana Patch Studios** (3865 Hanapepe Rd., 808/335-5944, www.bananapatchstudio.com, 10 A.M.–4:30 P.M. Mon., Tues., Wed., Thurs., and Sat., 10 A.M.–9:30 P.M. Fri.) you will see art being made through a large window looking right

NI'IHAU SHELLS

Diamonds and platinum may be a sign of luxury in the U.S. Mainland, but in Hawaii it's Ni'ihau shell jewelry. The rare and highly valued shells (*kahelelani, laiki, momi,* and *kamoa*), are found on the beaches of Ni'ihau and crafted by the island's residents into various styles of lei, earrings, and bracelets, equaling one of Polynesia's most precious art forms. Captain Cook returned from Hawaii with a Ni'ihau shell lei that now resides in the British Museum. The jewelry is mostly sold on Kaua'i, while some of it makes it to shops on other islands. A large amount is sold in stores on the west side and made by the shop's owner or relatives on Ni'ihau. It's not uncommon to encounter a clerk at one of Waimea's shops and ask where she got her jewelry, only to hear that her niece or nephew made it. Here's an opportunity to purchase the jewelry directly from its crafter, as many of these people are happy to give you a phone number to contact the person who made it.

The shells wash up on the beaches mostly October–March, when winter swells bring waves big enough to wash them ashore. This is when islanders rush to gather the shells and either make the jewelry on the island or send the shells to family on Kaua'i to craft. The tiny shells are sorted by size and color, and only the best are kept; around 80 percent are thrown away. Many of the pink *kahelelani* that are found are a dull flesh color, worn rough, or are broken. The shell colors include bright pink, deep red, white, yellow, blue, and, rarely, gold. Holes are delicately drilled into the small shells, and they are then strung in a traditional fashion to make various types of jewelry. Most common are the necklaces and lei. Roughly twice as many shells than go into a lei are needed because around half are expected to break during the process. The lei are usually a combination of many strands, either hanging below each other or spiraling around each other.

The making of the jewelry, along with the entire process, is an intricate task and can take up to six months to complete. The Ni'ihau women usually do the work, and whole families are involved in collecting, but I recently had a Waimea Big Save cashier tell me that her nephew made the beautiful earrings she was wearing and that he sells them, too. Ni'ihau shell lei are the only shell necklace in the world that can be insured. Shells are used for Ni'ihau lei because the dry island doesn't have a sufficient environment to grow the abundance of flowers the other islands have.

To see a museum-type collection of Ni'ihau shell work, visit the Hawaiian Trading Company in Lawa'i, visible from Highway 50. For a rare and valuable souvenir, Ni'ihau jewelry is the perfect thing. The best book on Ni'ihau jewelry is *Ni'ihau Shell Leis*, by Linda Paik Moriarty, published by the University of Hawai'i Press.

© JADE ECKARDT

an untouched beach on Ni'ihau

into the studio. This is a great place for souvenirs such as ceramic tiles saying "please remove shoes," and "aloha." Owner Joanna Carolan creates the tiles, an array of jewelry, and nature-inspired paintings. Island-style trinkets and home decor from other crafters are also in stock.

Traditional watercolors and out-of-this-world island photography capturing nature's spectacular moments can be found in the **Arius Hopman Gallery** (3840C Hanapepe Rd., 808/335-0227, www.hopmanart.com, 10:30 A.M.–2 P.M. Mon.–Fri., 6–9 P.M. Fri.), where the artwork can be printed up to 12 feet long. Both the paintings and photos reflect Kaua'i's beauty, life, and energy. Hopman's artistic ability is in his blood; his mother was a world-renowned artist who was commissioned to sculpt Mahatma Gandhi twice. The native of India moved to Hawaii in 1985 and lives in Hanapepe.

Crafts and Books

There's something warm and cozy about independently owned bookstores, and **Talk Story Bookstore** (3785 Hanapepe Rd., 808/335-6469, www.talkstorybookstore.com, 10 A.M.–5 P.M. Mon.–Thurs., 10 A.M.–9:30 P.M. Fri.) doesn't disappoint. The family-run business is Kaua'i's only new and used bookstore and is located in the historic Old Yoshiura Store. Over 40,000 used, rare, and collectible books are available, along with Hawaiian gifts, crafts, records, and Hawaiian slack-key and ukulele lesson courses. Any books you may be done with can be traded in for in store credit. The shop stays open late on Art Night offering live entertainment.

Crafts and jewelry decorate **JJ Ohana** (3805-B Hanapepe Rd., 808/335-0366, www.jjohana.com, 8 A.M.–6 P.M. Mon.–Thurs., 8 A.M.–9 P.M. Fri., 8 A.M.–5 P.M. Sat.). The highlight here is the Ni'ihau shell jewelry made by the owner, whom you may find overseeing the shop when you visit. She makes beautiful earrings, necklaces, and bracelets that are some of the most valuable Kaua'i souvenirs.

PORT ALLEN
Clothing

At the **Red Dirt Factory Outlet** (4350 Waialo Road, 800/717-3478., www.dirtshirt.com, 9 A.M.–5 P.M. daily) in Port Allen, a natural resource has been used to create one of the most famous Kaua'i souvenirs. The shirts are dyed with real Kaua'i red dirt and there's an interesting story behind the making of the shirts.

When Hurricane 'Iniki unleashed its fury on Kaua'i in 1992, the staff at Paradise Sportswear returned to the shop to find the warehouse roof completely torn off. The storm left a large stock of shirts dyed red from the island's dirt. What could have led to a bleak future for the company suddenly became a blessing as a person with a "glass half full" outlook on life said, "These shirts look pretty cool." Next thing you know the Red Dirt Shirt was created and is maintained by local families taking regular old white shirts home and dipping them in vats of Kaua'i's red dirt. They bring them back and other locals apply silk-screen designs on shirts that are distinct from one another because the color ranges from a deep reddish brown to a light orange. Self-guided tours are available at the factory store daily 9 A.M.–noon and 1–4 P.M. to watch the silk-screening process. There is also a smaller red dirt store in Waimea and on each island.

WAIMEA
Gourmet Treats and Beauty Products

Known as one of the tastiest tropical flavors and used across the culinary board from desserts to entrées, the *liliko'i,* or passion fruit, is used in all of its glory at **Aunty Liliko'i** (9633 Kaumuali'i Hwy., 808/338-1296, www.auntylilikoi.com, 10 A.M.–6 P.M. daily). The sweet and sour fruit is the highlight in jams, jellies, mustards, dressings, syrups, and even skin-care products. Drop by the quaint shop in Waimea to pick up a snack.

Antiques

Antiques from around the islands can be found at **Collectibles and Fine Junque** (9821 Kaumuali'i Hwy., 808/338-9855). An array of Hawaiiana, books, trinkets, jewelry, and so much more fills the small shop to the brim. The staff is usually happy to "talk story" with shoppers, and even just browsing here can be fun. The small building that houses the shop is an antique itself. Those looking for it may question if the run-down building is being utilized, but the historic look adds to the shop's spirit.

THE WILD WEST
Souvenirs

Located at the bottom of Koke'e Road is the Waimea Canyon Plaza, with a **Menehune Food Mart** (808/337-1335), **Waimea Canyon General Store** (808/337-9569), and **Thrifty Mini Mart** (808/337-1057). These markets are good for last-minute souvenir shopping.

Entertainment

If you're looking for nightlife, the west side isn't where you'll find it. Art Night in Hanapepe is really the only action at night other than a dinner out or stargazing on the beach (which is quite enjoyable).

◖ ART NIGHT IN HANAPEPE

Around 16 art galleries open their doors for a night of art celebration each Friday 6–9 P.M. on Hanapepe Road. Art Night is an opportunity to socialize with locals and other visitors, explore the town, and meet artists. A gallery manager recently said that any shops in the historic town that don't sell art (there aren't many) will tell you the celebratory night is called "Festival Night." Don't be fooled, he said—it's all about the art. The night can be enjoyed casually if you're coming straight from the beach but it can also be an opportunity to dress up for a night out on the small, historical town.

NIGHTLIFE

Your best bet for entertainment in Waimea would be live music at the **The Grove Cafe** (9400 Kaumualii Hwy., 808/338-1625,11 A.M.–10 P.M. daily), where local bands play for dinner guests most nights a week. You can also sit down for a meal on the plantation-style building's lanai or enjoy a locally brewed beer at the indoor bar.

CINEMA

The historic **Waimea Theater** (9691 Kaumuali'i Hwy., 808/338-0282, www.waime-atheater.com) was built in 1938. It closed in 1972 and was converted to a warehouse and

STARGAZING

Stargazing can be done anywhere on Kaua'i, but few take advantage of this opportunity. Joining a group of stargazers once a month is an inspiration to relax outdoors at night and revel in the light of the sparkling stars (*hoku* in Hawaiian). From June to September, the **Kaua'i Educational Association for Science and Astronomy** (808/332-7827, www.keasa.org) gathers stargazers together at the Kaumakani ball field to watch a celestial cinema. Heading west from Hanapepe, look for the Thrifty Mart Bakery in Kaumakani, take a right at the Kaumakani sign, then turn right again to the ball field. With no city lights around, the stars out here burn bright and glittery.

later survived damage from Hurricane 'Iniki in 1992. The building was leased in 1993 by West Kaua'i Main Street to prevent the owner from tearing it down, and this marked the beginning of a seven-year effort to save the landmark theater. In 1996 the County of Kaua'i purchased the building, and after years of restoration it was opened in 1999 as a functioning movie theater that now accommodates 270 patrons. Featuring a small stage, movie screen, sound system, and snack bar, it's the only movie theater from here to Lihu'e. A night at the Waimea Theater isn't just movie night, it's experiencing a part of the west side's history. Call for showtimes and movie listings.

Food

Good food isn't hard to find out west. There are a number of *ono* (delicious) places to eat, from snacks and desserts to local brews and dinner. For such small towns there's a wide array of cuisines and a decent number of vegetarian dishes scattered through the eateries.

HANAPEPE
American
The roadside **Grinds Cafe** (4469 Waialo Rd., 808/335-6027, www.grindscafe.net, 5:30 A.M.–9 P.M. daily) serves their entire menu all day long. They offer pizzas, sandwiches, pasta, salads, and more. Breakfasts options start at $6, while dinner entrée options range $18–20. Indoor and patio seating is available to enjoy a meal along with a glass of beer or wine, or passersby can take some food to go for the beach or a boat trip from nearby Port Allen. Here you will find a mix of locals picking up a cup of coffee and visitors passing through the area. *Grinds* is local slang for food.

Groceries
For groceries, alcoholic beverages, local deli food, and more drop into the **Big Save** (808/335-3127, 6:30 A.M. to 10 P.M. daily) in the 'Ele'ele Shopping Center (4469 Waialo Rd.). This is a good spot to stock up on extra drinks or snack before heading out on a boat cruise or jetting of to Ni'ihau for the day. The store offers limited pre-made food such as sushi and other local style dishes to eat on the road.

Local Food
If you're looking for a true local experience, have a meal at **Da Imu Hut** (1-3529 Kaumuali'i Hwy. Suite A, 808/335-0300) and try plate lunch local food. Their signature dishes include the Hawaiian plate lunch and the Imu Hut teri-fried chicken. *Ono, brah.*

Mostly Vegetarian
The **◖ Hanapepe Cafe and Bakery** (3830 Hanapepe Rd., 808/335-5011, 7 A.M.–3 P.M.

Mon.–Thurs., 5–8:30 P.M. Fri., $15–35) never fails to satisfy with their mostly vegetarian menu, which is backed up with local fish dishes and what the owner calls "the occasional turkey club sandwich." Pastries made on-site are available in many different forms of mouthwatering sweet goodness, and trying at least two is a must. The home-style café and bakery has a homey atmosphere in an old plantation building adorned with Hawaiian-style decorations and crafts. Service is good and friendly, and always comes with a smile. The bakery opens once a week for dinner on Fridays.

Thai
◖ Toi's Thai Kitchen (in the 'Ele'ele Shopping Center, 808/335-3111, 10:30 A.M.–2 P.M. and 5:30–9 P.M. Tues.–Sat.) is a local favorite and staple. The atmosphere is relaxed and lacking in ambience, but the food is tasty and portions are good. Service can be a bit on the slow side, but it's always friendly. They offer a substantial menu that will satisfy traditional diets as well as vegetarians with their seafood, meat, and tofu options. Lunch dishes come with a green papaya salad that I highly recommend, and the option of brown, sticky, or jasmine rice.

Treats and Desserts
Chocolate, especially local, is enough of a reason to stop at the **Kaua'i Chocolate Company** (4341 Waialo Rd., 808/335-0448, www .kauaichocolate.us, 8 A.M.–6 P.M. Mon.–Fri., 11 A.M.–5 P.M. Sat., noon–3 P.M. Sun.). Serving up truffles, macadamia nuts, and ice cream, the shop will either fill your belly on the spot or your suitcase for gifts at home. The small shop is like a mini version of Willie Wonka's factory, and it's nearly impossible to leave without a treat.

Wong's (13543 Kaumaualii Hwy., 808/335-5066, 9:30 A.M.–9 P.M. Tues.–Sun.) claims to serve up Kaua'i's best *liliko'i* (passion fruit) pie. Wong's is a Chinese restaurant, but I'm citing them for the pie. The light *liliko'i* chiffon pie is delicious, and it actually tastes like real *liliko'i*.

Stop in and enjoy a piece for under $3, or take a whole pie to go.

The tropical- and traditional-flavored ice creams and sorbets at **C Lappert's Ice Cream** (1-3555 Kaumuali'i Hwy., 808/335-6121 or 800/356-4045, www.lappertshawaii.com, 10 A.M.–6 P.M. daily, $4 for a single scoop) are the perfect cool accent to a warm Hawaiian day. Originating on Kaua'i, the shop now has outlets statewide and has about 16 percent butterfat in its regular flavors and around 8 percent in its fruit flavors, making for some pretty creamy ice cream. There's a wide array of delicious flavors, so I recommend sampling a few before making a decision.

The **Kaua'i Kookie Company** (1-3529 Kaumuali'i Hwy., 808/335-5003, www. kauaikookie.com, 8 A.M.–4 P.M. Mon.–Fri., 11 A.M.–4 P.M. Sat.–Sun.) is another local treat that makes a great snack or gift. At the Hanapepe factory outlet they sell their macadamia shortbread, Kona coffee, guava macadamia, and coconut krispies cookies and more. The cookies are also distributed around the island and can be purchased by mail order.

Farmers Market

A year-round, open-air market, the **Hanapepe Farmers Market** provides local produce and crafts. Located behind the Hanapepe fire station in **Hanapepe Park,** the market happens every Thursday 3–5 P.M. Try to remember to bring your own reusable shopping bag or a pre-used plastic bag from another store.

WAIMEA
American

The decor stays true to the name at **C Wrangler's Steakhouse** (9852 Kaumuali'i Hwy., 808/338-1218, for lunch 11 A.M.–4 P.M. Mon.–Fri., for dinner 4–9 P.M. Mon.–Sat., $17–28), where the restaurant is decorated with cowboy trinkets and gear. Indoor and outdoor seating are offered, and I've learned that with little ones who have a hard time sitting still, the outdoor seating in the back is a good idea. Wrangler's is known for their great steaks, and they offer a salad and soup bar with

each meal. A full bar is stocked with a variety of liquors, wines, and beers to please any palate. The menu offers a hefty assortment of red meats, poultry, and seafood, but surprisingly, vegetarians can enjoy a sufficient and tasty meat-free meal. Service is friendly and there is also a small *paniolo* (Hawaiian cowboy) museum as well as shell jewelry for sale.

To peel, or not to peel, that is the question at **C The Shrimp Station** (9652 Kaumuali'i Hwy., 808/338-1242, $11–12), where shrimp is served up in a number of ways. At this very laid-back eatery, seating is on picnic tables under a tent right on the side of the main road. The menu includes shrimp entrées, drinks, desserts, and ice cream. *Kama'aina* discounts are available and service is friendly but to the point. It's across from Island Tacos.

Breakfast
Obsessions (9875 Waimea Rd., 808/338-1110, 6 A.M.–2 P.M. Wed.–Sun.) is a home-style breakfast café with absolutely no frills. Eggs, sausage, pancakes, coffee and other usual breakfast dishes are served. The food is decent, simple, and perfectly satisfying. The atmosphere is very homey, with artwork and letters from the town's schoolchildren on the wall. Food is served on disposable plates.

Groceries
For usual supermarket needs there is a **Big Save** (9861 Waimea Rd., 808/338-1621, 6 A.M.–10 P.M. Mon.–Sat. and 6 A.M.–9 P.M. Sun.) in Waimea. They carry limited pre-made deli food, groceries, snorkel and dive gear, baby products, and more.

The **Ishihara Market** (9894 Kaumuali'i Hwy., 808/338-1751, 6 A.M.–7:30 P.M. Mon.–Thurs., 6 A.M.–8 P.M. Fri.–Sat., and 6 A.M.–7 P.M. Sun.) offers the usual supermarket finds, but they are well known with locals for their wide variety of local deli foods. Check out the deli in the back for *poke,* sandwiches, sushi, ribs, and a whole lot more. They even sell plain already-made rice and have a substantial selection of bowls, cups, and utensils, making it perfect for a last-minute camping stop. The store smells a little funky and fishy, but locals love the food.

Hawaiian Regional

The [**The Grove Cafe**](9400 Kaumualii Hwy., 808/338-1625,11 A.M.–10 P.M. daily, $11–25) brews different types of locally brewed beer from all over the islands and serves good food with a local twist. A plantation-style building has high ceilings, hardwood floors, and fans that enhance the breezy environment. The menu includes local seafood dishes, steak, spicy ahi roles, and various vegetarian options.

Italian

In the same building as Wrangler's is **Pacific Pizza and Deli** (808/338-1020, 11 A.M.–9 P.M. Mon.–Sat.). They serve really good pizza, calzones, deli sandwiches, drinks, and ice cream. The small shop puts a twist on traditional pizza with options such as Thai, Filipino, Portuguese, and Mexican tastes, reflecting the flavors of each country. Smoothies, coffee, and ice tea are offered to refresh you in the west-side heat.

Local Treats

Finely shaved ice and 60 flavors can be found at [**Jo-Jo's Clubhouse** (9734 Kaumuali'i Hwy. across from mile marker 23). What's commonly known as a snow cone in the Mainland is called shave ice in Hawaii. The line can be long, but it's a testimony to their great shave ice. Try some local flavor combos like lychee and coconut or *liliko'i* and *melona*.

An easy and healthy breakfast or snack in the hotel room or while camping can be found at **Kaua'i Granola** (9633 Kaumuali'i Hwy., 808/338-0121, www.kauaigranola.com, 10 A.M.–5 P.M. Mon.–Sat., 10 A.M.–3 P.M. Sun.). Unique flavors like pina colada, Hawaiian zest, and guava crunch are available and sold along with Waimea-made chocolate-dipped coconut macaroons, dried fruit, cookies, and pastries. Nestled in a small shop next to Island Tacos, it's another option to bring home a taste of paradise.

Mexican

[**Island Tacos** (9643 Kaumualii Hwy., 808/338.9895, www.islandfishtaco.com, 11 A.M.–5 P.M. Mon.–Sun., $3–12) in Waimea is a simple order-at-the-counter taco stand with seating, reminiscent of roadside taco stands in Mexico. The large menu offers local fish, pork, chicken, and even a wide variety of satisfying vegetarian and vegan options. Portions here are large, with unique toppings like a wasabi-spiked aioli sauce and the option of fat-free dishes. Perfect for a quick stop on a drive through Waimea or to satisfy a craving after camping at Polihale, this place is really good. As locals would say, 'nuff said.

Mostly Vegetarian

Organic, vegetarian, vegan, and natural breakfasts, lunches, smoothies, and desserts can be found at the new family-run [**Happy Mangos Healthy Hale** (Alawai Rd., 808/338-0055, www.happymangos.com, store 6:30 A.M.–5 P.M., café till 4 P.M. Mon.–Fri., 7 A.M.–3 P.M., café till 2 P.M. Sat., $3.50–8.25). The local owners serve freshly made food along with natural and organic groceries and produce. Located in a small plantation-style building across from Lucy Wright Beach Park, the health food store is the only natural and organic choice in Waimea. They serve non-vegetarian sandwiches too.

KOKE'E STATE PARK
Local Food

At the **Koke'e Lodge** restaurant (808/335-6061, www.thelodgeatkokee.net, $7–10), breakfast is served daily 9–11 A.M. and lunch 10 A.M.–2:30 P.M. The soups accent the cool weather nicely, and their banana bread and Koke'e corn bread are good for a treat. Meat entrées are common, but there are a few vegetarian options too, along with local dishes like *kalua* pork and *loco moco*. Wine, beer, and cocktails are also on the menu. The next eatery is about 15 miles away unless you bring a picnic lunch.

THE WILD WEST
Farmers Market

On Saturdays a farmers market happens at the

Kekaha Neighborhood Center on Elepaio Road from 9–11 A.M. Drop by on the way to the beach to see the assortment of local crafts, fruits, vegetables, and other local specialties. The market is open year-round.

Groceries

Located at the bottom of Koke'e Road is the Waimea Canyon Plaza, offering **Menehune** **Food Mart** (808/337-1335, 6 A.M.–8 P.M. Mon.–Sat., 6 A.M.–6 P.M. Sun.), **Waimea Canyon General Store** (808/337-9569, 9 A.M.–5:30 P.M. daily), and **Thrifty Mini Mart** (808/337-1057, 8 A.M.–9 P.M. daily). Each market offers basic small supermarket finds. These markets are good for cooler stocking before heading out to Polihale or when entering or leaving the parks.

Information and Services

BANKS
Hanapepe

In the 'Ele'ele Shopping Center is a **First Hawaiian Bank** (808/335-3161, www.fhb.com, 8:30 A.M.–4 P.M. Mon.–Thurs. and 8:30 A.M.–6 P.M. Fri.), offering walk-in and 24-hour ATM services and a notary service.

Bank of Hawaii has an ATM in the Big Save in the 'Ele'ele Shopping Center and the McDonalds at the shopping center.

In Old Hanapepe is an **American Savings Bank** (4548 Kona Rd., 808/335-3118, www.asbhawaii.com, 8 A.M.–5 P.M. Mon.–Thurs. and 8 A.M.–6 P.M. Fri.). The branch offers walk-in services and a 24-hour ATM.

Waimea

There are several banks in Waimea. **First Hawaiian Bank** (4525 Panako Rd., 808/338-1611, www.fhb.com, 8:30 A.M.–4 P.M. Mon.–Thurs. and 8:30 A.M.–6 P.M. Fri.) offers walk-in and 24-hour ATM services and a notary service.

Next to the Big Save is a **Bank of Hawaii** (9801 Waimea Rd., 808/338-1636, www.boh.com). Walk-in service and a 24-hour ATM are provided.

POSTAL SERVICES
Hanapepe

At Hanapepe's **United States Post Office** (3817 Kona Rd., 808/335-3641, 9 A.M.–1 P.M. and 1:30–4 P.M. Mon.–Fri.) regular shipping services are offered.

Waimea

There is a **United States Post Office** (9911 Waimea Rd., 808/338-9973, 9 A.M.–1 P.M. and 1:30–4 P.M. Mon.–Fri. and 9–11 A.M. Sat.) in Waimea. They provide shipping services, limited packaging materials, and stamps.

INTERNET SERVICES
Waimea

Internet is available at **Aloha-n-Paradise** (9905 Waimea Rd., 808/338-1522, 7 A.M.–noon Mon.–Fri., 8 A.M.–noon Sat.), where you can surf the net on their computers or bring in your own laptop and use their wireless. The **Waimea Public Library** (9750 Kaumuali'i Hwy., 808/338-6848, noon–8 P.M. Mon. and Wed., 9 A.M.–5 P.M. Tues. and Thurs., 10 A.M.–5 P.M. Fri.) and the **West Kaua'i Visitor and Technology Center** (9565 Kaumuali'i Hwy., 808/338-1332) both offer Internet access. Printing is available at each location.

EMERGENCY SERVICES
Waimea

A fire station is located along the highway at the bottom of Menehune Road, and a short distance up Waimea Canyon Drive is **West Kaua'i Medical Center** (4643 Waimea Canyon Dr., 808/338-9431) and its clinic (808/338-8311). It is the only hospital on the west side and offers 24-hour emergency services.

WEST SIDE

CLASSES
Waimea

There's no better way to experience local culture than to learn some of the traditions. Hula and art classes give visitors a unique window into the Hawaiian culture and the island's natural beauty.

Hula at **A Hideaway Spa** (9400 Kaumuali'i Hwy. Waimea, 808/338-0005, www.ahideawayspa.com) will expose you to an art that is a foundation of the Hawaiian culture. Located on the property of Waimea Plantation Cottages, the 90-minute classes are a perfect way to relax, learn, and have fun on your vacation. Call for a class schedule.

Create your own souvenir at **Kaua'i Art Classes** (808/631-9173, www.Kauaiartclasses. com). All materials are provided for creating silk paintings, acrylics, and pastels at Waimea Plantation Cottages. Classes are offered at multiple locations on the west side so check the website for directions and addresses.

To get the most out of your photo opportunities on Kaua'i, take a **digital photography class** from Hanapepe painter and photographer Arius Hopman (808/335-5616).

Getting There and Around

BY AIR

After arriving at the Lihu'e Airport visitors have the choice of catching the bus around the island, renting a car, having a friend pick them up, or even hitchhiking. Most visitors will arrive in Lihu'e via a stopover in Honolulu, where they will connect from their large commercial airline to either Hawaiian Air or Go! Airlines.

BY CAR

The most convenient way to get around the west side is by car. Highway 50 heads west straight out of Lihu'e and runs all the way to the end of the road to Polihale. Rental cars are the best bet here and are available at the airport. Gas prices go up the farther west you go, so it's a good idea to fill up in Lihu'e.

BY BUS

The **Kaua'i Bus** (808/241-6410, www.kauai .gov/Transportation, 5:27 a.m.–10:40 p.m. Mon.–Fri. and 6:21 a.m.–5:50 p.m. Sat., Sun., and holidays) runs island-wide as far west as Kekaha, and is a green, convenient, and affordable way to get around. But with Kekaha as the last stop, and no routes up to the parks, taking the bus out west means you are far away from the biggest draws of the west side—the far west beaches and the state parks. It does stop at the Kaua'i Coffee Company Visitor Center and in Hanapepe, allowing for a visit to the art galleries. Fares are $1 for children and seniors, and $2 for the general public. Monthly passes are also available.

BY TAXI

Pono Taxi (808/634-4744, www.ponotaxi. com) offers west shore sightseeing and dining tours.

HITCHHIKING

Hitchhiking is legal on Kaua'i, as long as you stay off the paved part of the road, but if you try to thumb it all the way out to Polihale, there's a good chance of walking a very long way in the scorching sun. For safety reasons, it is recommended that women and children do not hitchhike alone.

ACCOMMODATIONS

Kaua'i is home to many different types of accommodations, with most of them on the south, east, and north sides. You'll find a substantial array of vacation rentals, condominiums, resorts, bed-and-breakfasts, smaller hotels, and mainstream, big-name resorts. Those who are planning on being outdoors exploring the island may prefer a lower-priced place to leave belongings and shower without planning on spending much time in the room. Visitors who would like to spend a lot of time relaxing at their accommodations may find a large resort or luxury condominium with a lot of amenities suitable. Visitors with bigger groups may do well at a vacation rental, a residence with the usual amenities a home has to offer that enables privacy. For nature lovers or travelers on a budget, camping shouldn't be overlooked as an option. It's an extremely affordable way to enjoy the best of Kaua'i's natural beauty, even if just for one night.

It's a good idea to make accommodation reservations well in advance, especially if you're visiting in the busy season. A good thing to take into consideration when booking a place to stay is location. If you've been to Kaua'i before and know you'll be spending most of your time in your favorite area, that of course would be the place to stay. For those who are making their first visit to the island and who will be exploring all sides of Kaua'i, a place in Kapa'a or Lihu'e may be sufficient since the island is so small that driving most places doesn't take long. The east side generally offers more affordable accommodations than the north or south shore. Remember to always inquire about *kama'aina* rates (special rates for Hawaii residents); hotels offer them often.

© POIPU OCEAN VIEW RESORTS, INC.

East Side

WAILUA
Under $100

Easy on the wallet is the **Rosewood Kaua'i Bunk House** (872 Kamalu Rd., 808/822-5216, www.rosewoodkauai.com, $50–60), where you can choose from three studios with kitchenettes and private entrances with shared bathroom and outdoor shower. Very cute and clean with hardwood floors and bright white walls. Two rooms rent for $50 a night and one for $60, all with a $25 cleaning fee.

Located in a private home in Wailua is the **Whispering Ferns Studio Apartment** (808/822-5216, www.rosewoodkauai.com/whispering_ferns, $95). Renting for $95 a night with a three-night minimum and $50 cleaning fee, it offers 350 square feet of space with its own entrance. A nice treat is that the owners provide daily breakfast and a welcome basket. You'll have wireless Internet and a kitchenette. The apartment has an elegant island decor.

A good deal is **The Garden Room** (808/822-5216, www.rosewoodkauai.com/garden, $75), an affordable studio apartment in a private home in Wailua. It's just three miles from the ocean, and you'll find a welcome basket upon arrival. The studio is very clean with a well-kept interior and lovely manicured grounds with a fishpond. Beach gear is available here, along with Internet access and a private entrance. The place rents for $75 a night with a $50 cleaning fee.

A privately owned apartment dubbed the **Traditional Room** (808/822-5216, www.rosewoodkauai.com/traditional, $95) is located in the hills of Wailua and is an immaculately maintained unit with a private bathroom. You'll wake up to breakfast each morning here. It sleeps two for $95 a night with a three-night minimum and $35 cleaning fee. It's a gorgeous room with an elegant island style.

On three acres on the Sleeping Giant mountain is **Lani Keha** (848 Kamalu Rd., 808/822-1605, www.lanikeha.com, $55–65), which offers very casual accommodations perfect for the traveler who is looking to meet others. They offer three rooms with a communal kitchen and living room. You can rent one room at $55 a night for a single or $65 for a double, or the whole house for $250 with a two-night minimum. No frills but nice, simple, and clean.

The lovely **Sleeping Giant Cottage** (5979 Heamoi Pl., 505/401-4403, www.wanek.com/sleepinggiant, $95) is a one-bedroom simple cottage with three lanai nestled in a lush yard. It's about a 10-minute drive down to the ocean, and they require a three-night minimum. The rate is $95 a night but they offer specials for weekly and monthly stays with a one-time $50 cleaning fee. It has a homey simple island style with full bathroom and kitchen, cable TV, washer and dryer, some beach gear, gas grill, king-size bed, and a queen-size sleeper sofa.

At the **(Kaua'i Sands Hotel** (420 Papaloa Rd., 808/822-4941 or 800/560-5533, www.kauaisandshotel.com, $59–80) you'll find a perfect blend of simple island style and great affordability in 200 rooms on six oceanfront acres. Reminiscent of a 1970s hotel in the simple style and color mix, the hotel is quite nice, although simple with no frills. Each room has a small refrigerator, TV, air-conditioning, and either one king-size or two double beds. Service is always friendly, and out by the usually uncrowded pool the lawn opens up to the ocean. The hotel is extremely affordable, with standard mountain-view rooms going for $59 a night, superior garden views for $65 a night, deluxe pool view for $69 a night, and a kitchenette for $80 a night.

$100-200

Inn Paradise (6381 Makana Rd., 808/822-2542, www.innparadise.com, $85–120) has three suites. The King Kaumualii Suite can house up to four people and is a two-bedroom one-bath unit. With a full kitchen it runs for $120 a night for a three-night minimum. The

WORLD WIDE OPPORTUNITIES ON ORGANIC FARMS (WWOOF)

Become one with nature by WWOOFing on youre Kaua'i vacation. World Wide Opportunities on Organic Farms (WWOOF) is a world-wide program that offers accommodations and food on organic farms in trade for volunteer work. Visit www.wwoofhawaii.org to sign up for the program. It's only $25 a year per person or $40 a year for a couple. There is around 20 farms on Kaua'i that serve as WWOOF host farms, and more throughout the islands. They usually ask for a certain amount of hours of volunteer work in exchange for a place to stay and meals. Accommodations can vary from pitiching a tent on the property to a basic cabin. It's a good idea to try and book a couple of months in advance as the spots can fill up quickly. Check out the website for host information.

Queen Kapule Suite is a one-bedroom that can hold up to four people. It has a small kitchen and a three-night minimum stay is required. It costs $100 a night. A cute studio that accommodates two people perfectly, the Prince Kuhio Suite is decorated in island-style decor and is $85 a night with a three-night minimum. Personalized welcome baskets, beach gear, and a Jacuzzi are all offered.

Opaeka'a Falls Hale (120 Liahu St., 800/262-9912, www.bestbnb.com/OpaekkaUpper.html, $110–130) has two units. The upper is called the Royal Palm and the Queen Emma is on the lower level. The Royal Palm rents for $130 a night and sleeps two people. The Queen Emma rents for $110 a night for two. Both have a $50 cleaning fee and require a five-night minimum. There's a beautiful pool on-site and it's a short drive from the ocean. Both have a full kitchen, lanai, and washer and dryer.

The **Fern Grotto Inn** (4561 Kuamo'o Rd., 808/821-9836, www.ferngrottoinn.com, $99–149) consists of three cottages and a house. All are remodeled simple plantation-style homes with shared laundry and either full or limited kitchens. The friendly owners live on-site and it's near the Wailua River. All of the accommodations are decorated with a clean island style. The River Cottage is a cute and clean studio for $149 a night with an $80 cleaning fee. The Canal Cottage is divided into two studios, one renting for $99 a night and one for $109. The Garden Cottage studio rents for $99 a night with a $60 cleaning fee.

Four clean cottages make up the **Hale Lani B&B** (283 Aina Lani Pl., 808/823-6434, www.halelani.com, $125–195). Kanoa's Cottage has a private hot tub and costs $185 a night. Melia's Suite is a two-bedroom with kitchenette and private hot tub for $165 a night or $195 for four adults. Nani's Retreat is a studio with kitchenette for $135 a night. Lani's Studio is $125 a night. All have private entrances, personalized gift baskets, and home-cooked meals left outside your door in a cooler if you choose. Three-night minimums are required for all. If it works out they offer a half-day rate of $45 if you have a late return flight home.

A great deal is **Kapa'a Sands** (380 Papaloa Rd., 808/822-4901 or 800/222-4901, www.kapaasands.com, $90–185) along the ocean with under 30 units. It's just off the beach with a nice lawn between the units and the ocean, and you'll find a pool, barbecue area, and free Internet access. Oceanfront and ocean-view studios and two-bedroom units are available with lanai and maid service. Studios can be rented for $90–135, two bedrooms for $130–185, and can house up to four people. A three- or seven-night minimum stay is required.

A steal of a deal is at **Wailua Bayview** (320 Papaloa Rd., 800/367-5242, www.wailuabay.com, $163–175), where fewer than 50 units are located just off the beach. Condominium amenities include pool, free Internet access, and a barbecue area. One-bedroom units are $163–175. A four-night minimum stay is required.

At the **Courtyard by Marriott** (650 Aleka

EAST SIDE ACCOMMODATIONS

Name	Type	Price	Features	Why Stay Here	Best Fit For
Aloha Hale Orchid	studio	$55	mini-fridge	on orchid farm, affordable	budget travelers
◪ Aston Aloha Beach Hotel	hotel	$200-315	pool	affordable, good location	families, couples
Courtyard by Marriott	hotel	$100-200	pool, business center	friendly service	families, couples
Dilly Dally House	B&B	$115-185	pool, breakfast	amenities	couples, no children allowed
Fern Grotto Inn	cottages	$99-149	kitchens	privacy	families, couples
Garden Island Inn	small inn	$135-160	kitchenettes, beach gear	affordable, central location	couples
The Garden Room	apartment	$75	welcome basket	affordable	couples
Green Coconut Studio	private home	$110	overlooks the ocean	affordable	couples
Hale Lani B&B	B&B	$125-195	breakfast, hot tub	privacy, home-cooked meals	couples
Hotel Coral Reef	hotel	$110-175	pool	oceanfront	couples
Inn Paradise	B&B	$85-120	laundry, beach gear	friendly, homey	couples
Kaha Lani	condos	$235-500	tennis court, pool	oceanfront	families, couples
Kapa'a Sands	condos	$90-185	pool, barbecue	oceanfront, affordable	families, couples
Kaua'i Beach House	hostel	$30-70	kitchen area	near the water	budget travelers
Kauai Country Inn	B&B	$129-179	Beatles museum	breakfast	couples

Name	Type	Price	Features	Why Stay Here	Best Fit For
Kaua'i Inn	small inn	$85-139	pool	free breakfast	budget travelers
Kauai International Hostel	hostel	$25-65	common kitchen area	affordable	budget travelers, young people
◪ Kaua'i Marriott Resort	large resort	$220-429	full resort amenities, child care	full-service resort	families, couples
Kaua'i Palms Hotel	budget hotel	$75	free muffins and coffee	affordable	budget travelers
◪ Kaua'i Sands Hotel	budget hotel	$59-80	pool	oceanfront, affordable	budget travelers
◪ Lae Nani	condos	$204-355	pool, tennis court	oceanfront	families, couples
Lani Keha	rooms	$55-265	communal kitchen	affordable	budget travelers
◪ Motel Lani	hotel	$64	showers	affordable	budget travelers
No Ka Oi	studio	$79-99	beach gear, barbecue	affordable	budget travelers, couples
Opaeka'a Falls Hale	vacation rental	$110-130	pool	affordable	couples
Orchid Tree Inn	studios	$85-110	full kitchen	location	budget travelers
Rosewood Kaua'i Bunk House	rooms	$50-60	kitchenettes	affordable	budget travelers
Sleeping Giant Cottage	private home	$95	beach gear, grill	privacy	couples
Traditional Room	apartment	$95	breakfast	affordable	couples
Wailua Bayview	condos	$163-175	pool	affordable	couples
Whispering Ferns Studio Apartment	apartment	$95	breakfast	welcome basket	budget travelers, couples

Loop, 808/822-3455, www.courtyardkauai. com, $100–200) in Kapaʻa you'll find very nice accommodations. The rooms have a clean-cut island-style feel, with lovely furniture made from coconut wood and really comfortable beds. They have a business area with free Internet access and a computer and printer for guests. It was renovated in 2011. The property is along the ocean, and rooms have ocean or mountain views. Oceanfront rooms max at a little over $200, and rates vary with season, but this is generally a very affordable hotel. A pool, spa, tennis courts, fitness center, and lounge decorate the centrally located hotel. Check for *kamaʻaina* rates here; they make a big difference.

Over $200

Backing the wonderful Lydgate Beach Park is the **(Aston Aloha Beach Hotel** (3-5920 Kuhio Hwy., 808/823-6000 or 888/823-5111, www.abrkauai.com, $200–315). The location is great for anyone who loves swimming in the calm ocean, especially families. Consisting of 216 rooms, the hotel boasts two pools, a tennis court, a jet spa, an on-site restaurant, fitness room, high speed Internet, and coin-operated laundry. Rooms have sliding doors but no balcony, and offer small refrigerators. Two-room cottages are also available here. One wing has bathtubs while the other has showers. Garden views run $201, ocean views $215, junior suites $252, one bedrooms $324, and cottages $315.

Between the Wailua golf course and Lydgate Beach Park, location is just one of the appeals of **Kaha Lani** (4460 Nehe Rd., 808/822-9331, www.castleresorts.com, $235–500). The complex is luxury on the ocean, but with ample space between the units and the water. There is a pool, a lighted tennis court, and all units have full kitchens and a lanai. One-bedroom units rent for $235–375, two bedrooms for $250–400, and three bedrooms for $375–500, and prices vary slightly between seasons.

A real treat is the condominium **(Lae Nani** (410 Papaloa Rd., 808/822-4938, $204–355). All nicely decorated units have full kitchens, a lanai, TVs, and one and a half baths.

Guests are also treated to a pool, poolside grill, and tennis court. Bookings can be done through different companies, but the average price for a one-bedroom is $204–300, and two bedrooms cost $240–355. A minimum stay of two nights is required.

KAPAʻA
Under $100

Proof of a round-trip ticket or continuing voyage is required to stay at the **Kauai International Hostel** (4532 Lehua St., 808/823-6142, www.kauaiinternationalhostel.com, $25–65), where bunk beds are available for $25 a night. Private rooms that share a bathroom with the dorm are available for $50, deluxe rooms and the suite are $60, and for $65 you'll get hallway bedrooms or the master bedroom with a private bathroom in the main house. Check-in is from 11 A.M. to 10 P.M. Kitchen and main house common areas are open from 8 A.M. to 10 P.M., and it's lights out at 11 P.M. Key and linens are issued without a deposit and expected to be returned at checkout. Bring your own bath supplies and towels; kitchen utensils and use of the communal kitchen are provided. There is an in-office safe for valuables, and the hostel is pretty well kept and clean. A coin-operated washer and dryer are on-site.

Another hostel-style place to stay is the **Kauaʻi Beach House** (4-1552 Kuhio Hwy., 808/822-3424, www.kauaibeachhouse.net, $30–70). Originally a real beach house converted into accommodations similar to a hostel, most rooms look out across a lawn and out onto the water. There is a separate mini kitchen area that is for guest use. Shared rooms run $30 per night for a single and $45 a night for a double. Private rooms and apartments rent for $65–70 a night. Females and couples have priority for beds that have complete privacy and curtains in a dorm. There are shared bathrooms and a gathering place on the second-level lanai.

The **Aloha Hale Orchid** (5087-A Kawaihau Rd., 808/822-4148, www.yamadanursery.com, $55) offers simple and clean accommodations for the low price of $55 a night with a three-night minimum. It's a very simple and affordable studio with a queen-size bed, shower and tub, fan, TV, and mini refrigerator. It's located on a functioning orchid nursery.

Meaning "the best" in Hawaiian, the **No Ka Oi Studio** (4691 Pelehu Rd., 808/651-1055, www.vrbo.com/125884, $79–99) has a two-night minimum and a $75 cleaning fee. It's a studio that can fit two to three people. It is comfortable with a kitchenette, videos and books, barbecue, great ocean views, and beach gear for guest use.

The **Orchid Tree Inn** (4639 Lahua St., 808/822-5469, www.vrbo.com/118213, $85–110) is made up of two very small but simple and functional units right in Kapa'a that sleep 4–6 with the addition of convertible beds. The good thing about this place is its central location, allowing for guests to catch the bus around and save money there. A full kitchen is offered, along with washer and dryer. Rates vary $85–110 a night with an average of a $100 cleaning fee. Weekly or monthly rates are available.

$100-200

Hotel Coral Reef (1516 Kuhio Hwy., 808/822-4481 or 800/843-4659, www.hotelcoralreefresort.com, $110–175) was one of the first hotels in Kapa'a, and it has recently undergone renovations that have brought a modern island style to the rooms. The hotel is rather small with around 20 rooms and a pool. It sits right on the ocean. All rooms have air-conditioning, microwaves, in-room refrigerators, and flat-screen TVs, and guests receive a continental breakfast. Mountain-bike rentals and barbecue facilities are also offered. Garden-view suites start at $110, oceanfront suites start at $245, and garden-view deluxe suites start at $175. Check the website for pretty good "eSpecials"; they also offer *kama'aina* and senior citizen discounts.

On a bluff overlooking the ocean is the **Green Coconut Studio** (4698 Pelehu Rd., 808/647-0553, www.greencoconutstudio.com, $110). Decorated with a bright clean island style and bamboo furniture, the studio

also has a lanai with great views. Rates are $110 a night for two people with weekly and monthly rates. They charge an additional $20 for a third person. There's no cleaning fee for stays of four nights or longer but a $100 fee for under three nights.

Located inland in the lush interior, the **Dilly Dally House** (6395 Waipouli Rd., 808/631-9186, www.lolohale.com, $115–185) is an impressive collection of units in a nice house with a large pool with tables by it. Five rooms are offered with a welcome basket and wonderful breakfast of local themed dishes, such as taro or macadamia nut pancakes. The grounds are immaculate, very classy plantation style. A two-night minimum stay is required, and no children are allowed. Rooms are all very high end with elegant island-style decor. Amenities include Hawaiian toiletries, beach gear, wireless Internet, and a grill with sauces and stuff.

The **Kauai Country Inn** (6440 Olohena Rd., 808/821-0207, www.kauaicountryinn.com, $129–179) has a unique twist—the only private Beatles museum in the United States! A simple continental breakfast is supplied every morning, and all units have private entrances and bathrooms, and a full kitchen or kitchenette. Wireless Internet is available in each of the four gorgeous suites. The Green Rose rents for $169–179 a night, the Plumeria Suite for $169 a night, the Yellow Ginger for $149, and the Orchid Suite for $129.

LIHU'E
Under $100

The **◖ Motel Lani** (4240 Rice St., 808/245-2965, $64), consisting of only eight rooms, provides usually clean and very simple rooms with shower only, and no TV or phone. They only take cash—no credit cards—and it's very affordable. This is the type of place to stay if you are planning on being outdoors all the time and looking for a cheap place to store your stuff. This is a very good option for leaving stuff while hiking for days along the Kalalau Trail, since you don't want to risk it getting stolen out of your car at the trail parking lot. They don't have a website; just call.

CONDOS, VACATION RENTALS, AND BED-AND-BREAKFASTS

Vacation rentals can be found island-wide. They range from small studios to elaborate, luxury, high-end beach-front large homes. When booking a vacation rental, take into account the minimum night requirement and the cleaning fee when determining cost. For vacation rental listings and reservations visit **www.vrbo.com** for a huge selection of legal vacation rentals island-wide. The site has thorough listings, good detailed information, availability calendars, and good photos. Another option is **www.vacationrental.com,** with sufficient information to help you with your choice. **Summit Pacific Inc.** (www.summitpacificinc.com) also lends booking help and has information for Kaua'i vacation rentals.

More options include **R&R Realty and Rentals** (800/367-8022, www.r7r.com). They have a variety of oceanfront and inland accommodations with the usual amenities from $630 to $1,500 a week. Many come with a pool, sauna, and kitchen and are near the beach. For one- to five-bedroom rentals contact **Garden Island Rentals** (800/247-5599, www.kauairentals.com). They have units all over Po'ipu and offer a range of options as well as prices and bookings. Another good resource is **Kauai Vacation Rentals** (800/367-5025, www.kauaivacationrentals.com). They offer assistance with booking low- to mid-range condos and mid- to upper-level vacation rentals on the south side.

High on a bluff, **Princeville** is loaded with condominiums. Many are privately owned and have been turned into timeshares. Since there isn't just one central management company for all of them, to get the best rates and up-to-date information it's a good idea to go online and work with one of the recommended booking companies. A good and reliable source for Princeville condos is **Pacific Vacations** (800/800-3637, www.princeville-vacations.com), which has a thorough listing of vacation rentals and condos on Kaua'i. They will help

you with availability and reservations. Another good source is **Rentals on Kaua'i** (800/222-5541, www.kauai-vacation-rentals.com). **Hanalei Vacations** (www.800hawaii.com) is a great source for vacation rentals and condo listings. They'll book you and give you travel info. Remember that most condos require a minimum number of nights and charge a cleaning fee. Try **www.oceanfrontrealty.com** for good prices and lots of options.

For a lengthy listing of condos and to make reservations visit **www.astonhotels.com/kauai.** Another option is **www.diamondresorts.com,** also reachable at 808/742-1888. Both websites have information on condos and vacation rentals. At **www.greathawaiivacations.com** there is a wealth of options for the south side. This site offers condos from $84 a night to $1,650 a night. You'll find overview photos, reviews, and room info. **Poipu Connection Realty** (800/742-2260, www.poipuconnection.com) can connect visitors with an array of condos from one to three bedrooms all over Po'ipu. They have up-to-date information on all of Po'ipu.

For thorough listings of vacation rentals and condominiums consult **Kauai Vacation Rentals and Real Estate** (800/367-5025, www.kauaivacationrentals.com). They have over three decades of experience with booking travelers places to stay. **Garden Island Properties** (800/801-0378, www.kauaiproperties.com) is a good source for vacation rentals and condos on the east side. They manage vacation rentals and can help you find the right place.

Bed-and-breakfast fans should check out **Hawaii's Best Bed and Breakfasts, Private Inns, and Vacation Rentals** (800/262-9912, www.bestbnb.com). They provide thorough listings of the aforementioned types of accommodations on the island with bookings of three nights or longer. From the north to the west this site offers an array of beautiful homes to stay in while on Kaua'i.

The **Kaua'i Palms Hotel** (2931 Kalena St., 808/246-0908, www.kauaipalmshotel. com, $75) offers very simple and affordable rooms without many amenities (no phones). There are full kitchens in the higher priced rooms. Another good option for the outdoors type since the hotel itself doesn't offer the lap of luxury. There's free wireless Internet throughout the property and a coin-operated laundry, and it's a good place to stash your stuff and explore the island. They offer complimentary muffins and coffee in the lobby in the mornings. Amenities include refrigerators and TVs, and some rooms have air-conditioning, so check when booking. Rooms have a standard rate of $75 for one king-size bed or two queens.

Located on the south end of Lihu'e past Nawiliwili Bay, the **Kaua'i Inn** (2430 Hulemanu Rd., 800/808-2330, www.kauai-inn.com, $85–139) is another rather simple place. Rooms include a small refrigerator, microwave, and air-conditioning. There's a shallow swimming pool, and ground floor rooms have lanai. A little bonus here is a free continental breakfast each morning. Mountain views are seen from the property. Rooms have a king, queen, or two double beds.

$100-200

You'll feel the *aloha* at the **Garden Island Inn** (3445 Wilcox Rd., 800/648-0154, www.gardenislandinn.com, $135–160), where you'll find more simple rooms at a decent price. Flat-screen TVs, kitchenettes, air-conditioning, and complimentary use of a variety of beach gear are what you'll find here. Rooms have a modest tropical decor, and discounts are offered for three nights or more.

Over $200

The **◖ Kaua'i Marriott Resort** (3610 Rice St., 808/245-5050, www.marriott.com, $220–429) overlooks beautiful Kalapaki Bay and is fronted by the large beach, with two more smaller ones nearby. The immaculate resort makes a home on hundreds of acres over the bay with nearly 600 rooms on-site. The high-end Kaua'i Lagoons Golf Course is here too, offering world-class golf on 18 holes. The hotel offers a complimentary airport shuttle. You'll find a spa, fitness center, and six restaurants right there, including the option for private cabana dining. The hotel is within walking distance to some shopping and other eateries. All rooms offer high-speed Internet access, a mini refrigerator, and safe. There is a huge, centrally located swimming pool where you can easily spend the entire day lounging and sunning. Guests have the option of one king or two double beds in the rooms, many with balconies. They offer child care on-site, freeing up parents to relax, golf, or enjoy a romantic dinner. Features include a business center, tennis courts, and wedding services, and the hotel has a smoke-free policy.

North Shore

KILAUEA

Large hotels and condominiums are absent in the lush jungle area of Kilauea. Accommodations here are limited to vacation rentals and small cottages, which is a good thing in hopes of maintaining the country feel. Staying in Kilauea is convenient, and enables guests to be very close to everything the north shore has to offer but be within a quick driving distance to the other sides of the island.

Under $100

Enjoy the scent of citrus at **Green Acres Cottages** (5-0421 Kuhio Hwy., 808/651-6173 or 866/484-6347, www.greenacrescottages.com, $75–90), where three free-standing studios (no shared walls) are nestled among 300 citrus trees. Each studio has a queen-size bed with a kitchenette, wireless Internet, cable TV, and barbecue supplies, as well as access to beach gear and a shared hot tub. You'll find

NORTH SHORE ACCOMMODATIONS

Name	Type	Price	Features	Why Stay Here	Best Fit For
☑ Ali'i Kai	condos	$100-175	pool, tennis	location	couples, families
Bamboo Cottage	apartment	$175	spa tub, kitchen	privacy	couples
Bed, Breakfast and Beach in Hanalei	B&B	$120-170	breakfast	location	couples
The Cliffs at Princeville	condos	$290-380	pool, tennis	views, location	couples, families
Emmalani Court	condos	$125-150	pool, barbecue	affordable	couples
Green Acres Cottages	B&B	$75-90	studios	location, affordable	budget travelers
☑ Hanalei Bay Resort	condos	$200-550	pool, tennis courts	location, decent price	families, couples
Hanalei Bay Villas	stand-alone homes	$150-175	mountain views	location	families, couples
☑ Hanalei Colony Resort	condos	$204-352	pool	oceanfront location	honeymooners, couples
Hanalei Inn	motel	$139-149	barbecue, TV, hammock	simple, location	couples
Hideaway Bay	cottage	$295	hot tub	privacy	couples
Kaua'i Coco Cabana	private home	$125	beach gear, outdoor shower	location	couples
☑ Manu Mele Cottage	private home	$160	outdoor shower	privacy	couples
Mauna Kai	condos	$100-150	pool	affordable	families, couples
North Country Farms	cottages	$150	orchard	location	nature-lovers

ACCOMMODATIONS

Name	Type	Price	Features	Why Stay Here	Best Fit For
Ohana Hanalei	studio	$115	private outdoor shower	location	couples
Plumeria Moon Cottage	cottage	$295	hot tub, beach gear	privacy	couples
Plumeria Vacation Rental	private home	$230	near beach	privacy	couples, families
Puamana	condos	$100-150	pool	affordable	families, couples
The River Estate	private homes	$275-300	hot tub	location	couples, families
◐ SeaLodge	condos	$110-150	pool, barbecue	location, price	couples, families
St. Regis Princeville Resort	luxury resort	$425-1,100	pools, beach, restaurants, spa	luxurious stay	lovers of luxury
Westin Princeville Ocean Resort Villas	villas	$250-800	pools	resort amenities	luxury-seeking families and couples
YMCA Camp Naue	cabins, tents	$15	oceanfront	affordable, simple	budget travelers

ACCOMMODATIONS

North Country Farms

complimentary danishes, coffee, and teas inside and can help yourself to picking fruit on site. They don't charge for cleaning fees, and two of the cottages (16 by 20 feet) both sleep two for $75 per night while the third cottage (around 500 square feet) sleeps up to four for $90 a night.

$100-200

Self-proclaimed ecotourism destination **North Country Farms** (808/828-1513, www.north-countryfarms.com, $150) offers two cottages on a four-acre farm. A stay on the farm enables guests to stroll the land and pick fruit to eat and flowers to enjoy. Both cottages are cute, clean, and decently priced for the north shore.

On six and a half lush acres lies the **◖ Manu Mele Cottage** (808/828-6797 or 808/651-9460, www.kauaibirdsongcottage.com, $160). The picturesque cottage is perfect for two and decorated with hardwood Asian furniture. The free-standing structure has a private outdoor shower and tub as well as its own driveway.

They charge a $100 cleaning fee and have a three-night minimum, with discounts for seven nights or longer. This is a very cute cottage, with an elegant Asian island decor.

Cozy up near the fireplace at the **Bamboo Cottage** (808/828-0812, www.surfsideprop.com, $175), a one-bedroom located upstairs of the owner's home. Private facilities are offered, and it's a short walk to the beaches, with ponds and a waterfall in the lush yard. The home has a full kitchen, TV, and wireless Internet access, and the bathroom has a spa tub. It rents for $175 a night with a three-night minimum or $1,100 a week. The Bamboo Cottage also offers guests the use of beach gear.

Over $200

The secluded homes **Plumeria Moon Cottage** and **Hideaway Bay** (4180 Waiakalua St., 888/858-6562, www.kauaivacationhideaway.com, $295) are perfect for visitors looking to be alone for a romantic getaway. Located on a three-acre farm, each cottage has its own hot tub, and a unique feature is free long-distance calls to the Mainland and inter-island. Hideaway Bay is a two-bedroom vacation rental with everything a visitor could need. There is a spa tub in the bathroom, and lovely ocean views can be taken in from the home. It's decorated with an Asian Pacific elegant yet relaxed decor. Plumeria Moon Cottage has a deck for sunning with great ocean views and a hot tub. The home has full amenities, including a washer and dryer and a barbecue on the deck.

The **Plumeria Vacation Rental** (808/828-0812, www.surfsideprop.com, $230) is just 300 yards from Anini Beach, which usually has peaceful, calm waters. The home has a master suite, a loft bedroom, and a den with more sleepers. A lanai wrapping around three sides of the home offers a place for enjoying the sunsets and a screened-in area for dining. There are two bathrooms along with a private outdoor shower. The home rents for $1,625 a week (which is about $230 per night), offers use of beach gear and bicycles, and sleeps up to five people.

PRINCEVILLE

Princeville accommodations are made up of luxury hotel rooms and a huge number of condominiums. As with most accommodations, prices are lower in the off-season. One might assume that with so many condos in one area, finding a place to stay would be easy. But since there isn't one main booking agency, one condominium complex can have a high number of booking agents, all with different contact info and rates. With each condo privately owned, it's up to the owner to find someone to manage it. Another thing that's happened in Princeville is that many of the condos have turned into time shares exclusively. There are a lot of condos in Princeville, and frankly, in addition to the accommodations listed here the Internet is the best resource to explore the thousands of condos and the many management companies. One thing to remember with condos is that you'll most likely have a minimum-night requirement and a cleaning fee.

$100-200

For condominiums with an unbeatable ocean view on the cliffs of Princeville, try **(SeaLodge** (3700 Kamehameha Rd., 866/922-5642, $110–150), which offers nearly 100 units along the cliffs, most with great ocean views. A real treat here is the location near SeaLodge Beach, a wonderful hidden cove below the cliffs. It's accessible by a roughly 15-minute easy hike down a dirt path and along the coast. Features include a pool, places to barbecue, coin-operated laundry and washer and dryer in many units, Internet access, and full kitchens. One- and two-bedroom units are available, and prices are pretty good.

Mauna Kai (search for Mauna Kai phone numbers on www.vrbo.com, $100–150) isn't on the cliffs and doesn't have an ocean view but offers a pool and is within walking distance of the Princeville Center and Anini Beach.

Puamana (search for Puamana phone numbers on www.vrbo.com, $100–150) has a pool but no views, and offers one-, two- and three-bedroom units. There are 26 units and a clubhouse in the collection of condos, and a few are right on the golf course.

With great ocean views, the **(Ali'i Kai** (3830 Edward Rd., 877/344-0692, www.aliikairesort.com, $100–175) offers proximity to Hideaways Beach and Queen's Bath. All units are two-bedroom, two-bath, with full kitchen, washer and dryer, lanai, and living room. On-site facilities include a barbecue area, tennis courts, and a pool. Rates vary between units and booking agencies but run from a real steal of $100 per night up to $175.

At the bottom of Princeville are the **Hanalei Bay Villas** (5451 Ka Haku Rd., 800/222-5541, search for Hanalei Bay Villas on www.vrbo.com, $150–175). Lovely mountain views can be taken in from these two-story villas offering two- and three-bedroom options in stand-alone homes. Two bedrooms rent for $150 a night and three bedrooms for $175. The rental company offers the seventh night for free with weekly rentals. Location is the appeal here, with a short drive to the lovely beaches of the north shore, and Hanalei town nearby.

At the affordable **Emmalani Court** (5200 Ka Haku Rd., 808/826-7498 or 808/826-9675, www.kauai-vacations-ahh.com, $125–150) you'll find a pool, hot tub, and barbecue area. Again the units are individually owned, so decor will vary. Rates change slightly with season. Discounts are offered for week-long and month-long rentals.

Over $200

[**Hanalei Bay Resort** (5380 Honoiki Rd., 808/826-9775 or 800/826-7782, www.hanaleibayresort.net, $200–550) offers privately owned condo units as vacation rentals on over 20 acres at the bottom of Princeville. Accommodations range in size from one bedroom plus loft to three bedroom plus loft, adding up to nearly 300 rooms. There are eight tennis courts on-site with a full-time tennis pro, as well as a swimming pool with a small waterfall. The suites have the added convenience of kitchens. The resort is located sort of behind the St. Regis Princeville Resort, and guests have access to the white-sand Pu'u Poa Beach. Just about any type of beach gear can be rented on-site, including chairs. Rates vary greatly, from $100 without taxes and cleaning fees up to $550, and most have a three-night minimum.

The high end **The Cliffs at Princeville** (3811 Edward Rd., 808/826-6219 or 800/367-8024, $290–380) offers one-bedroom units with two bathrooms, fully equipped kitchens, large living rooms, and two lanai. You'll be treated to on-site tennis, swimming pool, hot tub, putting green, volleyball court, recreation room, laundry room, and barbecue pavilion near the ocean. One-bedrooms range from $290 to $350, and the units with lofts run $350 to $380.

Quite an elaborate collection of units is the **Westin Princeville Ocean Resort Villas** (3838 Wyllie Rd., 808/827-8700, www.westin-princeville.com, $250–800). The grounds feature many amenities, including a main pool, a kids' pool, hot tub, a kids' club, fitness center, plunge pool, and more. Entertainment is offered by the pool nightly, barbecue areas are offered for your enjoyment, and they even have daily activities offered like hula. Rates for the one-bedrooms and studios vary greatly depending on seasons and specials. The lowest priced studios start around $250, one-bedrooms around $300, while villas can go up to about $800.

True to its name, the **St. Regis Princeville Resort** (5520 Ka Haku Rd., 808/826-9644, www.stregisprinceville.com, $425–1,100) will have you feeling like royalty during your stay at the north shore's premier resort. Resting above Hanalei Bay, which is in full view from the ocean-view rooms while others look out to a garden or the lush green mountains, Princeville can provide enough awe, comfort, and intriguing moments for the whole vacation. While staying at Princeville, guests can venture off the hotel property to experience activities like surfing, hiking, and exploring nearby historical Hanalei town. Or they can remain in Princeville indulging in ocean-side spa treatments, staying cool in the pool while the kids play in the adjacent children's pool, sunning on the white-sand beaches in front of the hotel, or playing a round of golf while the children are looked after by the on-site Keiki Aloha program. Other hotel features include day and night child care, three restaurants and bars, spa lounge, pool and beach, ballrooms and boardrooms, and valet parking. Princeville is a destination within itself.

The mountain- and garden-view rooms offer approximately 540 square feet of modern Hawaiian decor. Each room has a queen- or king-sized bed, marble bathroom, oversized tub, double vanity, and unique transparent glass electronically controlled for views or privacy. These rooms are located on floors two through seven and nine. Rooms with the same views and features are also available with a terrace on floors one, four, nine, and ten.

Ocean-view rooms offer beautiful Pacific and garden views. Features are similar to the other rooms but include a sitting room. Located on floors two through seven and nine, these rooms offer an oversized tub and shower combination. The ocean-view rooms with terrace are the beginning of the high-end rooms. Located on the ground floor at pool level, with wonderful views of the ocean and gardens, you'll have either two queen beds or a king bed covered with 300-thread-count linens. The rooms have a sitting area with a loveseat and coffee table. Each of these rooms offers an entertainment console that contains a 42-inch HD flat-screen TV, and business travelers will be happy to find an elaborate work space with a large desk and high-speed Internet access. Privacy is enhanced with a glass partition between the bathroom and sleeping area that can be electronically controlled, and plush bathrobes and slippers wait here for guests.

The premium ocean-view rooms have many of the same features and decor as the garden-view rooms, along with spectacular views of Hanalei Bay. In front of the large window looking out on the ocean is a seating area perfect for taking in the breathtaking views and relaxing. These rooms are located on floors four through eleven.

The top-tier suites are nothing short of amazing. The Prince Junior Suite has a foyer, bedroom, entertainment system, sitting and dining area, and bath suite all serviced by a 24-hour butler. The suites climb through four more levels of luxury to the St. Regis Ocean View Suite, the Bali Hai Signature Suite, the Presidential Suite, and finally to the Royal Suite, all with butler service. The Royal Suite is more like a high-end apartment, with a large walk-in shower for two, a royal spa with a whirlpool bathtub, an entertaining room, master bedroom, kitchen, wet bar, and more.

Room prices start from $375 for mountain views and go up to $750 for premium ocean views. Suites start at $1,100 for the Junior Suite and top off at $6,200 for the Royal Suite.

HANALEI TO THE END OF THE ROAD
$100-200

Hanalei Inn (5-5468 Kuhio Hwy., 808/826-9333 or 877/445-2824, www.hanaleiinn.com, $139–149) offers five quaint and cute rooms just a block from beautiful Hanalei Bay. The

rooms are simple without frills, and provide queen-size beds, homey local style decor, air-conditioning, TV, and a covered lanai to take in the mountain views. Rooms without a kitchen are priced at $139 and with a kitchen go for $149. The kitchen is a nice touch for those who are looking to save money by grocery shopping and cooking at home. The great thing about the Hanalei Inn is that it's right out in Hanalei, just minutes from snorkeling, hiking, and all of the spectacular north shore beaches at the end of the road. In the yard you'll find a barbecue pit, hammocks, and a picnic bench to enjoy the outdoors. There are no phones in the rooms here, only a pay phone outside, but since most people travel with cell phones that doesn't seem to be a problem. This is a good choice for those who intend to stay on the north shore while in Kaua'i, and they offer a small discount for booking four nights or longer. They also have no minimum-night requirement, which is quite nice. There isn't much going on in the rooms, but being outdoors on the north shore is heaven.

Located just a short walk from both the beach and Hanalei town, **Ohana Hanalei** (Pilikoa Rd., 808/826-4116, www.hanalei-kauai.com, $115) is centrally located, but in a quiet neighborhood near the ocean. A studio that is under the friendly owner's house, it rents for $115 a night with a three-night minimum and a $35 cleaning fee. Weekly rates are available for $750 a week with a $55 weekly cleaning fee. Nearly 500 square feet with a king-size bed, the place has both indoor bathroom and private outdoor shower. Quite a good deal and great location.

Good location and a tasty breakfast are the highlights at **Bed, Breakfast and Beach in Hanalei** (5095 Pilikoa Rd., 808/826-6111, www.bestvacationinparadise.com, $120–170). The home is a very short distance from Hanalei Beach but doesn't offer ocean views. Only one or two people are allowed to stay in the three rooms available. The three-story house with a large lanai makes for a good place to stay if you don't mind meeting others. Breakfast is served daily 8:30–9 A.M., including local fruits,

© JOE JENKIN/REZSTREAM

Hanalei Colony Resort

banana pancakes, lemon coconut coffee cake, and more. Beach gear is available for use. The Country Cedar room is on the second floor with a queen bed and private bath just steps outside the door for $120 a night with a two-night minimum. The Pua Lani room has a king bed on the second floor and a private bath for $135 with a two-night minimum. The Bali Hai suite is 700 square feet on the third floor with a king-size bed and large private bath for $170 a night with a three-night minimum. Not super private but nice, clean, and friendly.

The location can't be beat at the **Kaua'i Coco Cabana** (4766 Ananalu Rd., 866/369-8968, www.kauaivacation.com/coco_cabana.htm, $125), a one-bedroom, one-and-a-half-bath home on a lush two acres in a wonderful area in Wainiha toward the end of the road. The home sleeps one to two people and is placed along the Wainiha River, which you can swim in. This is a great spot for those who want to enjoy the peace and solitude of the Hanalei area and beaches near the end of the road and is a short drive from Hanalei and the

Na Pali Coast. It's a fully equipped home for $125 a night with a $125 cleaning fee. The home is not suitable for children but is a great place for honeymooners with a private outdoor shower, hammock, and beach gear.

Over $200

Nearing the end of the road and all of the north shore's wonderful beaches is the **◖ Hanalei Colony Resort** (5-7130 Kuhio Hwy., 808/826-6235 or 800/628-3004, www.hcr.com, $204–352). The hotel stakes claim to one of the best locations to stay. Here you will find 48 condominium units on five oceanfront acres with ocean or mountain views. Each condo features the same size and floor plan with a full kitchen, dining and living room area, two bedrooms with sliding louvre doors (one has twin beds), and one and a half or two bathrooms. Each unit has a lanai to enjoy the ocean breeze, large picture windows, and is decorated with a relaxed and classy island theme. You are very close to the ocean here no matter what room you're in, but the premium ocean rooms house you just

© THE RIVER ESTATE

The River Estate

a few yards from the sand. To enhance the experience of Kaua'i's raw nature, units do not have televisions, stereos, or phones, although pay phones are located outside. Cell phones generally work out here but may be a little unreliable. High-speed wireless is available. There is a pool outside, a long beach to walk on out front, and many other beaches in the immediate area. Rates change a bit throughout the year, and rooms in low season from just after Labor Day range $204–352. From Christmas through the rest of the year is the high season, and rates are $220–352. The resort is beautiful, the location couldn't be more convenient for enjoying the north shore, and everything is peaceful. Every seventh night is free.

Two glorious homes make up **The River Estate** (Ala Eke Rd., 800/390-8444, www. riverestate.com, $275–300), composed of two high-end and immaculate homes on lush green land along a stream. The two-bedroom, two-bathroom Guest House is perfect for honeymooners for $275 a night for two. Additional guests are allowed for $15 a night. The River House is a three-bedroom, two-bath home with a hot tub on a screened-in lanai for $300 a night. Both are gorgeous, perfectly kept, unique, and fun with a great location. Located in Wainiha, the land itself is green, vibrant, and a tropical experience of its own. Everything you could need can be found here.

Camping

Unless you're motivated to haul camping gear miles across the Kalalau Trail, there are two main campsites on the north shore. **Anini Beach Park** on Anini Road offers ample camping space. Here you'll also find bathrooms, barbecue pits, and showers. The campgrounds can get pretty crowded here, and daily beach goers fill up the area fast. Past Hanalei nearing the end of the road is **⟨ Ha'ena Beach Park.** Here you'll have access to showers, bathrooms, and a covered pavilion. Daily beach goers do crowd in here, but it's an ideal place to camp because you'll be close to all the north shore beaches, Hanalei, and the Na Pali Coast for hiking. The campgrounds can get crowded here too, but the gorgeous beach makes it worth it. You'll need camping permits for both of these spots.

Not far past the Hanalei Colony Resort between mile markers 7 and 8 is **YMCA Camp Naue** (808/246-9090, www.ymcaofkauai.org) in Ha'ena. It's a quick stroll to the wonderful snorkeling of Tunnels Beach. You'll be able to spend the night in bunk-bed-filled structures with a toilet area and cooking facility on-site. Reservations are only taken for groups of 20 or more; smaller groups are served on a first-come, first-served basis. Bunking or tent camping costs $15 per night per person.

South Shore

The south shore is known as Kaua'i's resort area. Large resorts can be found along the coast, along with condominiums and vacation rentals. The relaxed small town of Kalaheo has modest and generally affordable accommodations that are ideal to stay in while visiting the south or west side of the island. Koloa is a nice, green, lush area with a few cottages to stay in to avoid the bustle of large resorts in nearby Po'ipu. Po'ipu is great to stay in if you're looking to be a beach bum during your stay on the south side.

KALAHEO
Under $100
Affordable studios can be found with **Sea Kaua'i** (3913 Ulualii St., 808/332-9744, www.seakauai.com, $75–95). The modestly decorated and clean Ti Room is a roomy studio with living area, kitchenette, lanai, and king-size bed. It rents for $75 a night. It's really a great deal and perfect for those looking for a place to stay while exploring what nature has to offer on the south or west side. The Ti Room is right next to the Seaview Suite, and they can be rented together for friends or family. The Seaview Suite has a large full kitchen, two-person shower, and a king bed with two convertible twin beds. It rents for $95 a night with a three-night minimum and has a simply decorated and clean, spacious interior.

In laid-back Kalaheo the ◖ **Kalaheo Inn** (4444 Papalina Rd., 808/332-6023, www.kalaheoinn.com, $87–187) offers 15 private suites in a lush garden setting. Studios with a kitchenette go for $87, a one-bedroom with a kitchenette for $97, a one-bedroom with a kitchenette and lanai for $107, a two-bedroom with a kitchenette and lanai for $137, and a three-bedroom, two-bathroom house with a full kitchen for $187. Rooms are simple with a quaint island theme, and the inn rests in very quiet and small Kalaheo town. Here you'll be a short drive from the beaches of Po'ipu and not too far from the west side. Seventh-night-free specials are available for certain months, and other discounts depend on the length of your stay. It's a perfect and affordable place to stay on the south side if you're looking for simple accommodations without frills.

$100–200
A mix of island style and elegance, **Kauai Garden Cottages** (5350 Pu'ulima Rd., 808/332-0877, www.kauaigardencottages.com, $100–135) is on two acres with a small stream. The two suites are in an elevated home with separate access. The Torch Ginger Suite measures about 500 square feet and is a one-bedroom with lovely green views from lanai. The Orchid Suite is over 400 square feet and has one bedroom. Both suites have wireless, full bathrooms, and kitchenettes. Each room opens onto a large shared open lanai with valley and tree-top views, and some beach gear is available for guest use. Each suite rents for $135 a night for 3–6 nights, and $100 a night for 7–13 nights. Different rates are available if renting both rooms or for over two weeks.

The island-decorated **Hale O Nanakai B&B** (3726 Nanakai Pl., 808/652-8071, www.nanakai.com, $75–170) offers a mix of Hawaiian style and luxury. The Kahili Suite

ACCOMMODATIONS

© HALE O NANAKAI B&B

view from the deck at Hale O Nanakai B&B

rents for $125–135 a night with a $53 cleaning fee. The suite boasts nice teak furniture and a private entrance. Hina's Bed Chamber is affordable at $110–120 a night with a $35 cleaning fee. Named after the goddess of hula, Laka's Garden is an 800-square-foot *'ohana* (family) unit with two bedrooms. It has a screened-in lanai, is wheelchair accessible, and offers a welcome basket. The unit rents for $140–150 a night for two guests, $160–170 for three, $180–190 for four with a three-night minimum and $65 cleaning fee. The most affordable room here is the Maile Room. It's a single bedroom that rents for $75–85 a night and has a $35 cleaning fee. Units include breakfast daily, and all rates go down if multiple rooms are booked.

At the **Bamboo Jungle House** (3829 Waha Rd., 888/332-5115, www.kauai-bedandbreakfast.com, $130–150) you'll find three rooms: the Waterfall Room, Jungle Room, and the Bamboo Garden Room. Rates are $130–150 a night with a $35 cleaning fee. There is a three-night minimum for Jungle and Waterfall Rooms and a five-night minimum

for the Bamboo Room. There are no children allowed here as the place is very couple- and honeymooner-oriented. Breakfast is provided daily, and there is a swimming pool and hot tub. The owners consider the inn a "green" inn.

There's a variety of options with **Classic Vacation Cottages** (2687 Onu Pl., 808/332-9201, www.classiccottages.com, $80–150) which offers nine different accommodations—a combination of cottages, vacation rentals, and studios. Each place has either a kitchen or kitchenette and lanai and sleep 1–7 people total. Rates range $80–150 a night depending on season. All have TV, free use of beach towels, chairs, and mats, snorkel gear, tennis gear, golf clubs, bikes, barbecues, coolers, boogie boards, hot tub, and unlimited free use of the tennis courts at the Kiahuna Swim and Tennis Club in Po'ipu.

KOLOA
Under $100
A very short drive from historic Koloa town, the **Boulay Inn** (4175 Omao Rd., 808/742-1120, www.boulayinn.com, $85) is a one-bedroom,

SOUTH SHORE ACCOMMODATIONS

Name	Type	Price	Features	Why Stay Here	Best Fit For
Bamboo Jungle House	B&B	$130-150	pool, hot tub	romantic	couples
Boulay Inn	apartment	$85	beach gear, private room	affordable	budget travelers
Classic Vacation Cottages	vacation rentals	$80-150	beach gear, hot tub	lots of options	families, couples, groups
Grand Hyatt Kaua'i Resort and Spa	spa	$290-910	two pools, golf course, restaurants, spa	location, luxury	families, couples
Hale Kua	B&B	$120-175	kitchenettes, beach gear	private units	families, couples,
Hale O Nanakai B&B	B&B	$75-170	breakfast, welcome basket	affordable, location	families, couples, groups
Hale Pohaku	private homes	$195	pool	privacy, good for gatherings	families, couples, groups
Hideaway Cove Villas	high-end villas	$205-250	Jacuzzi tubs, kitchens, beach gear	high end, amenities	luxury-lovers
☑ Kalaheo Inn	inn	$87-187	kitchenettes	affordable, location	families, couples
Kaua'i Banyan Inn	private suites	$130-225	kitchenettes	location	families with children 10 and older
Kaua'i Cove Cottages	cottages	$99-185	kitchens	honeymoon cottages	couples

Name	Type	Price	Features	Why Stay Here	Best Fit For
Kaua'i Garden Cottages	private home suites	$100-135	lanai	privacy	couples
◪ Kiahuna Plantation Resort	cottages	$179	gardens, restaurant	lovely grounds	couples
Kuhio Shores	condo	$150-300	oceanfront	location	families, couples
Marjorie's Kaua'i Inn	B&B	$130-195	pool, hot tub	affordable	couples
Nihi Kai Villas	condos	$145-238	heated pool, oceanfront, hot tub, tennis	full amenities	families, couples
Poipu Kapili	condos	$250-500	pool, oceanfront	luxury	families, couples
Poipu Shores	condo	$250-650	pool	location	families, couples, honeymooners
◪ Prince Kuhio	condo	$64-145	pool, barbecue	affordable, location	families, budget travelers
Sea Kaua'i	rooms in home	$75-95	kitchenette	location, affordable	groups, nature-lovers
Sheraton Kaua'i	resort	$209	two pools, spa, shopping	full-service resort	families, couples
Turtle Cove Cottage	private home	$1,350 weekly	lanai, full home	close to beach	families, couples
Waikomo Stream Villas	condos	$130-211	pool, hot tub, kiddie pool, tennis	amenities	families, couples
◪ Whalers Cove	condo	$400-700	pool, hot tub, oceanfront	location	couples

private, 500-square-foot unit. It is at the owner's home but is on top of the garage, so it has a private entrance and no shared walls with the owners. Free beach gear use is available. There is a three-night minimum and the place rents for $85 a night with a $50 cleaning fee. Weekly and monthly rates are also available.

$100-200

Five options are available at **Hale Kua** (800/440-4353 or 808/332-8570, www.halekua.com, $120–175). The Vacation Cottage sleeps four and is a full house. The Coral Tree has three bedrooms and sleeps six. The Gardenia Unit sleeps four and overlooks a citrus farm. The Banana Patch has a wraparound lanai and sleeps four with a separate bedroom. The Taro Patch sleeps four and has a separate bedroom and a wraparound lanai. All have kitchenettes and access to beach gear and barbecue facilities.

Overlooking lush Lawa'i Valley is **Marjorie's Kaua'i Inn** (P.O. Box 866, 808/332-8838 or 800/717-8838, www.marjorieskauaiinn.com, $130–195), where all rooms include breakfast. The Sunset View Room fits two people and has a lovely view, mini kitchen, and queen bed with pull-out couch. It rents for $195 a night. The largest room at Marjorie's is the Valley View Room for $140 a night. The Trade Wind Room rents for $130 a night and has a mini kitchen. On the grounds of the inn you'll find a pool, hot tub, Bali-style hut bar, surfboard, bikes, and use of a kayak and snorkel gear.

Located on one acre in Lawa'i is the **Kaua'i Banyan Inn** (3528-B Mana Hema Pl., 888/786- 3855, www.kauaibanyan.com, $130–225). There are six self-contained private suites on the property. All are clean, with an elegant Hawaiian-style decor. No children under 10 years old are allowed to stay. All have kitchenettes and wireless Internet access.

PO'IPU
Under $100

Bordering Prince Kuhio Park is **◖ Prince Kuhio** (5061 Lawa'i Rd., 800/367-5025 or 808/245-8841, $64–145), which offers studios and one-bedroom units close to beaches with a five-night minimum stay. The grounds are nice, and there's a pool and barbecue area. It's a great location to enjoy sunsets, and units run $64–125 for studios and $105–145 for one-bedrooms.

$100-300

Decorated like luxury island jungle escapes, the accommodations at **Kaua'i Cove Cottages** (2672 Pu'uholu Rd., 808/742-2562 or 800/624-9945, www.kauaicove.com, $99–185) are the ideal honeymoon cottages. The Plumeria cottage has woven bamboo on the walls, full kitchen, canopy bed, and a tasteful tropical decor. The Wild Orchid has an island decor, tiled bathroom, and kitchen. The Hibiscus is a studio with a canopy bed, kitchen, and porch with barbecue. Rates vary $99–185 a night with a $50–85 cleaning fee.

The condominium complex called **Waikomo Stream Villas** (2721 Po'ipu Rd., 808/742-2000 or 800/742-1412, www.parrishkauai. com, $130–211) is a small place of 60 units with a pool and hot tub. It's not on the ocean but a short walk, drive, or bike ride from it and is directly across from a shopping center. One- and two-bedroom ($270) units with one or two bathrooms are available with covered lanai, along with several barbecue areas, a three-foot-deep kiddie pool, and tennis courts. Units range in size from 1,000 to 1,500 feet and include free parking. A nice accent is toiletries from the local Malie Organics line. The majority of units are managed by Parrish Kauai.

The **Nihi Kai Villas** (1870 Ho'one Rd., 808/742-2000 or 800/742-1412, www.parrishkauai.com/kauai-condos/nihi-kai-villas, $145–238) are steps away from the ocean, just a bit over 300 yards to Brennecke's Beach and Po'ipu Beach Park. Here you'll be treated to a large heated oceanfront pool and hot tub, along with tennis courts, paddleball court, and barbecue area. Units are individually owned, so interior decoration varies, but Parrish Kauai manages the majority. Units range from 1,000 to 1,800 square feet with oceanfront, ocean-view, or garden-view options, including

Kaua'i Cove Cottages

one-bedroom ($145–238), two-bedroom ($159–380), and three-bedroom ($300–625) units. The wonderful local body products from Malie Organics are found in the units.

On the water is **Kuhio Shores** (5050 Lawa'i Rd., 800/543-9180 or 808/742-7555, www.kuhioshores.net, $150–300). One-bedroom ($150–260) and two-bedroom ($200–300) condos are available, and many beaches and a surf break are nearby. There isn't a pool here, but it is near the beach.

Just a step away from Po'ipu Beach is **Hale Pohaku** (2225-2231 Pane Rd., 808/212-9749 or 866/742-6462, www.vacationrental-kauai.com, $195). On a half acre near Po'ipu Beach village are four separate homes. Two are fully restored two-bedroom, one-bath historical Kaua'i plantation cottages. The Jungle rents for $195 a night with a two-night minimum, and the Orchid Cottage goes for $195 a night with a two-night minimum. The two-bedroom, one-bath Beach Rose rents for $195 a night with a two-night minimum. For large groups the five-bedroom, three-bathroom Manager's

Home rents for $475–595 a night and was built in 1954. On the property is a private swimming pool. The managers are happy to accommodate weddings and business meetings here.

The lovely ◖ **Kiahuna Plantation Resort** (2253 Poipu Rd., 866/733-0587, www.outriggerkiahunaplantationcondo.com, $179) is operated by Hawaii's own Outrigger, although some units are managed by Castle Resorts and Hotels. The grounds have history connecting to the sugar industry, which is the foundation of the area. Before the grounds opened to the public in 1972, they were the estate and gardens of Mr. and Mrs. Hector Moir, a manager of the Koloa Sugar Company. What is now the reception building was once the owner's private home, and the dining area of the Plantation Garden Restaurant is located in the home's living room and other rooms. In the yard is the Moir Garden, where cactuses and tropical flowers flourish. Lying on 35 acres, the gardens have had more foliage added to them and now have over 3,000 types of tropical flowers, trees, and plants. Just over 300 units make up

© KEN POSNEY/HIDEAWAY COVE VILLAS

Hideaway Cove Villas

the resort. Because each unit is individually owned, they are all decorated differently. They have queen or full-sized beds. Each unit has its own lanai with patio furniture, one bedroom or two, bathroom, living room, and dining area. Concierge service can book anything on the island, and there's daily maid service. Room rates vary between seasons; garden-view one-bedrooms start at $179 without tax and max out at $620. All are a very short walk from the beach.

The exquisite units at **Hideaway Cove Villas** (2307 and 2315 Nalo Rd., 866/849-2426, www.hideawaycove.com, $205–250) are high-end, extremely nice places to stay. Smaller studio units go for $175 and up a night with a $100 cleaning fee, while one-bedrooms with one bath cost $205 and up a night with a $115 cleaning fee, and two-bedrooms with two baths are $250 and up with a $145 cleaning fee. Larger units are offered with three bedrooms and three baths for $375 and up a night with a $195 cleaning fee, and with five bedrooms and four baths for $635 and up a night with

a $345 cleaning fee. Features include kitchens with granite countertops, entertainment centers, Jacuzzi tub in the bathrooms, high-speed wireless throughout the property, covered lanai, barbecues, beach chairs and towels, and coolers.

Along the ocean is the **Sheraton Kaua'i** (2440 Ho'onani Rd., 808/742-1661 or 800/782-9488, www.sheraton-kauai.com, $209), wonderfully placed on Po'ipu Beach. A total of 394 rooms make a home on the property, boasting a casually upscale island-style decor. Each has a private lanai. The hotel was one of the last to reopen after the devastating effects of Hurricane 'Iniki. The resort is elegantly decorated but not over the top, and is also home to retail shops and a fitness center. There are two freshwater pools. The Beach Pool lies near Po'ipu Beach and has a hot tub, while the Garden Pool is slightly inland and surrounded by exotic koi ponds and a waterfall. Both pools have a children's pool. Two restaurants, child care, a spa, and beach rentals and gear are available on-site. Rooms start at $209 based on availability and run up to $785. Prices vary greatly between the high and low seasons.

Over $300

At **Poipu Kapili** (2221 Kapili Rd., 888/699-0354, www.poipukapili.com, $250–500) you'll find one- and two-bedroom condos and suites. A very, very nice place, it's high class, well maintained, and luxurious. The oceanfront property has a large pool. Prices change with the season, but one-bedrooms run $250–350 a night, two-bedrooms are $395–500 a night, and penthouse suites cost $500–650 a night. All rates depend on views and season. Well-equipped kitchens are offered in each, along with free wireless Internet, cable, and queen or king beds. You can walk to the beach from here.

Poipu Shores (1775 Pe'e Rd., 808/742-7700 or 800/367-5004, www.castle-poipu-shores. com, $250–650) offers condo units with a swimming pool and is very close to the ocean. Units are individually owned, so upkeep varies, but they're generally well kept. One- and two-bedroom units are available ranging $250–650. There's a penthouse available for around $500 a night.

Po'ipu's **Grand Hyatt Kaua'i Resort and Spa** (1571 Po'ipu Rd., 808/742-1234 or 800/633-7313, www.grandhyattkauai.com, $290–910) has been recently renovated and boasts a grand, elegant, magnificent, luxurious air from nearly every element. The four-level hotel is home to 602 rooms, but it isn't any taller than the palm trees waving in the wind outside. The hotel holds four restaurants, lounges, and bars that offer excellent food and nightly entertainment. Resort shops are also within the hotel walls, enticing those in need of a break from the beach. Both fresh- and saltwater pools lie in the oceanside grounds, complete with slides, waterfalls, and whirlpools. Rooms are entered through heavy hardwood doors and boast minibars, an entertainment center, robes, and lanai sitting area with Hawaiian quilts and other island themes. You can even kayak the hotel's lagoons. Bathrooms are constructed of elegant marble and you will find iPod docks and stereos in the room. On-site child care is available, along with golf and a luxury spa. There are many types of rooms available, from garden views to the presidential suite, but a unique one is the hypo-allergenic room for allergy sufferers. All rooms come with the option of two beds or one king. Prices vary greatly between seasons and start at $290 for rooms and range up to $910. Suites range $1,570–5,100.

At 🄲 **Whalers Cove** (2640 Puuholo Rd., 800/225-2683, www.whalerscoveresort.com, $400–700) you'll find condos right on the ocean. On-site treats include a heated pool, hot tub, and barbecue area. The individually owned units have free wireless Internet, jacuzzi tubs, and are all well kept. One- and two-bedroom units run $400–700 a night.

Just 80 feet from the ocean is **Turtle Cove Cottage** (831/479-3885, www.vrbo.com/292422, $1,350 a week, six-night minimum), a plantation-style cottage that was built in 1992, with ocean views from the kitchen, living room, and deck. The neighborhood is peaceful and close to Po'ipu's lovely beaches, including Lawa'i Beach for snorkeling, Baby Beach for children, and PK's for surfing. You'll find queen beds here along with a full kitchen, barbecue grill, wireless Internet, linens, and washer and dryer. The home is wheelchair accessible. There is a $150 cleaning fee and a $500 deposit.

West Side

Accommodations on the west side are somewhat limited, as the area is perhaps the least-busy locale on the island. The west side does offer some of the best places to camp though, both along the ocean and up in the mountains.

HANAPEPE
Under $100

For those who appreciate quiet locales, **Hanapepe Riverside** (4466 Puolo Rd., 808/261-1693, http://affordable-paradise.com/accommodation.php?unit=74, $85), located on the Hanapepe River, is a newly built upstairs one-bedroom hideaway that boasts river views. It includes a full kitchen, a bedroom with king-size bed, a living room with a sofa bed that sleeps two, and a washer and dryer. Salt Pond Beach Park is only about a half mile down the road. Rates start at $85 daily with a three-night minimum.

$100-200

A very unique and "green" place to stay is **Coco's Kaua'i Bed and Breakfast** (P.O. Box 169, Makaweli, 96769, 808/338-0722, www.cocoskauai.com, $110–130). Owned by the Robinson family, the owners of Ni'ihau, the bed-and-breakfast offers single or double occupancy on the 12-acre estate. There are two rooms. A private nearly 600-square-foot guest room has a king-size bed, couch, kitchenette, a living room area, and a connecting private full bath. Another bedroom is across the hall, perfect for two people, and futons can be put on the floor for children. Wireless Internet and use of beach gear are included, along with laundry and barbecue facilities. The place is off the electrical grid and uses hydroelectric power, compact fluorescent light bulbs, and plant-based cleaners, and makes sure to recycle. Rates are $110 a night without breakfast or $130 a night with breakfast.

WAIMEA
Under $100

The affordable **Kaua'i Rock Cabin** (Menehune Rd., 808/822-7944, www.holiday-rentals. co.uk/p227308, $50) is located on a citrus farm. The simple but nice single-walled home is a one-bedroom, one-bathroom that sleeps three or four with children. A kitchen, towels, TV, and dinner table and porch dining make for a homey feel. A great deal at $50 a night, $350 a week, or $800 a month.

The Boathouse (4518-A Nene St., 808/332-9744, www.seakauai.com, $85) is a private studio with an extra-large wraparound lanai to enjoy wonderful west-side sunsets. The studio has a kitchenette, full bathroom, and an extra large outdoor shower as well. A king-size bed is found here, along with light fishing tackle for guests. It rents for $85 a night with a three-night minimum.

$100-200

Close to the heart of Waimea town is the **West Kaua'i Vacation House** (808/346-5891, www.westkauaihouse.com, $100), a fully furnished home with two completely separate two-bedroom, one-bathroom guest apartments with air-conditioning. You'll find cable TV, Internet access, a full kitchen, washer and dryer, beach gear, and a grill. Each apartment is $100 per night with a three-night minimum stay and $50 cleaning fee.

A uniquely designed place to stay is the **Monolithic Dome** (808/651-7009, www.vrbo.com/204885, $109), a one-bedroom, one-bathroom home that sleeps 1–2 people. It has a kitchenette and is very quiet and private. A river lines the back of the property, and it has TV, a washer shared with the main house, queen bed, lanai, and wireless Internet. It is a good location for relaxing in solitude and spending time on the west-side beaches. The home rents for $109 a night with a three-night minimum and $75 cleaning fee.

Sprawling on 30 acres of oceanfront land adorned with coconut trees, **【 Waimea Plantation Cottages & Spa** (9400 Kaumuali'i Hwy., 808/338-1625, www.waimeaplantation. com, $176) is a combination of contrasting

ACCOMMODATIONS

WEST SIDE CAMPING

One of the best ways to get in touch with the island's natural rhythms and beauty is by camping, and the west side is the perfect place. Camping is possible island-wide, but the west side's drier weather and often clear skies make it the ideal location to be hotel free. Something that makes camping on the west side unique from the rest of the island is that you can camp up in the mountains or down by the sea.

In **Koke'e State Park** tent camping is allowed with a permit that costs $5 per campsite and can be obtained at the state parks office in Lihu'e. Picnic tables and toilets are available in the area, and two forest reserve campgrounds are located along Camp 10-Mohihi Road. There are four very basic campgrounds in Waimea and Koai'e Canyons that can be utilized as long as you have a permit from the State Division of Forestry and Wildlife, which are free. The main camping area is in the open meadow past the museum. Campers can spend up to three days at Sugi Grove off of the road in Koke'e, and the Pihea Trail leads to the Kawaikoi campsite.

In **Waimea Canyon State Park** the Kukui Trail leads to the Wiliwili campsite. About a half mile up the Waimea River from here is the Kaluahaulu Camp at the beginning of the Koai'e Canyon Trail. Three miles past this are the Hipalau and Lonomea campsites. These require substantial hikes in, so hauling in food and other gear is a must. There won't be any running in and out here.

Along the coast on the west side camping is allowed by permit at the county parks of **Salt Pond Beach Park** in Hanapepe and **Lucy Wright Beach Park** in Waimea. Lucy Wright Beach Park isn't the most ideal camping area. It's directly off the highway, and there are much prettier and more secluded places to camp. At these parks, restrooms, cold water showers, grills, pavilions, and drinking water are provided.

By far the nicest beach camping is at **Poli-hale State Park.** Waking up early at Polihale is to wake up to a silence and feeling of peace in the world that will stay with you forever. An early stroll down the beach is a great way to start the day, especially before the sun comes over the cliff. When it does, it instantly brings an intense heat. Polihale has cold showers, somewhat rough bathrooms (you'll want to bring your own stash of toilet paper), pavilions, picnic tables, and trash cans. Camping in an RV is allowed here, and campsites are on top of the dunes at the back of the beach. Shade is one of the most important things for camping at Polihale. Unless you plan to leave in the morning, some form of shade, either an EZ Up or another pop-up tent, is a necessity. The sun out here gets scorching midmorning and lasts till midafternoon. If you're camping with children, it's a good idea to secure the inside door zipper with a paper clip or something similar so the kids can't leave the tent without you knowing. I've been there when a seven-year-old girl got up to use the bathroom in the middle of the night and wandered down the beach. The parents didn't know until, thankfully, she was returned by some friendly campers who had noticed her while on a midnight driving spree.

The state requires that tents are used at these campsites instead of camping under the stars, although many locals sleep in the back of trucks. Permits, which are obtained at the **Division of Parks and Recreation** (4444 Rice St., Pi'ikoi Bldg., Ste. 350, Lihu'e, 808/241-4463, Mon.-Fri. 8:15 A.M.-4 A.M.p.m.) are good for up to seven days. More information can be found at www.kauai.gov, under the Camping Information link on the Visiting page.

Camping permits for Polihale or Koke'e are obtained at the **Department of Land and Natural Resources** (Division of State Parks, 3060 Eiwa St., Rm. 306, Lihu'e, 808/274-3444, www.hawaii.gov/dlnr/dsp, 8 A.M.-3:30 P.M. Mon.-Fri.). Permit costs vary, so please call for more information.

WEST SIDE ACCOMMODATIONS

Name	Type	Price	Features	Why Stay Here	Best Fit For
The Boathouse	studio	$85	kitchenette, fishing tackle	affordable	budget travelers
Coco's Kaua'i Bed and Breakfast	B&B	$110–130	breakfast, off grid	unique	green travelers
Hale Puka 'Ana	suites in home	$169–229	private rooms, communal living area	location	couples
Halepule Suites	B&B	$110–120	lanai, near beach	friendly service	couples
Hanapepe Riverside	apartment	$85	full kitchen, washer and dryer	affordable, location	budget travelers
Kaua'i Rock Cabin	private home	$50	kitchen, citrus farm	affordable	budget travelers
☑ The Lodge at Koke'e	cabins	$64	wood-burning stoves, cooking utensils	affordable, in nature	outdoors types or budget travelers
Monolithic Dome	private home	$109	lanai, kitchenette	private and relaxing	solitude-seekers
PMRF Beach Cottages	cottages	$80–95	barbecue, restaurant	oceanfront	budget travelers, military
☑ Waimea Plantation Cottages & Spa	hotel	$176	pool, oceanfront	historic, unique	families, couples
West Inn Kaua'i	small hotel	$199–249	kitchenettes	location	families, couples
West Kaua'i Vacation House	apartments	$100	kitchen, beach gear	affordable, location	budget travelers
YMCA Camp Sloggett	tents, cabins	$15–300	fireplace, kitchen	time in nature	outdoors types

elements and styles. A collection of quite a few original sugar plantation cottages from the 1900s, the homes exude a unique blend of history and elegance, island style, and luxurious comforts. The homes still have their original layout, style, and wood but have been refurbished and are very clean. Set along a black-sand beach and swimming pool where hammocks stretch from one original plantation coconut tree to another, cottages range in size from one to five bedrooms, providing guests with the space and privacy of their own home and fully equipped kitchen, with the comforts and ease of being guests. Live in the lap of luxury lounging at the pool, napping in a oceanside hammock, indulging at the spa, and exploring the hotel's museum. Or you can go low-key and local style here with a backyard barbecue in a yard with an old mango tree, watch the sunset over Ni'ihau from your porch while sipping a locally brewed beer from the on-site Waimea Brewery, or make dinner in a classic plantation kitchen in your own home. Cottages range from one bedroom home for $176 to a five-bedroom oceanfront home for $892.

Nestled in the small town of Waimea, **Halepule Suites** (4469 Halepule Rd., 808/338-1814, www.innatwaimea.com, $110–120) offers four quaint suites near the ocean. The home-turned-inn was once the residence of the pastor of the Waimea Japanese Christian Church and was renovated in 2001 as a four-suite inn. A lanai allows guests to take in the breeze, and it's a very short walk to the ocean, although the beach here isn't ideal for swimming. The Banana Suite holds one king bed, a Jacuzzi tub, and a living room and rents for $120 a night. The ocean-view Bamboo Suite ($110) has one queen bed, a living room, and a normal shower. In the Hibiscus Suite ($110) you'll find one queen bed, a mountain view, a shower, and living room. The Taro Room ($110) has a king bed, living room, and renovated bathroom. All rates are for two or more nights. All rooms have Internet access, coffee-maker, and small refrigerator. The Hibiscus Suite and Taro Room have TVs.

Located in the very relaxed west-side neighborhood of Kekaha is **Hale Puka 'Ana** (8240 Elepaio Rd., 808/652-6852, www.kekahakauaisunset.com, $169–229), a large home with three suites for rent. While the rooms are private the communal areas include a living and dining area and ocean-view lanai. The Ali'i Suite has a king bed, private bathroom, and private entrance. A highlight here is the large double-head shower. It rents for $229 a night. The Hoku Suite has a king bed, private bath, and private entrance. It's an ocean-view suite, and sliding glass doors open to the ocean and a large private lanai; it rents for $199 a night. The Ku'uipo Suite has a queen bed, private bath, and private entrance. The suite rents for $169 a night and the seventh night is free for all suites.

Over $200

The **West Inn Kaua'i** (9690 Kaumuali'i Hwy., 808/338-1107, www.thewestinn.com, $199–249) is directly across from the historic Waimea Theater. It has a two-night minimum (it will take guests for one-night reservations but only on short notice the day before). Rates vary by the season, and a room with a king bed or two double beds ranges $199–249, a one-bedroom suite with one king bed ranges $219–249 with a seven night minimum, and the two-bedroom suite with two king bedrooms rents for $239–349 with a seven-night minimum.

KOKE'E
Under $100

In the cool mountain air is ◖ **The Lodge at Koke'e** (3600 Koke'e Rd., 808/335-6061, www.thelodgeatkokee.net, $64), offering cabins up in Koke'e State Park. The wooden cabins are nice and clean with wood-burning stoves and mattresses and often remind visitors of Mainland mountain cabins. Hot showers, cooking utensils, bedding, and wood for the stoves are provided. There is a five-night maximum stay and two-night minimum stay if one night is a Friday or Saturday, which be perfect for hiking and enjoying overlooks the park. The cabins cost $64 a night and provide all you need for a simple frills-free weekend in the forest. Call between 9 A.M. and 3:30 P.M. to make a reservation.

Camping

At **YMCA Camp Sloggett** (Kumuwela Rd., 808/245-5959, www.campingkauai.com, $15–300) you'll find different options for spending the night in nature in Kaua'i's mountains. Built in 1925 by the Sloggett family for a personal mountain retreat, the camp offers a beautiful and relaxing escape from the busyness of everyday life. It's a great place to stay for a break from the beach and heat, and for those who plan to explore many of the Koke'e trails and hikes. For $15 a person you can pitch your own tent on the campgrounds and have access to a kitchenette and bath facilities. It's the same price per person for a night in the simple Weinberg bunkhouse. Here you'll spend the night on bunk-style beds and have access to a kitchenette and bath facilities. No-frills mattresses are provided but it's the guest's responsibility to bring a sleeping bag and towels. For camping or staying in the bunkhouse children 5 and under are free and ages 6–12 are $5 per person.

Also at the camp, up to four people can stay in the Mokihana studio with two double beds for $95 per night Monday–Thursday and $110 Friday–Sunday. Here you'll also have access to a kitchenette and bath facilities in the Weinberg bunkhouse.

A group of 24 people can stay in the Hale, a combination of 10 bunk beds and two double beds in the Mokihana wing of the Weinberg bunkhouse and the Mokihana end unit studio for $175–200. Here you'll have a private kitchenette and bath facilities, but it's up to you to bring sleeping bags and towels. The Cottage, a cabin with a king bed, a queen sofa sleeper, a complete kitchen, wood-burning fireplace, and a bathroom with shower, is available for four guests for $125–150. This accommodation provides linens and towels. The Sloggett Lodge houses up to 15 people, who stay in two bedrooms, each with a double bed and a bunk bed, and a main living room with sleeping couches and mattresses. There is also an 800-square-foot covered patio for dining and recreation, a complete kitchen, wood-burning fireplace, and a bathroom with shower. You'll need to bring your own blankets and towels but mattresses are provided. Prices range from $250 a night for Monday–Thursday to $300 for Friday–Sunday. Really large groups can rent the entire grounds for $1,350 a night Monday–Thursday and $1,500 a night Friday–Sunday. If you're planning on anything other than a tent try to book a few weeks in advance because the cabins fill up often. There is a two-night minimum requirement for the Lodge, Cottage, Mokihana, and Hale. Check the website for various organization-related discounts.

THE WILD WEST
Under $100

For those who belong to the armed forces, **PMRF Beach Cottages** (1293 Tartar Dr., 808/335-4752, $80–95) is a great option. Nineteen cottages are located right on the beach at the PMRF military base. For those who have access to the base, this is a great and affordable place to stay. Barbecues are provided, along with free wireless Internet and computers at the restaurant. A tennis court is on the grounds, along with a driving range, fitness center, pool, racquetball, handball, air-conditioning in bedrooms, and a restaurant. Each cottage stands alone and is about 1,000 square feet for only $80–95.

BACKGROUND

The Land

As the eldest of the Hawaiian islands, Kaua'i has had time on its side to shape lush green mountains, create nutrient-rich fine red dirt, and produce amazing long beaches of fine white sand. The island lies 100 miles northwest of O'ahu and is the northernmost and westernmost of Hawaii's six main islands. The Garden Island is the fourth largest of the islands, measuring approximately 33 miles long and 25 miles wide. With 90 miles of coastline, Kaua'i is the most circular of all the islands. In fact, the good news for beach lovers is that nearly half of the coastline is actually beautiful white-sand beaches. You'll find many of Hawaii's beast beaches on Kaua'i, and it has much more sand than the Big Island or Maui. The coast is also dotted sections of cliffs (most notably the Na Pali Coast), bays, a port, and crashing waves.

Approximately 90 percent of Kaua'i's land is unlivable thanks to the mountainous interior. This means that the population lives along the coast, with a very small number of people residing in Koke'e State Park on long leases. It's believed by some that Ni'ihau, a separate and smaller private island off the coast of Kaua'i's west side, may have once been connected to Kaua'i. Legend says the small island was the afterbirth from Kaua'i being born.

Built by one huge volcano that became

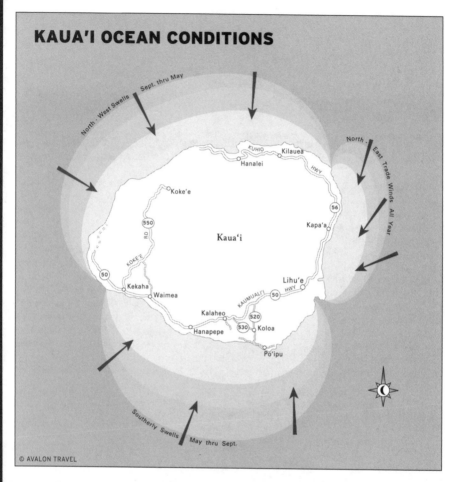

KAUA'I OCEAN CONDITIONS

North - West Swells   Sept. thru May

North - East Trade Winds All Year

KUHIO   Kilauea
Hanalei

Koke'e

550

KOKE'E RD

Kaua'i

56

Kapa'a

50

Kekaha
Waimea

Lihu'e

KAUMUALI'I   HWY   50

Kalaheo   520
Hanapepe   530   Koloa

Po'ipu

Southerly Swells   May thru Sept.

© AVALON TRAVEL

extinct about five million years ago, Kaua'i was once farther south, on the hot spot that is now under the Big Island. It's this hot spot that erupts magma and builds islands, and as the Earth's plates move, so do the islands. That's why Kaua'i is the oldest, at the top of the chain, and the Big Island is still active and on the bottom of the island chain.

A legend regarding the geological activity tells of the myth of Pele. It tells of the fire goddess as a young and beautiful woman who visits Kaua'i during a hula festival and falls in love with Lohiau, a handsome and mighty chief. She wants him as a husband and determines to dig a fire-pit home where they can reside in contented bliss. However, her unrelenting and unforgiving sea-goddess sister pursues her, forcing Pele to abandon Kaua'i and Lohiau. So Pele wandered throughout the islands and sparked volcanic eruptions on O'ahu, Maui, and Kilauea Crater on Hawaii, where she now resides.

GEOGRAPHY

The interior of Kaua'i is a high and wet mountainous area. The two highest points on Kauai,

RED DIRT

The Big Island is still rocky, O'ahu has a lot of reddish dirt, and Maui has a mix of rock and dirt, but Kaua'i is covered with deep, vibrant red dirt. Thanks to its high mineral bauxite content, the dirt has a color that has become representative of Kaua'i itself. Dirt is abundant on Kaua'i as a result of the island's age; time enabled the elements to break the lava rock down to soft, fine dirt.

Red Dirt, a local company that decided to use the dirt as a dye, did so after a storm blew the roof off of its T-shirt factory and stained the shirts red. The crew thought, "Hey, this looks kind of cool" and started the shirt line. It can stain, and red-tinged feet and shoes aren't an uncommon sight after a hike. Don't get the dirt on your favorite clothing, because you'll probably see a hint of it even after a wash.

© JADE ECKARDT

Mount Kawaikini (5,243 feet) and **Mount Wai'ale'ale** (5,148 feet), are thought to be the western rim of the island's collapsed main volcanic crater. Mount Wai'ale'ale's claim to fame is being the wettest spot on earth due to its 450 inches of rain per year. The only way to look in the crater is by helicopter, and the views are exceptional.

A hospitable environment to flora and fauna found nowhere else on earth, the **Alaka'i Swamp** draws water from the abundance in Mount Wai'ale'ale. Old *'ohi'a* trees and unique tropical flowers decorate the enchanting swamp. Bordering the swamp on the west is **Waimea Canyon,** where weather and geological activity have worn a 3,000-foot-deep, two-mile-wide canyon aptly nicknamed the Grand Canyon of the Pacific. The **Waimea River,** which runs through the floor of the canyon, is just under 20 miles long and is the

one of Kaua'i's many rivers

island's longest river. The Wailua River is the only truly navigable waterway; however, passage by boat is restricted (although it's a popular place to explore in a kayak).

Towering over the ocean near Waimea Canyon is the stunning and hardly touched **Na Pali Coast,** where amazing cliffs reach up to 4,000 feet high over the Pacific. Here, deep lush valleys, caves, secluded beaches, and waterfalls sit above some of the best snorkeling in Hawaii.

Inland, north of Koloa, is the human-made **Waita Reservoir,** which is the largest body of freshwater in Hawaii, covering 424 acres with a three-mile-long shoreline.

A few unique mountain formations in Kaua'i have been identified by their notable shapes. Some say the **Ha'upu Ridge** (elevation 2,000 feet), which divides the south side and Lihu'e, forms a profile of Queen Victoria. Resting above Wailua is the Sleeping Giant, traditionally known as the **Nounou Range,** which takes the shape of a man resting on his back.

Between O'ahu and Kaua'i is the **Kaua'i Channel.** It reaches a depth of almost 11,000 feet and is 72 miles wide. The channel is the deepest and widest in all of Hawaii. Off of the west side of Kaua'i, between Kaua'i and Ni'ihau, is the nearly 4,000-foot-deep **Kaulakahi Channel,** a favorite place for humpback whales to spend time while visiting the islands. The two islands are just 17 miles apart.

CLIMATE
Temperatures and Rainfall

Warmth from the sun is the most common climatical mood on Kaua'i. The average temperature is 75–85 degrees Fahrenheit in the spring and summer, and dips only a few degrees down to about 75–80 degrees the rest of the year. From Lihu'e heading west is the warmest area, and it gets increasingly dryer in that direction. It's not uncommon for nights to drop 10–15 degrees, and they can even get down to the upper 50s in the wintertime, even along the coast. Humidity is usually in the 60s and low 70s, so although it's not unheard of to have a very muggy day, it's usually pretty nice. Very

HURRICANE STATISTICS

Various types of storms hit Hawaii, and of course they range in severity. A **tropical depression** is a storm system characterized by a large low-pressure center accompanied by thunderstorms that produce strong winds and heavy rain. A **hurricane** is defined as a storm with violent winds exceeding 64 knots or 74 miles per hour. Heavy rains, huge waves, high water, and storm surges usually come along with hurricanes.

Hawaii has an elaborate warning system for natural disasters. You will notice large green alarms that look similar to stacked, thick plates on top of poles. There are the alarms that go off for tsunamis, hurricanes, and earthquakes. They are tested the first day of every month very early in the morning. So if you hear a siren, check the date; if it's the first of the month, you're probably safe.

MAJOR HURRICANES IN HAWAII SINCE 1950

Name	Date	Islands Affected	Damages
Hiki	Aug. 1950	Kaua'i	1 death
Nina	Dec. 1957	Kaua'i	$100,000
Dot	Aug. 1959	Kaua'i	$5.5 million
Fico	July 1978	Big Island	$200,000
'Iwa	Nov. 1982	Kaua'i, O'ahu	1 death, $234 million
Estelle	July 1986	Maui, Big Island	$2 million
'Iniki	Sept. 1992	Kaua'i, O'ahu	8 deaths, $1.9 billion

muggy days are usually the ones with on and off light rain.

Although the west side appears to be very dry, it gets a somewhat sufficient amount of rain out in the arid Mana Plain before Polihale Beach in the west. The dry west side holds the wide and always-flowing Waimea River. From there across the south shore to the Po'ipu beach resort area, rainfall runs 5–20 inches per year, and just past that area it gets increasingly greener; Lihu'e receives about 30 inches of rain a year. And more northward toward Kapa'a and around the coast past Kilauea toward Hanalei, rainfall becomes more frequent at about 45 inches per year, which is evident in the vibrant green jungle and many waterfalls cascading down the back of Hanalei Valley. Farther down the coast it may reach 75 inches per year, raining more during the winter months.

Due to the **trade winds** (breezes from the northeast that blow 5–15 mph), temperatures in Hawaii are constant and moderate. Blowing an average of 300 days a year, the trade winds are a factor in keeping down the humidity. The **Kona winds** (hot winds coming from the south) blow less often and bring hot, sticky air.

Hurricanes

Severe damage was done to the island during Hurricanes 'Iwa and 'Iniki. On Thanksgiving of 1982, **Hurricane 'Iwa** brought 80-mph winds and was the fourth storm of this severity to be recorded in Hawaii. A total of $200 million in damages was done to Kaua'i during

'Iwa. Homes were destroyed and beaches washed away, but the residents moved on.

A decade later, on September 11, 1992, **Hurricane 'Iniki** struck Kaua'i with unimaginable force and top wind speeds of 175 miles an hour, destroying everything it hit. A third of the homes on the island were demolished, boats were thrown about, and over 4,000 hotel rooms were destroyed. In Hawaiian, *'iniki* can mean either piercing winds or pangs of love. Director Steven Spielberg and the cast of *Jurassic Park* were stuck inside the hotel that is now the Kaua'i Marriott Resort, weathering the storm with other guests and hotel staff. While trying to heal the island and its people, the mayor of Kaua'i and her staff worked in her office, which was missing its roof, while trying to help with recovery. Eight people were killed, although many people were emotionally scarred from the trauma and their losses.

ENVIRONMENTAL ISSUES
GMOs
A GMO (genetically modified organism), also known as a GE (genetically engineered) or transgenic organism, is created by scientists in a laboratory, where they insert genes into an organism to create new traits, such as insect resistance. GMO crops are a common sight on Kaua'i these days, with many acres on the west side out toward Polihale covered in GMO corn grown for feed. Many people are split on how they feel about GMOs. A lot people think they're okay, while a huge number aren't comfortable with the idea of living by these crops or ingesting genetically modified foods.

Hawaii has more experimental field trials of genetic engineering than any other state in the nation. Also on the west side you'll notice the large and looming workplaces of the GMO manufacturers, and many Kaua'i residents are extremely unhappy about the number of them on the island. West-side residents speak of sicknesses and water pollution as byproducts of the GMO crops in the area. Another point anti-GMO activists make is that the corn feed is shipped out of state and fed to animals; they feel the acreage involved should be used to grow food for people instead.

Flora and Fauna

Originally landmasses of barren lava 2,000 miles from the nearest continent, the Hawaiian Islands gradually eroded, slowly creating soil. Eventually, Polynesian settlers arrived with 27 varieties of plants that would feed them, serve as medicines, and provide other stuff. Around 90 percent of the plants found on the Hawaiian Islands today weren't introduced until after Captain Cook first set foot in the islands. Flowers were few; coconuts weren't found here; and vegetables, fruits, edible land animals, mangroves, and banyans didn't exist in the chain. Today, Hawaii's indigenous plants and animals have the highest rate of extinction on the planet. At the beginning of the 21st century, native plants growing below 1,500 feet in elevation were almost completely extinct, replaced by introduced species.

Some of Hawaii's indigenous and endemic plants existed on the island long before the first Hawaiians arrived, while others were brought over on ocean vessels with the first settlers. The island's beautiful flowers and trees have been disappearing over the generations, like many other native things. The majority of flora considered "exotic" to visitors was introduced by Polynesians or white settlers. Polynesians brought foodstuffs such as bananas, coconuts, taro, breadfruit, etc. Others brought mangos, papayas, passion fruit, pineapples, and other tropical fruits and vegetables that are now associated with the islands.

TREES
The beautiful koa tree still exists on Kaua'i. The **koa,** a form of acacia, is Hawaii's most valuable native tree and can grow to over 70 feet high, with a strong, straight trunk that

MARIJUANA

Marijuana has been a lucrative industry in the Hawaiian Islands for nearly half a century, and business is still booming. Puna on the Big Island, certain parts of Maui, and areas of Kaua'i have been home to marijuana growing more than other parts of the islands. Known in Hawaiian as *pakalolo*, marijuana has found an environment very hospitable to its needs in the islands. Even though it's still illegal, marijuana is a large and profitable cash crop in the islands. Hawaii is one of the top five marijuana-producing states in the country.

On Kaua'i, marijuana started off as a hippie crop, with hippies in the communes and living on the north shore in the early days cultivating in the jungle and even in their yards. Locals wanted a part of the profits and soon learned how to grow it. There were times that staking claim to a crop became an outright battle. One person would plant and maintain it, and others would come along and simply help themselves to it. Stories of booby-trapped crops are true, and of growers guarding a near-harvest crop with guns. If you happen to stumble across a crop while hiking (you probably won't these days), just keep on moving.

can measure 10 feet in circumference. The pricey wood is used to make furniture and other crafts. Koa is believed to have originated in Africa, and when it came to the Pacific islands, instead of reverting to the true leaf it broadened its leaf stem into a sickle-shaped, leaf-like foliage that produces a pale yellow flower. Historically, koa was used mainly for the construction of canoes, paddles, spears, and surfboards, and today it is considered excellent and quite expensive furniture wood. It resembles eucalyptus.

The beautiful native **'ohi'a** can live in wet lush areas as well as dry lands covered only in lava, and therefore is the most abundant of all the native Hawaiian trees. Red is the most common color of the flowers on the 'ohi'a tree, but yellow and orange 'ohi'a blossoms do exist, although they are much rarer. Shape varies too; many trees are narrow and straight, while others have large, far-reaching branches. These trees are often the first life in new lava flows. Legend says that Lehua and Ohia were lovers, and out of jealousy Pele turned them into the flower and tree. Whenever a lehua blossom is picked, legend says it will rain because the two lovers are crying because they've been separated.

The multipurpose **kukui** tree can grow to a height of 80 feet. Historically, its nuts, bark, and flowers were ground into salves to treat skin ulcers and cuts as an antibiotic, or to be taken internally for various reasons. The nuts were used as candles, the oil holding a steady flame, and they were also ground and eaten as a condiment called 'inamona. The nuts are also sanded and polished and strung into lei, something you'll most likely come across while shopping around Kaua'i.

GECKOS

Accepted by Hawaii residents as a friendly roommate is the gecko. Known as *mo'o* in Hawaiian, geckos have become a symbol for Hawaii. They generally don't get in your way, and they flock to lights and eat insects. You'll now notice two main types of geckos: the traditional, light gray brownish gecko, which comes out at night, and the Madagascar gecko, which has made a home in Hawaii in the last decade or so. They have quickly become dominant in the islands and are noticeable by their bright green color and orange spots on their backs. Because they come out in the daytime, they're said to eat the traditional geckos. Neither species is harmful to humans, and they are actually quite cute.

MAMMALS

Hawaii has only two indigenous mammals: the Hawaiian monk seal and the Hawaiian hoary bat. **Hawaiian monk seals** ('ilio holu i ka auau) travel along and are infrequently seen, but you

the endangered Hawaiian monk seal

may get lucky and see one on a beach. They like to sunbathe on the beach, sleeping, relaxing, and being left alone. Females are somewhat larger than males and can weigh up to 600 pounds and measure up to 8 feet long. There are around 1,500 throughout the island chain, and they enjoy Kaua'i. If you see one, please stay at least 10 feet away and don't throw anything at it, not even water. Sadly, I've seen people toss water, sand, and other items at the seals.

The **Hawaiian hoary bat** *('ope'ape'a)* is a relative of the North American bat, which flew to the islands long ago, over time evolving into a new species. Small populations of the bat are found on Maui and Kaua'i, but most are on the Big Island. Wing spans get up to 13 inches wide, and they are solitary creatures that live in trees. Hoary means frosted, which refers to the white tips of the body hairs. They are found in both wet and dry areas from sea level to about 13,000 feet.

Humpback whales migrate to Hawaii every year from November to May. Here they relax, mate, give birth, and care for their young until returning to food-rich northern waters in the spring. Watching them breach, their large yet graceful bodies emerging from the ocean

before splashing down, is one of the greatest sights on Kaua'i. An uncommon but not rare treat is hearing their songs from shore at night.

The role of whales and dolphins in Hawaiian culture seems quite limited. Unlike fish, which were given individual names for each species, whales had only two general names in Hawaiian: *kohola,* meaning whale, and *palaoa,* meaning sperm whale. Dolphins were called *nai'a.*

BIRDS

Birds can be seen all over Kaua'i, which is home to the largest number of indigenous birds in Hawaii, even though they are endangered. An estimated 70 native species of birds existed before the arrival of humans on the island, and since Captain Cook arrived in 1778, 23 species have become extinct, with 31 considered endangered. The island is on a main bird migratory route, and some land has been reserved for the well being of these birds in the form of wildlife refuges. Along with the wildlife refuge centers, the inland regions surrounding Mount Wai'ale'ale and Alaka'i Swamp have provided a natural sanctuary for Hawaii's birds. Approximately 15 of the original 70 species of birds that thrived in Hawaii before the

COCK-A-DOODLE-DOO: KAUA'I'S WILD CHICKENS

The mystery of Kaua'i's feral roosters and hens is addressed in a couple of urban legends. Some say the chickens multiply and roam free because there aren't any mongooses (rodents that love to eat chickens) on Kaua'i. Others say that Hurricane 'Iniki set the chickens free from their cages and they just haven't been contained since.

No matter what the reason, reality is that all of Kaua'i is covered in wild chickens, roosters, hens, and chicks, running amok. They're at the beach, around the hotels, in shopping center parking lots, on golf courses, pretty much everywhere. You'll see a colorful variety of roosters and many mother hens finding food for their chicks.

They can be noisy, but they generally mind their own business. But it's not unheard of to find a chicken getting out of an open bag of chips someone's left open on the beach.

© JADE ECKARDT

coming of humans have disappeared. There are multiple factors for the decline in bird species in Hawaii, ranging from ancient Polynesians—who used the feathers for *kahili* fans (which indicated rank among the elite), lei, feather capes, and helmets—to rats and disease.

Kauai upland forests are still home to many Hawaiian birds. You may be lucky and get to see some of the following: Hawaiian owl *(pueo)*, *'elepaio*, *'anianiau* (found only in Kaua'i's native forests) or *nukupu'u*. Some extremely rare species are found in Alaka'i Swamp, such as the *'o'u*, Hawaiian creeper, and *puaiohi*.

Along with the birds that live inland, beautiful seabirds fly offshore, and many can be seen at Kilauea Point National Wildlife Refuge. Some Kaua'i seabirds include the Laysan albatross, wedge-tailed shearwater, red-footed booby, white-tailed tropicbird, great frigate bird, Hawaiian stilt, Hawaiian coot, Hawaiian duck, and Hawaiian gallinule. Many of these birds live in areas you can visit, while others are rare and very difficult to spot.

History

Kaua'i is the first of the Hawaiian Islands in many ways. Besides being the oldest main island geologically, Kaua'i was possibly the first island to be populated by Polynesian explorers. Even Pele had chosen Kaua'i as her first home until her sister drove her away, and she took her fires with her.

DISCOVERY OF THE ISLANDS

Anthropologists believe that Kaua'i was the first of the Hawaiian Islands to be settled by Polynesian explorers. It's believed that the island was first settled as early as 200 A.D. Although the island was most likely settled as early as 200 A.D., what's considered the first

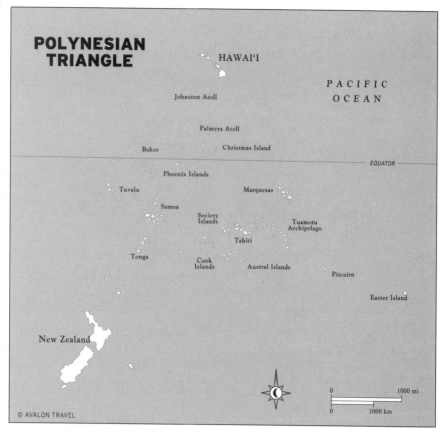

POLYNESIAN TRIANGLE

HAWAI'I

PACIFIC OCEAN

Johnston Atoll

Palmyra Atoll

Baker   Christmas Island

EQUATOR

Phoenix Islands

Tuvalu   Marquesas

Samoa

Society Islands   Tuamotu Archipelago

Tahiti

Tonga   Cook Islands   Austral Islands

Pitcairn

Easter Island

New Zealand

0   1000 mi

0   1000 km

© AVALON TRAVEL

"deliberate migrations" from the southern island are believed to have been as early as 500 to 800 A.D. Yet as new archaeological discoveries are made, academics keep pushing the date back of the first settlement. Old Hawaiian chants tell of returns to Tahiti, believed to be the homeland of the people who became Hawaiians. The travelers were great ocean-going people, using the stars, the sun, and the winds to navigate their way across the Pacific.

Archaeological evidence has led researchers to believe that voyagers were originally from Taiwan, and the people began their voyage into the Pacific on bamboo rafts with outriggers, which resembled early Polynesian outrigger canoes. Crossing the Pacific from Taiwan across

the Polynesian Triangle and eventually getting to Hawaii has been estimated to have taken them 35,000 years.

They lived on the islands for 500 years, creating an advanced civilization. Travel back and forth between Hawaii and Polynesia was a regular thing and has been proven by archaeological evidence. A new life was brought in the 12th century when voyagers from Tahiti made their way to Hawaii and conquered the islands. A Tahitian priest named Pa'ao introduced the god Ku and brought the *kapu* system of rigid taboos. Travels between Tahiti and Hawaii continued for around a century but then stopped. Hawaii returned to being an isolated chain of islands.

A CREATION TALE

Hawaiian legends tell of the days before humans settled on Kaua'i, when two brothers and their sister traveled to Kaua'i in the form of rocks. It's said they stopped at islands along the way but, having not found a suitable home, continued on until they reached Kaua'i. They decided they would like to make a home on the island. The eldest brother said, "Not under the water. I want to feel the rain on my face, the sun on my body, and the breeze at night." So they all traveled onto land looking for a place to rest. As they emerged from the water the sister saw the reef, and it called to her. "Brothers, I want to rest on the reef until my energy comes back. I want to be with the waves and spend time with the fish, birds, and crabs," she said. The brothers tried to stop her, but she resisted and laid to rest on the reef. It's said that this is how O'o A'a the sister came to Ha'ena.

As the two brothers walked over the beach and through the dunes, they came to a hala tree forest. The youngest brother said, "Brother, I am tired and this looks like a comfortable place to rest. The breeze is nice and the earth is strong." The older brother warned him, "Vines will grow over you and leaves will scratch you; come with me to the mountains." But his younger brother laid down and slept. This is how Pohaku Loa came to Ha'ena.

The eldest sibling continued on and began the intense climb up the mountain. Many times he grew exhausted and tried new routes to reach the top. After falling down to the bottom many times, the great god Kane saw the eldest, still in the form of a rock, and asked him why he didn't give up and rest with his siblings. "I can see the birds and clouds and feel the winds from the top of the peak. I can see the trees grow and the sea life in the ocean from up there," he explained. The brother said he wouldn't sleep like his siblings, but would stay awake and watch. So the god picked up the rock and, before setting him down on the peak of the mountain, said, "When I see you again you must tell me what you have seen. When you are ready to move on the island will sink beneath the ocean, the water will be upon you, and you and your brother and sister can travel again." Far below the eldest brother, O'o A'a slept on the reef, and Pohaku Loa slept in the hala forest. This is how Pohaku o Kane came to Ha'ena.

Almost 500 years of isolated tropical life went by undisturbed by outsiders until the arrival of Captain James Cook. For the Hawaiians, life would never be the same. Cook set eyes on O'ahu from the sea on January 18, 1778, and first set foot on Hawaiian soil in Waimea on Kaua'i.

COOK'S VISITS

Captain Cook left Plymouth, England, in 1776 for what would be his third and last voyage into the Pacific. On January 18, 1778, the crews of Cook's 100-foot flagship, the HMS *Resolution,* and its 90-foot companion, HMS *Discover,* saw O'ahu from sea. Two days later they arrived on Kaua'i, their first time on Hawaiian land. Cook landed to get new supplies for his ships, and he noted in his diary that the Hawaiians looked similar to other people he had seen across the Pacific, such as in New Zealand. He trade brass medals for a mackerel and noted that the Hawaiians were quite enamored with the ships. Once ashore, sailors immediately began mixing with the women, bringing the first venereal diseases to the islands, which spread quickly. The highlights of the first meeting included mutual interest in each other, a few of the sailors' items being stolen, trades of sex and venereal disease, and that was pretty much it.

It wasn't until nearly a year later that Cook returned, and his impact would become much more significant. Cook named Hawaii the Sandwich Islands after one of his patrons—John Montague, the Earl of Sandwich. Cook first viewed Maui from the sea on November 26, 1778, but could not find a suitable port in nearly two months of searching. So, they

KOOLAU THE LEPER

Leprosy spread throughout the Hawaiian Islands during the 1870s and 1880s. Those affected, or believed to be affected, were taken from their lives and families and sent to the leper colony on Moloka'i. Kaluaikoolau was a leper was born on Kaua'i's west side in Kekaha in 1862. He was nicknamed Koolau. Koolau refused to be banished to the leper colony and took his family to live deep in the Kalalau Valley. He stood up against authorities for years. He killed the people sent out to the valley to take him away and died a free man living off the land. His story went down in history as a tale of resilience and resistance, and Jack London made it famous in his short story "Koolau the Leper." In 1906, Koolau's wife told his story, and in 2001 the University of Hawai'i Press published an account of it titled *The True Story of Kaluaikoolau: As Told by His Wife, Piilani.*

moved on. The *Discovery* and *Resolution* anchored in Kealakekua Bay on the Big Island's Kona Coast.

Coincidentally, when Cook landed on the Big Island it was the time of the *makahiki,* a celebration dedicated to the beloved god Lono. For a few days, as Cook circled the island, the Hawaiians circled it too, parading a structure held overhead of a cross beam with two flowing white sheets of tapa (it resembled a ship's mast). On January 16, 1779, as the Hawaiians reached Kealakekua Bay, Lono's sacred harbor, Cook's ship came into the port. Because of the timing with the *makahiki,* the Hawaiians believed Cook to be a god and welcomed him to shore with respect. They brought him to Lono's sacred temple and offered him the utmost respect.

In the following weeks the Englishmen overstayed their welcome. When they left, the *Resolution* broke down at sea. Cook returned to the Big Island but was no longer welcomed. Hawaiians stole random items from the sailors, and the sailors became violent with the

Hawaiians. Cook lost control after Hawaiians stole a cutter that had been moored to a buoy to protect it from the sun. Cook became furious, a change in temper that would cost him his life. He went ashore with backup, intending to take Chief Kalani'opu'u hostage for ransom, but after taking the advice of his wife, the chief remained on shore. Soon, the violence escalated and Cook was eventually killed. His men sailed back to England.

At the time of Cook's visits, Hawaii was in a state of political turmoil. In the 1780s, the islands were divided into three kingdoms: Kalani'opu'u ruled the Big Island and the Hana District of Maui; Kahekili ruled Maui, Kaho'olawe, Lana'i, and eventually O'ahu; and Kaeo ruled Kaua'i. Soon after, the great warrior Kamehameha conquered all the islands under one rule. This dynasty would last for a century, until the Hawaiian monarchy would fall forever.

It became known that Hawaii was a convenient stop in the route between the Pacific Northwest, Canada, and China, leading to an influx of westerners. Hawaii was no longer a secret.

KAMEHAMEHA'S UNIFICATION OF THE ISLANDS

Kamehameha was born on the Big Island, after a prophecy that he would become a "killer of chiefs." Because of this, other chiefs ordered the child to be killed, so his mother had to sneak off to the royal birthing stones near Mo'okini Heiau. After giving birth, she gave the child to a servant, who took him down the coast to raise him in solitude. As he grew and matured, Kamehameha proved himself a fierce and hardy warrior.

In 1790, Kamehameha invaded Maui with the assistance of cannons from the *Fair American,* a ship he had gained control of. Kamehameha killed so many commoners in battle that the bodies dammed the waters. He had conquered Maui. By the time Kamehameha took over the Big Island it was a popular stop for ships dealing in the sandalwood trade with China. The area of Kawaihae on the Big Island was covered in sandalwood trees (it is now nothing but dry grass and bare old lava). Over the next two decades, foreigners remained in Hawaii, and whaling become popular in Hawaiian waters with the French, Russians, English, and Americans.

Kamehameha's final victories over all of the islands came later. In 1794, a huge battle happened on Oʻahu, between Kamehameha (and around 16,000 of his warriors) and Kalanikupule and his army, who had hold over Oʻahu. The final showdown took place along the Nuʻuanau Pali, giant cliffs behind where Honolulu is today. Kamehameha's men pushed Kalanikupule's warriors over the cliff to their demise. After hiding, the other chief was found and eventually put to death. Kamehameha now ruled Oʻahu. In 1796, Kamehameha put down a revolt on Hawaiʻi, and Kaumualiʻi, the king of Kauaʻi, recognizing his strength, gave up the island, choosing not to suffer attack. Kamehameha now ruled all of the Hawaiian Islands.

Under Kamehameha, social order was medieval, with the *aliʻi* (royalty) owing their military allegiance to the king and the serf-like *makaʻainana* paying tribute and working the lands. *Kahuna* (priests) were respected and turned to for advice.

The great king ruled until his death on May 8, 1819. Hawaii knew a peaceful rule under Kamehameha. After years on Maui, he returned to his home in Kona on the Big Island, where he passed away. His burial place is unknown. His son, Liholiho, gained the kingdom, but Kamehameha's wife Kaʻahumanu had a strong influence and power. A truly memorable year for Hawaii, 1819 held the great king's death and the overthrow of the *kapu* system of societal rules. Missionaries from New England arrived, dedicated to converting the natives. Eventually the islands got the first American school, printing press, and newspaper west of the Mississippi. Lahaina on the Big Island grew to be a huge whaling port, accommodating over 500 ships during its peak years.

NO MORE *KAPU*

As Kaʻahumanu used her strength to counsel Kamehameha's son and successor Liholiho, she

The Hawaiian term *kapu* (taboo) refers to a rigid system of rules that were eliminated in 1819.

knew that the old ways would not carry Hawaii into the future. In November 1819 she inspired Liholiho to eliminate the *kapu* system. Men eating with women was *kapu,* and women were forbidden to eat certain food, such as bananas and particular fish. Kaʻahumanu and Liholiho ate together in public, breaking these important taboos and marking the demise of the old ways.

MISSIONARIES

On April 4, 1820, the first missionaries landed on the Big Island and were granted a one-year trial missionary period by Liholiho. On Oʻahu and the Big Island they began to convert Hawaiians and were quite successful. Even Kamehameha's first wife and Liholiho's mother, Chieftess Keopuolani, was converted. To defy Pele, she stood in front of erupting volcano Kilauea, ate the *'ohelo* berry that was reserved for Pele, and announced that Jehovah was her god.

Keopuolani died in 1824 and had a Christian burial. Many commoners and *aliʻi* followed her to the new faith, and the missionaries continued to be successful with their intention to wipe out all parts of the Hawaiian culture.

SAILORS

Generally the most dirty, uneducated, drunk, and filthy men from their own countries, the whalers themselves took a huge toll on Hawaii. They flaunted their drunkenness in front of Hawaiians, who tried alcohol themselves. They spread serious venereal diseases, along with regular ones like measles, cold, flu, and smallpox. With no immunity, the Hawaiian population dwindled fast. Cook estimated a population of around 300,000 in 1778, and by the 1850s, it was at an estimated 60,000. The whalers fathered *hapa haole* (half white) children, and they were simply very bad influences.

MISSIONARIES TAKE OVER

Kamehameha III, also known as Kauikeaouli, the brother of Kamehameha II who was the second king of the Kingdom of Hawaii from 1819 until 1824, began to rule after his brother's death in 1824. In 1823, the first mission in Hawaii was established in Lahaina. In 1828 Waine'e Church began construction, the first on Maui. The missionaries were motivated to stop the women from sleeping with the sailors, and also to prevent the sailors from being drunk in public. They put a curfew on sailors and prevented native women from boarding ships, which had become a common thing. Over the years there were several incidents where sailors attacked the reverend's home and shot cannons at it. The new rules didn't stop the rendezvous, but they did instill some societal control.

THE GREAT *MAHELE*

In 1840 Kamehameha III installed a constitutional monarchy, bringing about the Hawaiian Bill of Rights. The biggest change was the privatization and division *(mahele)* of land. Before this, it had all belonged to the ruling chief, who allotted pie-shaped parcels called *ahupua'a* to the people, who could utilize the resources from land to sea. Now, suddenly, people could own land, a hard concept for Hawaiians to understand. They believed no one could own land, just use and care for it. In 1847 Kamehameha III and his advisors divided up the land into three types: the crown land that belonged to the king, the government land for the chiefs, and the people's land, the largest allotment.

In 1848, *ali'i* entered land claims into the Mahele Book and got ownership. Two years later commoners were given title in fee simple to land they used and lived on as tenants, and those without land could buy small farms from 50 cents an acre. In that same year foreigners were able purchase land in fee simple. The *aina* (land), such a part of the spirit of its people, was forever gone from the hands of its people.

SUGAR

Kaua'i stakes claim as the first island to be successful with sugar production. The Koloa Sugar Plantation successfully refined the sweet stuff in 1835. Some success was seen on Maui, and people saw promise in the business. Labor was the issue, and Hawaiians became indentured servants, with contracts lasting up to 10 years that didn't pay much. Chinese laborers were brought in, but rather than slaving for three dollars a month they often abandoned their contracts and went on to start other businesses. Another company brought in Japanese laborers, who worked out well. They worked 10 hours a day, six days a week for $20 a month plus housing and medical care. Eventually, sugar was doing so well the industry seemed promising to foreigners who needed work. Boatloads of people from Japan, Portugal, Germany, and Russia came to the islands. Religions, foods, beliefs, and other cultural aspects mixed.

END OF THE MONARCHY

Kamehameha IV (Alexander Liholiho) ruled 1855–1863, and his only child died in 1852. He was succeeded by his older brother, Kamehameha V, who ruled until 1872. When he died, the line of Kamehameha ended. Lunalilo was elected in 1873 and left no heirs when he died in 1874. David Kalakaua ruled until 1891 and was replaced by his sister, Lydia Lili'uokalani, the last Hawaiian monarch. She began her reign in 1891, and the Hawaiian population was down to 40,000 people. When the McKinley Tariff of 1890 brought a decline in sugar profits, she didn't attempt to solve the issue and got on the bad side of the planters, who said she was hindering their financial growth. With a mission to get rid of her, Lorrin Thurston, a Honolulu publisher, gathered about 30 men and challenged the Hawaiian monarchy. Also, U.S. president Benjamin Harrison wanted Hawaii to be annexed, so there was motivation from different powerful people. Lili'uokalani had limited support and the coup was successful.

Lili'uokalani surrendered not to the conspirators but to the U.S. ambassador, John Stevens, because she thought U.S. leaders would be outraged and come to her aid. They weren't entirely in approval of the coup, but when Lili'uokalani was asked about what she would do with the conspirators if she were reinstated, she said they would be hanged as traitors. Considering that the traitors were the most powerful people in Hawaii, this didn't go over well. On January 17, 1893, the Hawaiian monarchy came to an end. In the new Hawaiian republic, the provisional government was guided by Sanford Dole.

In January of 1895, a small counterrevolution by the queen didn't work, and she was placed under house arrest in Iolani Palace. She was forced to abdicate her thrown and swear allegiance to the new republic. She died in 1917 loyal to her people. The book *Hawaii's Story* is a wonderful read of the queen's story.

ANNEXATION

The majority of Hawaiians didn't want annexation to the United States to be successful, and a large petition was signed. However, they were prevented from voting in the new republic because they couldn't meet the property and income qualifications, which were imposed to control the majority. A big proponent of annexation was Alfred Mahon, a naval strategist who with support from Theodore Roosevelt said that the U.S. military must have Hawaii to be a viable force in the Pacific. On July 7, 1898, President William McKinley signed the annexation agreement and that was that.

By now, as it entered the 20th century, Hawaii was Americanized. Hawaiian language, religion, and culture were nearly gone. Everyone dressed like westerners and was Christian, and Asians made up 75 percent of plantation workers. By 1900 almost 90 percent of all Hawaiians were literate, and everyone was encouraged to attend school. Interracial marriage was accepted, and Hawaii was a true melting pot.

PEARL HARBOR ATTACK

On December 7, 1941, the Japanese carrier *Akagi* listened to a broadcast over its PA system of island music from Honolulu radio station KGMB. Yet the Japanese were secretly listening for a different message of code coming from the Japanese mainland. When they heard "east wind rain," an attack on O'ahu was launched. By the end of the day, 2,325 U.S. servicemen and 57 civilians were dead, 188 planes were destroyed, 18 warships were sunk or severely damaged, and the United States was in World War II. It roared on for four years through the Nagasaki and Hiroshima bombings. When it was over, Hawaii was considered part of the United States.

STATEHOOD

During World War II, Hawaii was placed under martial law, but no serious attempt to do anything to the Japanese population was made. There were simply way too many Japanese, many of whom gained the respect of Americans with their efforts during the war. Hawaii's 100th Battalion became the famous 442nd Regimental Combat Team, which saved the Lost Texas Battalion during the Battle of the Bulge and went on to be the most decorated battalion in all of World War II. When they got back, they were respected and not about to be turned away from their country. When the vote happened, approximately

132,900 voted in favor of statehood, with fewer than 8,000 against.

Congress passed the Hawaii State Bill on March 12, 1959, and on August 21, 1959, President Dwight D. Eisenhower announced that Hawaii was officially the 50th state.

Government and Economy

GOVERNMENT

The government in Hawaii is limited to two levels, the state and county. You'll hear of state beach parks, county beach parks, and state and county land. There are no town or city governments. Hawaii has somehow managed to keep turning out the best national voting record per capita, and the state generally supports Democrats. In the first state elections, 173,000 of 180,000 voters actually voted, a surprising 94 percent. When the election to ratify statehood occurred, 95 percent of the voters opted for statehood. The bill carried on every island except for Ni'ihau, which at the time had a population of approximately 250 who were of pure Hawaiian blood. Honolulu is the capital of Hawaii and has been so since Hawaii became a state.

Former governor Linda Lingle was the first Republican to be voted into the position, as well as the first woman; she broke a 40-year Democratic hold on power in 2002. Elected in 2010, Democrat Neil Abercrombie is the current governor, and Hawaii is represented in the U.S. Congress by two Democratic senators, Daniel K. Akaka and Daniel K. Inouye.

Kaua'i County

Kaua'i and Ni'ihau are the two inhabited islands that belong to Kaua'i County, in addition to Lehua and Ka'ula, both uninhabited islands. The owners of Ni'ihau originally owned Lehua but turned it over to the county years ago because it served no purpose, and taxes were too high. Lihu'e is the county seat and is represented by two state senators elected from the 6th district (a split district including north Kaua'i and portions of the South, Upcountry, and Hana regions for Maui) and the 7th district (which includes all of southern Kaua'i and Ni'ihau). The current mayor of Kaua'i is

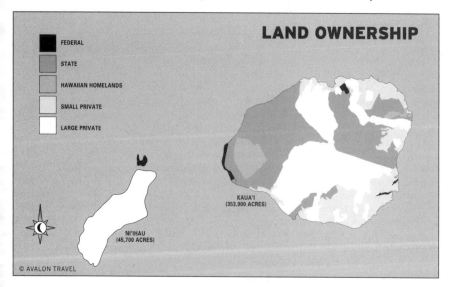

LAND OWNERSHIP

FEDERAL

STATE

HAWAIIAN HOMELANDS

SMALL PRIVATE

LARGE PRIVATE

KAUA'I
(353,900 ACRES)

NI'IHAU
(45,700 ACRES)

© AVALON TRAVEL

Bernard P. Carvalho Jr., elected in 2008 and re-elected in 2010.

State Government

Each county has its own mayor. While Kaua'i County consists of Kaua'i and Ni'ihau, Maui County consists of Maui, Moloka'i, Lana'i, and Kahoolawe. O'ahu makes up Honolulu County, and the Big Island makes up the County of Hawaii. There is also a governor for the whole state, and the Hawaii State Legislature is composed of the Senate and House with senators and district representatives.

ECONOMY

Today, tourism and the military are the two prime sources of income for Hawaii. Although the slow economy has taken a toll on the tourism industry in Hawaii, resulting in sometimes-empty hotel rooms, the industry is still going strong. The reason may be not only the appeal of year-round warm weather and beautiful beaches, but also the increasing appeal of staying within the United States but traveling to a tropical area. Tourists are become more interested in staying in the country as issues keep happening world-wide. Although damaging hurricanes have affected tourism on Kaua'i, it is the fourth most visited island in Hawaii.

Around one million visitors come to the state annually. On any given day there are an estimated nearly 20,000 visitors on Kaua'i. The earliest tourists came to Kalapaki Beach in Lihu'e and soon after spread to the Coconut Coast. After that, Po'ipu was the next tourist destination to become the island's first major resort area. Princeville followed, bringing people to the north shore, and is now the second major resort area on the island. The west end is still undeveloped, but it attracts many visitors looking to go slightly off the beaten path.

The military has a strong presence on the islands, too, and on Kaua'i. The Pacific Missile Range Facility (PMRF) military base has an exclusive hold on miles of beach on Kaua'i's west side, where they test missiles. There are about 125 military personnel and nearly 1,000 civilian contract workers on the island. A tracking facility associated with PMRF is on the Makaha Ridge overlooking the south end of the Na Pali Coast.

Both tourism and the military bring over $4 billion a year to Hawaii. Agriculture, including marijuana, also brings money to the state, especially as GMOs gain popularity. Hawaii is one of the top five marijuana-producing states in the nation.

People and Culture

POPULATION

Hawaii is a true ethnic melting pot. More than 50 ethnic groups are represented throughout the islands, and it's the only state where Caucasians are not the majority. It's estimated that around 56 percent of people in Hawaii were born here, while around 25 percent are from the U.S. Mainland and around 18 percent are foreign born. The influx of workers for the plantation days is one of the reasons for the varied ethnic groups, and current social strife such as unsuitable living conditions in Micronesia has caused Hawaii to see an influx of Micronesians.

The population of Kaua'i is currently around 62,000 people, including the very

small population on Ni'ihau. The population of Kaua'i County accounts for around 5 percent of the total population of Hawaii, and it is the least populated county in the state. The largest town on the island is Kapa'a with 7,600 people; next is Lihu'e with 5,200 people. Around 18,500 people live along Kaua'i's east coast, 12,000 in Lihu'e and the suburban area, 5,400 people in the Koloa/Po'ipu region, 16,000 along the south coast, and 6,400 on the north shore.

PEOPLE
Hawaiians

To put it bluntly, it's quite sad to look at the

LOCAL CUSTOM: NO SHOES IN THE HOUSE

One of the local customs that visitors often find a bit shocking is the generally set-in-stone removal of shoes before entering a house. Unless you're directly told otherwise, no shoes in the house is a definite rule. There are a few theories as to where this custom originates. Some say it's simply common sense to not trek added dirt and germs into a home, while others say it's a Japanese custom relating to not following in other people's shoes (or paths or footsteps). Whatever the origins may be, make sure to follow it if you visit a local's home, and it's even usually requested by the management of vacation rentals. The rule doesn't extend to hotels or businesses, but if you happen to notice a pile of shoes at the door of a small business, it's probably a sign that the owner prefers the no-shoes rule. If you are a fan of the custom or already practice it at home, locally made "please remove shoes" signs and tiles can be purchased around the island.

demise of the Hawaiian people. In 1778 Cook estimated a Hawaiian population of around 300,000 living on the islands. Only 100 years later, only 50,000 Hawaiians remained, having been demoralized and disrespected, their culture torn away from them. Although nearly 250,000 people claim to have some amount of Hawaiian blood, it's estimated that at maximum only 1,000 have pure Hawaiian blood, and the number is dwindling.

Hawaiians are part of a larger ethnic group called Polynesians of the Pacific. They are from certain islands located inside the Polynesian Triangle, including New Zealand, Rapa Nui, Tahiti, Fiji, Tonga, Pitcairn, the Tuamotu Archipelago, Marquesas, Tokelau Islands, Samoa, Niue, Tuvalu, and Hawaii. The islands and people within the Polynesian Triangle are considered Polynesian. The islands outside of it are home to Micronesians and Melanesians.

THE CASTE SYSTEM

Traditional Hawaiian society was divided into rankings by a strict caste system determined by birth and from which no one could escape. The *ali'i* ranked highest, including chiefs and royalty. Both the mother's and father's ranks were passed on, and it was a set rule that the first mating of an *ali'i* be with a person of equal status.

Kahuna were highly talented people whom others would go to for advice for serious moves like offering a prayer or building a home. They were very powerful and respected. There were also *kahuna* of the commoners. The healers were called *kahuna lapa'au,* and the dark magicians were *kahuna 'ana'ana;* it was said they could pray a person to death. The healers used plants for extraordinary medicinal purposes and could cure over 250 ailments. The magicians could cast love spells or curses.

Commoners were known as *maka'ainana,* meaning the people of the land, and that they were. They were farmers, crafters, and fishermen. They lived on *ahupua'a* land owned by *ali'i* but were not enslaved. If the situation wasn't good they were able to move on to another area. Commoners who could be called on in time of battle were called *kanaka no lua kaua,* meaning men for the heat of battle. Families, or *'ohana,* were the immediate circle of people. Farmers inland would trade their goods with those down by the sea, and this way everyone could get what they needed.

The lowest caste was the *kauwa,* a landless caste of people who were put on reservation-like land. If anyone went onto the *kauwa* lands they would be killed. If the community needed someone for a human sacrifice, the *kauwa* lands were the go-to spots. Calling someone *kauwa* is still a huge insult today.

THE *KAPU* SYSTEM

The functioning of everyday life was based on the rigid *kapu* system of rules. Men and women were assigned to certain duties, which were absolutely forbidden to the opposite sex. Men were the only ones allowed to work with taro, and this food was so sacred that there were more *kapu* concerning taro than concerning people. Men would work the taro into poi and serve it to the women. They also fished and built canoes, homes, and walls. Women worked the gardens, fished along the shoreline, and made tapa cloth. The whole *'ohana* (family) lived together in a common house called the *hale noa*.

Men and women could not eat together, and women couldn't enter the men's eating house. Pork, coconut, red fish, and bananas were *kapu* for women. Men were not allowed to partake in sex before fishing, going to battle, or going to a religious ceremony. A settlement area was made up of a men's eating hut, a communal sleeping hut, a women's menstruation hut, a prayer hut, and a women's eating hut.

Some *kapu* were only temporary. Fishing areas or certain lands would be temporarily deemed *kapu* so the wildlife or plants could replenish, a traditional sustainable method found throughout the Pacific. Commoners had to lie on the ground when a high-ranking *ali'i* came into their presence, and lesser *ali'i* required that commoners at least sit or kneel when they were around. Commoners were also not allowed to let their shadows fall on an *ali'i*. Breaking a *kapu* meant immediate death.

TODAY'S HAWAIIANS

Hawaiians make up only approximately 13 percent of Hawaii's population, with very few being pure-blooded. Ni'ihau has the highest concentration of pure-blooded Hawaiians today, numbering around 125. And, Moloka'i has the second largest population of pure-blooded Hawaiians, along with nearly 3,000 Hawaiians living on a 40-acre piece of Hawaiian Home Lands, meaning it's property is dedicated to housing Hawaiians. O'ahu has the highest population of Hawaiians total, with around 240,000 or so.

Chinese

The Chinese are a dominant ethnic group in Hawaii and are the oldest immigrants next to Caucasians from New England. It's estimated there are nearly 60,000 in the islands, with the largest concentration on O'ahu. As a group they have done well and have succeeded in starting businesses lasting generations. The first Chinese were brought to Hawaii to work on sugar plantations and arrived in 1852. They were contracted to work for $3 a month plus room and board. Working 12 hours a day six days a week, the Chinese nearly always moved on when their contracts were done and started their own businesses or shops.

Japanese

The first official Japanese to come to Hawaii were ambassadors sent by the Japanese shogun to go to Washington who stopped in Honolulu on the way in 1860. A small group came eight years later to work on the plantations, and a large influx came in 1885. After an emigration of Japanese farmers who were of a very low caste and were sent over because of the famine, from 1897 to 1908 there was a steady influx. By 1900 there were over 60,000 Japanese in the islands.

Caucasians

White people are lumped under the blanket term *haole*. It can be used with the strongest intent of insult behind it, or it can simply mean a white person with no offense at all. Tone and the situation really determine how it's used in each situation. Types of Caucasians don't matter here. *Haole* is the name for Germans, Irish, Greeks, whoever. It also doesn't matter if it's someone straight off the plane in Hawaii for the first time or someone born and raised in the islands; you're still a *haole*. White people are the longest-standing ethnic group in the islands besides Hawaiians. They have been around since the 1820s, with the first missionaries. They became a dominant group, acquiring an extensive amount of land, power, and cultural influence. They owned huge plantations and businesses and eventually gained places in political power. Historically the white population that came to the island tried to wipe out Hawaiian cultural practices. And there is a certain level of racial tension between Hawaiians and *haole* to this day because of the racism of *haole* ancestors.

Portuguese

Between 1878 and 1887 around 12,000 Portuguese came to Hawaii. Later on, between 1906 and 1913, 6,000 more came. They were put to work on plantations and gained a reputation as good workers. Although they were European, for some reason they weren't seen as *haole,* just somewhere in between. Nearly 27,000 Portuguese made up 11 percent of Hawaii's population by 1920. They intermarried, and Portuguese remain an ethnic group in Hawaii today. One item they brought that would influence local culture was the *cavaquinho,* a stringed instrument that would become the ukulele.

Filipinos

Hawaii saw a large influx of Filipinos because they had been American nationals ever since the Spanish-American war of 1898 and therefore weren't subject to immigration laws that other immigrants were affected by. In 1906, 15 Filipino families came, with many more following in 1924. They were looked down upon by the other ethnic groups in the islands, especially the Japanese. They were the last hired for jobs. Women didn't come with the male immigrants, so by 1930 there were 30,000 men and only 360 Filipino women. The men took part in prostitution, homosexuality, and drunkenness, and hung out at cock fights.

Today there is a large Filipino population in Hawaii of around 170,000 people, with most living on O'ahu. Today they are seen as equals with the other ethnic groups. Although they're illegal, the cock fights still happen, mostly on O'ahu. They take place secretly in neighborhoods but have huge turnouts with thousands of Filipinos and other people. They're known to be like fairs, with treats for kids, food, and socializing. Winning roosters can win up to $30,000, sometimes more.

FOOD

Although modern Hawaiian food is extremely meat based, traditionally Hawaiians were nearly vegetarian, reserving meats for celebrations rather than daily meals. Traditional Hawaiian food can still be found—your best bet would be at a *lu'au*—but a lot of it is now "local food," with foods from the other cultures found in Hawaii.

With ancient Hawaiians, the ocean was a great source for food. Yet they still cultivated successful crops on land of taro, sweet potatoes, breadfruit, and sugarcane. This took a lot of time, more so than fishing. They raised pigs for celebratory meals, as well as chicken, but didn't eat the eggs. The 'o'o (a digging stick) was their only farming tool.

The taro root was their staple crop, and it was the first thing they got going when settling the island. They believed the taro root was where people came from. They would pound it into poi, another meal staple that was eaten with other foods. Taro is nutritious and starchy, and women avoided the starch while pregnant in hopes of avoiding growing a large baby. Kaua'i has its very own brand of poi, Hanalei Poi. It is really good if you like poi. It can be found in nearly all supermarkets.

Another wonderful Hawaiian thing to eat is *haupia,* a wonderful sweet treat. It's a custard-like substance made from coconut that is usually found at *lu'au* or other social gatherings as a dessert. *Laulau* is another *lu'au* food and is a small package of meat, fish, or vegetables wrapped in ti leaves and baked or steamed. A dish made with fresh fish, usually ahi, is *poke.* Available at most delis and other stores, the fish is mixed with soy sauce, onions, seaweed, and other flavors and enjoyed as a snack, appetizer, or side dish.

FESTIVALS AND EVENTS

While in Hawaii, you'll notice respect paid to all the usual American national holidays, in addition to the state's own festivals, ethnic and cultural fairs and celebrations, and other events that are Kaua'i specific. Kaua'i is home to a number of fun events, many based on the Hawaiian culture, while others pay respect to music, and even a Native American powwow happens on the island. A wonderful source for festivals and events on Kaua'i is **www.kauaifestivals.com.** The site offers a thorough listing of one-time and annual events up to a year in advance.

January

Kauaian Days is dedicated to He Inoa no Kaumualii, Kauai's king from 1794–1810. A parade, food, workshops, games, and other cultural festivities take place at various locations. Call 808/338-0111 for more information.

February

Each February the **Waimea Town Celebration** is held by the West Kauai Business and Professional Association. For two days the community comes together in Waimea to enjoy food, entertainment, games, canoe races, a rodeo, and live music. The event has been held for over three decades. Find out more at www.wkbpa.org.

March

Located at Prince Kuhio Park in Po'ipu, the **Prince Kuhio Celebration of the Arts** provides cultural festivities relative to the time of the prince himself. Education on the Hawaiian culture, a *lu'au,* and live dance and music are all offered at the park, most free of charge. Other entertainment takes place at nearby resorts. Visit www.princekuhio.wetpaint.com for more details.

The **Kaua'i Orchid and Art Festival** takes place in Hanapepe. Various music events and other performances happen here in honor of the flowers and local artwork. Visit www.hanapepe.org for more information.

April

Buddha Day, traditionally known as Wesak, happens on the Sunday closest to April 8 and celebrates the birth of the Buddha. Many flower festivals, dances, and other programs take place at temples across the islands, such as the **Kapaa Hongwanji Dharma School** (4-1170 Kuhio Hwy., 808/822-4667, www.kapaahongwanji.org) on the east side.

May

The **Banana Poka Festival** takes place yearly at the **Koke'e Natural History Museum** (3600 Kokee Rd., 808/335-9975, www.kokee.org). In the cooler upland air this outdoors educational festival offers basket making, crafts, face painting, and other games and races for entertainment.

In Hawaii May 1 is known as **Lei Day,** or May Day in other places. Various celebrations take place around the island, including ones at the **Kaua'i Museum** (4428 Rice St., 808/245-6931, www.kauaimuseum.org) and **Kaua'i Community College** (3-1901 Kaumuali'i Hwy., 808/245-8311, www.kauai.hawaii.edu).

June

King Kamehameha Day on June 11 honors Kamehameha the Great with celebrations on each island. Look in the local paper, or keep your eye out for flyers announcing activities. Kaua'i has a parade, a *ho'olaule'a* (celebration), and arts and crafts fairs.

Known as the ultimate Sunday brunch, **Taste of Hawaii** (www.tasteofhawaii.com) is offered by the **Kapaa Rotary Club** (www.clubrunner.ca/kapaa). The event provides food and beverages created by chefs from throughout Hawaii, along with music, vendors, and other entertainment at **Smith's Tropical Paradise** (174 Wailua Rd., 808/821-6895, www.smithskauai.com).

July

The **Fourth of July** is celebrated in Hawaii, and it's a popular day for beach going and barbecues for locals. Check the local paper or with your hotel concierge for fireworks shows and other festivities. This is the day when beach parks are packed with grills, chairs, and families hanging out.

Celebrating plantation life and times is **Koloa Plantation Days** (www.koloaplantationdays.com). A parade, food, crafts fair, music, dance, and more pay homage to a time that is a strong part of Kaua'i's history.

August

The **Kauai County Farm Bureau Fair** (P.O. Box 3895, Lihu'e, 808/337-9944, www.kauaifarmfair.org) offers agricultural displays, a petting zoo, carnival rides, live music, circus acts, an array of food, and much more. It's fun for the whole family and worth checking out.

Recognizing the day Hawaii became a state, **Admission Day** is acknowledged on August 17.

September

Named after the flower that is native to Kaua'i, the annual **Mokihana Festival** (www.maliefoundation.org) is a weeklong event featuring a wonderful array of cultural crafts, hula, workshops, and entertainment. It's worth finding out what's offered and dropping by the events that interest you, or exploring it all.

Another weeklong event is the **Aloha Festivals** (www.alohafestivals.com), which celebrates the spirit of *aloha*. Through hula, music, arts, parades, *lu'au*, and other entertainment, everything *aloha* is celebrated.

October

In Koke'e the annual **Emalani Festival** (3600 Kokee Rd., 808/335-9975, www.kokee.org/festivals/the-emalani-festival) is an authentic and powerful Hawaiian cultural experience. Hula masters and dancers from Hawaii and other countries present the sacred dance at a festival held on the second Saturday of each October. The festival pays respect to Hawaii's Queen Emma, the wife of Alexander Liholiho, Kamehameha IV, who reigned from 1856–1863. She made a trip to Kaua'i's Koke'e State Park in 1871, which is why the festival is held there.

Polynesian- and coconut-themed entertainment, food, crafts, games, and more can be found at the **Coconut Festival.** It's in Kapa'a Beach Park each year, and you can learn cooking tips along with cultural education and just have fun.

November

Keeping up with the Mainland U.S., **Veterans Day** is celebrated statewide. Check the local paper for parade times, which usually takes place through Kapa'a.

The annual **Hawaiian Slack Key Guitar Festival** (www.slackkeyfestival.com) gathers a lineup of some of Hawaii's best slack-key artists for your enjoyment. Local food, island crafts, and other entertainment are provided.

December

To get the Christmas spirit while on Kaua'i, check out the **Waimea Christmas Parade** in historic Waimea Town. Check the local paper for the date so you can listen to carols sung in Hawaiian and enjoy light displays and decorations.

Enjoy the **Lights on Rice Parade** and **Kaua'i Museum Craft Fair** (4428 Rice St., 808/245-6931, www.kauaimuseum.org) for a huge variety of crafts, classes, food booths, hula, and other cultural displays. The fair precedes the evening parade, and it's quite a community gathering.

Avid bird watchers will enjoy the annual **Audubon Christmas Bird Count** held at **Koke'e Natural History Museum** (3600 Kokee Rd., 808/335-9975, www.kokee.org). Call for more information on specifics and the types of birds seen up here.

If you spend **New Year's Eve** on Kaua'i, check the local paper for fireworks displays and other events. There's usually a celebration taking place, but they can vary.

THE ARTS
Canoes

Considered a highly functional piece of art, Hawaiian canoes were built with few tools besides an adze and could carry 200 people. They lasted for generations and could travel thousands of miles. They were made with a small hut in the middle and were called double hulls with two canoes bound together.

Carvings

Wood was the most popular material with Hawaiian crafters, and they could turn it into canoes, tikis, furniture, and bowls. Koa was the favorite wood because of its strength and beauty, and is still highly prized today. Certain types of rock were carved into poi pounders, fish sinkers, and small idols.

Featherwork

Ancient Hawaiians loved bird feathers, and the chief's head pieces and cloaks were made of them. Their favorite colors were red and

CREATIVE KAUA'I: THE ISLAND'S BEST ARTS AND CRAFTS

Kaua'i is known for its inspiring scenery and beautiful surroundings, which serve as the muse for many artists. The island's galleries are loaded with locally made arts and crafts, and there are endless locations to visit yourself with a sketch pad or easel and paints.

An art fan's trip to Kaua'i wouldn't be complete without a stop at **Art Night in Hanapepe,** which happens each Friday night. From 6 to 9 P.M. around 16 galleries open their doors for a celebratory evening of everything art. You can browse local art and socialize with locals, meet artists, and sometimes enjoy live music.

Historic Kapa'a town has a good share of galleries, although the art focus isn't nearly as centralized as in Hanapepe. From a glass gallery to numerous shops with paintings, prints, and other items featuring the art of local artists, a stroll through the town offers art browsing or buying. Also in Kapa'a is the **Kaua'i Products Fair** on the northern end of town. The majority of the products here aren't locally made (many are made in Indonesia or Thailand) even though they may have a Ha-

waiian style. Yet it's still a fun place to shop around for craft souvenirs.

For classes and instruction in making your own art, there are several choices. At the **Kilohana Plantation** in Lihu'e there is a nice array of shops featuring local arts and crafts, along with a really nice pottery studio; at **Clayworks of Kilohana** (3-2087 Kaumualii Hwy., 808/246-2529, www.clayworksatkilohana. com, 10 A.M.–6 P.M. Mon.-Sat. and 11 A.M.–2 P.M. Sun.) you can make your own clay piece and take it home with you or have it shipped. Local artist **Marionette** (www.kauai-artist.net) offers art classes around the island. She offers instruction with a variety of mediums, including watercolors, silk painting, acrylics, and more at various locations on the west and east sides of the island. Hanapepe's **Arius Hopman Gallery** (3840 Hanapepe Rd., 808/335-5616, www.hopmanart.com) offers digital photography classes by the artist himself. Hopman takes beautiful photos of the island's natural beauty, and looking at his work will make you want to take some pictures yourself.

yellow, which only came from certain birds. The *'o'o, 'i'iwi, mamo,* and *'apapane* were birds whose feathers were often used. Feathers were attached to woven nets and made into helmets, idols, and capes and cloaks. They were worn only by men, often during battle. Very special and limited lei were also made from feathers and reserved for high ranking *ali'i* women.

Lei Making

The lei is a classic Hawaiian symbol. Any type of flower can be made into a lei, along with kukui nuts, shells, ferns, leaves, and the rare mokihana flower. Some of the most common flowers used in lei today are plumerias, which are wonderful because they smell great, and purple orchids. There are different methods of lei making, which result in flat lei, round lei, and even head (hair wreath) lei. Today, people of varying ethnic groups receive lei in real

life for various celebrations. Birthdays, graduations, weddings, and other celebratory moments are all times when a lei is given.

Tapa Cloth

A very beautiful creation, tapa cloth is made from tree bark and stamped with different meaningful designs. It's found throughout Polynesia and was also popular with Hawaiians. Women worked it, and mamaki bark was one of the best to use. They women would pound the bark to a pulp and then beat it into strips. It was dried and then painted and marked. You'll still see it today, but most comes from other places in Polynesia and isn't made with the same traditional methods. Tapa makes a lovely wall-hanging souvenir.

Tattoos

Tattoos were very popular throughout Polynesia,

and groups from different islands had their own meanings and styles. Hawaii was no less appreciative of skin art than other groups, and tattooed men and women were a common sight. Different designs signified different things, such as family and things ocean related. Today Hawaiian tattoos have a made a comeback, and many tattoo parlors do them. You may see men with legs or backs covered in traditional tattoos. They are intricate and abstract.

Weaving

The *lau hala* (*lau* meaning leaf, and *hala* the pandanus tree) was used to make wonderfully beautiful and strong mats and baskets. The spine of the leaf was removed and the leaves stored in rolls. When it was time to use them they were soaked in water and pounded to soften them and then woven into various items. *Hala* bracelets are a great find today, and you can also find women's purses made of it.

ESSENTIALS

Getting There and Around

BY AIR

You'll land at the **Lihue Airport** (3901 Mokulele Loop, 808/274-3800, http://hawaii.gov/lih), roughly an equal distance from the farthest point north and the farthest point west, which is roughly 35 miles. Here you are among the large shops and supermarkets if you need any last-minute items before heading to your accommodations or first adventure in either direction. When choosing your seat on the plane, it's a good idea to remember to sit on the left side of the plane in an A seat, or if you can't then a B seat. You'll get views of the island as you fly in during the daytime. If you happen to be flying at the crack of dawn (this is usually the cheapest time to fly inter-island if you booked your ticket last minute), then sitting on the right side of the plane will treat you to a magnificent sunrise view. Check with your hotel before arrival regarding airport shuttles.

BY CAR

To the west from the airport, Route 50 runs from Lihu'e to the end of the road on the west side. To the north, Route 56 runs to Princeville, where it soon becomes Route 560, reaching to the very end of the road at the Na Pali Coast. Although the route numbers change a bit, it's basically one road that can lead you around the island, with smaller roads jutting off to take

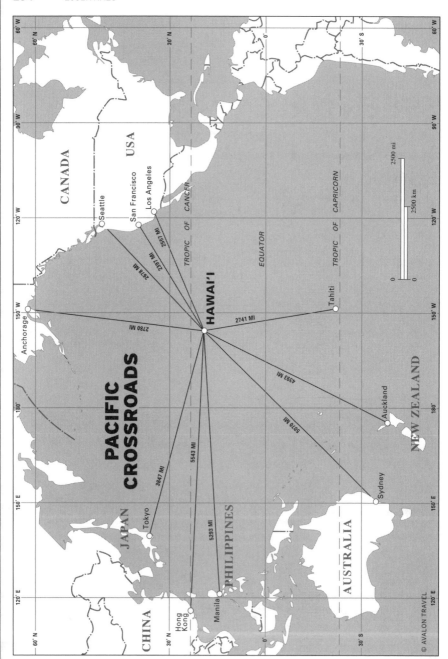

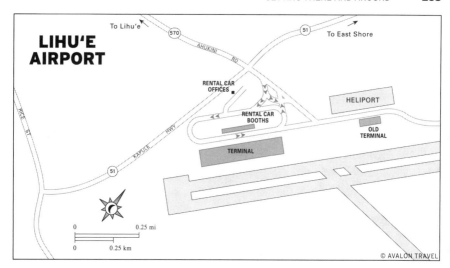

you to beaches or sights. Before you go, there are a few things to take into consideration. If you're under 25 years old, you will most likely be charged an extra $20 a day by major rental car companies. If you cannot afford this, you may want to consider other modes of transportation, which are pretty much limited to a moped, the bus, or thumbing it, although I'm not recommending that as a reliable mode for the whole trip. That said, rental cars are the best way to get around the island. Kaua'i is pretty small, but not small enough to walk everywhere you want to go. Make sure to book your car in advance.

Rental Cars

All rental agencies are located at the Lihu'e Airport. Upon arrival cross the street in front of baggage claim to the rental kiosks, and shuttles will take you to the main offices to pick up your car.

- **Alamo** (808/246-0645 or 800/327-9633, www.alamo.com)
- **Avis** (808/245-3512, 808/241-4384, or 800/381-8000, www.avis.com)
- **Budget** (808/245-1901, 808/245-903, or 800/527-7000, www.budget.com)

- **Dollar** (808/245-3652, 808/246-1150, or 800/800-4000, www.dollar.com)
- **Hertz** (808/246-0027 or 800/654-3131, www.hertz.com)
- **National** (808/245-5636 or 800/227-7368, www.nationalcar.com)
- **Thrifty** (808/245-7369 or 800/847-4389, www.thrifty.com)

CLEAN-ENERGY RENTAL CARS
GreenCar Hawaii (P.O. Box 223684, Princeville, 877/664-2748, www.greencar hawaii.com) offers clean-energy car rental options. They rent hybrid electric SUVs and a battery electric sedans. They provide hourly or daily GreenCar use.

BY BUS
The **Kaua'i Bus** (808/241-6410, www.kauai. gov/Transportation, 5:27 A.M.–10:40 P.M. Mon.–Fri. and 6:21 A.M.–5:50 P.M. Sat., Sun., and holidays) runs island-wide, with stops from Hanalei to the west side. The bus is a green, convenient, and affordable way to get around. The last stop in Hanalei is the old Hanalei courthouse, so the bus doesn't go out to the end of the road, and on the west side it runs to

© GREENCAR HAWAII

A good clean-energy rental car option is GreenCar Hawaii.

Kekaha, not out to Polihale. Fares are $1 for children and seniors, and $2 for the general public. Monthly passes are also available.

BY TAXI

Most taxi services run island-wide, since it's quite small. One option is **Pono Taxi** (808/635-3478, www.ponotaxi.com). It offers taxi, airport shuttle, and tour services island-wide and provides spacious and clean minivans.

North Shore Cab Co. (808/639-7829, www.northshorecab.com) provides island-wide rides and sightseeing tours.

For a more upscale ride, **Kaua'i North Shore Limousine** (808/828-6189, www.kauainorthshorelimo.com) offers limousine service for special dates, weddings, and corporate travel.

Island Taxi (808/639-7829) is based out of Lihu'e and provides island-wide rides. Service is prompt and friendly. **Ace Kaua'i Taxi Services** (808/639-4310) will take you wherever you need to go. Hawaii taxi rates are $3 per mile and $0.40 a minute. Prices are per minivan not per person.

BIKING

Although you *could* bike the whole island, Hanalei, Princeville, and Kapa'a are the best areas for biking. After Hanalei there are numerous one-lane bridges and a narrow winding road to Ke'e Beach that could push bikers into the traffic. Princeville is the safest and most convenient place for a leisurely ride, although the steady incline heading up can be rough. To rent a beach cruiser to explore Hanalei, stop at **Pedal-N-Paddle** (Ching Young Village, 808/826-9069, www.pedalnpaddle.com, 9 A.M.–6 P.M. daily) for hybrid road bike and cruiser rentals for $12 daily or $50 for the week. Biking accessories are also available, along with water-sport supplies.

On the east side you get lucky with the **Ke Ala Hele Makalae** bike path. The name translates to "the path that goes by the coast," and true to its name, the bike path stretches along part of the east coast while staying almost entirely level. Multiple beaches, swimming places, and picnic spots are located along the path. The path begins at the Lihi

DRIVE WITH *ALOHA*

A situation where local customs specifically come into play is driving. You'll notice that even on the highways drivers cruise along at a generally leisurely speed. Even some of the speed limit signs are below the minimum speed on O'ahu, for example. Off the main roads, it's essential to go very, very slow in residential neighborhoods, or on any side streets, especially when there are homes around. Going fast, even if it's not *really* speeding, can result in an angry fist shaken at your car or a call for you to slow down.

Driving customs in Hawaii extend to the casual wave. It's highly common for two drivers who don't know each other to wave at each other as they slowly pass. This goes for slow side roads, drivers on one-lane bridges, and the like, not for each person on the highway. If you're cruising through a residential neighborhood, it's likely a person in a yard will look up and give you a casual wave, so go ahead and return it. These small efforts can go a long way, especially if you're in an area locals prefer to keep visitors out of.

Boat Landing to the south and winds north to Kealia Beach. In Kapa'a, at **Coconut Coasters Beach Bike Rentals** (4-1586 Kuhio Hwy., 808/822-7368, www.coconutcoasters. com, 9 A.M.–6 P.M. Tues.–Sat., 9 A.M.–4 P.M. Sun.–Mon.), you will find a variety of bikes: classic and three-speed cruisers ($22 half day, $25 full day, $95 weekly) for adults and children, tandem bikes (half day $36, full day $45, weekly $190), mountain bikes (half day $25, full day $30, weekly $120), trainers that attach to adult bikes for 6–9 year olds, and covered trailers for toddlers that connect to the back of the bike. The classic beach cruiser is slightly less expensive, but I would recommend the three-speed; it makes it a lot easier to go uphill. Rates for kids' mountain bikes and cruisers vary. Reservations are required for rentals.

Also, **Kauai Cycle** (934 Kuhio Hwy., Kapa'a, 808/821-2115, www.kauaicycle.com, 9 A.M.–6 P.M. Mon.–Fri. and 9 A.M.–4 P.M. Sat.) offers cruisers, road bikes, and mountain bikes for rent. It also provides maps, trail information, clothing, accessories, and guidebooks. Rentals include a helmet and a lock and start at $20 per day. Multiday rates are also available, as well as car racks. It also has a full certified repair shop in case your own bike needs help.

In Lihu'e, long-time bike doctor **Bicycle John** (3142 Kuhio Hwy., 808/245-7579, 10 A.M.–6 P.M. Mon.–Fri. and 10 A.M.–3 P.M.

Sat.) offers a thorough selection of road and mountain bikes to rent and own. Also available is a selection of other biking gear, including bikes, helmets, lights, repair services, and more. Bicycle John himself is known to be a straight-to-the-point kind of guy, no bells (except for bikes) or whistles, but he knows what he's doing.

SCOOTERS

Hop onto a moped to zip around the north side and save on gas at **Island Scooter Rentals** (5-5134 Kuhio Hwy., Kilauea, 866/225-7352, www.mobilemopeds.com, 9 A.M.–5 P.M. daily). In Kapa'a it's located at **Coconut Coasters** (4-1586 Kuhio Hwy., 808/822-7368, www.mobilemopeds.com, 9 A.M.–5 P.M. daily). If you rent by the week the company offers free airport pickup. Four-hour tours are offered for $100. Call for prices and reservations.

HITCHHIKING

Hitchhiking is legal on Kaua'i, as long as you stay off the paved part of the road. This could work well in areas like Hanalei and Kapa'a, where streets are busy and it's a short distance between a lot of beaches, sights, and shopping. If you try to thumb it all the way out to Polihale, there's a good chance of walking a very long way in the scorching sun. Remember; hitchhiking can be dangerous, so women and children should never hitchhike alone.

Tips for Travelers

WHAT TO TAKE

Visiting Kaua'i doesn't require multiple large suitcases. You can get a lot of the basics right on Kaua'i, which can be a good idea depending on your airline's baggage fees. In the past travel supplies may have been cheaper at home since things are generally higher priced in Hawaii, but today airlines, including Hawaii's inter-island carriers, have ever-increasing fees for baggage, so it's a good idea to check with the airline and weigh your options. If you end up paying $50 for two additional bags filled with sunblock (a necessity), snorkel gear, toiletries, and the like, you may save money picking that stuff up at local shops (it will generally be more affordable in Lihu'e). Then again, if you're a highly experienced diver you may not mind the cost to bring your premium gear. Nearly all beach gear can be rented on Kaua'i, so again it's rental fees versus baggage fees.

The clothing you'll need while on Kaua'i is pretty much limited to shorts and T-shirts for men, and sundresses, skirts, and shorts for women for daily outings. Nearly everyone can get by wearing flip-flops, or slippers as they're called locally, unless you're going on a hike. Sneakers just get too hot in Hawaii unless you need the arch support. Casual wear is fitting for most places on Kaua'i unless you'll be spending time on a high-end golf course or going out to one of the few very formal restaurants where collared shirts and closed shoes are required for men. Sunglasses are a must while on sunny Kaua'i, and since many people have a favorite pair they're a good thing to bring with you.

Self-serve laundries can be found in Lihu'e. You can wash your clothes when needed, canceling out the need to bring two weeks worth of attire. They're also more affordable than hotel laundry services. A light jacket or cover-up should suffice for the usual island evenings or rainy days, and you'll only really want a jacket when visiting the high elevation inland areas on the west side or on the beach at night. Generally, one pair of jeans should work for a one- or two-week trip, if you're planning on doing laundry. Kaua'i is usually very warm, and those used to changing seasons and cold weather usually feel warmer in Hawaii than the locals, who may find anything less than 75 degrees reason for a jacket.

Visitors in search of long intense hikes will need good shoes or hiking boots and other hiking gear. Mosquito repellent is also a good idea, mainly for a few hikes. If it is rainy, a small fold-up umbrella can be a good idea for shopping around or visiting sites. Covered shoes and protective pants are also a good idea for adventure sports like riding an ATV. Again, all of this can be found on Kaua'i, so weigh the options with your luggage fees. Make sure to bring your camera, and binoculars are a good idea for overlooks and whale-watching.

TRAVELING WITH CHILDREN

While doing research for this book I hauled my 18-month-old to nearly every spot on Kaua'i in a baby carrier, save for the mile-long hikes. Kaua'i is a wonderful place to travel with children and babies, and they can visit most places on the island with you. While strollers serve their usual purposes, I highly, highly recommend a baby carrier for newborns up to about age three. A carrier enables you to go many places your stroller can't, or where it may be too tough or long for your toddler to walk. They're great for short and long hikes, beach walks, and even shopping around town. I used a carrier made by Ergo, which is known to be the strongest. It can be worn front or back and is designed to fit your body ergonomically, lessening chances of a back or neck ache. My son has climbed rocks, gone on hour-long hikes, and strolled miles on beaches thanks to our carrier. You'll see a lot more of the island with one.

Playgrounds are all over the island, and there are many beaches with calm waters for the little ones. The nice thing about Kaua'i and children is that on an island so small, you're never in the car for too long to get anywhere.

DISCOUNTS

Possible discounts for shopping, accommodations, and car rentals are generally limited to four different options. *Kama'aina* (Hawaii residents), military personnel, seniors, and college students are sometimes offered discounts at various locations. Businesses that offer discounts like these vary widely, and there's no list of each one, so check wherever you are or glance around the checkout counter for signs stating which ones, if any, they offer. *Kama'aina* discounts count for all islands, not just the one you live on, as long as you have a Hawaii driver's license or state ID. Student and senior discounts are usually offered on a certain day of the week and require ID or a student ID issued. Military discounts also require proper identification.

To save energy and money on airline baggage fees, contact **Ready Rentals** (800/599-8008, www.readyrentals.com) to rent various baby supplies. Cribs, tents, strollers, high chairs, and more are available to rent during your stay.

TRAVELERS WITH DISABILITIES

Travelers with a disability won't be missing out on a wonderful experience on Kaua'i. A little pre-planning will help, though. For a smooth trip make as many arrangements ahead of time as possible to suit your needs. Let transportation and tour companies, as well as hotels, know about the nature of your disability so they can arrange to accommodate you. If you might be needing medical attention while on the island, bring medical records. Traveling with friends or family might make it easier, or arrange for an aide before arriving. Some airlines will board those in a wheelchair with a lift if they know you're coming, as some carriers board passengers via steps. Many of the island's hotels and restaurants can accommodate

persons with disabilities, but you may want to call in advance to make sure. Overall, there are many accessible sites on Kaua'i for those with disabilities, and even many beaches that are easily accessible.

Commission on Persons with Disabilities

Created with the purpose of aiding those with disabilities, the commission is a source of valuable information and distributes self-help booklets that are published by the **Disability and Communication Access Board** (808/586-8121) and the Hawaii Centers for Independent Living. A person with a disability would only benefit by writing or visiting the offices once on the island. Pick up the *Aloha Guide to Accessibility* (the first part is free; there's a charge for the second and third parts) from the **Hawaii Centers for Independent Living** (4340 Nawiliwili Rd., Lihu'e, HI 96766, 808/345-4034).

Kaua'i Services

Handicapped parking is available at Lihue Airport across from the main terminal building. Car rental companies can install hand controls on their cars if they're given enough notice, around 48 to 72 hours. If you need a special parking permit, visit the **Drivers License Division** (4444 Rice St., Lihu'e, 808/241-4242) and use your own state placard while parking here. **Gammie Homecare** (808/632-2333, www.gammie.com) provides various medical equipment rentals.

Some travel service companies make special efforts to provide services for those with special needs. Contact Greg Winston at **Water Sport Adventures** (808/821-1599, www.watersportsadventures.ws), Chuck Blay of **Kauai Nature Tours** (888/233-8365, www.kauainaturetours.com), and Debra Hookano at **Liko Kauai Cruises** (808/338-0333).

LGBT TRAVELERS

Gay and lesbian travelers are welcome throughout Hawaii and on Kaua'i. While acceptance is part of the general state of mind, Kaua'i has a smaller gay and lesbian community in the way of nightclubs, bars, or other gathering places for members of the LGBT community than on O'ahu for example. In early 2011, Hawaii became the seventh state to legalize civil unions for same-sex couples.

The only accommodations option specifically geared to same-sex couples is the beautiful **Mahina Kai Ocean Villa** (4933 Aliomanu Rd., 800/337-1134 or 808/822-9451, www.mahinakai.com) in Anahola. Five rooms are offered in the style of a Japanese home, and the grounds are complete with a saltwater swimming pool and a hot tub.

To tap into the LGBT community on Kaua'i, visit www.lambdaaloha.com, the website for Lambda Aloha, a gateway for almost everything gay or lesbian on Kaua'i. Another option is to consult the **International Gay and Lesbian Travel Association** (954/630-1637, www.iglta.org). It can connect you with gay-friendly organizations and tour help.

Health and Safety

A report published by Health Trends said that life expectancy at birth in Hawaii is among the longest in the nation. In 2000, people born in Hawaii had a life expectancy of 80.8 years, more than three years longer than the U.S. average. When Hawaii's life expectancy for 2000 was compared to that of other countries it came in fifth, behind Andorra, San Marino, Japan, and Singapore. Possibly the fresh air and somewhat relaxed lifestyle have a positive effect on health.

Hawaii's location above the malaria belt has blessed the state with a malaria-free existence. The islands are also free of cholera and yellow fever. Although dengue fever doesn't call the islands home, several cases were confirmed a few years ago; they were brought to the islands by people who had contracted it out of the country. Animal quarantine laws are quite strict in Hawaii, and they have kept rabies out of the islands.

Due to a diet high in sugar and processed food that is different from what Pacific islanders traditionally consumed, diabetes and obesity have become rampant health problems for native Hawaiians. The great news is that the food and tap water are safe to consume, there is no need for vaccinations, and air quality on Kaua'i is top notch.

SUN
Sunburned skin is a common sight on Kaua'i, and for the sake of health and a good night's sleep, you don't want that to be you. Simply put, the sun on Kaua'i is intense. It's recommended that you put on sunblock with a SPF of at least 25 to 30 for any prolonged sun exposure. From 10 A.M. to around 3 P.M. the sun is at its strongest. If you do get sunburned, find some aloe fresh from the bush or an aloe gel to help with relief. Another great option is kukui nut oil, which offers great relief for sunburned skin.

Skin isn't the only body part affected by the sun, and sunglasses are a must while on Kaua'i. It's not uncommon to end up with red-tinged eyes after a day at the beach without glasses, and they enhance safety while driving. Hats are also a good idea, as well as something covering the neck while hiking. Some people prefer to hang a piece of fabric or a T-shirt over their neck or a towel over their head.

MOSQUITOS, ROACHES, AND CENTIPEDES
Insects are just as big of fans of Hawaii as people are. They breed well in the warm weather. Luckily, there aren't many that are dangerous or bite. Mosquitos didn't exist here until larvae were accidentally brought over in water on a ship named the *Wellington* in 1826 to Maui. Since then they have bred and multiplied and spread rapidly to all islands. Luckily, there is no malaria in Hawaii. However, the annoying insects are all over Kaua'i, especially in any forested area or yards at homes. They're usually rare right on the beach, but there's always the possibility one or two could sneak over.

Mosquito repellent is a good idea. Citronella is a natural option, and commercial repellents are available at supermarkets, drugstores, and the like. Health food stores carry an array of natural options too.

The centipede is most likely Hawaii's nastiest insect, but it's unlikely that you'll come across one because, although they're not uncommon, they're not seen daily or even weekly by most people. Just step out of the way if you come across one. You can most likely let it continue on its merry way to wherever it's going, but if you see one in your car or your tent, get it out. Their bites really hurt.

I've lived with cockroaches my entire life, as have most people in Hawaii. In fact, they're so common that I now consider them roommates and don't bother killing them or screaming and running in the other direction. They occupy most places in Hawaii, even if you rarely see one. But the good news is, they don't bite and they generally leave you alone. The worst they'll do is munch on your food if you leave it out and uncovered overnight.

HAOLE ROT

You may hear of or even come down with a case of *haole* rot while on the island. Its name hints that only Caucasians come down with it, but those with dark skin are no less prone to it. Although it does have a fancy scientific name if you were to go to a dermatologist, the local term refers to a type of fungus that infects only the surface of the skin. Spots that are lighter in color than the person's normal skin color appear on various parts of the body and don't tan with the rest of the skin. While some say it's caused from the sun, more evidence points to moisture, and some people are very susceptible to it while others never get it. If you're visiting for a few days or a week you probably won't get it, but those who spend months or move to the islands may pick it up after a while in the moist and humid climate.

While it's not harmful at all to your health, it is contagious. Don't share towels or unwashed clothes with a friend who has *haole* rot. To treat it, dry all towels and swimwear well.

After a swim put on dry clothing. Many people use Selsun Blue shampoo to treat it, but a much less toxic and often effective alternative is dabbing tea tree oil on the spots a few times a day.

SEA URCHINS

At beaches with reefs, both exposed and underwater, sea urchins are a common sight. They're painful if stepped on. They're called *wana* in Hawaiian, and you'll recognize them as the spiky balls usually nestled in the reef. Color varies; they can be black, white, or pinkish, but generally you should avoid any sea creature you see that is round and protruding a huge number of spikes. Water shoes are a good idea, but the spikes can penetrate a lot of shoes. It's best to keep an eye out for them. Surfers are prone to stepping on them on shallow reefs. If you do step on one, pull out the spike. Oftentimes a little piece will get stuck, and all you can do is wait until it comes out on its own, which can be very painful.

PORTUGUESE MAN-OF-WAR

Locally called the man-o-war, this relative of the jellyfish can't swim like its cousins and simply floats with the tide. Recognizable by the blue bubble that serves as a body and by their long blue tentacles, they should absolutely be avoided if you see them first. Although they're not common and you usually don't need to worry about them, they are sometimes washed ashore after a heavy storm. If you see one on the beach there are most likely more in the water. Tentacles can be a couple feet long even when the body is the size of a nickel, which means that they can wrap around your arm and make it hard to get them off without touching them more. If you get stung, try to remove them with a gloved hand, T-shirt, stick, or whatever's around. On the sting, rub alcohol—rubbing alcohol or the kind for drinking—lemon juice, meat tenderizer, or after-shave lotion.

LEPTOSPIROSIS

This is a very good reason not to drink river water. Found in streams, ponds, muddy soil, and rivers, leptospirosis is a freshwater-borne bacteria in water that infected cattle, wild boars, and other animals have urinated in. It can make you very sick. From two to 20 days after the bacteria enters the body, fever, chills, sweats, headaches, diarrhea, and/or vomiting suddenly strike. To prevent contracting it, do not drink river water or water from standing pools, and stay out of murky rivers if you have an open cut.

EMERGENCIES
To reach the police, fire department, and ambulance anywhere on the island call 911 from a land line or cell phone. The **Coast Guard Search and Rescue** can be reached at 800/552-6458. In case of a natural disaster like a hurricane or tsunami, call 808/241-6336. The **Sexual Assault Crisis Line** can be reached at 808/245-4144.

MEDICAL SERVICES
Hospitals
In Lihu'e stands the island's main medical center, **Wilcox Memorial Hospital** (3-3420 Kuhio Hwy., Ste. B, 808/245-1100 or 808/245-1010 for emergencies). The smaller **West Kaua'i Medical Center** (4643 Waimea Canyon Dr., 808/338-9431) is open for emergency care and surgical needs. Both facilities are open 24 hours.

Medical Clinics
Associated with Wilcox Memorial Hospital and located at the same address is the **Kaua'i Medical Clinic** (3-3420 Kuhio Hwy., Ste. B, 808/245-1500). It has an urgent-care walk-in clinic (8 A.M.–5 P.M. Mon.–Fri. and 8 A.M.–noon Sat.). There are other branches in 'Ele 'Ele (808/335-0499), Kapa'a (808/822-3431), and Koloa (808/742-1621).

In Hawaii, calling 911 will connect you with emergency services 24 hours a day. This can be the fastest way to get medical attention if you are far from the hospital because various fire stations are located around the island and they, or EMTs, can respond.

Alternative Health Care
Kaua'i draws an array of people, and therefore it has a good selection of people practicing alternative healing methods. Hawaiians traditionally utilized plants from the land and sea to heal ailments and disease, and they used the traditional massage method of *lomilomi* to work on muscles and heal bones. While many massage therapists have learned and practice *lomilomi,* you can also find it at just about any independent spa or hotel spa on the island. Asian healing arts, such as acupuncture and herbal medicine, are also practiced on Kaua'i. Western massage modalities, naturopathy, reflexology, chiropractic care, and other alternative forms of medicine can be found here too.

Since new practices open and old ones close, it's a good idea to look in the Yellow Pages or online if you need alternative medical attention while on Kaua'i. A good place to start is **Kauai Center for Holistic Medicine and Research** (4504 Kukui St., Kapa'a, 808/823-0994, www.holisticmedicinehawaii.com). It offers acupuncture, Indian Ayurvedic medicine, homeopathy, gem lamp therapy, biofeedback technology, and more.

Information and Services

TOURIST INFORMATION
Hawaii Visitors and Convention Bureau
The Hawaii Visitors and Convention Bureau, which has a **Kaua'i Visitors Bureau** (4334 Rice St., Lihu'e, 800/262-1400, www.gohawaii.com/kauai), is a great resource for travel information while on Kaua'i. Dropping by the office or visiting the website offers a wealth of information and will most likely answer any question you may have. Free maps, planners, brochures, and information on accommodations, restaurants, entertainment, transportation and more are available at the office. On the site you can explore each region visually and gain information on all aspects of the island.

Free Travel Literature

To further your knowledge of activities and places to eat, the island offers ample free magazines acting as directories and informational resources. Beginning at the airport (you can't miss the large kiosk at baggage claim loaded with publications) you'll see *This Week Kaua'i, Kaua'i Gold,* and *Kaua'i Activities and Attractions.* Other magazines include *101 Things to Do on Kaua'i, Kaua'i Menu,* and *Kaua'i Drive Guide.* In these you can find money-saving coupons, maps, information on monthly events, and more.

MONEY
Currency

U.S. currency is counted by the dollar and the cent. The drab green bills, decorated with the images of past presidents, are accompanied by coins. Bills in use these days are the $1, $2 (although rare), $5, $10, $20, $50, and $100. Coins include pennies worth once cent, nickels worth five cents, dimes valued at 10 cents, quarters worth 25 cents, and half dollars worth 50 cents, although these are uncommon. New designs have come out for the paper money since 1996 in an effort to battle counterfeiting. When you hand a salesperson a bill larger than $10, it's common to see them draw a black line on it that will disappear fast. This is a test for counterfeit bills.

ATMs (automated teller machines) are located at numerous locations around the island. You can find them in stores, at banks, gas stations, shopping centers—you get the idea. Although they're convenient, keep in mind that withdrawing money from an ATM that does not belong to your bank will usually result in charges both from your bank as well as the bank that owns the ATM. Discuss ATM fees with your bank before traveling to see if they have affiliate ATMs that you can identify by certain logos.

Travelers Checks

Travelers checks are widely accepted at many shops, hotels, restaurants, and car rental companies, but you may want to check with them to avoid an inconvenience. Your travelers checks should be in U.S. currency, since generally only select large hotels will accept Japanese or Canadian travelers checks. Foreign travelers checks are accepted at banks, but it adds an inconvenience.

Credit Cards

Credit cards are widely accepted on Kaua'i, with most shops, businesses, hotels, and restaurants accepting Visa and Mastercard. American Express is also widely accepted, but it's not uncommon to find out that certain small merchants don't accept it. If you're planning on using your card while on Kaua'i, let your credit card company know before you arrive. Banks will often put a stop on your credit card or bank-issued debit card when they notice out-of-state or -country activity to prevent fraud. Also, write down your card numbers in case they get stolen, and it's always good to ask in advance if an outfitter or business takes credit cards. Some very small and local businesses don't, but they'll usually post a sign stating so.

COMMUNICATIONS AND MEDIA
Telephone

Phone service is as modern and equal in quality as any Mainland phone system. Calling numbers on Kaua'i is considered local, while any calls to other islands are considered long distance. Inter-island long distance usually has different rates than long distance to the Mainland. Although public phones that charge 50 cents for local calls can be found around the island, they are slowly disappearing. You'll most likely have a phone in any hotel room or condominium, but those will cost more than other lines. A cell phone your best bet. Make sure to check with your carrier before you leave home about changing rates and times while on Kaua'i. If your phone breaks or you need help with service while traveling, all major carriers have stores on Kaua'i, and Walmart also sells phones and accessories. The area code for the entire state is 808, 911 will reach emergency services, 411 will reach directory assistance, and 800/555-1212 will reach a directory for toll-free numbers.

Newspapers

The main local paper is *The Garden Island* (www.thegardenisland.com), which is published daily with a Sunday edition. It is available at many stores and paper dispensers around the island.

The main daily newspaper in the islands is the *Honolulu Star-Advertiser* (www.staradvertiser.com), the product of a recent consolidation of the two papers. It is published daily with a Sunday edition. National papers such as *USA Today* and the *New York Times* are available at certain shops and Starbucks Coffee.

Kaua'i Radio Stations

If you want to take a break from the iPod (rental cars have auxiliary cable connectors) you can tune into one of the local radio stations. There are some broadcast on Kaua'i, and some stations from O'ahu can also be picked up.

- **KKCR 91.9 and 90.0 FM:** community radio
- **KONG 93.5 FM:** the hot station on the island, playing popular music and requests
- **KITH 98.9 FM:** island music
- **KSHK 103.3 FM:** classic rock and roll
- **KTOH 99.9 FM:** oldies from the '50s to the '90s
- **KUAI 720 AM:** music, news, and sports
- **KFMN 96.9 FM:** adult contemporary
- **KSRF 95.9 FM:** island music

WEIGHTS AND MEASURES

Like the rest of the United States, Hawaii uses the "English method" of measuring weights and distances. Ounces and pounds measure dry weight; ounces, quarts, and gallons measure liquids; and inches, feet, yards, and miles measure distances.

Electricity

If you're visiting from the continental U.S., you don't have to worry about bringing an adaptor for your electronics. The same electrical current is used in Hawaii as on the Mainland. Electricity here functions on 110 volts, 60 cycles of alternating current (AC). Visitors from other countries should get the right adaptor

so they can charge cameras and phones while on the island.

Time Zones

Daylight saving time does not apply to Hawaii. When the Mainland isn't on daylight saving, Hawaii is two hours behind the West Coast, four hours behind the Midwest, and five hours behind the East Coast. Many cell phones and computers these days have apps that calculate the difference in hours between countries and states.

LOCAL RESOURCES
Weather Reports and Surfing Conditions

For a recorded weather report call 808/245-6001. For the surf conditions call 808/245-3564. It's a great resource for serious surfers who come to Kaua'i for the waves, since surf breaks and places vary with conditions. For those booking surf lessons, the schools should know about the conditions and the best places to guide you.

Camping and Hiking Permits

County park camping permits are obtained through the **Department of Parks and Recreation** (Park Permits Section, 4444 Rice St., Ste. 105, Lihu'e, 808/241-4463, www.kauai.gov, 8:15 A.M.–4 P.M. Mon.–Fri.). Camping permits are issued for the following county beach parks:

- Anahola Beach Park
- Anini Beach Park
- Ha'ena State Park
- Hanalei Black Pot Beach Park
- Hanama'ulu Beach Park
- Lucy Wright Beach County Park
- Lydgate Park Campground
- Salt Pond Park

Camping permit fees are $3 per adult, per night for nonresidents and free for residents of the State of Hawaii who can show proof of residency. Children under the age of 18 years are also free and must camp with at least one adult 18 years of age or older.

Permits are also available on the south side at **Kalaheo Neighborhood Center** (4480 Papalina Rd., Kalaheo, 808/332-9770) and **Hanapepe Recreation Center** (4451 Puolo Rd., Hanapepe, 808/335-373), on the east side at the **Kapa'a Neighborhood Center** (4491 Kou St., Kapa'a, 808/822-1931 or 808/822-0511), and on the north shore at **Kilauea Neighborhood Center** (2460 Keneke St., 808/828-1421). They are available for pickup Monday through Friday except for holidays from 8 A.M. to noon. Call ahead to make sure they are open. These offices accept only money orders as payment for camping permits.

For state beach parks such as Polihale, Koke'e Park, and state campgrounds along the Na Pali Coast, contact the **Hawaii State Parks Office** (3060 Eiwa St., room 306, Lihu'e, 808/274-3444, www.hawaiistateparks. org, 8 A.M.–3:30 P.M. Mon.–Fri.) They can be obtained in person or in advance by mail. For Hawaii residents it is $12 a night per campsite per night for up to six people, and $2 a night for each additional person. The maximum fee per site is $20 a night. For non residents it's $18 a night per campsite per night for up to six people, and $3 a night for every additional person. The maximum fee per site is $30 a night. For state campgrounds along the Na Pali Coast fees are $15 per person per night for Hawaii residents and $20 per person per night for non-residents.

To obtain permits for the extremely far-off-the-beaten-path campsites in Waimea Canyon and Koke'e State Park, visit the **Division of Forestry and Wildlife** (3060 Eiwa St., room 306, Lihu'e, 808/274-3444, www.hawaiistate-parks.org, 8 A.M.–3:30 P.M. Mon.–Fri.) for permits at no cost.

Consumer Protection

The **Kauai Chamber of Commerce** (808/245-7373, www.kauaichamber.org) is the place to contact for reporting bad service, trouble finding a place to stay, or if you get ripped off by a business. For other issues with businesses, try the **Better Business Bureau of Hawaii on O'ahu** (808/536-6956, www.hawaii.bbb.org).

RESOURCES

Glossary

HAWAIIAN

There was once a point in time when it was illegal to speak Hawaiian. The language was reserved to the home, and wasn't spoken in school. However, along with the rest of the Hawaiian culture it has experienced a renaissance in recent years. It's being taught in colleges, and many more people are fluent in the language now than in years past. While it's far from being the state's official language, certain words and phrases have remained common in everyday conversation. Many Hawaiian words explain concepts, rather than having one simple meaning like words in the English language. The following words are most of the commonly used words in daily life. For a great language resource, pick up Elbert and Pukui's *Hawaiian Dictionary.* You'll see that a glottal stop or *'okina,* represented by the reversed apostrophe, is used in many Hawaiian words. This reversed apostrophe is used to indicate the separate pronunciation of two vowels that appear next to each other.

'a'a gray, crumbly, old lava
'ae yes
ahupua'a a traditional land division running from the mountains to the ocean, enabling those living there to have access to all resources
aikane buddy or friend
'aina land
akamai smart, clever, or wise
akua spirit or god
ali'i Hawaiian royalty
aloha common greeting or word of parting; means hello, good-bye, love, or welcome

anuenue rainbow
'a'ole no
'aumakua a personal or family protective animal spirit
auwe alas
'awa a plant found throughout Polynesia; a calming, mildly intoxicating drink is made from the root (also known as kava)
halakahiki pineapple
halau long house; when used with hula it means group or school
hale house
hana work
hanai literally means to feed; commonly used as a term for adopted parents or children, but not in a formal or legal sense (used also to describe a close relationship)
haole literally means no breath; used to describe Caucasians
hapa indicates mixed ethnicities, such as part Hawaiian part Caucasian
hapai pregnant
he'e nalu literally wave sliding, or surfing
heiau a sacred rock structure used as a temple and to worship the gods
honu sea turtle
ho'olaule'a a celebration, usually a party or gathering
huhu angry or irritated
hui a group of people or meeting
hukilau a fishing gathering where everyone helps pull *(huki)* the fish into shore in a huge net; everyone who helped gets to enjoy the food
hula a native Hawaiian sacred dance
huli huli to turn over, as in "*huli* the canoe";

chicken on a rotisserie barbecue is called *huli huli* chicken

i'a fish

imu an earthen oven

ipo sweetheart

kahuna priest, sorcerer, or doctor

kai the sea

kala the sun

kalua roasted underground in an *imu*

kama'aina a child of the land or longtime resident of any ethnic group; essentially, a local

kanaka Hawaiian (to discern from other ethnic groups)

kane man

kapu taboo, forbidden; do not touch

kaukau slang for eating or food

keiki child or baby, children

kiawe a tree that grows along the shoreline and is covered in long, sharp thorns (Local lore says missionaries planted the tree to coerce natives into wearing shoes. It's a good wood for fuel and adds flavor to barbecue.)

kokua help

kolohe rascal

konane a traditional Hawaiian game similar to checkers

Kona wind a subtropical wind that blows from the south hitting the leeward (dry) sides of the islands; usually brings muggy warm weather

kukui candlenut tree; the nuts are polished and strung into lei (The oil-rich nuts were strung on the rib of a palm frond and used as candles. The oil is also wonderful for various skin treatments, from rashes to sunburns.)

kuleana a person's right

Kumulipo an ancient Hawaiian genealogical chant that speaks of gods, creation, and the beginning of humankind

kupuna a grandparent or ancestor

lanai a commonly used term for porch or veranda

lani sky or heavens.

lau hala the leaf *(lau)* of the pandanus *(hala)* plant; used often in mat weaving

lei a necklace or garland made with flowers, shells, or nuts

limu seaweed

lomilomi traditional Hawaiian massage

lua bathroom

lu'au a celebratory party; thrown for birthdays, graduations, or other reasons to feast and enjoy dance and music

mahalo thank you

mahele division; the Great Mahele of 1848 broke up the traditional common lands and enabled private ownership of property

mahina moon

mahu traditionally referred to a third gender, similar to a transvestite; today it generally refers to a gay man; can be used in a neutral or negative light

maile a fragrant green vine used in lei making

makai toward the ocean ("The house is on the *makai* side of the road.")

make death, died

malo a traditional loin cloth

mana a person's spirit, power, or energy

manini small, or frugal

mauka toward the mountains, as in directions ("The house is on the *mauka* side of the road.")

mauna mountain

mele a song or chant

menehune the mystical "little people" of Hawaii; said to only come out at night (Some say they are completely made up, while others cite Hawaiian legends saying *menehune* are believed to have been Micronesians that settled the islands before Hawaiians.)

moa chicken

moana the ocean

moe moe sleep

mu'umu'u a long dress with a high neckline made from aloha print fabric

nani beautiful

nui big, large

'ohana family

oli chant

ono delicious

'opihi a limpet that clings strongly to rocks and gathered to eat; often found in pupu platters or at delis

'opu stomach

pahoehoe black, ropey lava that is younger than *'a'a*

pakalolo marijuana

pali cliffs

paniolo a Hawaiian cowboy

pau finished, done
pilau sticky or a bad smell
pilikia trouble, bad news
pono peaceful, righteous
pua flower
puka hole
pupule crazy
tapa a traditional cloth made from bark and stamped with intricate designs
ti a plant with red or green leaves used for wrapping food and offerings
tutu grandmother
ukulele a small guitar-like take on the Portuguese instrument called a *cavaquinho;* very connected to the islands and used in local music
wahine woman
wai water
wiki fast or speedy

Useful Phrases

Aloha ahiahi. Good evening.
Aloha au ia 'oe. I love you.
Aloha kakahiaka. Good morning.
Aloha nui loa. Much love.
E komo mai. Please come in; welcome.
Hau'oli la hanau. Happy birthday.
Hau'oli makahiki hou. Happy New Year.
Mahalo nui loa. Thank you very much.
Mele kalikimaka. Merry Christmas.

PIDGIN

A blend of the original immigrant languages and English, local pidgin is English based with an array of foreign terms and slang mixed in. Many locals are raised speaking it as their primary language, and most residents can speak it although they speak normal English often. It can be fun to learn, especially useful to decipher what a local might be saying.

an'den and then
auntie a respectful term for a woman of any age older than the speaker
braddah brother, male friend
brah used to call a male's attention
bumbye later, after a while
da'kine used to describe something really good, or when searching for the right word ("I went there with da'kine, you know who I mean? I forget her name.")
geev um go for it, give them hell
grinds food
hana hou again, encore
hele on let's move, let's do it
Howzit? How are you?
kau kau eat
li'dis an' li'dat like this and like that
mo' bettah good, great, better than
sista sister, female friend
slippa slippers, flip-flops
stink eye a glare of dislike
talk story chatting, catching up with someone
tanks 'ah brah thank you
Wea ste? Where stay? Where is he? Where is it?
we go let's go

Suggested Reading

There is a huge array of books published on Hawaii and the Pacific. From history and archaeology to can't-put-down novels, many books are published by local companies as well as mainstream large companies. Cookbooks, novels, and history books make great reads on vacation as well as wonderful souvenirs to take home.

Those interested in Hawaiian and Pacific literature should visit www.uhpress.com, the website of the **University of Hawai'i Press.** Other publishers that offer Hawaiian- and Pacific-themed books include the **Bishop Museum Press** (www.bishopmuseum.org), **Kamehameha Schools Press** (www.kamehamehapublishing.org), **Bess Press** (www.besspress.com), **Mutual Publishing** (www.mutualpublishing.com), and **Petroglyph Press** (www.basicallybooks.com).

ASTRONOMY

Rhoads, Samuel. *The Sky Tonight: A Guided Tour of the Stars over Hawaii.* Honolulu: Bishop Museum, 1993. This book contains a collection of star charts for every month in Hawaii.

COOKING

Beeman, Judy, and Martin Beeman. *Joys of Hawaiian Cooking.* Hilo, Hawaii: Petroglyph Press, 1977. A nice collection of local and Hawaiian-style recipes from Big Island chefs.

Choy, Sam. *Little Hawaiian Cookbook for Big Appetites.* Honolulu: Mutual Publishing, 2003. A collection of the famous chef's favorite recipes to execute in your own home is a great take-home souvenir.

Fukuda, Sachi. *Pupus, An Island Tradition.* Honolulu: Bess Press Inc., 1995. A roundup of tasty and famous pupu, or appetizers, to entertain with back at home can be found in this book.

Tuell, Bonnie. *Island Cooking.* Honolulu: Mutual Publishing, 1996. With this book you can find an array of tasty island recipes, including pupu, dinner, and desserts.

Wong, Alan. *New Wave Luau.* Berkeley: Ten Speed Press, 1999. With his book, Hawaii's prized chef shares wonderful recipes across the board of Hawaiian and local food.

CULTURE AND HISTORY

Cordy, Ross. *Exalted Sits the Chief.* Honolulu: Mutual Publishing, 2000. An archaeologist and professor at the University of Hawai'i West O'ahu, Cordy offers wonderful insight into the forming of the Hawaiian culture and society up until the pre-contact period. Although it focuses on the Big Island, the book integrates the history of all islands and is a great read.

Hartwell, Jay. *Na Mamo: Hawaiian People Today.* Honolulu: Ai Pohaku Press, 1996. This book is an intriguing collection of profiles of 12 people practicing Hawaiian traditions around the world.

Kamehameha Schools Press. *Life in Early Hawaii: The Ahupua'a,* 3rd ed. Honolulu: Kamehameha Schools Press, 1994. The book was written to educate schoolchildren on the basic organization of old Hawaiian land use and its function. It offers a good overview of Hawaiian history to those new to the subject.

Kirch, Patrick V. *Feathered Gods and Fishhooks: An Introduction to Hawaiian Archaeology and Prehistory.* Honolulu: University of Hawai'i Press, 1997. This book offers easy reading and great illustrations to share a wonderful insight into the pre-contact period.

Mills, Peter R. *Hawai'i's Russian Adventure: A New Look at Old History.* Honolulu: University of Hawai'i Press, 2002. A professor at the University of Hawai'i at Hilo, Mills offers a new take on the uses of Waimea's Russian Fort Elisabeth.

Moriarty, Linda Paik. *Ni'ihau Shell Leis.* Honolulu: University of Hawai'i Press, 1986. This beautiful, comprehensive book with color photos covers the social, cultural, modern, and historical aspects of the valued lei.

FAUNA

Denny, Jim. *The Birds of Kaua'i.* Honolulu: University of Hawai'i Press, 1999. An overview of the birds of Kauai, this is a must for any birder exploring the island.

Fielding, Ann, and Ed Robinson. *An Underwater Guide to Hawaii.* Honolulu: University of Hawai'i Press, 1987. Photos and well-written text lead you on an adventure through Hawaii's underwater world. A great companion for those who love to snorkel and dive.

Kay, Alison, and Olive Schoenberg-Dole. *Shells of Hawaii.* Honolulu: University of Hawai'i Press, 1991. A collection of great color photos of shells of the islands, this is a must for ocean lovers.

Mahaney, Casey. *Hawaiian Reef Fish, the Identification Book.* University of California: Planet Ocean Publishing, 1999. This book provides photos and descriptions of common feef fish you may see while snorkeling. It's the best way to identify the underwater life.

Van Riper, Charles, and Sandra van Riper. *A Field Guide to the Mammals of Hawaii.* Honolulu: Oriental Publishing. The book is a guide to the mammals introduced to Hawaii.

FICTION AND PERSONAL NARRATIVES

Davenport, Kiana. *House of Many Gods.* New York: Ballantine Books, 2007. Davenport tells a beautiful story of love, change, and growth of a woman raised in poverty on O'ahu. It ties in to Kaua'i when the woman travels to the island during a devastating hurricane and falls in love. Like all of Davenport's books, this one is a real page-turner.

Davenport, Kiana. *Shark Dialogues.* New York: Penguin Books, 1995. The author weaves a tale of several generations of a family of women experiencing life in Hawaii. A wonderful read.

Hamilton, Bethany. *Soul Surfer.* New York: Pocket Books, 2004. Having lost her arm to a shark attack while surfing, the Kaua'i surfer shares her story of getting back in the water and back on waves. It's an inspiring read.

Kaluaikoolau, Piilani, and Frances Frazier, translator. *The True Story of Kaluaikoolau: As Told by His Wife, Piilani.* Honolulu: University of Hawai'i Press, 2001. Kaluaikoolau was a Kaua'i leper. He refused to be banished the leper colony and took his family to live deep in the Kalalau Valley. His story went down in history as a tale of resilience and resistance, and Jack London made it famous in his short story "Koolau the Leper."

Liliuokalani. *Hawaii's Story.* Honolulu: Mutual Publishing, 1990. The beloved queen tells her story, as well as the story of the fall of the Hawaiian throne. Truly a wonderful read that sheds light on Hawaii's history and present in the form of a novel, not a textbook.

McKinney, Chris. *The Tattoo.* New York: Soho Press, 2007. Now a professor at an O'ahu community college, the author tells a tale of the darker side of Hawaii that visitors don't get to see.

FLORA

Kepler, Angela. *Hawaiian Heritage Plants.* Honolulu: University of Hawai'i Press, 1998. A focus on plants used by the early Hawaiians for medicinal and cultural uses.

Miyano, Leland. *A Pocket Guide to Hawaii's Flowers.* Honolulu: Mutual Publishing, 2001. A good guide small enough to keep on you that sheds light on the commonly seen flowers throughout the state.

Teho, Fortunato. *Plants of Hawaii: How to Grow Them.* Hilo, Hawaii: Petroglyph Press, 1992. A useful book for those who want instruction on successfully growing tropical plants. Some can be grown on the continental United States.

Valier, Kathy. *Ferns of Hawaii.* Honolulu: University of Hawai'i Press, 1995. This is one of the few books that focus on Hawaii's beautiful ferns.

Wagner, Warren L., Derral R. Herbst, and H. S. Sohner. *Manual of the Flowering Plants of Hawaii,* revised edition, vol. 2. Honolulu: University of Hawai'i Press in association with the Bishop Museum Press, 1999. The bible for Hawaii's botanical world is a very thorough scientific and technical read.

LANGUAGE

Pukui, Mary Kawena, and Samuel H. Elbert. *Hawaiian Dictionary.* Honolulu: University of Hawai'i Press, 1986. Provides Hawaiian to English and English to Hawaiian translation. This is the best comprehensive dictionary.

Pukui, Mary Kawena, Samuel H. Elbert, and Esther T. Mookini. *Place Names of Hawaii.* Honolulu: University of Hawai'i Press, 1974. A comprehensive listing of Hawaiian and foreign place names in the state. The book offers pronunciation, spelling, meaning, and locations.

Simonson, Douglass. *Pidgin to Da Max.* Honolulu: Bess Press, 1981. A great and humorous guide to speaking pidgin. It's fun and funny, and actually educational because it's accurate.

MYTHOLOGY AND LEGENDS

Beckwith, Martha. *The Kumulipo.* 1951 reprint. Honolulu: University of Hawai'i Press, 1972. This is the most comprehensive book of Hawaii's folklore. It tells the creation myth.

Pukui, Mary Kawena, and Caroline Curtis. *Hawaii Island Legends.* Honolulu: The Kamehameha Schools Press, 1996. Hawaiian tales and legends for youths, or anyone really.

Pukui, Mary Kawena, and Caroline Curtis. *Tales of the Menehune.* Honolulu: The Kamehameha Schools Press, 1960. This book is a collection of various stories about Hawaii's mythical little people.

Wichman, Frederick B. *Kaua'i: Ancient Place Names and Their Stories.* Honolulu: University of Hawai'i Press, 1998. A compilation of stories and legends relating to places on Kaua'i, this book can add depth to an understanding of the island and accent any visit.

Wichman, Frederick B. *Kaua'i Tales.* Honolulu: Bamboo Ridge, Press, 1985. A compilation of Hawaiian myths and legends related to Kaua'i with simple yet lovely pen illustrations.

Internet Resources

GOVERNMENT
County of Hawaii
www.kauai.gov
The official website of Kaua'i offers a wealth of information, including a calendar of events and information about parks, camping, and island bus schedules.

Hawaii State Government
www.hawaii.gov
Visit this website for comprehensive information about the state of Hawaii. Among other things you will find information for visitors on government organizations, health, living in Hawaii, education, and many other public topics.

TOURISM
Alternative Hawaii
www.alternative-hawaii.com
Check out this website for a guide to the path less traveled. It offers a calendar of eco-cultural events, a list of Hawaii heritage tour guides, travel services, and a lot more.

Best Places Hawaii
www.bestplaceshawaii.com
Best Places Hawaii provides information on the best places in Hawaii. It has very thorough information on places to see, things to do, places to eat and stay, and even a vacation planner.

Hawaii Ecotourism Association
www.hawaiiecotourism.com
The Hawaii Ecotourism Association website is a good source for eco-friendly information on traveling in Hawaii, with information on individual sites and links to organizations related to ecotourism.

Hawaii Visitors and Convention Bureau
www.gohawaii.com
This website has thorough information from the state-run tourism organization about all of the major Hawaiian islands. Information on accommodations, transportation, activities, and shopping, as well as a calendar, a travel planner, and a whole lot more can be accessed here.

Kaua'i Visitors Bureau
www.gohawaii.com/kauai
This section of the HVCB site is specifically about Kaua'i.

Index

A

accessibility: 239
accommodations: 179-208; east side 180-187;
    north shore 187-196; south shore 196-203;
    west side 204-209
Admission Day: 230
adventure sports: east side 48-50; north
    shore 98-99; south shore 127-128; west side
    165-166
agriculture: 214, 225
ahi: 65
air travel: 233; map 234
Alaka'i Swamp: 163-164, 211
Alaka'i Swamp Trail: 19, 21, 163-164
Alakoko Fishpond: 54
Alexander Day Spa and Salon: 51
Aliomanu Beach: 38
Allerton Garden: 133-135
Aloha Festivals: 230
Anahola: 33, 38
Anahola Beach Park: 38
Anahola Marketplace: 62
Anara Spa: 130
animals: 217, 250
Anini Beach: 16, 78, 80, 86
Anini Beach Park: 80
annexation: 223
area: 209
area code: 243
Arius Hopman Gallery: 231
art galleries: see arts and crafts
Art Night in Hanapepe: 13, 173, 231
arts and crafts: 230-232; classes 71, 178;
    galleries 60, 136-137, 170-172, 173; see also
    shopping
astronomy: 173, 249
ATMs: 243
ATVing: 20, 49, 127
Audubon Christmas Bird Count: 230
Awa'awapuhi Trail Loop: 164

B

Baby Beach (east side): 37
Baby Beach (south shore): 122
Backdoor Surf: 77, 89, 107
baggage: 238
Banana Joe's: 13, 109
Banana Poke Festival: 229

banks: east side 71; west side 177
Bar Acuda Tapas and Wine: 12, 77, 112
Bay, The: 90
beaches: 14-17; east side 33-38; north shore
    76-85; south shore 118-124; west side 149-
    154; see also specific beach
Beach House Restaurant: 13, 28, 119, 133, 140
bed-and-breakfasts: 186; see also
    accommodations
Bellstone: 58
Better Business Bureau of Hawaii: 245
Big Save: 23, 108, 136, 139, 147, 174, 175
biking: 236-237; east side 47-48; north shore
    97-98; west side 164
birds/bird-watching: 21, 98, 164, 216-217, 230,
    250
Birds in Paradise: 21, 165
Black Pot: 82
Blue Dolphin Charters: 20, 28, 127, 155
boat tours: 13, 28, 127, 155-157
books/bookstores: 172, 249-251; see also
    libraries
Bouchons Hanalei: 77, 108, 111
Brennecke Beach: 121
Brick Oven Pizza: 119, 120, 142
Bubba Burgers: 11, 112, 140
Buddha Day: 229
bus travel: 235-236

C

Caffe Coco: 12, 69
camping: 22-23, 195-196, 205, 208, 244-245
Cannons: 90
canoes: 230
Canyon Trail: 161-162
Captain Andy's Sailing Adventures: 20, 127,
    155
car travel: 114, 233-235, 237; see also specific
    place
caste system: 226
Caucasians: 227-228
cell phones: 243
centipedes: 240-241
ceramics: 231; see also arts and crafts;
    shopping
chickens: 217
Children's Media Center: 148
children, traveling with: 78, 120, 148, 238-239
Chinese: 227

Ching Young Village: 107-108
chocolate: 59
cinemas: 63, 173
Clayworks of Kilohana: 231
Cliff Trail: 161
climate: 10, 212-214, 244
clothing: 238; see also shopping
cockroaches: 240-241
Coconut Coast: 29-30
Coconut Marketplace: 61
coconuts: 64
Coco's Kaua'i Bed and Breakfast: 22, 204
coffee: 166, 167
Commission of Persons with Disabilities: 239
communications: 243-244
condos: 186; see also accommodations
Cook, James: 168, 219-220
Country Moon Rising Bakery: 32, 67
crafts: see arts and crafts; shopping
credit cards: 243
cruises: 28, 127, 155-157
currency: 243
customs, cultural: 226
cycling: see biking

D
demographics: 225-228
Department of Parks and Recreation: 244
disabilities, tips for travelers with: 239
Disability and Communication Access Board: 239
discounts: 239
diving: east side 38-39; north shore 86-88; south shore 124-125; west side 155-157
Division of Forestry and Wildlife: 245
doctors: 242
Donkey Beach: 13, 14, 37-38
driving: 114, 233-235, 237; see also specific place
drugstores: east side 62
Duke's: 12, 32, 65

E
Echo Beach: 153, 159
economy: 225
electricity: 244
Emalani Festival: 230
emergency services: 242; east side 71; west side 177
entertainment: east side 63; north shore 108; south shore 138; west side 173
environmental issues: 22-23, 214
ethnicity: 225-228

etiquette: 226
events: 228-230

F
farmers markets: 22; north shore 110, 113; south shore 139, 142; west side 175, 176-177
fauna: 250
Faye Park: 148
Faye Trail: 163
featherwork: 230-231
Fern Grotto: 42, 56
festivals: 228-230
Filipinos: 228
films/film-making: 54; see also cinemas
fish/fishing: 65; east side 43; north shore 92; west side 159
flora: 101, 102, 104, 133-135, 214-215, 250-251
food: 66, 228, 249; east side 64-70; north shore 109-113; south shore 139-142; west side 174-177
Fort Alexander: 73, 76
Fort Elisabeth State Historical Park: 24, 167-168
Fourth of July: 229

G
gardens: 101, 104, 133-135
gay/lesbian travelers, tips for: 239-240
Gaylord's: 12, 32, 64
geckos: 215
genetically modified organisms: 214
geography/geology: 209-212
Gillin's Beach: 118
Glass Beach: 147, 148, 150
glossary: 246-248
GMOs: 214
golf: east side 50-51; north shore 99-100; south shore 128-129
government: 224-225, 252
Grand Hyatt Kaua'i Lu'au: 138
GreenCar Hawaii: 23, 235
groceries: east side 62-63; north shore 110-111; west side 174-177
Grove Cafe, The: 13, 147, 173, 176
Grove Farm Homestead: 25, 54-55

H
Ha'ena Beach Park: 15, 84-85
Halele'a Spa: 100-101
Halemanu-Koke'e Trail: 164
Hamilton, Bethany: 90
Hanakapi'ai Beach: 19, 85, 96-97
Hanakapi'ai Falls: 19, 26-27, 96

Hanakoa: 97
Hanakoa Beach: 85
Hanalei: 11, 76; accommodations 193-195; beaches 82-83; entertainment 108; food 111-113; information/services 114; map 83; recreation 87, 90, 91, 94-95, 98, 100-101; shopping 106-108; sights 102-104
Hanalei Bay: 11, 15, 18, 77, 78, 82, 90
Hanalei Center: 107
Hanalei Colony Resort: 108
Hanalei Day Spa: 100, 101
Hanalei Dolphin Restaurant: 13, 109
Hanalei National Wildlife Refuge: 98
Hanalei Pavilion: 82
Hanalei River: 77, 90
Hanalei Surf Company: 77, 86, 89, 107
Hanalei Taro and Juice Co.: 77, 111
Hanalei Valley Overlook: 11, 77, 102-103
Hanama'ulu Beach: 35
Hanapepe: 12, 144-147; accommodations 204; beaches 150-152; food 174-175; information/services 177; map 150; recreation 155, 165-166; shopping 170-172; sights 167
Hanapepe Cafe and Bakery: 12, 147, 174
Hanapepe Farmers Market: 175
Hanapepe Park: 22, 175
Hanapepe Swinging Bridge: 12, 148, 167
Hanapepe Valley and Lookout: 167
hang gliding: 21, 165
Harvest Market Natural Foods and Cafe: 23, 107, 111, 112
haole rot: 241
Ha'ula Beach: 120
Hauola O Honaunau: 57
haupia custard: 228
Ha'upu Ridge: 212
Hawaiian hoary bat: 216
Hawaiian language: 65, 66, 246-248, 251
Hawaiian monk seal: 215-216
Hawaiians: 225-227
Hawaiian Slack Key Guitar Festival: 230
Hawaii Centers for Independent Living: 239
Hawaii State Parks Office: 245
Hawaii Visitors and Convention Bureau: 242
health: 240-242
Heavenly Creations 28, 111
helicopter tours: 13; east side 49-50; Ni'ihau 156; north shore 98; west side 165
Hideaways Beach: 82, 86-87
Hideaway Spa: 166, 178
hiking: 18-19, 244-245; east side 44-47; north shore 93-97; south shore 127-128; west side 159-164

history: 24-25, 217-224, 249-250
hitchhiking: 143, 178, 237
Ho'ai Heiau: 24, 133
Holoholoku Heiau: 24, 58
Honopu Beach: 85, 97
Ho'opi'i Falls: 12, 26, 44-45
Ho'opulapula Haraguchi Rice Mill: 24, 103-104
horseback riding: north shore 99; south shore 128
hospitals: 242
hotels: see accommodations
hula: 178
huli huli chicken: 66
humpback whales: 216
hurricanes: 213-214
hydrofoil rides: 43

IJ

Iliau Nature Loop: 18-19, 159
'Iniki, Hurricane: 213-214
International Gay and Lesbian Travel Association: 240
Internet access: east side 71; south shore 143; west side 177
Internet resources: 252
Irons, Andy: 89
Island Tacos: 147, 176
itineraries: 11-28; east side 32; north shore 78; south shore 119; west side 147
'Iwa, Hurricane: 213
Japanese: 227
jewelry: 171-172; see also shopping

K

Ka'ahumanu: 221
Kahaule Center: 106-108
Kahili Beach: 79
kahuna: 227
Kalaheo: 118; accommodations 196-197; entertainment 138; food 142; information/services 143; recreation 129, 130; shopping 137-138; sights 135
Kalaheo Cafe: 13, 119, 142, 143
Kalaheo Neighborhood Center: 22, 142
Kalaheo Yoga: 130
Kalalau Beach: 85, 97
Kalalau Overlook: 12, 147, 170
Kalalau Trail: 19, 85, 95-96
Kalapaki Beach: 33-34, 39-40
Kalihiwai: 80
Kalihiwai Beach: 13, 80, 89-90
kalua pig: 66
Kaluapuhi Trail: 21, 164

kama'aina discounts: 239
Kamalani Playground: 12, 36
Kamehameha V: 222-223
Kamehameha I: 220-221
Kamehameha IV: 222
Kamehameha III: 222
Kamokila Hawaiian Village: 24, 56-57
Kamuwela Trail: 21
Kapa'a: 12, 33, 225; accommodations 184-185; beaches 36-38; food 67-70; information/ services 70-71; map 36; recreation 40-43, 44-47, 48, 52; shopping 60-63; sights 58-59
Kapa'a Beach Park: 37
Kapaa Hongwanji Dharma School: 229
Kapaa Rotary Club: 229
Kapakaiki Falls: 46
Kapakanui Falls: 46
kapu system: 221, 226-227
Kauaian Days: 229
Kaua'i ATV: 20, 127
Kaua'i Backcountry Adventures: 21, 48
Kauai Center for Holistic Medicine and Research: 242
Kauai Chamber of Commerce: 245
Kaua'i Channel: 212
Kauai Coffee Company Visitor Center and Museum: 166, 167
Kaua'i Community College: 229
Kaua'i County: 225
Kauai County Farm Bureau Fair: 229
Kaua'i Educational Association for Science and Astronomy: 173
Kaua'i Hindu Monastery: 58-59
Kaua'i Lagoons Golf Club: 50
Kaua'i Medical Clinic: 71, 242
Kaua'i Mini Golf: 78, 99
Kaua'i Museum: 11, 25, 52-54, 229, 230
Kaua'i Museum Craft Fair: 230
Kaua'i Orchid and Art Festival: 229
Kauai Plantation Railway: 56
Kaua'i Products Fair: 62, 231
Kaua'i Visitors Bureau: 70, 242
Kaua'i Water Ski and Surf Co.: 20, 41, 43
Kaua'i Yoga on the Beach: 52
Kauapea Beach: *see* Secret Beach
kau kau (food): 66
Kaulakahi Channel: 212
Kaulu O Laka Heiau: 105
Kaulu Paoa Heiau: 105
Kaumakani: 148
Kawaikini, Mt.: 211
Kawailoa Bay: 120

kayaking: 20; east side 41-43; north shore 91-92; south shore 127
Ke Ala Hele Makalae: 48, 236-237
Kealia Beach: 37, 40
Kealia Kountry Market: 62
Ke'e Beach: 12, 16, 77, 78, 85, 88
Keiki Beach: 123
Kekaha: 149
Kekaha Beach Park: 148, 153
Kekaha Neighborhood Center: 22, 177
Keoki's Paradise: 13, 139
Keopuolani: 221
Kepuhi Beach: 84
Kiahuna Beach: *see* Po'ipu Beach
Kiahuna Golf Club: 128-129
Kiahuna Swim and Tennis Club: 129
Kikiaola Boat Harbor: 148, 153
Kilauea: 11, 21, 73; accommodations 187-191; beaches 76-80; food 109-110; information/ services 114; recreation 86, 89-90, 93-94, 98-101; shopping 105-106; sights 101
Kilauea Bakery & Pau Hana Pizza: 13, 77, 109
Kilauea Fish Market: 13, 109
Kilauea Lighthouse: 11, 25, 101
Kilauea National Wildlife Refuge: 98
Kilauea Neighborhood Center: 22, 110
Kilauea Plantation Center: 105
Kilauea Point National Wildlife Refuge: 11, 77, 101
Kilohana Plantation: 25, 32, 55-56, 60, 231
King Kamehameha Day: 229
King Reef: 82
King's Highway: 33
Kintaro: 12, 70
Kipu Kai Beach: 120
kneeboarding: 43
koa: 214-215
Koai'e Canyon Trail: 161
Koke'e Natural History Museum: 161, 169-170, 229, 230
Koke'e State Park: 12, 21, 159, 161-164; accommodations 207-208; food 176; map 162
Koloa: 20, 115-116; accommodations 197-200; food 138-139; information/services 143; map 131; recreation 127-128, 130; shopping 136; sights 131-132
Koloa Ball Park: 22, 139
Koloa Heritage Trail: 132-133
Koloa History Center: 131-132
Koloa Plantation Days: 229
Koloa Sugar Plantation: 132
Kona winds: 213
Kong Lung Historic Market Square: 105-106

Koolau: 220
Kountry Kitchen: 12, 32, 67
Kuamo'o Heiau: 57-58
Kuamo'o-Nounou Trail: 44
Kuhio, Prince: 133
Kuilau Trail: 18, 46
kukui: 215
Kukui Grove Shopping Center: 59-60
Kukui Heiau: 57-58
Kukuilono Golf Course: 129
Kukui O Lono Park: 25, 119, 135
Kukui Trail: 18-19, 159-161
Kukui'ula Small Boat Harbor: 13, 119, 124, 133
Kumuwela Trail: 163, 164

L

language: 65, 66, 246-248, 251
Larsen's Beach: 14, 77-78
laulau food: 228
laundry: 238
Lawa'i: recreation 127; shopping 137; sights 135
Lawa'i Bay: 124
Lawa'i Beach: 17, 123, 124
Lawa'i International Center: 135
Lei Day: 229
lei making: 231
leprosy: 220
leptospirosis: 241-242
LGBT travelers, tips for: 239-240
libraries: 71, 114
Lights on Rice Parade: 230
li hing mui: 68
Liholiho: 221
Lihu'e: 11, 21, 29, 185-187, 225; adventure
    sports 48-50; beaches 33-35;
    entertainment 63; food 64-67; information/
    services 70-71; map 53; recreation 39-41,
    43, 48, 50-51; shopping 59-60; sights
    52-56
Lihue Airport: 233; map 235
Lili'uokalani, Lydia: 223
Limahuli Botanical Garden: 12, 25, 104
literature: 250
loco moco: 66
lomilomi salmon: 66
lu'au: 228; east side 63; north shore 108; south
    shore 138
Luau Kalamaku: 63
Lucy Wright Beach County Park: 152-153
luggage: 238
Lumahai Beach: 18, 83
Lumahai Overlook: 12
Lydgate Beach Park: 16, 36, 38

M

Maha'ulepu Beaches: 13, 14, 118-120
mahele: 222
mahimahi: 65
Makai Tennis: 100
Makua Beach: 84, 87-88, 91
Malae Heiau: 57
malasada pastry: 68
Manawaiopuna Falls: 165
Maniniholo Dry Cave: 77, 104
marijuana: 215
Marionette Art Classes: 71, 231
McBryde Garden: 133-134
measurements: 244
medical services: 242
Mediterranean Gourmet: 28, 108, 113
Menehune Fishpond: see Alakoko Fishpond
Mermaids Cafe: 12, 32, 69
military discounts: 239
military installations: 153, 225
Miloli'i: 97
Milosky, Sion: 125
missionaries: 221-222
Moalepe Trail: 46
moi: 65
mokihana: 33
Mokihana Festival: 230
Mokolea tide pools: 94-95
Moloa'a Beach: 13, 76-77
Moloa'a Sunrise Fruit Stand: 13, 109
money: 243; see also banks
mosquitos: 240-241
Mount Kawaikini: 211
Mount Wai'ale'ale: 18, 19, 46, 211
movies: 54; see also cinemas
mythology: 251

NO

Na 'Aina Kai Botanical Gardens: 101
Nani Moon Meadery: 59
Na Pali Coast: 13, 17, 20, 76, 85, 88, 92, 95-97,
    155-157, 212
National Tropical Botanical Garden: 13, 119,
    133-135
Nature Trail: 163
naupaka: 102
Nawiliwili: map 34
Neide's Brazilian and Mexican Food: 11, 112
newspapers: 244
New Year's Eve: 230
nightlife: see entertainment
Ni'ihau: 156-157, 171; map 157
Ninini Beach: 34

Niumalu Beach Park: 33
Nounou: 59
Nounou Mountain Trails: 18, 44
Nounou Range: 212
Nu'alolo Kai: 97
Nu'alolo Loop: 164
Oasis: 28, 68
Oberg, Margo: 20, 126
'ohi'a tree: 215
'Okolehao Trail: 94
Old Hanapepe: 147
Olokele: 148
ono: 65
Opaeka'a Falls: 12, 27, 57
outfitters: *see specific activity; specific place*
Outfitters Kauai: 20, 21, 40, 42, 48, 92, 127, 164

P

Pacific Island Bistro: 32, 68
Pacific Missile Range Facility: 153, 158-159,
     208, 225
packing: 238
Pakala: 148
Pakala's: 151-152
Pali Ke Kua: 82
Papa'a Bay: 38
Papaya's: 23, 62, 69
Pearl Harbor: 223
Pele: 102, 210, 215, 217
people: 225-228
photography: 143, 178, 231
pidgin: 248
Pihea Trail: 19, 21, 163, 164
Pila'a Beach: 80
Pineapple Yoga: 100
Pine Trees: 78, 82, 90
PK's: 17, 122-123, 125
planning tips: 9-28
plants: *see flora*
Pohako Ho'o Hanau: 24, 58
poi: 66, 228
Po'ipu: 20, 118; accommodations 200-203;
     beaches 118-124; entertainment 138; food
     139-142; map 122; recreation 124-130;
     shopping 136-137; sights 132-135
Po'ipu Bay Golf Course: 128
Po'ipu Beach: 13, 14, 16, 20, 119, 120, 121-122, 125
Po'ipu Beach Park: 119, 120-121, 125, 130
Po'ipu Day Spa: 130
poke: 66, 228
Po'omau Canyon Ditch Trail: 163
Poliahu Heiau: 12, 24, 58
Polihale Beach Park: 12, 159

Polihale State Park: 14, 28, 147, 153-154
politics: 224-225
Polynesian dance: 63
Polynesian migration: 217-218
Pomodoro Restaurant: 28, 142
population: 225
Port Allen: 144, 155, 172
Portuguese: 228
Portuguese man-of-war: 241
postal services: east side 70; north shore 114;
     south shore 143; west side 177
Postcards Cafe: 77, 111
pottery: 231
Powerline Trail: 45-46, 94
precipitation: 10, 212-213
Prince Course: 99-100
Prince Kuhio Celebration of the Arts: 229
Prince Kuhio Park: 24, 133
Princeville: 73, 76; accommodations 191-193;
     beaches 80-82; entertainment 108; food
     110-111; information/services 114; map 81;
     recreation 86-87, 94, 98-101; shopping 106;
     sights 102
Princeville Center: 106
Princeville Makai Golf Course: 99
Princeville Playground: 78
Princeville Public Library: 114
Princeville Yoga: 100
Puakea Golf Course: 50-51
publishers: 249
pupu: 68
Pure Kaua'i spa: 100
Pu'u Ka Ohelo Berry Flat Trail: 163
Pu'u Lua Reservoir: 159
Pu'u O Kila Overlook: 12, 147, 170
Pu'u Poa Beach: 82

QR

Quarry Beach: 79, 89-90
Queen Reef: 82
Queen's Bath: 11, 77, 81-82, 98
Queen's Pond: 147, 154
radio stations: 244
rainfall: 10, 212-213
recreation: 14-21; *see also specific activity;
     specific place*
recycling: 22-23
red dirt: 211
Red Hot Mama's: 11, 77, 113
rental cars: 235, 239; *see also specific place*
resorts: *see accommodations*
restaurants: *see food*
roaches: 240-241

S

safety: 240-242
sailing: see boat tours; cruises
Salt Pond Beach Park: 17, 148, 151, 158
scooter rentals: 237; see also specific place
SeaLodge Beach: 11, 15, 77, 80-81, 87
sea urchins: 241
Secret Beach: 13, 14-15, 18, 78-79, 93-94
Secret Falls: 26, 28, 42
senior discounts: 239
shave ice: 68
shell jewelry: 171
Sheraton Beach: see Po'ipu Beach
Shipwreck Beach: 120
shopping: east side 59-63; north shore 105-108; south shore 136-138; west side 170-173
Skydive Kauai: 21, 165
skydiving: 21, 165
Sleeping Giant: 18, 59
Small Town Coffee: 12, 68, 71
Smith's Tropical Paradise: 57, 63, 229
snorkeling: 16-17; east side 38-39; north shore 86-88; south shore 124-125; west side 155-157
Soul Surfer: 90
South Pacific Dinner and Theater: 63
Spa by the Sea: 52
spas: north shore 100-101; south shore 130; west side 166
Spouting Horn: 13, 119, 120, 132
stand-up paddling (SUP): 39; east side 39-41; north shore 88-91; west side 157-159
stargazing: 173
statehood: 223-224
Steelgrass Chocolate Farm: 59
Storybook Theatre of Hawaii: 148
student discounts: 239
sugar industry: 132, 222
sunburn: 240
Sunshine Farmers Markets: 22, 110, 139
SUP: see stand-up paddling
supermarkets: see food
surfing: 13, 20, 244; east side 39-41, 61; north shore 88-91; south shore 125-127; west side 157-159
Swimming Pool Trail: 19, 28, 46-47

TUV

Tahiti Nui: 107, 108
tapa cloth: 231
taro chips: 68
taro root: 228
Taste of Hawaii: 229

tattoos: 231-232
taxis: 236; see also specific place
Taylor Camp: 85
telephone services: 243
tennis: east side 50; north shore 100; south shore 128-129
Tennis Garden and Sports Center: 129
theater: 63
tide pools: 93-95
time zones: 244
Titus Kinimaka Hawaiian School of Surfing: 77, 89
tourism: 225, 252
tourist information: 242-243; see also specific place
tours: east side 47, 48-50; north shore 92, 98-99, south shore 127-128; west side 155-157, 165-166
trade winds: 213
transportation: 233-237; see also specific place
travelers checks: 243
Tropics Day Spa: 166
tubing: 21, 48-49
Tunnel of Trees: 13, 131
Tunnels Beach: 12, 16, 77, 84, 87-88, 91
ulua: 65
Uluwehi Falls: 42
vacation rentals: 186; see also accommodations
Veterans Day: 230

WXYZ

Wahiawa Beach: 150
Waiakalua Beach: 79-80
Wai'ale'ale, Mt.: 18, 19, 46, 211
Waikanaloa Wet Cave: 105
Waikapala'e Wet Cave: 77, 104-105
Waikoko Beach: 82-83, 87, 90
Wailua: 12, 29-30, 44; accommodations 180-184; beaches 36; entertainment 63; food 67-70; information/services 70-71; map 35; recreation 38-39, 43, 44, 51; shopping 60-63; sights 56-58
Wailua Beach: 36
Wailua Falls: 12, 27, 57
Wailua Municipal Course: 51
Wailua River: 12, 20, 24, 26, 30, 41-42
Waimea: 12, 148-149; accommodations 204-207; beaches 152-153; food 175-176; information/services 177; map 152; recreation 156-157, 158, 166; shopping 172-173; sights 167-170
Waimea Canyon State Park: 12, 147, 159-161, 169, 211; map 160

Waimea Canyon State Park Overlook: 147, 169
Waimea Canyon Trail: 161, 164
Waimea Christmas Parade: 230
Waimea River: 157-158, 211-212
Waimea Theater: 173
Waimea Town Celebration: 229
Wainiha: 11
Wainiha Beach Park: 83-84
Wai'oli Hui'ia Church: 103
Wai'oli Mission House Museum: 103
Waipa Ranch Farmers Market: 22, 113
Waipo'o Falls: 26, 161-162
Waipouli Beach Park: 37
Waita Reservoir: 212
wakeboarding: 20, 43
waterfalls: 26, 28; see also specific waterfall
waterskiing: 20, 43
water sports: east side 38-43; north shore 86-
   92; south shore 124-127; west side 155-159;
   see also specific sport
weather: 10, 212-214, 244
weaving: 232

websites: 252
West Kaua'i Medical Center: 177, 242
West Kaua'i Technology and Visitor Center: 168
whalers: 222
whales/whale-watching: 20, 216; north shore
   92; south shore 127
Wilcox Memorial Hospital: 71, 242
wine/wineries: 59, 63, 136
wolf spider: 135
wood-carving: 230
World War II: 223
World Wide Opportunities on Organic Farms
   (WWOOF): 22, 181
Wrangler's Steakhouse: 13, 147, 175
Wyllie Beach: 80
yoga: east side 51-52; north shore 100-101;
   south shore 130; west side 166
Yoga at Koloa Hongwanji: 130
Yoga Hanalei: 100
Yoga House, The: 52
ziplining: 21; east side 48-49; north shore 98;
   south shore 127

List of Maps

Front color map
Kaua'i: 2-3

Discover Kaua'i
chapter divisions map: 9
Best of Kaua'i in Seven Days: 11

East Side
East Side: 31
Nawiliwili: 34
Wailua: 35
Kapa'a: 36
Downtown Lihu'e: 53

North Shore
North Shore: 75
Princeville: 81
Hanalei: 83
The End of the Road: 84

South Shore
South Shore: 117
Po'ipu: 122-123
Koloa: 131

West Side
West Side: 146
Hanapepe: 150
Waimea: 152
Ni'ihau: 157
Waimea Canyon State Park: 160
Koke'e State Park: 162

Background
Kaua'i Ocean Conditions: 210
Polynesian Triangle: 218
Land Ownership: 224

Essentials
Pacific Crossroads: 234
Lihu'e Airport: 235

Acknowledgments

FROM THE AUTHOR

As I write this acknowledgments page, I am in awe of the 11-month journey of creating this guidebook, which took numerous people working together to make it happen. *Moon Kaua'i* isn't just a travel guidebook, it also represents my pure love for the island, which is present in the text and photos that attempt to share the serenity and beauty Kaua'i offers to those lucky enough to visit. So first, I'd like to thank the island of Kaua'i for being such a beautiful and inspiring muse.

I'd like to thank my two boys, Arlo and Kaulualoha, for being such easy-going children during the research and writing process. At just one-and-a-half years old, Kaulualoha happily accompanied me on my back in a baby carrier during nearly every experience I had while researching this book. At 12 years old, Arlo was a true lifesaver during the process and a wonderful writer's assistant. I'd like to thank Akila for his continued support from start to finish, and Carolyn Reich for the support and motivation during the book proposal period. I'd also like to thank fellow writer Samson Reiny for his words of inspiration during highly stressful, tear-inducing moments throughout the journey.

I'd like to thank everyone at Avalon Travel for their help and contributions to the book. I would have never been blessed with this wonderful opportunity if it wasn't for Acquisition Director Grace Fujimoto's faith in me, and for that I will always be thankful. Finally, a huge *mahalo* to Senior Editor Erin Raber for her understanding, input, and patience during slipping deadlines, overwhelming situations, and a sometimes difficult process.

FROM THE PUBLISHER

The first edition of *Moon Kaua'i* was published in 1989. Its original author was J. D. Bisignani (1947–1997), whose *Japan Handbook,* which was first published in 1983, was one of Moon's founding publications. The next five editions of *Moon Kaua'i* were revised by Bisignani and Robert Nilsen (also the author of *Moon South Korea*). Nilsen took over as the sole author of the book after Bisignani's death in 1997. They both brought the same spirit of adventure to their Hawai'i coverage as they did to Moon's pioneering coverage of Asia. We wish them both *aloha.*

Color Photo Credits

www.moon.com

DESTINATIONS | ACTIVITIES | BLOGS | MAPS | BOOKS

MOON.COM is ready to help plan your next trip! Filled with fresh trip ideas and strategies, author interviews, informative travel blogs, a detailed map library, and descriptions of all the Moon guidebooks, Moon.com is all you need to get out and explore the world—or even places in your own backyard. While at Moon.com, sign up for our monthly e-newsletter for updates on new releases, travel tips, and expert advice from our on-the-go Moon authors. As always, when you travel with Moon, expect an experience that is uncommon and truly unique.

KEEP UP WITH MOON ON FACEBOOK AND TWITTER
JOIN THE MOON PHOTO GROUP ON FLICKR

MAP SYMBOLS

▦	Expressway	【	Highlight	✕	Airfield	⚲	Golf Course
▦	Primary Road	○	City/Town	✈	Airport	🅿	Parking Area
▦	Secondary Road	◉	State Capital	▲	Mountain	▰	Archaeological Site
▤	Unpaved Road	⊛	National Capital	✚	Unique Natural Feature	⛉	Church
- - - -	Trail	★	Point of Interest			⛽	Gas Station
⋯⋯	Ferry	•	Accommodation	🕊	Waterfall	⬭	Glacier
▰▰▰	Railroad	▼	Restaurant/Bar	▲	Park	▨	Mangrove
▦	Pedestrian Walkway	▪	Other Location	◼	Trailhead	▨	Reef
▥	Stairs	⋀	Campground	⛷	Skiing Area	▱	Swamp

CONVERSION TABLES

°C = (°F - 32) / 1.8
°F = (°C x 1.8) + 32
1 inch = 2.54 centimeters (cm)
1 foot = 0.304 meters (m)
1 yard = 0.914 meters
1 mile = 1.6093 kilometers (km)
1 km = 0.6214 miles
1 fathom = 1.8288 m
1 chain = 20.1168 m
1 furlong = 201.168 m
1 acre = 0.4047 hectares
1 sq km = 100 hectares
1 sq mile = 2.59 square km
1 ounce = 28.35 grams
1 pound = 0.4536 kilograms
1 short ton = 0.90718 metric ton
1 short ton = 2,000 pounds
1 long ton = 1.016 metric tons
1 long ton = 2,240 pounds
1 metric ton = 1,000 kilograms
1 quart = 0.94635 liters
1 US gallon = 3.7854 liters
1 Imperial gallon = 4.5459 liters
1 nautical mile = 1.852 km

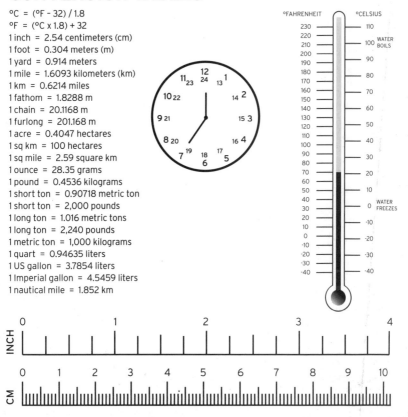

MOON KAUA'I
Avalon Travel
a member of the Perseus Books Group
1700 Fourth Street
Berkeley, CA 94710, USA
www.moon.com

Editor: Erin Raber
Series Manager: Kathryn Ettinger
Copy Editor: Deana Shields
Graphics Coordinators: Tabitha Lahr, Kathryn Osgood
Production Coordinator: Tabitha Lahr
Cover Designer: Tabitha Lahr
Map Editor: Mike Morgenfeld
Cartographers: Kat Bennett, June Thammasnong, Claire Sarraillé
Indexer: Deana Shields

ISBN-13: 978-1-61238-112-1
ISSN: 1091-3335

Printing History
1st Edition – 1989
7th Edition – June 2012
5 4 3 2 1

KEEPING CURRENT

If you have a favorite gem you'd like to see included in the next edition, or see anything that needs updating, clarification, or correction, please drop us a line. Send your comments via email to feedback@moon.com, or use the address above.